FUGITIVE LANDSCAPES

FUGITIVE LANDSCAPES

The Forgotten History of the U.S.–Mexico Borderlands

Samuel Truett

Published in cooperation with the William P. Clements Center for Southwest Studies, Southern Methodist University

Yale University Press
New Haven and London

Published with assistance from the Kingsley Trust Association Publication Fund
established by the Scroll and Key Society of Yale College.

The Library of Congress has catalogued the hardcover edition as follows:
Truett, Samuel, 1966–
Fugitive landscapes : the forgotten history of the U.S.–Mexico borderlands /
Samuel Truett.
p. cm.
"Published in cooperation with the William P. Clements Center for
Southwest Studies, Southern Methodist University."
Includes bibliographical references and index.
ISBN-13: 978-0-300-11091-3 (alk. paper)
ISBN-10: 0-300-11091-X (alk. paper)
1. Mexican-American Border Region—History. 2. Mexican-American
Border Region—Economic conditions. 3. Copper mines and mining—
Mexican-American Border Region—History. I. Title.
F786.T83 2006
972'.1—dc22
2006009071

ISBN: 978-0-300-14331-7 (pbk. : alk. paper)

A catalogue record for this book is available from the British Library.

This paper meets the requirements of ANSI/NISO Z39.48-1992 (Permanence of Paper).
It contains 30 percent postconsumer waste (PCW) and is certified
by the Forest Stewardship Council (FSC).

10 9 8 7 6 5 4 3 2 1

For Carmen

CONTENTS

Acknowledgments   ix

Prologue: Hidden Histories   1

Part I. Frontier Legacies

ONE Ghosts of Empires Past   13

TWO Borderland Dreams   33

Part II. Border Crossings

THREE Industrial Frontiers   55

FOUR The Mexican Cornucopia   78

FIVE Transnational Passages   104

Part III. Contested Terrain

SIX Development and Disorder   133

SEVEN Insurgent Landscapes   157

Contents

Epilogue: Remapping the Borderlands   178

Notes   185

Bibliography   229

Index   249

ACKNOWLEDGMENTS

A work rooted in two nations and multiple fields, this book owes a debt to many people. It began life in a much different form as a Ph.D. dissertation at Yale University. William Cronon and Howard Lamar steered that earlier work, and my larger passion for western U.S. and environmental history, toward new intellectual frontiers that I barely imagined at the outset. William Cronon laid conceptual foundations for this work by opening my eyes to the humanistic potential of environmental history, patiently guiding my journey from the world of anthropology (in which I earned my B.A.) to that of history and teaching me how to tell stories to make sense of the past. He has remained a reliable guide. Howard Lamar led me into the borderlands through his interest in the U.S. Southwest and its Mexican legacy and sent me south beyond the Americanist pale with characteristic encouragement, curiosity, and wisdom. This work builds on his legendary zeal for crossing frontiers and borders.

I likewise owe much to John Mack Faragher, Gilbert Joseph, and Sarah Deutsch, mentors at Yale, who were responsible for many of the turns the project later took. David Weber, an advocate of this project from the outset, has supported me in many ways. In 1997–98, I worked with Weber while a research fellow at the William P. Clements Center for Southwest Studies at SMU. In addition to giving me space and time for revisions, the Clements Center hosted a manuscript workshop with leading U.S. and Mexican historians. The participants—Richard White, Linda Hall, Thomas Sheridan, David Weber, William Taylor, John Chávez, Richard Francaviglia, Don Coerver, Miguel López, and James Miller—provided in one afternoon the initial guidance and courage to transform the dissertation into a completely different book: a transnational study based in the archives of two nations.

Since 1998, my debts have mounted. I received funding from the Latin American and Iberian Institute and the Research Allocations Committee at the University of New Mexico to conduct archival research in Mexico in 1999. A J. William Fulbright Lectureship at the University of Tampere, Finland, in 2000–01 gave me the distance and inspiration to finally cut the dissertation loose and start over. Such decisions are hard, especially in a world governed by the tenure clock, but I realize now that I could not have written this book otherwise. Those who supported me at this juncture deserve thanks, especially Pertti Haapala, Marjatta Hietala, Auvo Kostiainen, Pirjo Markkola, and Sari Pasto at the University of Tampere, and Markku Henriksson at the University of Helsinki.

Finally, a long-term Andrew W. Mellon Postdoctoral Research Fellowship at the Huntington Library in San Marino, California, gave me the resources and space to bring this work to completion in 2004–05. Robert Ritchie, Peter Blodgett, Romaine Ahlstrom, Dan Lewis, Carolyn Powell, Susi Krasnoo, and the remarkable staff of the Ahmanson Reading Room each supported this work in a special way. For intellectual support and their many conversations at the Huntington (and thereabouts), I wish to thank Clifford Ando, Thomas Andrews, Daniela Bleichmar, Flannery Burke, Karina Busto Ibarra, William Deverell, Elizabeth Fenn, Mary Fuller, Evan Haefeli, Karen Halttunen, Sarah Hanley, David Igler, Carina Johnson, Michael Johnson, Alexandra Kindell, Cheryl Koos, Rebecca Laroche, Peter Mancall, Elaine Tyler May, Larry May, Douglas Monroy, Walter Nugent, Felicity Nussbaum, Louise Pubols, Malcolm Rohrbough, Todd Romero, Charles Romney, Alison Sandman, Robert Self, Elaine Showalter, Laura Stevens, Steven Stoll, Mark Wild, and Kariann Yokota.

In its prior incarnation as a Yale dissertation, this project benefited not only from the financial support of the Ralph H. Gabriel Fellowship, but also fellowship donor and Ralph H. Gabriel "seminarian" Thomas W. Russell, Jr., who opened doors, with George B. Munroe and William C. Tubman, to Phelps Dodge archives. The Andrew W. Mellon Foundation, Yale Council on Latin American Studies, U.S. Department of Education, Yale Center for International and Area Studies, and the Mrs. Giles Whiting Foundation supported language study, research, and writing support. At all stages, I relied heavily on librarians and archivists at Yale University, Stanford University, the Universidad de Sonora, the University of Arizona, and the University of New Mexico. I am especially grateful to Peter Steere at the University of Arizona Library's Special Collections, Rose Byrne, Heather Hatch, Bruce Dinges, and Charles Herner, who helped at the Arizona Historical Society in Tucson, Boyd Nicholl at the Bisbee Mining and Historical Museum, David Farmer at the DeGolyer Library, Southern Methodist University, George Miles at the Beinecke Library and Bill Massa at the Sterling Memorial Library at Yale University, Ann Massmann, Teresa Márquez, and

Nancy Brown at the Center for Southwest Research at the University of New Mexico, and the able research librarians at the Archivo General del Estado de Sonora and the Centro INAH Sonora, in Hermosillo, Sonora.

I also thank the countless individuals whose friendship, conversations, and careful readings have helped guide me at all stages of the project. Karl Jacoby and Steve Pitti read my work and offered suggestions early on, as did Claire Fox, David Gutiérrez, Robert Pogue Harrison, Daniel Nugent, Karen Sawislak, and John Wirth. At the earliest stages of this project, I also benefited from conversations with Federico Besserer, Ned Blackhawk, Niklas Damiris, John Davis, Jr., William Deverell, William DeBuys, Henry Dobyns, William Doolittle, Alberto Durazo, Armando Elías Chomina, Richard Felger, Bernard Fontana, Ross Frank, Kurt Friehauf, Aaron Frith, Seth Garfield, Jay Gitlin, Greg Grandin, Reba Grandrud, James Griffith, Diana Hadley, Cindy Hayostek, Charles Herner, Yvette Huginnie, Ann Hyde, Richard Kamp, Chris Marín, Noel Maurer, Oscar Martínez, Alice Metz, James Miller, Pete Morris, Katherine Morrissey, Linda Nash, James Officer, Mike Parsons, Gina Pitti, Jenny Price, Raúl Ramos, Dolores Rivas Bahti, Kevin Rozario, Ramón Eduardo Ruiz, Jean Russell, Paul Sabin, Thomas Sheridan, Helga Teiwes, Miguel Tinker Salas, Martín Valadez, Louis Warren, Donald Worster, and Lane Witt.

Many of these same individuals have patiently supported, encouraged, and lent helping hands in the years since, as have many others: Jennifer Ahearn, Stephen Aron, Gabriela Arredondo, Conrad Bahre, Chad Black, Conevery Bolton Valencius, James Brooks, Rebecca Carter, Nathan Citino, Jon Coleman, Raymond Craib, Grace Delgado, Bruce Dinges, Tracy Duvall, Sterling Evans, Mark Fiege, Janet Fireman, Chief Goodman, Ramón Gutiérrez, Pekka Hämäläinen, John Hart, Sam Haynes, Evelyn Hu-DeHart, Peter Iverson, Elizabeth Jameson, Benjamin Johnson, Matt Klingle, Erika Lee, Brenna Lissoway, Alexis McCrossen, Maria Montoya, Kathryn Morse, Michelle Nickerson, Gunther Peck, John Nieto-Phillips, Jeffrey Pilcher, Ann Plane, Louise Pubols, Cynthia Radding, Andrés Reséndez, Mikko Saikku, Rachel St. John, Jeff Sanders, Christopher Schmidt-Nowara, Carlos Schwantes, Alexandra Stern, Jay Taylor, Omar Valerio-Jiménez, Paul Vanderwood, Marsha Weisiger, Richard White, Blair Woodard, John Wunder, and Elliott Young.

Books can never be finished without the cooperation, conversations, and humor of colleagues. At the University of New Mexico, I am grateful to Beth Bailey, Durwood Ball, Judy Bieber, Melissa Bokovoy, Cathleen Cahill, Margaret Connell-Szasz, Jennifer Denetdale, Angela Ellis, David Farber, Miguel Gandert, Kimberly Gauderman, Alyosha Goldstein, Felipe Gonzales, Timothy Graham, Linda Hall, Elizabeth Hutchison, Paul Hutton, Claudia Isaac, Enrique Lamadrid, Miguel López, Eric Morser, Tim Moy, Jonathan Porter, Noel Pugach, Cynthia Radding, Ann Ramenofsky, Bárbara O. Reyes, Pat Risso, Rob Robbins, Sylvia Rodriguez, Jay Rubenstein, Enrique Sanabria, Andrew Sandoval-Strausz, Virginia Scharff, Lynn Schibeci, Rebecca Schreiber, Jane Slaughter, Jake Spidle, Charlie Steen, Ferenc Szasz, Chris Wilson, and Mel Yazawa.

Some of the prose and ideas in this book appear elsewhere. Material from chapters 1 and 2 appeared as "The Ghosts of Frontiers Past: Making and Unmaking Space in the Borderlands," *Journal of the Southwest* 46 (Summer 2004), 309–50. Parts of chapter 6 can be found in "Transnational Warrior: Emilio Kosterlitzky and the Transformation of the U.S.–Mexico Borderlands," in *Continental Crossroads: Remapping U.S.–Mexico Borderlands History*, ed. Samuel Truett and Elliott Young (Durham: Duke University Press, 2004). They appear here with the permission of the *Journal of the Southwest* and Duke University Press.

For their careful readings of the manuscript, I would like to thank Katherine Benton-Cohen, Raymond Craib (from whose work I also borrow my "fugitive landscapes" metaphor), Pekka Hämäläinen, Karl Jacoby, Benjamin Johnson, Andrés Reséndez, and Rachel St. John. I would also like to thank Lara Heimert, my former editor, who inspired me to publish with Yale University Press, Chris Rogers, who stepped into the breach and helped me bring the project to completion, and Lawrence Kenney, an exemplary copy editor who helped keep my prose both honest and grounded.

My greatest debt goes to three people who have perhaps had the greatest hand in my intellectual growth, both in the writing of this book and in the greater work I do as a scholar. My father, Joe Truett, a wildlife ecologist and environmental historian, gave me the nudge I needed to go on to graduate school and write the kind of books I loved to read. He and my mother met in southern Arizona, and his passion for the ecological history of his new home—my birthplace—shaped my own vision of this borderland. My grandmother, Mary Schlentz, who lives in Tucson and valiantly defends my childhood home from the creeping condominiums, has done more than anyone else to keep me updated on what this place means. The reader owes it to her, as a former writer of advertising copy and a constant critic of scholarly writing, that this book is not longer than it is. My greatest intellectual guide, however, has been Carmen Nocentelli, who has introduced me to the realities of modern-day border crossings and has given me a chance to be an obsessive, curious scholar without being alone in the endeavor. She had to share countless hours with the characters and places in this book, and, more than anyone else, she understood why. In the end, it was she who kept me going, with her encouragement, keen intellect, and patience, to follow this book where it needed to go.

Prologue

HIDDEN HISTORIES

On a December evening in 1891, a well-dressed crowd of capitalists, intellectuals, and political elites ducked out of the cold into the Democratic Club on New York City's Fifth Avenue. They carried dinner invitations from Walter S. Logan, a Wall Street lawyer known in local business circles as a promoter of western investment. Some had attended a similar banquet that July, on Long Island, at which Logan had toasted the expansion of capital into the valleys and mining districts of Arizona. Now, stripping off their coats and scarves, they prepared once again to dream of distant sun-baked lands blessed by nature.[1]

Westward expansion was on the minds of many Americans in the 1890s. In 1893, masses gathered at the World's Columbian Exposition in Chicago to watch Buffalo Bill Cody reenact the epic of frontier expansion, while scholars convened nearby to hear Frederick Jackson Turner deliver a vision of U.S. history based on the same plot. The "peculiarity of American institutions," Turner argued, had been forged in "crossing a continent" and "winning a wilderness." Turner's frontier thesis, like Buffalo Bill's Wild West, painted a portrait of a vanished world: a continent crossed, a wilderness won. And yet for Walter S. Logan, gazing west from Wall Street, there was still work to be done. After his guests had cleared their plates, he raised his glass. "Capital has been flowing to her from every part of the world," he proclaimed; "her mines, her forests, and her fields are producing in abundance, and she is the favorite of all lands for the investor."[2]

Logan's guests were dreaming of expansion, but not of the kind that Turner had in mind in 1893. If the historian had attended Logan's banquet, he might have been surprised to find his fellow guests looking not to the western United States, but rather south across the border to Mexico. Logan's rhetoric had changed little from his efforts to promote Arizona, but everything else was different. The room was brilliantly festooned with the reds, whites, and greens of

1

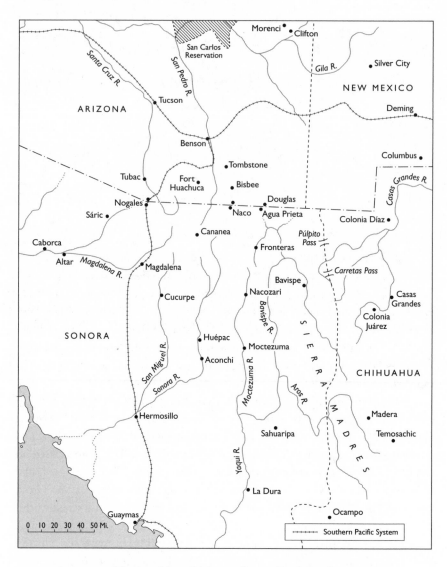

Figure 1. Map of Arizona–Sonora Borderlands

the Mexican flag, and the English pheasant and Blue Point oysters were served together with *mole de guajolote* and *frijoles a la veracruzana*. Turner might have been struck, moreover, at the ease with which Logan's guests shifted their attention south. They may have agreed with Turner about the peculiarities of the U.S. frontier, but, looking west, they also saw something more: a landscape of extraction that flowed across national borders.[3]

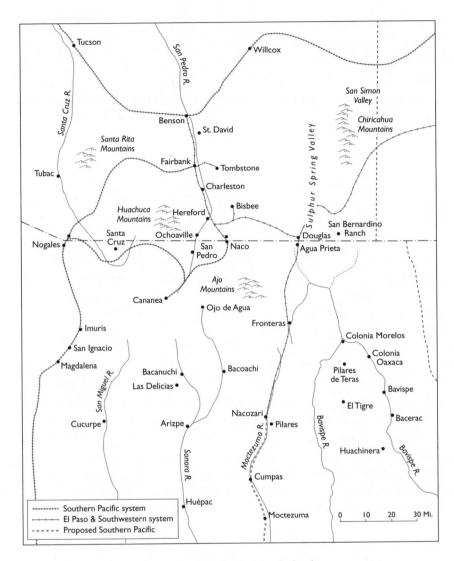

Figure 2. Map of copper borderlands.

This might have made perfect sense to Turner. Through the dim lights and cigar smoke, he might have recognized his buckskin heroes on a new frontier. Yet these men were anything but frontiersmen, and not everyone was looking west. After draining his glass, Logan turned to his special guest, Minister Matías Romero of Mexico. Romero had served as a diplomat to the United States since the 1860s, but Logan's guests knew him best as an advisor to President Porfirio

Díaz, a statesman whose views on economic development were similar to their own. Romero and Díaz felt the networks that linked Wall Street to the western United States might facilitate Mexico's own entry into the modern age. Romero had come to New York to forge ties between "Sister Republics," and he saw the borderlands as fertile terrain for economic connections. "Nature has made us neighbors," he said as he raised his own glass; "there is no reason, therefore, why we should not trade largely and to our mutual advantage."[4]

The idea of Mexico and the United States as neighbors by nature no doubt struck a chord with many of the guests, for boosters such as Logan often applied the doctrine of natural advantages—the idea that nature favored some places over others for economic development—in the promotion of western lands. Yet it resonated in a special way for Logan. The New York lawyer was involved in re-source extraction schemes on both sides of the border, from the silver mines of Chihuahua to the river valleys of Arizona and Sonora. And he would soon em-bark on his most famous venture yet. In 1899 he helped an entrepreneur named William Cornell Greene create a copper mining company at Cananea, Sonora, across the line from the rich copper district of Bisbee, Arizona. If nature had made the United States and Mexico neighbors, nowhere was it more apparent than in the hidden fields of red metal that tied Cananea to its sister mining towns in southeastern Arizona.[5]

More important, Cananea was one of those places where booster dreams came true. For whatever nature had to do with it, the industrial *transformation* of the natural world at Cananea joined the United States and Mexico together more intimately than Romero and Logan could have imagined in 1891. By the twenti-eth century, as a result of the electrification of modern America, copper attracted more capital to Arizona and Sonora than any other industry. Fueled by Logan's Wall Street connections and by railroad, banking, and corporate networks that stretched into nearby Arizona, Cananea grew overnight from a village of nine hundred into a city of twenty thousand. Together with Bisbee and the nearby copper towns of Nacozari, Sonora, and Douglas, Arizona, Cananea remade a formerly isolated region at the ragged edges of states and markets into an indus-trial crossroads fed by circuits of capital, labor, and transnational collaboration that extended deep into both nations.

Few of those at the Democratic Club in 1891 could have conceived of the scale of development in this region. It was hard enough to imagine the world of copper mining, which would demand concentrations of technology and labor far beyond those required in nineteenth-century precious metal mining. But it was even harder to imagine this in the borderlands. Outsiders in 1891 saw Ari-zona and Sonora as frontiers, places beyond the pale. Railroads had arrived, and

Apaches, long considered a chief obstacle to entry into the modern era, had been deported by 1886. Arizona and Sonora appeared ripe for incorporation, but mining, ranching, and agricultural development remained modest. It was not until the early 1900s—as Gilded Age corporations and the Porfirian state gained power on their respective sides of the line—that people saw the industrial reorganization of the borderlands as anything but a fragile dream.

What is most surprising is not how hard it was to predict this world in 1891, but how hard it is to remember it today. This is partly due to the power of national history: Mexicans and Americans usually take the border for granted when they think of the past. U.S. history includes Mexican history only before 1848 and 1854, the years that treaties turned the Mexican North into the U.S. West. U.S. history after 1854 includes Mexicans only after they cross the border. Similarly, Mexican history concerns itself with the United States only when it affects historical events in Mexico. This creates misunderstandings. One recent misunderstanding is that globalization and free trade are changing America such that the United States and Mexico will soon look nothing like they did in the past. "Delineated by a steel wall or a warning, the border always separated and rarely joined Mexico and the United States," proposes the journalist Anthony DePalma. With the passage of the North American Free Trade Agreement (NAFTA) and other trade accords, he writes, we are "creating a new history."[6]

Most Americans have forgotten transnational histories not only because they have trusted maps of the nation, but also because they have succumbed to the siren song of the state. Like their precursors they still see the borderlands as land that time forgot, places where renegades and bandits have given way to new barbarians: mercenary *narcotraficantes*, immigrant desperados, and camouflaged vigilantes. As one recent writer puts it, the borderlands remain ensnared in their "wild west past."[7] In this state-centered view, citizens are the legitimate bearers of history, and enemies of the state haunt the frontiers of the body politic like forces of nature, taunting the narrative logic of the nation. The historical borderlands are thus as unstable as they are divided. In a world ruled by nations, states, and their master tales, transnational history is by its very nature ephemeral, frequently hidden, and, at the very least, hard to pin down.

As a border native, I was drawn to this terra incognita. What began as a search for a lost history—a Wall Street banquet, a shadowy world rooted in copper—raised new questions. For instance, why did residents of my home state of Arizona, who celebrated their state's Spanish past and thought about current Mexican affairs, know so little about their common history with Mexico? As I dug into archives on both sides of the border, I learned that things were not always this way. In the early twentieth century, Arizonans viewed their neighbors to the south as siblings in an interlocking family history of sorts, a history that began with shared struggles on the "wild" frontier and pointed toward a shared modern future. National borders seemed to exert less power over the stories that people told about themselves, and this fascinated me.

This broader vision was particularly evident in the copper cities of Cananea, Nacozari, Bisbee, and Douglas, anchors of a historical landscape that the geographer D. W. Meinig has dubbed the "copper borderlands."[8] One cannot study an early twentieth-century map of this region without seeing connections: railroad lines, like strands of a spider's web, converge on, indeed, almost overwhelm, the line between nations. I wondered about these linkages. How had copper communities transformed space on both sides of the border as they consumed ore, coke, timber, water, crops, livestock, and human labor—and how had these local relationships reshaped U.S.–Mexico relations? How had the borderlands sustained transnational circuits of migration, extraction, and human exchange, even as they divided peoples and places? And what, in the end, had become of this landscape? If a frontier had become a modern crossroads between nations, why did divisions and frontier rhetoric still haunt the borderlands? It was as if an entire world, a vast web of human pathways, had vanished.

What follows is a history of this lost world, which became by the early twentieth century one of the most industrialized and urban places in the U.S.–Mexico borderlands. People dreamed about this landscape in ways that may seem remarkably familiar today, in an age of globalization and NAFTA. They expected economic development to knit Mexico and the United States together and carry them as progressive partners into a modern future. This is the history of what actually happened. Corporations, states, and regional entrepreneurs hoped to domesticate and modernize a fugitive landscape—what they saw as a wild and barbaric frontier—but it continually slipped out of their control. Their reorganization of the borderlands remained tenuous, uneven, and incomplete. Over the short term they often made impressive gains, but in the long run, their dreams were dashed and their stories were forgotten.

By recapturing this past, I hope to suggest new ways of moving U.S. and Mexican history onto a larger American stage. I also want to give dreamers today a sense of the contingency and messiness of transnational relations. If present and past dreams of integration and globalization have one thing in common, it is the notion that market forces and enlightened development will bring our planet under greater human control. Prophets of free trade see the world wrapped in a carefully woven cocoon of economic systems, business practices, and diplomatic alliances. With rational management, they propose, ideas, things, and people will migrate across borders to the greater global good. Yet looking back, we find two things that these dreamers have lost: memory and humility. History reminds us that efforts to control the world, especially in a transnational context, have rarely turned out as planned.[9]

To grasp these lessons, one must rethink borderlands history. The borderlands have seen many intellectual travelers, guided by a variety of compass bearings. Spanish borderlands history has told us a great deal about Spain's legacy in what is now the United States, while Chicana/o historians have examined the later history of Mexicans who either crossed a border or had a border cross them. Although they take the United States as their standard point of reference, Chicana/o historians have increasingly looked at migration, labor, and identity in a transnational context. Historians of the U.S. West have studied the U.S.–Mexico borderlands within a larger U.S. regional context, and Mexicanists have taken a similar regional perspective on northern Mexico. Historians of Native America, African America, and Asian America have likewise integrated the borderlands into their own histories of race, ethnicity, and postcolonialism.[10]

The result is a patchwork of histories with considerable overlap and conspicuous divides. The most visible boundary splits U.S. and Mexican history in two, but a similar line divides colonial and national borderlands. A reader interested in the Pimería Alta—a region that reached from Magdalena, Sonora, to Tucson, Arizona—can track its history through Mexican Independence in 1821 but loses the trail after 1854, when the northern half of this region was annexed to the United States. The social networks that supported the Pimería Alta persist, but they vanish from official maps and narratives: one has to follow their shadows through distinct U.S. and Mexican histories. This is largely a problem of scholarly perspective. Most Spanish borderland historians find the national era as foreign as Mexico is to a U.S. historian, whereas few modernists peer back into the colonial past far enough to see the borderlands as anything but divided.

To address these blind spots and develop the untapped potential of borderlands history, historians need to reclaim the center of the field. We need to start with the border itself and include spaces on both sides as our unit of analysis. Only then can we explore what Michiel Baud and Willem Van Schendel call the "paradoxical character" of borderlands, the fact that they both divide and connect.[11] Nation-centered histories can explain how Mexican villagers became workers in the United States or how U.S. corporations transformed the Mexican countryside, but they cannot say how these stories are interwoven. They cannot tell why capital and workers move between nations or why national distinctions still matter in the wake of these migrations. They cannot even tell what the nation means to many of its citizens. Border people cannot forget nations, but nation-bound histories often forget border people. Unless borderlands historians put the border at center, they will replicate this forgetfulness.

Failing to cross the divide between colonial and national histories poses a similar problem for borderlands historians. Just as Mexicans did not appear from thin air when they crossed into U.S. history, neither were border people blank slates for the inscription of new national identities. As locals reoriented themselves toward the United States and Mexico, they made sense of their new, modern borderlands in the light of an older colonial past. We cannot understand how they chose to adapt to this world, what they dreamed about when they looked north and south, and what their strategies were for dealing with modernity and its limits without referring to earlier times. By challenging the assumption of closure—by asking how colonial forms endured—Spanish colonial historians can show how their histories mattered in unexpected ways to later days. And by paying attention to colonial precursors, historians of recent borderlands can place their national and modern subjects in a richer and more complete context.

To fully understand the copper borderlands, we need to also cross other borders. We might cross into Asian-American history to better place the Chinese who ran mining town stores and raised produce on local truck farms. Historians have studied Chinese in Sonora and Arizona separately, but rarely together. Mormon history can help situate the transnational stories of European and Anglo-American Latter-day Saints in the river valleys of southern Arizona and exile colonies of northern Sonora and Chihuahua. And Native American history teaches about the Opata, Yaqui, Apache, Tohono O'odham, and other native communities who called the borderlands home for centuries before the advent of nations and copper markets. For borderlands history is more than just a story of Mexicans and Americans: it is a story of many peoples, shaped in distinct ways at the continental crossroads of empires, nations, markets, and cultures.

The copper borderlands were indeed not so much a discrete, coherent landscape as a shifting palimpsest of spaces, each with its own circuits and borders. The history of the region unfolds in various spatial registers, like transparent maps which can be read individually or stacked as a collective whole. One map might show webs of production and consumption that connected the mining towns of Bisbee and Cananea to hinterlands of farms, ranches, mills, smelters, coke ovens, and timberlands. Another might show the migrations of Mexican miners, smelter workers, and ranchers who entered the industrial orbit of copper but also traveled other pathways, on terms that had little to do with the modernizing dreams of copper elites. The cultural landscapes of Chinese workers might constitute a third map; migratory networks of Yaquis a fourth; the colonial homelands of Opatas and Spaniards a fifth; and so forth.

Thinking about the borderlands in this way lets one engage the transformations of market and state while keeping a transnational political economy from governing the ways we see the past. By treating the borderlands as a shifting mosaic of human spaces—some interwoven, others less so; some transnational, others national; some colonial, and others modern—we can avoid simply replacing one historical container with another. A history bounded by cross-border networks of corporate power would, just like national history, exclude much of the lived experiences of border people. We also need to track historical border crossers along their own, local pathways. For only then can we appreciate how ordinary people emerged from the shadows of state and corporate control to reshape the borderlands on their own terms.

Indeed, the ultimate goal of this book is to understand how the best-laid plans of states, entrepreneurs, and corporations repeatedly ran aground in fugitive landscapes of subaltern power. In part 1, I show how Mexicans and Americans tried but ultimately failed to domesticate Sonora and Arizona in the years before the coming of the railroad. Their frontier stories introduce foundational social relationships that would persist well into the modern era. In part 2, I explore how entrepreneurs, corporations, state elites, and ordinary people reorganized the borderlands at the turn of the century. I show how corporations and states worked to control transnational space, and how ordinary people forged alternative landscapes that eluded this control. In part 3, I examine how this land was contested and selectively unmade as social conflict and revolutionary struggles shook the foundations of the modern borderlands, dashing dreams of domestication and domination and conjuring the ghosts of frontiers past.

On one hand, this is a forgotten story of failed dreams, of the messy and often unintended consequences of crossing national borders to control nature and people. On the other hand, it is the story of people and places that endured, and why. If anything, I hope to reconstitute the historical tissue that connects the U.S. and Mexican past. In the shadow lands between nations, inhabited by dreams, ghosts, and hidden histories, what became of our flesh and kin? How did their transnational journeys shape our world? And what can they tell us about the fugitive landscapes that divide us still?

Part I

FRONTIER LEGACIES

GHOSTS OF EMPIRES PAST

In early 1853, the New York City bibliophile and ethnographer John Russell Bartlett set sail from Texas for New Orleans. He had just completed a two-and-a-half-year journey into the heart of North America with the U.S.–Mexican Boundary Commission, an expedition charged with surveying the new border between the United States and Mexico. While his subordinates had shouldered the technical burden of flattening territory onto maps, astronomical tables, and scientific illustrations, Bartlett chronicled their passage through exotic lands. He later devoted two volumes to the experience in his *Personal Narrative of Explorations and Incidents*, published in 1854 for a broad popular audience. Through his words and sketches, a vast terra incognita extending west from Texas to California resolved itself in the mind of an expanding nation.[1]

Like many travelers of his time, Bartlett gave nature his full attention. He noted the abundance of timber, soil, and water for immigrants, while also pausing to catch the particular and peculiar. Sketches of prairie dogs, lizards, and cacti placed his readers on alien terrain. In the borderlands, observed Bartlett, "nature assumes a new aspect." Soil dried out, water grew scarce, and familiar greens yielded to "that most unbecoming of all hues, yellow." Prospects for settlers often seemed bleak. "Here man . . . cannot live," he wrote of its extremes, "for there is no water to slake his thirst, no wood to supply him with fuel; nor can the domestic animals so necessary to him exist." At times, his wonder turned to frustration. "Is this the land which we have purchased, and are to survey and keep at such a cost?" he wrote at the end of one especially trying day: "As far as the eye can see stretches one unbroken waste, barren, wild, and worthless."[2]

This abstracted view of nature as an inventory of resources, a catalogue of exotic species, an "unbroken waste" permeated early U.S. accounts of the borderlands. Almost ritualistically, Bartlett and his cohort stripped the land of its human skin. This tendency says much about the mindset of exploration but profoundly distorts our understanding of the region, for border people had long turned nature to their advantage. Hardly a day passed that Bartlett's party did not walk across someone else's map of the world, oriented—for those who knew where to look—around fields, pastures, orchards, mines, hunting grounds, villages, roads, and trade centers such as Paso del Norte, Chihuahua, and Guaymas, Sonora, where nature was loaded into carts, wagons, mule packs, and the holds of ships and launched into the wider world.

If human landscapes hovered ghostlike at the edge of Bartlett's sight, specters of prior settlement haunted him more deeply. He came regularly upon crumbling vestiges of deserted villages, weed-choked furrows of neglected fields, and the ruins of missions and fortresses. He found the war-torn remains of Goliad, Texas, "novel and interesting" after an American squatting in a deserted church offered him a "fairy-tale vision" of the ghost town from his roof. In other places, ruins evoked less romantic sentiments. In San Antonio, U.S. soldiers had used the façade of the San José church for target practice, and weather had carried the job further, destroying its best frescoes and paintings. A nearby mission church had been turned into a livestock corral, its floors desecrated with animal feces. "Myriads of bats flitted about," Bartlett observed, "chatter[ing] and scream[ing] at our invasion of their territory."[3]

As he entered northern Sonora near its future border with Arizona, Bartlett spent the night among the ruined corrals of the San Bernardino ranch, whose owners had fled in the 1830s after Apaches swept down from their Arizona strongholds. "Such seems to be the case with all deserted places here," he declared. "A fatality or superstitious dread hangs over them, and . . . they are not again inhabited." The old ranch herds had fanned out across the surrounding countryside, turning "wild and more fierce than the buffalo." From the New Mexico border west to the San Pedro River and south to the abandoned silver mines of Cananea, herds of feral cattle and horses had severed ties to ranches and villages, reclaiming this battleground on their own terms.[4]

Empire's ghosts followed the travelers south into Sonora. Crosses lined the road where Apaches had killed Mexicans, marking their passage into a land of the dead. At the deserted church of Cocóspera, where Jesuits had once led an assault on native lives, bats had invaded the edifice, and swallows nested in the niches. This was a colonial landscape turned inside out, a land where the borders of civilization had been violated—where so-called *indios bárbaros* had replaced *gente de razón*, where domesticated animals had degenerated into wild beasts, where nature had reclaimed the inner sanctuaries of the human world. If these ghost landscapes intrigued Bartlett, they did so only in the most ambivalent fashion. It was sad, he wrote, "to see so beautiful a region reverting to the condition of a wilderness."[5]

Ruins like these haunted most Americans. Those coming west in search of virgin land and opportunity had to think again, for the region not only evoked a deep legacy of human residence but also was scarred by failed dreams. Yet not everyone wept over a lost land. For some, Sonora evoked a vision of bountiful reclamation. Former villages and ranches—though deserted—revealed nature's potential, and lost mines possibly led to lost riches. This was a vision of opportunity rooted not in virgin soil, but in squandered space. The British had once used similar language to claim lands they felt Indians had wasted in early America, but the rhetoric of manifest destiny gave this well-worn cant of conquest a fresh sheen. "Does not the certainty suggest itself," one U.S. newcomer to Sonora wrote, "that before many years the American people, proverbially ambitious and restless as they are, will spread themselves over this hidden paradise?"[6]

Seen this way, the U.S.–Mexico borderlands represented the meeting place of two opposing narratives: the history of Spanish and Mexican decline and a prophecy of U.S. expansion. Sonora's ghosts were nothing if not the symbolic ashes for the Phoenix-like rebirth of empire. Nostalgic reminders of a Spanish golden age played foil to dreams of a modern nation that many felt would absorb Sonora, if not all of Mexico. Even Bartlett, as he fixed the new border in place, shared the expansionist spirit of his times, dreaming of worlds beyond national boundaries. "There is no project too great for the Californian of the present day," he proclaimed after completing his journey to the west coast. "He is ready for any undertaking, whether it be to make a railroad to the Atlantic, to swallow up Mexico, or invade the empire of Japan."[7]

Motivated by visions of expansion, U.S. travelers failed to appreciate the deeper meaning of northern Mexico's haunted landscapes. Sonora was, in many ways, a failed enterprise. Apaches and Americans had checked Mexican expansion, shattered dreams of empire, and disrupted efforts to domesticate the frontier. Yet there was more to this unsettled land than met the eye. This was a place where relations of empire had always been unstable. If authorities in Madrid and Mexico City saw their dreams dashed, local residents were far more pragmatic. Ruins evoked failure, but they were also symbols of a fugitive landscape, one characterized by mobility and flexibility, that survived by eluding the scrutiny of empire and resisting incorporation. For it was easy enough to dream, but as U.S. newcomers would soon learn, one needed more than prophets to pin this land down.

Yet prophecy is a good place to begin, for if the first Spanish colonists shared one thing with John Russell Bartlett, it was the ability to see the borderlands in their imperial mind's eye long before they called it home. Not long after the conquest of Mexico, in 1521, Spaniards heard tales of wealthy cities to the north, their streets lined with silversmiths' shops. The conquistador Núño Beltrán de Guzmán sent troops along the Pacific coast as far north as present-day Sonora to claim what he called a Greater Spain and to search for these cities. They returned with reports of a land ripe for the harvest of captives, but little else. Then one day in 1536, as Guzmán's men were taking captives in Sinaloa, four unknown men, three Spaniards and an African, stumbled into camp, seemingly out of nowhere, with a fantastic new story about lands beyond the colonial fringe.[8]

In 1528, these men had sailed from Cuba as part of an expedition to claim Florida for Spain. After becoming separated from their ships and hopelessly lost, they had built rafts and tried to navigate the coast of the Gulf of Mexico toward New Spain but were shipwrecked off the coast of Texas. For the next eight years they lived as slaves, traders, and healers, wandering west across present-day Tamaulipas, Nuevo León, and Coahuila to Chihuahua, where they threaded their way through high passes of the Sierra Madres and entered the irrigated lands of the Opata and Pima Indians of Sonora. Native trade routes and a retinue of some two hundred Indian guides would eventually lead the men back to the frontiers of Spanish America and "out of so sad and wretched a captivity" in the heathen north.[9]

Most of the stories told by their leader, Álvar Núñez Cabeza de Vaca, challenged dreams of wealthy civilizations. Unlike Bartlett, who traced a similar path centuries later, Cabeza de Vaca and his companions had lost the accoutrements of empire and had to rely on the modest kindness of strangers. They learned from their hosts the value of prickly pear fruit, pine nut mash, and mesquite bean flour, and in lean seasons necessity drove them to the frontiers of culinary propriety. One group in the Texas border region offered them "spiders and ant eggs and worms and lizards and salamanders and snakes . . . and everything that they can find and deer excrement and other things that I refrain from mentioning," wrote Cabeza de Vaca. Sonora, with its sedentary Pima and Opata communities, provided welcome relief. "They gave us many deer and many robes of cotton, better than those of New Spain," he recalled. This was a land where economic transformations ran deep: if not brimming with gold and silver, it still had much to offer Spanish colonists.[10]

But in their colonial dreams, Spaniards were not farmers. What attracted them to Sonora was not what Cabeza de Vaca saw but what he did not see, for there was more to this land than fields. There were also tales, heard among the Pimas, of larger villages to the north. The Pimas gave the four castaways arrowheads made of turquoise and malachite (Cabeza de Vaca called them emeralds) traded from these villages, and even though they lost them, the tales endured. Architecture and population grew by the telling, until the north was again filled with lost cities.[11] In 1539, Viceroy Antonio de Mendoza of New Spain sent the frontier elite Francisco Vázquez de Coronado north to retrace Cabeza de Vaca's path through Sonora and learn more. Coronado spent two years wandering across New Mexico and the southern plains, only to verify the power of dreams to lead adventurers astray.[12]

When Coronado returned empty-handed, Spain's fascination with the far north waned. Not only lack of treasure, but also native rebellions that swept across the region dampened their zeal. By the late 1540s, too, Spaniards were distracted by the real discoveries of silver in Zacatecas, to the northwest of Mexico City. Second in population only to Mexico City, the boomtown of Zacatecas redefined the search for El Dorado. Adventurers chasing elusive cities of gold were replaced by a new generation of professional miners, merchants, and prospectors bent on deciphering the countryside for clues to subterranean wealth. Starting from Zacatecas, prospectors began to migrate north once again, this time along the foothills of the Sierra Madres into Nueva Vizcaya, a new province to the east of Sonora.[13]

Leading the way was Francisco de Ibarra, a nephew of one of Zacatecas's founders and a member of a new Basque immigrant fraternity of mining men. In the early 1560s, Ibarra was made governor of Nueva Vizcaya, which by then included Sinaloa and Sonora, and in 1565 he set out to reassess the wealth of his new holdings. Following the paths of Guzmán, Cabeza de Vaca, and Coronado into Sonora, Ibarra read the landscape for signs that prior explorers had overlooked in their search for refined wealth. Drawing on expertise developed in the mountains around Zacatecas, he not only paid attention to topography, vegetation, and settlement patterns, but also kept his eyes to the ground, looking for "signs and traces" and "colors and kinds" of underground gold, silver, and lead. As a mining country, he concluded, the region had enormous potential.[14]

The question was not whether Sonora measured up to the dreams of empire, for clearly it did, but rather how to bring the empire to Sonora. A network of roads, finance, labor, and expertise had begun to radiate outward from Zacatecas, but this infrastructure was still in its infancy in 1565. Mining discoveries on the east slopes of the sierras, closer to Mexico City, kept men of Ibarra's professional class busy for years to come. It wasn't until 1584 that Baltasar de Obregón, a soldier under Ibarra, wrote the official chronicle of Ibarra's expedition of 1565, the first to promote Sonora as a field for mining investment. By then, things were changing. Miners were moving into Chihuahua, and explorers began to reconsider the far northwest. As the failures of earlier generations were forgotten, Sonora found itself once again at the doorstep of empire.[15]

As some began to imagine a new, subterranean Sonora, others began to re-assess its more visible human landscape. These new dreamers included members of the Jesuit order, founded in the 1540s when Coronado was chasing shadows of El Dorado. In the 1570s, Jesuits sailed to New Spain and soon thereafter began to claim the far northwest as their own. Working from bases in Sinaloa, a land de-populated by Spanish slavers in the 1530s, they plunged north. They established their first Sonora missions in the 1610s among the Mayo and Yaqui Indians, then leapfrogged north across the Pima and Opata homelands, following the Bavispe, Moctezuma, Sonora, San Miguel, and Fronteras river valleys of eastern Sonora. By the 1650s, a tenuous chain of Jesuit missions reached to the northern borders of Opata territory, near the present-day Arizona border.[16]

Above Opata territory, Jesuits faced a new spatial divide. This was a border-land between watersheds: the San Pedro and Santa Cruz rivers started here and ran north to the Gila River, and the Sonora and Yaqui rivers (and the Fronte-ras, Bavispe, Moctezuma, and San Miguel tributaries) washed south to the Gulf of California. An arid savanna fed by riverine capillaries, it supported semino-madic groups such as the Sumas, Janos, and Jocomes—groups that were later replaced by or incorporated into the advancing Apache populations from the north. Farther west were the Pimas, Sobas, and Sobaipuris of the San Pedro, Santa Cruz, upper San Miguel, and Magdalena rivers, and Tohono O'odham of the Sonoran desert. In the 1680s, under Eusebio Francisco Kino, Jesuits pressed north into this land (which they called the Pimería Alta, or upper Pima land), joining it to their multiethnic constellation of mission landscapes to the south.[17]

Closely behind the Jesuits came Spanish miners, merchants, and ranchers. Pedro de Perea, commander of royal troops in Sinaloa, was authorized to settle Sonora in 1637, and several of his soldiers established an outpost on the San Miguel River, near present-day Cucurpe, and began prospecting in the nearby hills. Meanwhile, miners began to migrate north and west across the Sierra Madres from Nueva Vizcaya, where the silver boomtown of Parral had emerged as an administrative, trade, and shipping center in the 1630s. By the 1660s, impor-tant silver towns—San Juan Bautista, Bacanuchi, and Nacozari among them—had taken root in the eastern highlands, often overlooking missions in the nearby river valleys. Spanish and mestizo ranchers, for their part, moved into the hilly grasslands between the missions and silver boomtowns to graze cattle, sheep, and other livestock for mining town markets.[18]

Yet there was more to these migrations than the lure of profit, for Crown officials expected miners, merchants, and ranchers to defend as well as trans-

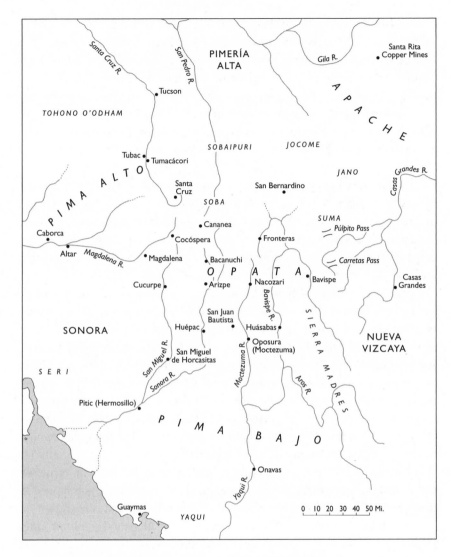

Figure 3. Map of colonial borderlands.

form space. To hold the borders of the body politic, whether against Indians or other empires, colonists also went north as civilian warriors, with gun in hand. As resistance to empire mounted, the state supplemented these militias with *presidios,* or self-supporting garrisons, in places turning the frontier into a literal military front. Settlers faced increasingly well-mounted and well-armed adversaries, whose seminomadic practices made their homelands hard to invade. To incorporate and domesticate these fugitive terrains, settlers and soldiers—like missionaries—had to rely on a mixture of persuasion and limited force and the help of native allies. Violence unsettled the frontier, but it also created new opportunities, especially for the region's emerging military elite.[19]

To understand how these newcomers remade the far north, one should start with the landscapes they unmade in the process. Early accounts suggest that Sonora was not a place to enter lightly. When Coronado passed through the province in 1540, he set up his base camp among the Opatas of the Sonora River. After soldiers began to take native supplies and rape native women, Indians destroyed the settlement. When Francisco de Ibarra visited in the 1560s, the Opatas boasted of their expulsion of the Spanish, warning Ibarra to pass with care. "They are a warlike people," Obregón said of one village: their homes were heavily fortified against outsiders, and trophies—"dead bodies, heads, arms, legs, tongues, and ears"—were prominently displayed in the streets.[20]

Obregón was struck not only by Opata military prowess, but also by their numbers. Larger towns such as the stronghold of Arizpe, he claimed, contained up to seven hundred terraced adobe homes and stone-and-adobe temples. And if anything, these lands had been even more heavily populated in the past. Crossing into Chihuahua, the expedition found the remains of Casas Grandes, a trade center that had fallen over a century earlier. Obregón compared its multistory ruins to those of Rome. When he asked the "wild, coarse, and roaming people" among the rubble where the previous inhabitants had gone, they said enemies from Sonora had forced them out. In the far north of Sonora, Jesuits later found similar "vestiges of settlements" with Opata names, hinting at cultural outposts that had "existed so long ago that no living soul remembers them." One ancient Opata place-name, Chirigagui (modified to Chiricahua), was applied to the Apaches that reclaimed this unsettled land in the sixteenth century.[21]

This was a world in flux; shifting territories and migrations and ghosts of former civilizations evoked a profoundly nomadic landscape. Anthropologists suspect that the Opatas either migrated into Sonora from Casas Grandes or were culturally reshaped by refugees from this trade center well before the Spanish conquest. There is also evidence that Opatas were still expanding south and west into Pima territory in the sixteenth and seventeenth centuries. And there is another layer to this spatial tectonics. According to seventeenth-century accounts, Pimas and Opatas lived in small, fluid settlements that fragmented seasonally to hunt and gather in the nearby countryside. The large towns Obregón remembered from the 1560s were nowhere to be seen, and no evidence of such places exists today.

A Jesuit reading Obregón's chronicle before coming to Sonora would have felt disoriented by the conspicuous absence of these places.[22]

Most historians dismiss Obregón's descriptions precisely because they do not square with seventeenth-century realities, but a few wonder if Old World epidemics might not have made an appearance in Sonora well ahead of the Jesuit *entrada*, reducing its population significantly. Given the paucity of evidence about Sonora at this time, we might never know. But we can say this: the Spanish conquest of a once-formidable military society took place in the wake of smallpox, typhoid, and measles epidemics, which profoundly unmade native space in the seventeenth century. When delegates from highland Sonora traveled south after 1610 to ask for missionaries, it may have been in a desperate attempt to reconstitute shattered communities. The lands described by early colonists in Sonora were already ghost landscapes, not only owing to the terrible deaths that haunted them but also because entire villages had vanished, as if into thin air.[23]

Even before Spaniards came, native groups in Sonora had been moving toward smaller, less centralized communities, for whom mobility was a crucial practice. For the Tohono O'odham, who shifted seasonally between the mouths of arroyos and upland hunting and gathering camps, mobility was a way of life. Pimas were also relatively mobile, whereas Opatas invested heavily in fixed settlements based on irrigation. Yet when the time came to gather mescal and mesquite beans or hunt deer and antelopes, even the most dedicated farmers dispersed across sierras and savannas to supplement crops—or, in years of droughts or floods, to stay alive. Pima and Opata place-names evoked this world beyond the domesticated fields: Babiácora (place of Babícori, an herb), Nacozari (honeycomb), Cuquiárachi (place of doves), Tumacácori (pepper bush), and Cocóspera (onion mountain). Jesuits called many of these people *naciones errantes*, or wandering peoples, because they were often difficult to congregate around the more fixed terrain of the mission.[24]

As they entered these shifting landscapes, newcomers remade them into places of their own. For Jesuits, the incorporation of humans and nature were part of the same equation. To attract converts and build the mission economy, they sought to transform Sonora into a world of pastures and fields. "Besides spiritual duties the missionary has continually to take care of worldly business," wrote one missionary: "where there is no bread the children do not appear." Their success depended on plants and animals that came with them, for if disease organisms destroyed native Sonora, other species offered means for renewal. The wealth of nature also gave Jesuits the means to clothe and pay converts, sustain the church and its ceremonies, and map out new geographies of labor, discipline, and economic exchange. By controlling nature and natives in tandem, Jesuits hoped to turn Sonora into a landscape worthy of God.[25]

Yet natives responded to the colonial world on their own terms, and the selective incorporation of Old World species into their local rounds often curbed Jesuit efforts to remake natural and social space. Pimas and Opatas took new crops into their fields but not always in ways that missionaries saw fitting. "No one knows how to plow a regular furrow," grumbled one frustrated father. "Sonora could have a superabundance of . . . produce if the inhabitants would diligently engage in agriculture. But they are much too lazy for such labor." This complaint, reflecting an Enlightenment obsession with order, also betrayed a poor appreciation of local wisdom that favored diversity and flexibility over supposed efficiency: unnecessary work in the fields could eat into the time for hunting and gathering. Native norms also shaped the use of animals. Some refused cows and horses because they threatened crops, while others, like the Tohono O'odham and Apache, lumped them with deer and elk as animals to be hunted, not herded.[26]

Efforts to transform the borderlands were stymied not only by what missionaries considered barbaric customs, but also by nature. "When brooks dry up or are exhausted and the plantations can no longer be watered, everything wilts," wrote Father Philipp Segesser, who also recalled a wet year when the Yaqui River rose so high that it "destroyed entire mission villages." Often natural disorder followed in the wake of social disorder. When Pima rebels killed a friend, Segesser took over his mission, which had been "reclaimed" by nature. Trees and shrubs had invaded the garden, the orchard had withered owing to lack of irrigation, and "everything had been devastated by ants." Missionaries also had to contend with that most fickle of allies, Old World disease. Measles were the "harvest of Heaven," wrote one father. "By it populated villages are suddenly reduced. Indians fear it very much and great effort is required to keep them together, for they flee and try to hide in the woods."[27]

Jesuits saw these environmental obstacles as problems of spatial control. Beyond the mission, claimed Father Ignaz Pfefferkorn, "the absence of both order and a civilized existence was the rule," whereas Indians on the inside "were so improved in their customs that they retain almost nothing of their former aspect than their brown skin." Borders of the Jesuit landscape, in this view, marked off the wild from the tame, the pure from the corrupt. Horses and cattle that wandered from the mission's pastures "became wild and timid in the wilderness," joining the same conceptual geography as "barbarous" Indians whose lives were, in Pfefferkorn's words, "more like those of animals than of reasoning human beings." There was also the constant danger of losing converts to lay Spaniards,

notably miners, "godless men" who offered Indians "every freedom and per-
mitted them the most shameful excesses."[28]

The missionary's ability to domesticate the frontier was also compromised by
his distance from colonial markets. Each Jesuit received a yearly subsidy of three
hundred pesos, Pfefferkorn noted, but this was quickly spent. By Spanish law,
European goods—including vestments and ceremonial objects—had to enter
New Spain through the port of Veracruz and then take an arduous overland journey, first to Mexico City, then north via Guadalajara or Parral to Sonora. Goods
frequently changed hands, facing multiple sales taxes and customs duties. "It is
easy to understand how goods which have made such a journey . . . must finally
come to an enormous price in Sonora," wrote Pfefferkorn; "one can easily imagine that the above-mentioned three hundred pesos did not go far." Their subsidy
barely covered liturgical costs, forcing Jesuits (like other colonists) to depend on
local resources, together with native knowledge and practices, to survive.[29]

Missionaries thus faced a paradox: to sustain a European island of civilization
in a supposedly barbaric American sea, one had to sink roots into both worlds.
Some compromises were cosmetic. As much as he wished to build churches of
stone, Pfefferkorn had to rely on locally made "sun-dried bricks," and, unlike
churches to the south, their ceilings were "not arched but instead were flat, con-
structed of logs." In the fields, visitors took note of the unusual use of wooden
plows. "The iron plowshare is not used for plowing," wrote Pfefferkorn, "because
iron is much too expensive in Sonora." If he dreamed of "regular furrows" of Old
World wheat and a loaf of bread for dinner, he gradually devoted space to native
corn, which yielded better harvests. Driven to make this a land worthy of God,
Jesuits yielded to environmental constraints and native wisdom, interweaving
American and European landscapes.[30]

Such pragmatic, hybrid spaces abounded in Sonora. Not only had native
peoples incorporated Old World crops and animals into their rounds, but newcomers—especially poor mestizos—also blended landscapes. "There is little difference between the food of the Indian and that of the common Spaniard in
Sonora," Pfefferkorn remarked. "Spaniards do not eat rats, snakes, and other such
Indian delicacies, but they get along with posole, pinole, atole, and tortillas, and
they are completely satisfied if with these dishes they have a piece of dried cow-
beef. . . . Mutton, chicken, and other good dishes are only for the tables of the
wealthy."[31]

Prickly pear, saguaro, agaves, wild grapes, and acorns expanded the harvest;
and native spices lent new flavors to Old World soup, lentil, and bean recipes.
Settlers also learned from local Indians, who especially in the Opata region became cousins and godparents, about native roots, herbs, fruits, and plants that

could be put to medicinal uses. "The providence of nature or should I say the Divine Providence?" noted the Jesuit Juan Nentvig, with respect for this new borderland, "has endowed Sonora, devoid of physicians, surgeons, and apothecaries, with excellent medicinal herbs, shrubs, gums, fruits, mineral and animal products of such quality that there is no collection like it in Europe."[32]

Miners and ranchers often had greater success than religious orders in achieving their dreams of social and environmental control. By the late seventeenth century, silver camps had sprung up all across the Pima and Opata highlands. As Spaniards, mestizos, and Indians flocked to the mines, the demand for food, clothing, and housing put a new value on nearby river valleys and grasslands. With the assistance of native *peones* and *vaqueros*, native landscapes were transformed into pastures and fields to feed the growing mining population. In some places Jesuits and native converts monopolized these rural markets; in others, lay entrepreneurs took the lead. Mining camps and their rural hinterlands also remade less domesticated spaces: wild plants and animals supplemented crops, while oak, pine, and mesquite forests entered a growing frontier network of mines, ranches, and farms as building materials and fuel.[33]

Town and countryside thus emerged in tandem. Ranchers who brought beef and butter to miners' tables also produced tallow for candles burned underground. "Herein lies the principal profit to be derived from cattle raising," noted Pfefferkorn. Local rawhide went into the bags used to carry ore (and water, when the mines flooded) to the surface. Woodcutters hauled timber from nearby mountainsides to build the machinery for the stamp mills and to shore up larger mines with timbers. Most of the wood, however, went to make charcoal for smelting, which led to the rapid denudation of nearby forests. Lead mines provided reagents for the reduction of silver, mules supplied the power for the *arrastras*, or ore-grinding mills, and salt and copper—gathered from local river deltas and mined in the nearby highlands, respectively—were also used as reagents when silver ores required the additional step of amalgamation.[34]

The mining landscape also depended on long-distance trade networks, whether south along the coast to Guadalajara or east across the sierras to the mining entrepôt of Parral. From the outside, merchants and miners brought sheepskin bellows for smelting furnaces, quicksilver to extract silver in the *arrastras*, and the iron tools—picks, hammers, and crowbars—used in the mines. Paths leading south were also conduits for wine, olive oil, tobacco, pottery, silks, and tailored clothes, often produced thousands of miles away. Frontier merchants, largely from Parral, controlled this traffic. They were responsible for buying and selling and for freighting silver south to Mexico City. Since Sonora, like most frontiers, was cash-poor, these merchants doubled as bankers, loaning money to prospectors and other mining entrepreneurs. Their special access to outside markets and investment capital gave them a control over the borderlands rarely matched by their native and immigrant neighbors.[35]

Yet this control was often ephemeral. Mining ventures could collapse overnight if workers depleted surface deposits, lost a vein, or hit porous rock below the water table and flooded the shafts. "In the absence of pumps water must be carried out of the mines in tubs," one local explained. "This labor doubles the cost so that even the richest mines, whose bright silver glistens in the water, must be abandoned." Even after extracting the metal and preparing it for market, the battle was only half won. Shipping silver over the highlands was hard. "There are no freight wagons," wrote Segesser; "rivers are not navigable, and roads are so narrow, rough, and steep in many places that one dreads looking down the precipices." Often, freighting was out of the question. In the summer monsoon season and during less violent (but often more debilitating) winter rains, camps could be cut off for weeks at a time.[36]

Mining elites found workers just as hard to control as nature. "Everywhere there are people who seek metal up hill and down dale, but there are few persons who wish to work," wrote Segesser of *vagabundos*, usually prospectors who drifted from place to place. Catching wind of a new bonanza, even disciplined workers vanished, added Nentvig: "They are much like the mastiff that, letting the piece of meat he carried in his mouth drop, ran after its own image reflected in the water." Most mine workers left in the planting and harvest seasons, and after the rains they could also be found with their families in communal placers near Bacoachi, Saracachi, and Huásabas, digging for *pepitas de oro* (gold seeds) and *oro en polvo* (gold dust). Mobility, a strategy that was already familiar to Pimas, Opatas, and Yaquis, allowed newcomers to smooth the wrinkles of an uneven frontier economy. Colonists thereby reinforced Sonora's fugitive nature, making it harder for their enterprising countrymen to pin this province down.[37]

Nothing unsettled Spanish enterprise more than Apache Indians. During the seventeenth century, Apaches had become expert mounted raiders and were starting to move into Sonora and Chihuahua. By century's end, Spaniards realized that a vast land between Zuni Pueblo and the Opata homeland, a blank spot on their mental map of the region, was far from vacant. This territory, which they now called the Apachería, was home to a wide range of families, bands, and fluctuating alliances, whose heterogeneity and fluidity baffled Spanish officials. In a region that was already a land of intermittent warfare among Opatas, Spaniards, Janos, Jocomes, and Sumas, Apaches became a new contesting force. Soon Apaches, Spaniards, and Opatas entered an unprecedented cycle of raids, feuds, battles, and captive taking. Although not as deadly as the epidemics that had destroyed earlier generations, this contest profoundly unsettled Sonora, limiting the ability of all sides to transform space as they wished.[38]

Apaches were drawn to the animals, people, and goods that collected around the mines. When they attacked Nacozari in the 1690s, they carried off the mules that hauled ore to the smelter, along with the town's cattle and horse herds. Freighters taking silver over the sierras were also at risk. Carretas Pass, leading east to Chihuahua, was "made famous by the numerous Apache outrages committed on the lives and property of travelers and traders," observed Nentvig. Mobility gave them an edge. "Where there is no house to ransack nor any livestock to confiscate," revenge expeditions were pointless, he wrote. It was like tracking ghosts across "a land as vast as an ocean," added a Spanish military officer. Meanwhile, Sonora was shrinking. Near the abandoned mines of Bavispe, "we see the Apaches' fires almost every night," Nentvig wrote in 1764. Horses were confined to corrals, gardens were forgotten, and the roads were "strewn with crosses," in memory of those killed by these "masters of the country."[39]

Ranchers faced many of these same problems of control. By the late seventeenth century, the Spanish ran cattle, horses, and mules all across the savannas and foothills of northeastern Sonora, as far north as the Santa Cruz River. When silver was found near present-day Nogales, Sonora, in the 1730s, Spanish miners, ranchers, and farmers began to move into what is now Arizona. Many began to follow their herds into the savannas along the Santa Cruz and San Pedro rivers. According to Pfefferkorn, Spaniards preferred ranching to all other pursuits. "In that work they are really indefatigable," he noted. "It seems not to tire them to ride around through woods and hills the entire day rounding up the animals." Sonora's grasslands were so well suited for cattle, he added, that Spaniards and Indians alike had "sizeable herds." By the eighteenth century, some reached twelve thousand head, not counting the hundreds of horses and mules that "ran free and completely uncared for" in the surrounding countryside.[40]

The proliferation of cattle, horses, and mules spoke to opportunities in this line of work, but as with mining, natural abundance did not ensure control over nature. "Wild mountain cats" often attacked livestock, wrote Segesser, and since entrepreneurs preferred to save their gunpowder to mine silver, "these harmful beasts of prey multiply unhindered." Ranchlands were frequently devastated by wildfires—some natural, others set by Pima and Apache Indians to drive game—and livestock at times simply wandered off, beyond their owner's control. This control diminished spatially in times of Apache–Spanish conflict. In places, cattle "can no longer be rounded up, much less confined in a corral," observed Pfefferkorn of mid–eighteenth century Sonora, whereas Spanish horses often grew "so wild and timid in the wilderness that they immediately take flight when they but catch sight of a human being."[41]

Like missionaries, ranchers faced what was ultimately a failure of spatial control, which they increasingly saw through the lens of Spanish–Apache struggles. "Nothing is safe from these 'birds of prey,'" Pfefferkorn wrote of Apache raiders, "except that which wanders around wild on the hills and in the bushes and does not let itself be run off." Horses were at greatest risk because Apaches valued them both as mounts and for their meat, which they preferred to beef. As these raids increased, ranchers began to retreat to lands immediately adjacent to the presidios, missions, and villages. Early eighteenth-century ranches that extended for leagues in all directions became a distant memory by century's end. "Only those areas which are in sight of villages are tilled and planted," Pfefferkorn claimed. "So the largest and best part of this beautiful and extremely fertile country lies uncultivated and deserted because of the fear of the barbarians."[42]

This fear of barbarians, more than anything else, motivated the Spanish Crown to see the frontier as a line dividing the empire from stateless forces of nature. The effort to patrol this line gave rise to another colonial landscape, one that was linked to the frontier presidio. In 1692, as native revolts swept across the north, officials established the presidio of Fronteras in northeastern Sonora. As Apaches began raiding in the province in years to come, others were founded at Terrenate, Tubac, Tucson, and Altar. Presidios evoked the authority of the state, but just barely. Presidio captains were usually merchants, miners, or ranchers who sought to increase their local power. At Fronteras, settlers complained that Captain Gregorio Álvarez Tuñón y Quirós used soldiers to herd cattle and mine silver rather than to defend territory, a practice that underscored the fragility of state authority in the region. "The presidial captain was as much a *patrón* as a *comandante*," one historian has argued, for he saw his subordinates less as "warrior-citizens" than as "personal vassals."[43]

Yet many officials expected to eventually overcome these local obstacles. A new generation of Bourbon leaders under King Carlos III began to pour subsidies into these military institutions in the late eighteenth century. Officials in Madrid and Mexico City began to see the far north as a frontier line, and they shifted and respaced presidios to match a new Euclidian geometry of defense. Officers negotiated new treaties, led fresh campaigns into enemy territory, and organized Opata and Pima auxiliaries to increase its armed frontier "citizenry" — even if these Indians fought as much for their own lands as for the interests of empire. Perhaps most significantly, Bourbon authorities offered gifts and rations to those who sought peace, and many accepted. By the 1790s, colonies of *Apaches de paz* (peaceful Apaches) lined northern Chihuahua and Sonora, helping to mark colonial distinctions between civilized and barbarous Mexico.[44]

Subsidies deployed to draw a frontier line and domesticate barbarous outsiders gave rise to a new era of colonial prosperity by the 1790s. Owing to a respite from Apache raids and the Jesuit expulsion of 1767, ranchers claimed former Apache and mission lands on both sides of today's border. Families like the Elías, Ortíz, Pérez, and Pesqueira, who hailed from a close-knit, prestigious military fraternity of presidio commanders and officers, obtained land grants and moved livestock north. Up to twenty thousand head were sent annually to Chihuahua through Carretas Pass, the Elías family alone branding thousands each year on their San Pedro ranch. Good times fueled a new privatization of space. Older mission commons were carved up and granted to individuals to encourage development. By repopulating and defending the far north, bureaucrats reasoned, these local elites would help regenerate the interior spaces of empire.[45]

Yet this bounding and privatization of land also limited the state's power, since it enabled frontier elites to monopolize space on their own terms, thereby undermining the relative power of Madrid and Mexico City. If Bourbon rulers saw authority and control through the lens of enlightened mercantilism, whose conduits led from the periphery to the core, frontier elites sought to keep power at the periphery through local, traditional circuits of marriage, custom, and patron–client relations. By the 1830s, when the Apache peace fell apart, military elites such as the Elías family, who owned much of the land that Apaches began to reclaim, asserted authority as defenders of a region that Mexico City could not control. When locals supported them as *caudillos*, or strongmen, they did so within the familiar context of military patronage. These elites persisted as a strong counterweight to central power, ironically drawing on authority as landed elites and warriors that had been granted in the hopes of building a stronger, more centralized state.[46]

Bourbon leaders never had a chance to control these *caudillos*. In 1810, the wars for Mexican independence broke out, and by 1821, Spanish authorities had been ousted. A new generation of national leaders found Mexico in ruins. The treasury was depleted, trade networks were severed, and presidio subsidies were spent. *Apaches de paz* faced hunger, disease, and renewed animosities (for frontier elites now had to pay for rations from their own pockets) and returned to raiding to survive. A generation of peace had made them stronger—they knew their enemies better, having lived and fought alongside them—and new trade ties to New Mexico and Chihuahua offered outlets for plunder and greater access to arms. Frontier residents watched in alarm as Apaches began to reclaim their old territory in the early 1830s. "Places now marked by agricultural and industrial development," claimed a committee of residents from Sonora, Chihuahua, Durango, and New Mexico in 1832, will soon "be converted into deserts of tears and terror."[47]

As Apaches gained a stronger sense of territorial authority, Sonora became more divided. The wars of independence weakened Sonora's ties to Mexico City, whereas the lifting of colonial trade restrictions in 1821 reoriented it toward the outside world—and especially toward European and North American merchants in the Pacific trade. Sonora now faced a dilemma: how to defend against outsiders while at the same time profiting from them. And who, moreover, should have the authority to sort these issues out: national or state elites? On one hand, locals wanted access to new federal subsidies and hoped to build a stronger nation. But they also wanted to preserve their autonomy, especially their freedom to profit from outside markets on their own terms. Nationally these tensions gave rise to a larger battle between centralists and federalists—who fought over the balance of national and provincial power—but in Sonora they often devolved into fights among rival *caudillos*, who used the rhetoric of national politics to defend their local authority. These contests further undermined efforts by the new nation and its statesmen to control Sonora.[48]

After taking office in 1849, Gov. José de Aguilar looked over his native state with some trepidation. As a teenager in the village of San Miguel de Horcasitas, he had watched as the Mexican eagle replaced the Spanish lion on the flag and as decades of peace with Apaches collapsed. "The decline in the state's security is unsettling," he wrote. Political revolts had created "civil war and the germ of anarchy" in Sonora, and yet this paled in contrast to the "incursions of the barbarians." The Apaches have "left our frontiers depopulated, the fertility of fields devastated, many towns abandoned, and numerous properties that previously formed the wealth of this state ruined," he wrote. Many residents had moved south to safer terrain, whereas the discovery of gold in California—now part of the United States—had emptied entire villages. Citizens had thus become wanderers, wrenched from their homes by tales of "exaggerated" riches or forced to flee to new lands, "where they could find work and the hope of compensation."[49]

Yet on the ground, things were never quite so bad. If statesmen worried about a frontier that seemed to be retreating, frontier residents were adapting to a new way of life among the ruins, just as their native and European forebears had years before. This was a different fugitive landscape: one that persisted rather than retreated, moving like an apparition at the corners of the state's eye. John Russell Bartlett caught glimpses of this shifting terrain in the 1850s. Along the

San Pedro River, where Apaches and feral cattle had reclaimed space formerly fixed by Spanish land grant, he encountered a party of Mexicans hunting wild bulls. He found hidden in a thicket downriver another group "engaged in drying meat" from cattle they had just killed. These were residents of the nearby Santa Cruz presidio who had taken to hunting rather than herding cattle—much like their native enemies.[50]

Residents of Fronteras likewise relied on a hybrid of Spanish and native practices until the harvest, subsisting "entirely upon dried meat from the wild cattle, and pinole." In this presidio community, Bartlett found scant evidence of late colonial reforms that had sought to standardize frontier defenses. Rather than a uniform army, he found a motley crew: the personification of frontier particularity and pragmatism. "Some were dressed in blue great coats and high caps," he observed, "and others in short jackets, while all wore the common loose white cotton drawers and shirts of the country. Every variety of costume seemed admissible." The ad hoc nature of this military frontier was more than sartorial. Its noncommissioned officers included an Apache Indian, held in high regard by his fellow soldiers. "Being familiar with the haunts of his people," Bartlett wrote, he was an indispensable guide, using his local knowledge to sustain an ephemeral military landscape that fell beyond the purview of the state.[51]

These fugitive landscapes—where Mexicans lived like Indians; and where Indians led Mexicans into battle—persisted because the state could not replace them. This was also true in more subterranean realms. As reformers set out to reorganize the frontier in the late eighteenth century, they had also turned to mining. The Bourbon state had created a centralized mining guild (Cuerpo de Minería), a set of mining ordinances, and a School of Mining directed by German-trained mining and metallurgical experts. They hoped to standardize a dizzying array of local mining practices, regenerate lost mines, and use Enlightenment thought to better incorporate space into the empire. By training the sons of mine owners, importing technologies and ideas from abroad, and gathering data from local mines, Bourbon elites hoped to domesticate these spaces and turn them toward the good of the state and the public treasury.[52]

But Mexican independence changed everything. Although political elites would try to revive the Bourbon-era reforms of the mining industry in the 1820s, the unsettled political and economic conditions of the postindependence era prevented these reforms from reaching Sonora. Instead, newcomers found the withered remains of what they considered a lost golden age of mining. The "crumbled walls of reduction haciendas, immense heaps of scoria from their furnaces, and decayed towns," wrote one mining engineer in 1866, spoke to "a higher grade of civilization than has since visited this unfortunate country." Most attributed the decline to a flight of foreign capital after 1821. "The first suicidal act of the Mexican government," wrote the U.S. mining entrepreneur Sylvester Mowry, was the expulsion of the Spanish in 1824, which removed most of the investment capital and "well-directed industry" that had kept mining alive.[53]

No less critical, added the Englishman John Hall, who moved to Sonora in the 1850s, was the decay of the royal ordinances of the 1780s, which had prohibited the destruction of deserted mines by so-called *gambusinos*, independent small-scale miners. In the absence of authorities to enforce the laws in the unstable climate following Mexican independence, Hall wrote, these "reckless men," who made a living by "working in the rubbish thrown out of the mines," hastened the process of subterranean "spoliation and destruction." In some places, they literally unmade mines by attacking the underground pillars required by law to prevent the mine ceilings from falling in on miners. These often contained the best and most accessible ore, and since these trespassers were "fearful of being caught *in flagranti*" they "took the easiest first." In this way, many of Sonora's mines were "caved in" and "lost."[54]

Hall's view of Spanish law and order was selective at best. Bourbon ordinances made the removal of mining supports illegal—"under pain of ten years' imprisonment"—but they also decreed that when owners let mines fall into decay, their "waste ground," "earth heaps," "scoria," and "refuse" became common property of nearby communities. Although Hall and some Mexican elites of his time perhaps wished differently, this was a loophole in legislation otherwise geared to the privatization and commodification of space that legalized traditional common land regimes. It also harnessed ruins legally to the control of space: that which was "left to decay" or became "waste ground" was, according to mining law, free for the taking. This no doubt had worrisome implications for landowners without the means to keep their mines in operation, since Sonora was beginning to enter the imperial gaze of the United States.[55]

By linking the practices of *gambusinos* to criminal acts, Hall also obscured the fact that they had generated much of Sonora's wealth, their small-scale operations being well suited to the unstable climate of the frontier. In many areas, they were simply farmers who launched scavenging raids into Apache-controlled lands between farming cycles, weaving them—much as Apache raiders did Mexican pastures—into a larger, diversified economy. In both cases, what outsiders perceived as a reckless unmaking of space was more often a highly skilled business. The same entrepreneurs who criticized *gambusinos* frequently used them as guides, relying on their knowledge of abandoned mines. So expertly had they picked clean one such mine, admitted a U.S. mining engineer, that "I could scarcely find a sufficient vestige of the ores to determine their character."[56]

These relationships exposed a larger middle ground that had emerged in Sonora. The province had slipped away from colonial dreamers to hover ambivalently between civilized core and barbarous periphery. Yet if missionaries, miners, military elites, and the colonial state were unable to transform Sonora as completely as they had hoped, this was not necessarily a sign of failure. For it was precisely the indeterminate, unfixed, and nomadic nature of this land that allowed residents to survive at the uneven fringes of state power. If the state was concerned with mapping out a coherent political space marked by dichotomies of subject and other, frontier residents learned to ride out the rough spots of this unruly terrain by pragmatically incorporating what the state had been unable to destroy. In a sense, they built immunities to a world in which the defenses of the state were weak by exposing themselves to and eventually internalizing a range of nonstate practices from beyond the colonial pale.

If a shifting world rooted in years of pragmatic wisdom limited the power of one nation-state, it posed a challenge to the next. As Bartlett wandered through Sonora's ghostly landscapes—its plundered communities, its abandoned cattle herds, its scavenged mines, its enduring hybrid spaces—it was the unfinished aspect of this world that caught his eye. He and his readers assumed that Anglo-Americans would complete what Spaniards and Mexicans had left undone. Yet although Mexico was forced to give up much of its northern frontier to new invaders in 1848 and 1854, its age-old dream of domesticating the frontier endured. The question facing future generations was not how U.S. dreams would replace Mexican dreams, but rather how Mexicans and Americans would dream in tandem about a newly divided land, and how in the end these dreams might bring them closer together.

2

BORDERLAND DREAMS

By the time Americans began to dream of Sonora, Sonora was a dream that had traveled across national borders, halfway around the world, and back again. It started with a journey of exploration. In 1799, the German geographer Alexander von Humboldt left Europe with royal permission to explore the Americas from Argentina to New Spain. He had become interested in New Spain several years earlier as a student at the Royal Mining Academy at Freiberg, Saxony. There he had heard glowing reports from two classmates, Andrés Manuel del Río and Fausto de Elhúyar, leaders of New Spain's Cuerpo de Minería. His interest in the Americas extended from astronomy to ruins to botany, but he convinced King Carlos IV to support his expedition by promising to report back on Mexico's mines and mineral deposits.[1]

Humboldt sailed north from South America to New Spain in 1803, where he spent a year, most of it in archives, libraries, and botanical gardens. He visited mines near Mexico City, but most of what he learned came from officials in the capital city and the Royal School of Mining. Like his hosts, he used Enlightenment science to make Mexico legible to administrators and entrepreneurs. The task was far from easy. "I could only give a very imperfect map of Mexico," he complained. It seemed to be an endless fugitive landscape, lacking fixity on formal maps of empire and in relation to astronomical coordinates. Above Durango, "we wander as it were in a desert, notwithstanding the show of manuscript maps," he wrote. If visitors would take sextants, repeating circles, achromatic telescopes, and other geographers' tools into Chihuahua, New Mexico, and Sonora, he proposed, they "would give a new face to the geography of New Spain."[2]

If Humboldt failed to fully pin this land down, his vision of colonial mining fixed Mexico firmly in the dreams of foreign investors. From its unmapped interior, which he compared to the heart of Africa, emerged a vision of wealth rivaling those of Coronado's lost cities. Humboldt's *Political Essay on the Kingdom of New Spain* was translated into English in 1811 with the goal of luring European capital to Mexican mines. And the idea of unfinished conquests appealed to a British capitalist class that was beginning to invest energetically at home and abroad. When Mexico achieved independence in 1821, British entrepreneurs coursed across the ocean, sending back a flurry of promotional pamphlets on mines and prospects. Their dream was the same across the board: British ingenuity and technologies, including steam engines to drain flooded mines, would reclaim these lost landscapes from both nature and a backward colonial past, thereby completing the domestication of Mexico.[3]

As the British followed Humboldt to Mexico, Mexico was turning to the world in new ways. During the colonial era, Sonora had suffered the economic consequences of a mercantilist system that prohibited trade along the frontier, undermining the economic power of local elites and forcing such men as Ignaz Pfefferkorn to depend on precisely those landscapes and customs they most hoped to replace. With independence in 1821, those trade barriers were dissolved, to the great relief of frontier entrepreneurs. On one side, Sonoran merchants reached out in a limited way to the Santa Fe trade between New Mexico, Chihuahua, and the U.S. West. On the other, they tapped a new maritime trade with Europe and Asia that entered Sonora at the port of Guaymas. Guaymas attracted a growing merchant class of Mexicans, along with foreign merchants and investors, whose attention soon turned toward the mining heartland of the state.[4]

British and Mexican dreams converged in Sonora in early 1826, when two British entrepreneurs sailed to Guaymas in search of hidden treasure. The first was Col. Simon Bourne, who had been sent west to explore the abandoned silver mines of San Juan Bautista and Nacozari. The second was Lt. Robert Hardy, who was assigned to report on pearl fisheries on the Sonora coast but who decided at the last minute to accompany Bourne into the interior. They saw only one brig and a handful of small schooners in the port of Guaymas, but officials assured them that commerce was on the rise: in the recent past, over two dozen ships had dropped anchor there. Many of these, Colonel Bourne observed, carried the fruits of the India and China trade from Acapulco, San Blas, and Mazatlán. It was a traffic that predisposed Sonorans to be charitable to outsiders. "Although there are no inns in the towns," Bourne reported, foreigners were always "well received."[5]

Following a warm reception, the men bought horses, mules, and provisions and headed east. In Pitic (soon renamed Hermosillo), their hosts gave them chocolate, white sugar, coffee, and tea from India, China, Peru, and the United States: additional signs of Sonora's new commercial bearings. Yet Sonora's isolation was also evident. Hermosillo was a trade gateway, where imports from coastal Sonora were exchanged for the mining and agricultural products of more traditional highland villages to the east. Burros, carts, and wagons of an older Sonora creaked west along the dusty mountain trails and wagon roads with their loads of gold, copper, silver, wheat, and hides, destined for the bustling trade centers of Loreto, Mazatlán, Acapulco, and China. For newcomers like Bourne and Hardy, these rustic beasts and vehicles seemed to be rattling out of Sonora's past into its future, thus marking a divide that was as temporal as it was spatial.[6]

The antiquity of highland Sonora was most evident at their final destination, the deserted mines of San Juan Bautista and Nacozari. In their heyday, they had supported some of the largest towns in the province; now one could hardly tell them from the land itself. To reach Nacozari, Bourne and Hardy rode through a valley "planted over with fig-trees, pomegranates, peaches, and other fruits with a variety of ornamental shrubs and plants, which were once arranged with order and taste, but now form a confused thicket." Farther on, they stumbled across ruins of churches, homes, and reduction works, "so dilapidated that it is impossible to judge of their former nature." Bourne turned to his Mexican guides from nearby Cumpas and Moctezuma for explanation. "The old men say their fathers used to speak of this spot . . . as being the most delightful place in all of Mexico," he wrote. It had since been "entirely destroyed by the Apaches."[7]

If their Mexican colleagues looked to the past to make sense of this place, Colonel Bourne and Lieutenant Hardy looked to the future. They measured the foundations of the reduction works, followed the paths of the veins, recorded the locations of the mines, and estimated how much they had flooded since they were deserted. These observations—indeed, Bourne's entire account—would later be published as part of a larger economic portrait of Mexico and its mines by Henry Ward, England's foreign minister to Mexico and the one person apart from Humboldt most responsible for feeding knowledge of Mexico back across the Atlantic. Bourne's report inspired future calculations by eager British and U.S. readers, who would mark down numbers, measurements, and equations, fragments of their own transnational dreams, onto the margins of the page.[8]

Bourne's hosts were probably more measured in their expectations. By 1826, the fragile peace between Apaches and Mexicans had begun to crack. Just two years earlier, Chiricahua Apaches had begun to raid north and west of Nacozari, and as elites desperately scraped together money for rations to keep the peace, most knew it was only a matter of time before these ad hoc subsidies would peter out. Nacozari's ghosts no doubt haunted Mexican communities more than ever. And if those who led Bourne and Hardy through the graveyards of their ancestors imagined reprieve in new transatlantic collaborations, they would be sadly disappointed. For barely had Hardy's and Bourne's accounts left the printing press when the Mexican investment bubble burst, and mining capital vanished with British dreams. Even though British merchants continued to dominate the trade of western Mexico, a generation would pass before outsiders again made the long overland journey to San Juan Bautista and Nacozari.[9]

If Humboldt's immediate impact was short-lived, the hope of attracting capital to regenerate Sonora lingered. From the 1820s on, Sonorenses looked abroad for the means to remake a landscape that many knew only from family stories. As Sonora was pulled into a larger oceanic trade, proposed the regional elites Juan M. Riesgo and Antonio J. Valdez in 1828, it might develop an entrepreneurial spirit it lacked under Spanish rule. Its mine owners might then see the "colossal fortunes" that had blessed their counterparts elsewhere in Mexico. "The day that Sonora has a society as economical and ingenious as that of the Jesuits for the working of their mines," added the Sonorense Ignacio Zúñiga in 1835, turning for his part to the past for inspiration, "it will be the best place in the world for precious metals." If Riesgo and Valdez gazed seaward, Zúñiga looked north. With the blazing of new roads to New Mexico and California, he suggested, Sonora might become a gateway for overland trade and thus harness its future to the fortunes of the continent at large.[10]

Zúñiga thought about roads to New Mexico and California because these places, more than Sonora, had been reoriented toward North American markets. After Mexico opened the north to trade in 1821, merchants from Missouri began to drive west across the plains to trade manufactured goods for silver and mules in Santa Fe and Chihuahua; and New England merchant ships sailed west to trade merchandise for California hides and tallow. Apaches to the north, a desert to the northwest, and British domination of coastal commerce kept Sonora isolated from these networks. Americans who came to the state were the exception rather than the rule. One such exception was John A. Robinson, a New York entrepreneur who had sailed to California in 1821 to sell sugar and tobacco. Finding the market glutted, he unloaded his shipment in Guaymas and decided to stay. He married into a prominent family and into the 1860s worked in Sonora as a merchant, trade broker, and consular agent for both the United States and England.[11]

Other Americans migrated west through Apache land. Half a dozen U.S. traders and trappers lived in the village of Moctezuma, near Nacozari and San Juan Bautista, by the 1830s. James Kirker and Robert McKnight were two such men; migrating west as fur trappers, they saw opportunity all across this borderland, managing mines for Mexicans, trapping beavers and smuggling pelts for U.S. markets, trading guns and ammunition to Apaches for plunder from Sonora and Chihuahua ranches (which they sold farther north in New Mexico), and sometimes fighting these same Apaches for Mexicans, who began to pay cash for Apache scalps in the 1830s. These liminal characters, who often married Mexicans and claimed both U.S. and Mexican citizenship, were agents of a new fugitive landscape between nations: fugitive not only because it resisted efforts to fix and police territory, but also because in its unsettled condition it represented an ambiguous, shifting blank space on most mental maps of North America.[12]

Soon after invading Mexico in 1846, the United States began to fill this space in. That same year, after claiming New Mexico, Gen. Stephen Kearny sent Capt. Philip St. George Cooke west to open a road to San Diego. Cooke hired Antoine Leroux and several other trappers who had lived in Sonora in the 1830s to guide them across northern Chihuahua, through the deserted San Bernardino ranch, to their former trapping grounds on the San Pedro River. From here they went to Tucson and then north to the Gila River, which led the army west to California. This was precisely the kind of road Zúñiga had dreamed of a decade earlier. Americans were in a unique position to carry the project out because the Apache groups who controlled this territory saw them as potential allies against shared enemies. "You have taken New Mexico, and will soon take California; go then and take Chihuahua, Durango and Sonora," one chief reportedly told Kearny: "We will help you. . . . The Mexicans are rascals; we hate and will kill them all."[13]

The United States saw Captain Cooke's road as a lifeline for military personnel, but after gold was found at Sutter's Mill in 1848, it became a thoroughfare for thousands of Argonauts and migrants traveling overland to California. For many Sonorans, the gold rush offered an early glimpse of their neighbors to the north. By 1849, merchants and farmers in Tucson had begun to enjoy a brisk commerce with the Americans, who traded for bread, flour, milk, and other goods from nearby fields and pastures. Yet these migrations also had a dark side. In 1849, Anglos sacked the town of Cieneguilla in northwestern Sonora, and a Texas mob ran roughshod over Santa Cruz, a former Spanish presidio community on the road below Tucson. If Americans held Sonora in low regard, the flight of Mexican and Opata refugees from the expanding Apache frontier to California's goldfields reinforced Anglo visions of the region as hostile, barren country.[14]

Like John Russell Bartlett's portrait of an empire in ruins, these visions fed into a larger cant of conquest. Sonora is "under the absolute dominion" of the Apaches, "who had more than a hundred years ago destroyed the early settlements of the Spanish, and driven them to the more southern provinces," wrote one migrant.[15] Such judgments assimilated the region to an older idea of frontier space, one peopled by savages, not real citizens, and thereby justified its annexation. But as the gold fever faded, some gradually revised their opinion of Sonora. A new wind was in the air, fanned by frustrations with California, but also by the circulation of older accounts—notably those of Bourne, Hardy, and Ward—that gave readers a fresh glimpse of their neighbors to the south. The United States began to see Mexico as Humboldt had fixed it in the European mind: a land of lost mines and forgotten treasure. In these textual terrains, Americans found themselves dreaming the dreams of empires past.

Among these new dreamers were a Kentuckian named Charles Debrille Poston and a German-born mining engineer named Herman Ehrenberg. Ehrenberg had moved from Germany to Mexican Texas in the 1830s, where he participated in the war for Texas independence and inspired later waves of German immigration west with his popular account, *Texas und Seine Revolution*. The 1840s found him on the road again, from Texas to Oregon, the Sandwich Islands, Polynesia, and finally California. Poston, for his part, left Kentucky in 1851 to accept a position as a clerk in the San Francisco customshouse, only to find the Golden State in an economic depression. As impoverished and restless fortune seekers began filling the streets, Poston joined Ehrenberg and others who sought to invest their dreams and limited funds elsewhere.[16]

The search for new frontiers began in the so-called Government Boarding House, at the corner of Stockton and Washington, a meeting place for government officials and entrepreneurs. As the United States and Mexico began the discussions that led to the Gadsden Purchase in 1853, "a new California was hoped for on the southern boundary," Poston wrote. Stories of lost mines, or mines soon to be lost to the United States, drew special attention. "Old Spanish history," Poston continued, "was ransacked for information, from the voyages of Cortez in the Gulf of California to the latest dates, and maps of the country were in great demand." Poston and his cohort devoured Bourne's descriptions of Nacozari and San Juan Bautista, yet were even more captivated by the fabled land of "Arizunea," said to be "full of minerals, with fertile valleys washed by numerous rivers, and covered by forests primeval." After convincing local investors to support an expedition, Poston prepared to sail for the Arizona–Sonora borderlands to find if this "new California" lived up to its reputation.[17]

In 1854, the British bark *Zoraida* left San Francisco with Poston and Ehrenberg on board, their heads swimming with visions of El Dorado. According to Poston's colorful (and distorted) version of events, the ship was ill prepared for travel, and after rounding Baja California it wrecked off the Sinaloa coast. Unshaken, the men rowed ashore and made their way up the coast to Sonora, where they struck inland to assess the state's abandoned mines. If we can take Poston at his word, landowners were eager to collaborate, offering partnerships "in consideration of furnishing machinery and means." With U.S. capital and technology, Poston argued, their mines could become "more permanent and regular in yield than the mines of California." When he learned that the Texas Western Railroad Company had surveyors in the northern part of the state, Poston's pulse quickened. The promise of railroad ties to eastern markets suggested that "machinery and means" might be closer at hand than imagined.[18]

Armed with great expectations, Poston traveled to the east coast to secure financial backing. With Samuel Peter Heintzelman, a mining developer and officer at Fort Yuma, California, he organized the Sonora Exploring and Mining Company in Cincinnati in early 1856. Among the company's backers was Robert J. Walker, a New York capitalist who had served as secretary of the treasury under President James K. Polk and now headed the Texas Western Railroad. Where Poston saw silver, Walker saw railroad traffic. Both supported the company's mandate: to return west to the Gadsden Purchase well armed against Apaches, explore the territory, and "recover and hold possession of old Spanish mines" wherever they might be found. As company agent and military commander of the exploring party, Poston was entrusted with the job of finding lost mines and putting them in working order.[19]

Poston left for the borderlands that spring. He stopped in San Antonio to outfit the expedition and obtain recruits, many of them German immigrants who had moved west after reading Ehrenberg's account of Texas in the 1830s. "There were plenty of educated German miners about New Bramfels [*sic*] working on farms and selling lager beer, and they enlisted joyfully," Poston wrote. He made up the balance with "frontiersmen" who "were not afraid of the devil." After securing arms, ammunition, and letters of reference from the U.S. War Department—in case they needed military assistance in Arizona—they continued to the deserted Mexican presidio of Tubac, Arizona, forty-five miles south of Tucson, where they made their headquarters.[20]

Tubac reflected Sonora's embattled past in microcosm. Established as a presidio at the northern edge of Spanish settlement in 1752, it offered a bulwark against Apache expansion. It defended a string of Spanish and Pima settlements in the San Luis Valley, where the Santa Cruz River dipped into what is today Sonora. In such places as Santa María Soamca, a Pima village that later became the Spanish–Indian town of Santa Cruz, settlers had farmed the valley, run cattle, and prospected in the neighboring highlands since 1680. For years, ranchers in the San Luis Valley produced hides, tallow, and meat for mining settlements to the south as well as for export to Chihuahua. Yet by the late 1760s, as Apaches began to pull this region into their own expanding territory, Pima and Spanish refugees left the countryside for the presidio walls of Tubac.[21]

Tubac's position was anything but secure. In 1776, as Apache power grew, royal administrators moved Tubac's troops north to the Pima village of Tucson. Apaches ran off Tubac's remaining residents by 1783, turning it into a ghost town. Yet war could remake as well as unmake space. In 1787, a contingent of Pima soldiers augmented by Opatas from the south was ordered back to Tubac, and as native troops gained control, residents returned. With the Apache peace of the 1790s, ranchers and miners spread out once again into the nearby highlands, and by the time of Mexican independence, former Indian lands were being swallowed by new land grants. The Tubac elites Tomás and Ignacio Ortíz gained titles to the Arivaca and Canoa land grants north and west of town in 1821 and 1833, León Herreras claimed former mission lands on the Sonoita Creek to the east, and other enterprising Mexicans similarly took over Apache and Pima land on the Santa Cruz and San Pedro rivers and the grasslands in between.[22]

Like its precursors, this new era of peace and prosperity was built on precarious foundations. When military funding dried up after independence, local armistices with Apaches faltered. As Apaches renewed their raiding and reclaimed land, Mexican control once again dissolved. By 1840, Mexicans had abandoned the Sonoita and Canoa ranches, and by decade's end Apaches had once again pushed residents out of Tubac and the neighboring Pima enclave of Tumacácori. Although Mexico established a new military colony in Tubac in 1851, authorities found it nearly impossible to convince residents to return, and by 1854 Apaches had severed its ties to the outside world. Weeks before Poston and his party arrived, demoralized Mexican troops packed their belongings and crossed the new national border to Santa Cruz, Sonora.[23]

This embattled past haunted Poston as he entered Tubac. "There was not a soul in the old presidio," he recalled. "It was like entering the ruins of Pompeii." Having access to eastern capital, however, he was confident he and his colleagues could bring Tubac back to life. They refurbished officers' quarters and vacant houses, repaired old corrals, and cut timber in the nearby mountains to rebuild the doors, windows, and furniture that former residents had carted to Mexico. That December, Poston purchased the 8,677-acre Arivaca land grant from the Ortízes, and within a year the company had converted its savannas into pastures for its cattle, mules, and horses. Meanwhile, mining experts fanned out in search of lost wealth: ruins of *arrastras* and smelters showed where the silver had been reduced, and half-hidden mine openings, rank with vegetation, led to the abandoned shafts.[24]

If linkages to Wall Street made Poston and his colleagues confident, their success was also due to makeshift arrangements with Apaches. The United States had not yet established a policy for dealing with Apaches, and to survive as a minority population entrepreneurs had to negotiate treaties locally. These so-called calico treaties, wrote the English border resident John Hall, protected newcomers from raids if they left Indians the "privilege of entering Sonora and despoiling its inhabitants." Poston agreed to such a treaty with the Chiricahua Apache leader Mangas Coloradas, owners of the nearby Patagonia mine made a similar treaty, giving gifts of beef, salt, and flour in return for peace, and Indian agents did the same in 1858 to protect the overland wagon road. Apaches had much to gain from these agreements. Knowing Mexicans could not legally pursue them across the border and counting on treaties, gifts, and markets for plunder in Arizona, Hall wrote, they "committed their depredations [into Mexico] with impunity."[25]

As raids around Tubac declined, former residents trickled back to their deserted homes, fields, and pastures along the Santa Cruz River. Although a new border divided the region, this did not seem to bother Mexicans, who migrated north "in great numbers to work." Poston later attributed the migration to the magic of Yankee enterprise, but this was the selective memory of someone who remembered himself as the Daniel Boone of Arizona. In reality, the power of the state, more than pioneering spirit, attracted workers. In 1856, well before the Sonora Exploring and Mining Company began operations, the U.S. Army established a new post at the Calabasas ranch, south of Tubac. According to reporters in Sonora, this gave Mexicans fresh confidence in the borderlands. With "protection from Indians, and market for their produce" at Calabasas, wrote a newcomer, the farmers of Imuris, Magdalena, and San Ignacio, Sonora, found "new life" feeding their new military neighbors just across the line.[26]

Migrants from the north, many from Tucson, came south to supply the new military community as well. Prices were as high as "the California prices of 1849," and cattle would fetch "more here than at any place in the west," the Tucsonan William B. Roods told a friend. For old-timers at Tubac, the economic benefits of war were nothing new. And nowhere were they more apparent than along nearby Sonoita Creek. Felix Grundy Ake, one of the first to resettle the Sonoita, had gone ahead of the troops with orders to "put up forage for the dragoons" and later supplied the troops with lumber. His neighbor William Wordsworth filled a contract for beef, while his son-in-law, Thomas Thompson, raised vegetables for the army. Elias Green Pennington and his sons cut hay for horses and mules, and his daughters sewed for the officers' wives. These farmers continued to feed troops after 1857, when the army established Fort Buchanan at the head of Sonoita Creek, and by this time they were supplying new mining contracts as well.[27]

If mining took longer than soldiering to transform the economy, it was because it took longer to get a mining venture in order. By 1857, the Sonora Exploring and Mining Company had begun enlarging one of its mines but then hit water and had to suspend operations until it could get pumping equipment from California. It began building reduction works by early 1858, but smelting and amalgamation machinery, ordered months before from San Francisco, had not yet arrived. Mountains of ore accumulated near the mine, waiting to be smelted. When the machinery came, "the rainy season had set in, the material on the mine, adobes, etc., had been destroyed, the contracts to deliver the timber broken, and the workmen employed in building the works . . . had left," wrote one official. "We had no goods in the *tienda*, and those ordered and bought in San Francisco did not arrive; we could not pay the Mexican peons regularly, and they were unwilling to work." And to top things off, the staves for the amalgamation barrels had dried out and no longer fit. All told, "unforeseen obstacles" delayed production for over two years.[28]

By this time, other companies had joined the field. In 1858, officers of the Sonora Exploring and Mining Company created the Santa Rita Mining Company to work mines in the Santa Ritas, east of Tubac. Another enterprise was the Patagonia mine, a deserted mine that officers from nearby Fort Buchanan tried to exploit in their spare time. These military men sank shafts that were, according to later reports, "badly opened and badly worked." Eventually the mine passed to the retired army officer Sylvester Mowry, who had greater access to capital. He invested two hundred thousand dollars in the mines and smelters, in houses for the Mexican workers, and in everything else required "for an extensive and permanent establishment." This new venture, the Mowry mine, joined the ranks of the top regional producers.[29]

By the late 1850s, mines and military posts had regenerated linkages to Sonora. Magdalena, Sonora, became a supply center for Tubac, wheat from Cucurpe fed troops at Fort Buchanan, and the town of Santa Cruz sustained the Mowry mine, just miles to the north. Mexican merchants sold wagons of flour, beans, fruit, and *panocha* (brown sugar cakes) for silver, and from these rural products Mexican and Indian miners made their traditional fare of *tortillas, frijoles,* and *pinole.* Such transactions were small scale but far reaching. In Sonora, wrote Mowry "almost every shopkeeper knew the value of the ore" from the Sonora Exploring and Mining Company's Heintzelman mine, which passed along webs of exchange that reached even to British merchant ships on the coast. Conversely, Fort Buchanan, Tubac, and other mining camps depended so heavily on Mexican fields, orchards, and pastures, wrote one local military officer, that one had to consider southern Arizona "a dependency of Sonora."[30]

Arizona's mining enterprises likewise leaned heavily on Mexican workers. Over 80 percent of the men in the Santa Rita and Heintzelman mining camps in 1860, and 94 percent of those at the Mowry mine in 1864, were from Mexico. Some were mestizos, others were Opatas, Yaquis, and Tohono O'odham. Their migrations into this region were nothing new. Tubac had nurtured ties for years not only to Santa Cruz and the San Luis Valley, but also to the borderland towns of Cucurpe, Magdalena, Onavas, Cocóspera, and Altar, Sonora, through genetic and ritual kinship, trade, and ceremonial networks. Pima and Opata soldiers in Tubac nurtured similar ties to their home villages in Sonora and the Pimería Alta, and many were linked to Spanish and mestizo networks, in turn, through ties of *compadrazco*, or godparentage. When Mexicans migrated north to work near Tubac after 1854, they retraced lifelines of an enduring regional community—invisible on most maps—that extended deep into Mexico.[31]

What made these networks appealing to U.S. elites was the cost of Mexican labor: Mexican workers tolerated lower wages than their U.S. counterparts. U.S. entrepreneurs also thought, often mistakenly, that Sonorenses were used to debt peonage. "The lower class of Mexicans, with the Opata and Yaqui Indians, are docile," Mowry wrote. "They have always been 'peons' (servants) for generations. They will always remain so, as it is their natural condition." Following this line of thought, the Santa Rita Mining Company paid Mexicans twelve to fifteen dollars monthly versus thirty to seventy dollars a month plus board for Anglos, and it even lowered these costs by paying Mexicans with marked-up items from the company store. Poston paid Mexican workers with *boletas*, or coupons, which he claimed were used "among the merchants in the country and in Mexico." Thirty-two percent of these Mexican "wages," noted a colleague, returned to the company as profits at the company store.[32]

Given Sonora's abandoned mines and cheap labor, one might imagine that mining officials leaped at the chance to expand investments south of the border. Curiously, in the 1850s at least, few did. Sonora entrepreneurs more readily crossed borders. The Magdalena merchant Francisco Padrés not only hauled freight to Tubac and Fort Buchanan, but also operated the nearby Cahuabi and Fresnal mines. When gold on the Gila River brought a rush of miners from Sonora in the 1860s, Hall recollected, merchants in Cucurpe "advanced money to the adventurers at 200 per cent, to be paid on their return from the new El Dorado." Hall was one of the few to find his fortune in the other direction. In 1850, he had moved to Cucurpe with Mexican and Opata acquaintances he had made in the California goldfields. Living and working with Sonorenses, he was struck by the selective nature of these transnational circuits. Americans looked south into Mexico, but Mexicans, more than Americans, crossed borders to their advantage.[33]

If U.S. businessmen seemed more constrained than their Mexican counterparts—if they relied on others to cross borders—they also lacked the pragmatism and flexibility that was second nature to Sonorenses. When they found this land hard to domesticate, they were more easily frustrated. Initially, things went their way. At the Mowry mine, "the sound of the axe reverberated from hill to hill," and the "smoke of many charcoal pits filled the air," noted the journalist J. Ross Browne in 1864. "It may very literally be said that the wilderness blossomed as the rose." But there was more to this picture than met the eye, added the mining engineer Raphael Pumpelly. "Seen through its wonderfully clear atmosphere, with a bright sun and an azure sky, or with every detail brought out by the intense light of the moon, this has seemed a paradise," he insisted, and yet "again, under circumstances of intense anxiety, it has been a very prison of hell." [34]

Among this landscape's more unsettling aspects was its isolation. Browne marveled that one could find a region "so completely isolated from the civilized world." Sonora, he claimed, is "practically, more distant from San Francisco and New York than either of those cities is from China or Norway. I made the trip from Germany to Iceland and back much more easily, and with much less expense and loss of time, than from San Francisco to Sonora and back." Distances from centers of supply were especially taxing, for the depletion of a single item could be crippling. When miners ran out of safety fuse at the Santa Rita mines, they had to shut down until more could be sent in. And when a mining engineer at the Heintzelman asked for nails, he found none could be had "short of Hermosillo." "Such neglects are unpardonable," Heintzelman wrote in his diary. In the end, the company had two choices: order the nails from San Francisco and wait months for them to arrive or make their own. [35]

Isolation also constrained food supplies. Farmers and merchants worked to feed miners, but their success depended on the season, availability of labor, and the nature of the roads—impassable during the rains, always vulnerable to raids. In light of the unprecedented demand, it was amazing everyone got fed. One manager claimed he had run out of flour and coffee, then later griped, "We have had nothing to eat for some time but flour and beans, no fat or grease of any kind." Many blamed shortages on ineptitude. "The store keeper don't know flour is wanted until he sells the last pound," wrote Heintzelman, and later: "Our men have had no meat for three days and we have none to-day, from the neglect of our worthless storekeeper." He complained that the oranges he bought were "not quite ripe enough and a little sour." Whether a problem of supply or demand, one thing was clear: distance from markets limited Heintzelman's ability to eat what he wanted, as it had for generations of colonists before him. [36]

U.S. managers faced a similar lack of control in the mines and smelters. Owing to a chronic scarcity of labor, veins went untouched and ore piled up. Men were competent as miners—breaking and hauling rock—but had limited metallurgical experience, at least with the latest U.S. methods. The roasting of ores "is performed too hurriedly," argued Mowry, and "the roving character of the Mexicans renders it very difficult to make them good workmen at the furnace." Yet more often than not, the largest problem was the complexity of ores, or the way the silver was bound chemically to the rest of the rock. Metallurgy was still in its infancy in the United States, and local Mexican expertise was often equal to if not better than imported knowledge. Mowry explained how efforts to use an expensive barrel amalgamation process from Freiberg, Saxony, yielded the loss of as much as 30 percent of the silver smelted at Arivaca. Had they used the cheaper Mexican patio process, he admitted, the outcome would have been the same.[37]

Managers were also frustrated by a lack of industrial discipline. After payday at the Mowry mine, "work is out of the question," claimed Browne. Relatives and friends from nearby Santa Cruz joined the miners, and the camp dissolved into endless games of *monte*. Managers saw these visits just as Jesuits had seen "wild" Indians and "godless" Spaniards: as corrupting influences. They felt the same way about religious festivals, which emptied the mines and smelters. When the *fiesta* of San Francisco came to Magdalena in October, even Americans joined the fun. Poston and his friends left to "attend the 'fiesta,' like a pack of children," grumbled Heintzelman in 1858: thus "our operations are suspended." New bonanzas also disrupted discipline. When gold was discovered on the Gila River in 1858, for instance, Mexicans abandoned the mines and smelters near Tubac. In such a climate, mining operators had to work around a schedule that was as Mexican as it was American.[38]

Even more unsettling was the volatility of race relations in the borderlands. The specter of social conflict shook investors' confidence in part because this land already had a reputation as disputed terrain. And nothing set tensions more on edge than the persistent U.S. rhetoric of annexation. Many local entrepreneurs predicted the eventual annexation of Sonora, but it was one thing to imagine such a future and quite another to carry these ideas to the streets. Things grew particularly tense in 1857, when the Californian Henry Crabb and an army of U.S. civilians invaded Caborca, Sonora, to the southwest of Tubac. After a brief battle, Mexican soldiers captured and executed the invaders, leaving their bodies to be devoured by wild animals. Distrust lingered on both sides, and for a time Mexican officials shut down all trade with Arizona. "Americans were not safe over the Mexican boundary, and Mexicans were in danger in the boundaries of the United States," Poston wrote. For months afterward "the country was paralyzed."[39]

The tensions provoked by the Crabb filibuster went underground in 1858, only to resurface in 1859 with the so-called Sonoita Massacre. Rumors had circulated that April that Mexican peons on the Reventon ranch near Tubac were plotting to rise in revolt, murder local Americans, and plunder the ranch. The Anglo fore-man, George Mercer, and others went after the leaders of the rumored rebellion, whom they caught, tied up, and whipped. Hall, visiting Tubac at the time, heard the story from friends. One of the Anglos, "an old Indian hunter, and half drunk, acted as a barber," Hall wrote. He "dressed their hair in a barbarous fashion" and cut one man's scalp and ear in the process. A few days later, a squatter named Greenbury Byrd, one of the men present at the whipping, was murdered in his cabin near Tumacácori, reportedly by the "shaved Mexicans."[40]

The news of the murder caused enormous excitement. On May 9, 1859, a mob of armed Anglos calling themselves regulators rode through the Sonoita valley, driving Mexicans from the ranches. At its head was a hell-raiser named William Ake, a nephew of the rancher Felix Grundy Ake who had come to Arizona with Crabb. As Ake and his regulators approached a local mescal distillery, Mexican and Yaqui workers began to run. The attackers opened fire, and a skirmish en-sued. When the dust cleared, three Mexicans and a Yaqui Indian lay dead. Sit-ting down to dinner that night at the nearby Patagonia mine, Hall heard a man shouting, "Mataron a todos! Mataron a todos!" (They killed everyone). It was his friend José Gándara, an owner of the distillery. Returning with him to the scene, Hall found everything "destroyed and deserted . . . the botas overturned and the peons' shanties gutted—their contents strewn in all direction." One of the victims still lay where he had fallen, "killed by the cut of a bowie knife, which disemboweled him."[41]

Just like the Crabb filibuster, the Sonoita Massacre disrupted the entrepre-neurial landscape of southern Arizona. News of the violence "spread like a prai-rie fire over the country," wrote a reporter. Almost a hundred Mexicans left the Heintzelman mine and smelting works at Arivaca, and others took their leave of the Santa Rita camp and farms on the Santa Cruz. They left the Sonoita valley completely deserted. In Santa Cruz, "the entire male population got under arms and prepared to resist an invasion," claimed one reporter, while "every fugitive from the American side [had] some horrid version of the murderous intention of the Americans, who it was declared intended to invade Sonora and extermi-nate the people." In Sonora, authorities were hard-pressed to prevent locals from exacting revenge on foreigners, noted Hall. He was preparing to return home to Cucurpe, but after the massacre he chose to wait, "as I did not consider it very healthy in Sonora for white men for some time."[42]

Mining entrepreneurs, ranchers, and merchants met and drew up a resolution to condemn the "gang of lawless men" who had led the massacre. It was pub-lished in Spanish and English and promised safe passage back to the mines for "all Mexicans who desire work." These elites also worried about the unmaking of trade networks. They assured Mexican merchants south of the border that "trains and property shall be safe from . . . bad Americans or Mexicans." They promised that soldiers at Fort Buchanan would take the lead in "ridding the country of the outlaws," not surprising since Capt. R. S. Ewell, the commanding officer, was an owner of the Patagonia mine. By late May, residents of southern Arizona were still feeling the impact of the Sonoita Massacre. The planting of crops was delayed, and hopes of attracting labor back to finish this job seemed slim after haciendas in Sonora began to pick up the workers for themselves.[43]

Despite the public outcry against "lawless men," traditional fault lines gradually reappeared. "Public opinion took a decided turn against Mexicans," Hall wrote, while Mexican violence against U.S. employers grew. Horse stealing, reportedly by "lawless" Mexicans, became so common that "it was not possible to keep an animal." The Sonoita murderers—those who were caught—were tried and released, and only one returned to Arizona. After a while, Hall got word from Sonora "that the excitement had abated, and that the Mexicans were on their return to the lines on the look out for work." Taking his cue, he decided to leave the tense racial climate of Arizona behind and return to his home in Cucurpe, "well knowing that although some hard feelings should remain against 'white men' . . . I was safe."[44]

As tense as border relations between Anglos and Mexicans were, more unsettling was the decay of the fragile Anglo–Apache peace. Local treaties held for a time: raiding parties were seen riding to Mexico, but they generally skirted Tubac's mines. Things fell apart after newcomers began to disregard the treaties. In 1858, lumberjacks working on the Canoa ranch helped Mexican ranchers recover horses and mules that Apaches had driven off. A month later, Apaches attacked the ranch, killing its residents, burning its buildings, and running off its stock. In 1859, when Apaches stopped at the Mowry mine to obtain customary rations of flour and tobacco, an armed miner ordered them to leave. In a subsequent flare of tempers, two men were killed. Military officials reported that the Apaches had not broken any treaties—they were "on their way into Sonora on a marauding expedition"—and that the blame lay with the miner. Yet it was also clear that tolerance between Apaches and Americans was wearing thin.[45]

In ways, this tolerance had always been thin. When Apaches pledged friendship to General Kearny in 1846, the trapper Kit Carson warned him against taking the promises too literally. Carson knew that treaties were always contingent. For instance, Apaches thought Americans hated Mexicans, but when Mexican and U.S. elites began to collaborate at Tubac they had to rethink this assumption. Conditions were also shifting on the Apache side. By the late 1850s, local chiefs such as Mangas Coloradas, Cochise, and Victorio were growing powerful because Mexicans could no longer chase them into their Arizona strongholds and because U.S. markets for Mexican plunder were booming. Yet Apaches were of different minds. Some raided Mexico with impunity; others sought to renew older peace treaties. Mexicans were also divided: some felt that Sonora could not afford to wage constant war, while others, such as the military elites José Juan Elías and Rafael Angel Corella, hated Apaches and sought their extermination.[46]

The migration to Apache lands of thousands of Americans, many with their own legacy of Indian hating, added more stress to these unstable foundations. If U.S. officials found treaties had to be negotiated on a local basis owing to the multiplicity of Apache bands, factions, and alliances, Apaches faced a similar, often unsettling diversity of U.S. attitudes and interests. Some tolerated their raids, some bought their booty, and some joined Mexicans against them. If some were respectful, others treated them in a cavalier fashion. It was hard to pin Americans down, and this made Apaches uneasy. U.S. gifts and rations also left much to be desired: some Apaches even considered casting their lot with Mexicans because they rewarded their allies better. This all added to the complexity of the situation near Tubac, where a diplomatic veneer was slowly being worn away by the weight of cross-border and cross-cultural contingencies.[47]

Officers at Fort Buchanan hoped to chastise the Apaches, but, like that of the fledgling mining enterprises they defended, their control over the region was little more than symbolic. Not only did they lack the manpower, the knowledge of Apache land, and the authority to pursue Indians south into their Mexican sanctuaries, but they also knew that direct military action would likely ensure retaliation against mines, settlements, and the overland mail, a crucial link between Arizona enterprise and eastern capital. These fears were well founded. In 1861, when Lt. George N. Bascom took Chiricahua hostages to force the recovery of cattle and of a boy taken by other natives, Apaches under Cochise attacked a wagon train, killing its Mexican drivers and taking three Americans. When Bascom refused to back down, they killed their hostages, and Bascom responded in kind. By year's end, avenging Chiricahua warriors had swept across Anglo-American Arizona, turning it into a mirror image of Mexican Sonora.[48]

By this time, national banking failures tied to the Panic of 1857 had begun to fray the tenuous cords of finance that sustained Tubac. As speculative ventures all across the United States lost backing and as the search for investors became desperate, silver entrepreneurs in southern Arizona found themselves unable to mine anything but optimistic rhetoric. No less unsettling were fresh sectional tensions in the east. In response to secession in February 1861, Congress discontinued the southern overland mail. Weeks later, the Civil War broke out and the United States began to recall troops from Arizona. Superiors wired officers at Fort Buchanan to abandon the post, burn its buildings, and destroy "anything that will feed an enemy." Apaches attacked the fort in June 1861, killing several soldiers and chasing its horse and mule herds into Mexico. But its fate was already sealed: a few weeks later, its troops tied up loose ends, set fire to the fort, and left for Santa Fe.[49]

Without the army, Tubac's managerial elite held out little hope. "The wisest said we could not hold the country," that "the Apaches would come down upon us by the hundreds, and the Mexicans would cut our throats," Poston later wrote. Most of the mines were already in dire straits because of indebtedness and Apaches. Pumpelly put it this way: "We were entirely out of money, owing a considerable force of Mexican workmen and two or three Americans, and needed means for paying the transportation of the property, and for getting ourselves out of the country." Desperate, he rode to the Heintzelman mine, one of his debtors, only to find them in a similar bind. Unable to get money, "for no one could afford to part with bullion," he agreed to accept a load of ore along with some flour and calico. Giving these last items to his workers, he took the ore to Tubac, where he and a few others spent nine weeks surrounded by Apaches but smelting the ore to pay the rest of the employees, "who without it could not escape."[50]

After the army left, wrote Poston, Mexicans began to cross the border, "declaring that the American government was broken up, and they had come to take their country back again." Managers redoubled their guard over their Mexican workers, even as they armed these same men to help guard against Apaches. After Americans deserted Tubac, Mexicans stripped the town of its doors and windows—as they had when they left Tubac in 1856—and carted machinery and ore across the border. The economy of Sáric, Sonora, thirty miles below Arivaca, boomed under this new trade in scavenged ore. Visiting the Heintzelman mine in 1864, Browne found the impact of this *gambusino* enterprise clearly etched on the landscape. Piles of silver ore had "been broken up ready for packing away," he observed, "and the fresh tracks of mule-trains and wagon-wheels, on the well-beaten road to Sáric, showed just how profitable this sort of enterprise must be to the Sonoranians."[51]

Southern Arizona in the early 1860s bore a haunting resemblance to the deserted Mexican landscapes of John Russell Bartlett's era. Tubac's plaza, once a vibrant center of U.S. enterprise, was "knee-deep with weeds and grass," and its silver mines were "silent and desolate—a picture of utter abandonment," wrote Browne. "The engines were no longer at work; the rich piles of ore lying in front of the shafts had been sacked and robbed by marauding Mexicans; nothing was to be seen but wreck and ruin, and the few solitary graves on a neighboring hill,

Tubac.

Figure 4. Tubac in ruins, 1864. From J. Ross Browne,
Adventures in the Apache Country (1869).

which tell the story of violence and sacrifice by which the pathway to civilization
has been marked in Arizona."[52]

Americans now came close to understanding what this land had meant to
their Mexican precursors. Gone were glowing prophecies of opportunity rooted
in the ashes of former empires. Americans saw instead the specter of their own
unfinished conquest of space. "It was sad to leave the country that had cost so
much money and blood in ruins," wrote Poston years later, "but the greatest blow
was the destruction of our hopes—not so much of making money as of making
a country." "Of all the lonesome sounds that I can remember," he recalled, the
"most distinctive is the crowing of cocks on the deserted ranches. The very chickens seemed to know that they were abandoned."[53]

Soon the Union was reunited, and Americans would spill into the borderlands
in unprecedented numbers, following new frontier dreams. Browne's account,
in fact, was not so much a melancholy tribute to failed dreams as a challenge to
a newer generation of borderland entrepreneurs. "Tubac is now a city of ruins,"
he acknowledged in 1864, "yet I can not but believe that the spirit of American
enterprise will revisit this delightful region, and re-establish, on a more permanent footing, all that has been lost. The mines are proverbially rich; and rich
mines will sooner or later secure the necessary protection for working them."
Even in 1861, when U.S. mining elites were first jolted awake from their border
reveries, few doubted this land would eventually yield to the twin forces of capital

and modernity. "That the region in question has a future that is both bright and near," wrote Pumpelly after leaving his own mining enterprise in ruins, "there can, I think, be little doubt."[54]

Yet if this future promised to pull Arizona toward the reconstructed body politic, it would pull in other directions as well. More than ever, Arizona mining entrepreneurs would find their gaze turned south as well as north, especially after railroads connected Arizona and Sonora in the early 1880s. These ties would be bolstered by the discovery of new copper deposits in both states, which in the railroad era attracted capital in ways that mining elites in the 1850s barely anticipated. By the early twentieth century, the rise of new transnational connections in the copper borderlands would profoundly change the ways economic elites saw Arizona and Sonora. For no longer was it possible to imagine one without feeling drawn, almost inexorably, to the other.

Part II

BORDER CROSSINGS

3

INDUSTRIAL FRONTIERS

In 1864, as civil war raged in the United States, a young Mexican diplomat named Matías Romero dined with U.S. capitalists at Delmonico's in New York City. Mexico was a different place from what it would be in 1891, when an older Romero met Walter S. Logan on Wall Street. Among other things, it was mired in a civil war of its own. France had invaded Mexico in 1862, setting up a client monarchy under Ferdinand Maximilian and forcing President Benito Juárez and his cabinet out of Mexico City. Romero, a twenty-five-year-old lawyer, was among the refugees. A spokesman for the Juarista cause, he was seeking support against the French, but he was also interested in reshaping U.S. visions of Mexico. It was this task that brought him to Delmonico's. If Americans could imagine common ground with Mexicans, he reasoned, they might support Juárez's fight for national autonomy. And what better way to make this argument than to present the U.S. business class with a portfolio of opportunities to be found in a restored liberal Mexico?[1]

"My country has been favored with all the blessings of nature," Romero told the crowd seated before him. Mexico had produced much of the silver in the world, and as for gold, "the wealth of California is nothing compared with that which still remains in Mexico." As Mexico's neighbor, he insisted, the United States was "called by nature" to develop his nation's mineral resources. His dream of a modern world that transcended national borders—which he later toasted with Logan in 1891—was already well formed in 1864. Economic ties would allow Americans to extract the "blessings of nature" to the benefit of both nations, he argued. Through trade and development "the United States will derive all the advantages which they might obtain from the annexation of Mexico, without suffering any of the inconveniences."[2]

Among Romero's most rapt listeners was a merchant named William E. Dodge Jr. of the New York import-export house of Phelps, Dodge, and Company (hereafter, Phelps Dodge). Dodge knew Romero well, for his father and name-sake had recently hosted the Mexican diplomat in his Madison Street mansion and would later invite him for a weekend at his country home on the Hudson. The connection was partly political, for within a context of U.S. disunity the elder Dodge embraced the Juarista battle as a model republican cause. But the family also had other things on its mind. Phelps Dodge was a leading manufac-turer of brass, a copper-zinc alloy, and was seeking new sources of copper. And copper might have been on Dodge's mind that night, for that same year min-ing promoters were beginning to gossip about a "monster mine" of copper that had been discovered near the colonial silver mining town of Nacozari, Sonora. Perhaps this reservoir of red metal figured among the "blessings of nature" that Dodge imagined as he gazed into Romero's crystal ball.[3]

It makes for interesting speculation because years later Phelps Dodge pur-chased this "monster mine," making Nacozari a cornerstone of a growing transna-tional empire in copper. Perhaps that night at Delmonico's William E. Dodge Jr. saw not just the future of Mexico but his own as well. Yet what mattered more in 1864 was not the particulars—a monster mine in Mexico, a curious capitalist—but the sea change in the way Americans thought about Mexico. When Dodge and Romero raised a glass to the future, they saw a new age of transnational con-nections. The annexationist visions of the previous generation, which led Henry Crabb and his fellow adventurers to a grisly death in Caborca and fueled mur-ders and racial tensions in the Sonoita valley, were gradually being replaced by a new sensibility. By 1864, the expansion of U.S. capital into Mexico was begin-ning to replace the appetite for territory. As one statesman put it, Americans were beginning to "value dollars more, and dominion less."[4]

San Francisco capitalists led the way. In 1863 and 1864, California poured over a million dollars into Sonora's abandoned mines, and millions more were spent on stamp mills, hardware, cloth, iron, steel, lumber, pumps, and steam en-gines, shipped from San Francisco to Guaymas. "The prospects of Sonora have much improved," wrote the mining entrepreneur Sylvester Mowry in 1864. He nodded to the growing stability of the state under Gov. Ignacio Pesqueira, a lib-eral Juarista. "The constitutional power of the state has been boldly asserted and maintained, [and] revolutions nipped in the bud," he observed. If annexation-ists had preyed on stereotypes of a weak, disordered Mexico, the new economic expansionists emphasized the opposite: a strong, reformed state with an interest in protecting investments. Many saw in Pesqueira and the liberal ascendancy in Hermosillo promising signs of a new era of cross-border collaboration.[5]

In 1862, a year after retreating soldiers set fire to Fort Buchanan, U.S. troops from California reoccupied Tucson and established new military posts nearby.

Mexicans and Americans gradually returned to the farms, ranches, and mines of southern Arizona, and by the late 1860s, trade with Sonora was stronger than ever. Most traffic passed from Hermosillo to Tucson, a new regional crossroads. When he arrived in Tucson in 1866, the immigrant John Spring found the main street "taken up by a long train of army wagons, and another of 'prairie schooners' carrying flour from Sonora, Mexico." Tucson was the "chief depot of supplies" for the army quartermaster, who redistributed goods from Sonora to military posts across southern Arizona, but some places looked directly across the border. Camp Wallen, for instance, a new fort on the San Pedro River, nudged aside the former Mowry mine as the chief beneficiary of the fields and pastures of Santa Cruz, Sonora.[6]

Like their precursors in Tubac, Americans found these ties constrained by nature and local custom. Soldiers seeking a familiar meal of beef and potatoes in Tucson were frequently disappointed. "Beef was not always easy to procure," explained the army officer John Gregory Bourke of Tucson, "but there was no lack of bacon, chicken, mutton, and kid meat." Potatoes did not grow well and "could not be had for love or money." Yet for those willing to eat by the custom of the country, "there was plenty of 'jerked' beef, savory and palatable enough in stews and hashes; eggs, and the sweet, toothsome black 'frijoles' of Mexico." Even the local money was Mexican: until the railroad arrived in 1880, wrote the immigrant John A. Rockfellow, Tucson merchants quoted prices in silver pesos.[7]

Despite these renewed border crossings, U.S. market penetration into Sonora was relatively shallow. The state saw a reversal of fortunes after the French took Guaymas in 1865. "Owing to the revolutions and disturbed condition of the country," reported U.S. Consul Alexander Willard in 1868, all but two of the U.S. mining companies founded in the early 1860s "are lying idle, and most of them abandoned." The economic depression following the French expulsion in 1867 only made things worse, as did renewed conflicts with Apaches. Military forces in Arizona did little to interrupt the flow of guns and ammunition to Apaches in return for Sonora livestock and booty. In the early 1870s the United States created a new reservation on the border for the Chiricahua Apaches, which offered refuge for raiders. Apache incursions in Sonora led to the desertion of mines, haciendas, farms, and ranches and spurred emigration, leaving fewer people to prevent the frontier from slipping out of Mexican control.[8]

Those dining with Romero in 1864 would have been discouraged by these trends. If Americans and Mexicans yearned for new, liberal connections of development and trade, then things were hardly moving as planned. Sonora was trapped in a vicious cycle of warfare and emigration, while Apaches had all but planted a flag on a growing territory that resisted U.S. and Mexican visions of economic expansion. And just as U.S. entrepreneurs prepared to make a second pass at the borderlands, bank failures in the 1870s undercut confidence. But at the centers of power, the gears of a new industrial era were nevertheless starting to move. And like its entrepreneurial precursors, it began to gather momentum in that western powerhouse of empire, San Francisco.

It all began with a battle over what many considered a worthless desert. In 1870, a group of tycoons, known in California as the Big Four—Collis P. Huntington, Leland Stanford, Mark Hopkins, and Charles Crocker—took over a railroad known as the Southern Pacific that was planned between San Francisco and San Diego. Initially they intended to build south, but things changed in the late 1870s when a competitor line, the Texas and Pacific, decided to run track west from Texas. The Southern Pacific advanced toward Yuma, on the Arizona border, to defend its California monopoly. Arizona offered little in the way of traffic, but momentum and competitive spirit took over. In 1878, the Big Four pushed on beyond Yuma to claim federal lands destined for their competitors. Railroad crews reached Tucson in March 1880, and one year later completed a transcontinental connection in the borderland village of Deming, New Mexico.[9]

The Southern Pacific rapidly transformed the border landscape. Goods that once took three weeks to reach Arizona from San Francisco now crossed California in three or four days. In Sonora, consumers continued to buy manufactured goods from California but unloaded them from trains in Arizona rather than from ships in Guaymas. By 1877—months before Southern Pacific crews had even left Yuma for Tucson—half the cotton and woolen goods bound for Sonora markets came across the border. By 1879, this trade, mostly clandestine, was over triple that which came by sea. If the Southern Pacific pinned commercial space down in new ways, it also gave rise to a new fugitive landscape in northern Sonora: a shadowy web of roads and trails leading across the desert to Tucson and other railroad stations, where border entrepreneurs hauled contraband back and forth across the line. The goods that evaded the customs inspectors included livestock, flour, tobacco, mescal, silver, and more than half the gold extracted in Sonora.[10]

Sonorenses began to consider the wisdom of bringing these steel pathways south across the border. Local elites had dreamed of a railroad in Sonora since the early 1850s, when the Texas Western Railroad sent surveyors into the borderlands. The surveyor Andrew B. Gray had proposed a branch of the Texas Western from Tubac to Guaymas, and others imagined a similar line from El Paso threading west through the Sierra Madres. In 1858, the topographical engineer Thomas J. Cram argued that a Pacific road would be shorter and cheaper if it ran to Guaymas rather than to San Diego. These visions had been renewed in the 1870s, when a British promoter named James Eldredge proposed a railroad "through the heart of Sonora" into Arizona. This railroad, promoters said, would allow Sonora to develop its mines, secure the Asian trade, and turn Guaymas into another San Francisco, or, as Eldredge predicted, "the New York of the Pacific coast."[11]

Governor Pesqueira and other Sonora statesmen supported Eldredge's dream. A railroad to Arizona, they argued, would make up for years of economic neglect. "Those who were rich proprietors of the soil, and lived in opulence, cannot preserve to-day that which was acquired by years of labor and severe economy," lamented local officials who backed the scheme. Was it not a cause for great national shame that "a great portion of our brothers, not finding work, abandon their homes, to seek in a foreign land a proper subsistence?" Others disagreed. Gaspar Sánchez Ochoa, chief of Mexico's Department of Engineers, argued that if there were a railroad to Arizona, "Mexico would see floating on the territory which belongs to her the banner of the stars and stripes." Residents of the highland districts of eastern Sonora were also skeptical. How would they benefit from a road built so far west of their farms, ranches, and mines?[12]

Ultimately, the opinion that prevailed came from the center. In 1876, the nation's reins passed to Porfirio Díaz, a prodevelopment statesman who felt Mexico's entry into the modern age could be achieved only with foreign capital. He supported cross-border connections, and in 1879 he granted the Eldredge concession. By this time it had passed to the Atchison, Topeka, and Santa Fe Railroad, who began work on the line in July 1880. Many saw in the new Sonora Railway a long-awaited liberation from an embattled past. With the railroad, wrote Carlos I. Velasco, editor of Tucson's *El Fronterizo*, "Sonora will be reborn like a Phoenix out of the ashes." After the road was completed in 1882, Anglo-Americans offered their own predictions. "The vast empire of trade, which has been for fifty years . . . extending in the west," one seer insisted, "has turned toward the tropics." With the help of U.S. capital, the U.S.–Mexico borderlands would become "the heart of the great commercial empire of the continent."[13]

It was neither the first time nor the last that people overestimated the power of technology to subdue the frontier. The Sonora Railway ushered in a spurt of investment in the mid-1880s, but conflicts with Apaches and Yaquis together with drought and an epidemic of yellow fever slowly pushed investors back. The road's peripheral position, its distance from the mines of eastern Sonora, and the inadequacy of Guaymas as a port for large ships further undermined its promise. The Mexican Central Railroad between Mexico City and El Paso and the Mexican National Railroad, which ran north to Laredo, Texas, were more profitable. When they were finished in 1884 and 1888, they opened a much larger region to investors. Only in the 1890s, when the Santa Fe turned the Sonora Railway over to the Southern Pacific, did the line begin to operate in the black—and only then because the Southern Pacific decided to extend the line south, transforming it from a regional branch into a major west coast trunk line.[14]

Yet all this was on the horizon in the 1880s. As the Sonora Railway simply made do and dreams of Guaymas's rise as a Pacific metropolis faded, border elites returned to the drawing board. The question was how to connect eastern Sonora, the cradle of the state's fabled mines, to outside markets. The new industrial pathways between Tucson, Hermosillo, and Guaymas had proven inadequate to the task. The answer came from an unexpected quarter, a region that in the early 1880s lay beyond the control of corporation and state: the Apachería of southeastern Arizona. It was in this contested landscape, in an isolated mining camp with the unpromising name of Tombstone, that border notables set their sights once again on the ghosts of eastern Sonora. Their story was also linked to railroad expansion but began in what many regarded as a no-man's-land, a blank space on the map of industrial America.

Seen from the inside, this land was anything but vacant. Years of U.S.–Apache warfare inaugurated in the 1860s had turned it into a violent cultural crossroads. Although increasingly subsidized by the state, much of this violence was local: U.S. "pioneers" joined Mexicans and other Indians in fighting Apaches, setting off bloody cycles of vengeance. The carnage was so horrible that "almost a new population has been introduced to fill the places of the dead," wrote a newcomer in the early 1870s. U.S. troops were no more able than their precursors to control this land. It fell under the sway of such leaders as Cochise, who had pledged to fight Americans "until the last one was exterminated." "There were hardly a thousand white people in the whole territory outside of the military posts," and most were "fugitives from justice," wrote one soldier, who felt hemmed in by strangers and enemies: "To go south was to invite murder at the hands of the Mexicans, and the interior was held exclusively by the Apaches."[15]

The tide began to turn in 1872, when the United States sent the Indian fighter Gen. George Crook to Arizona. Using Apache scouts, as the Mexicans at Fronteras had done in the 1850s, Crook broke the strength of most local Apache bands by 1873. Cochise agreed in 1872 to relocate with his fellow Chiricahuas to a reservation on the Sonora border that included traditional strongholds in the Chiricahua, Dragoon, and Mule mountains. Yet two years later, responding to Mexican complaints about Apache raids and to pressure from settlers who wanted access to mineral lands, the United States decided to relocate all Apaches to the San Carlos Reservation in the hot lowlands of east-central Arizona. In 1874, soldiers began to round up and relocate Chiricahua Apaches to San Carlos and in 1877 established Fort Huachuca at the western edge of the former Chiricahua Reservation, offering support to newcomers who wished to reclaim this region as their own.[16]

Encouraged by these displays of state power, entrepreneurs began to trickle east from Tucson. Among them was a prospector named Edward Schieffelin, who made Fort Huachuca a base of operations. Schieffelin found silver in the hills east of the San Pedro River in 1877 and located the Tombstone and Graveyard claims. The names echoed prior visions of failed dreams but also spoke to the still-fragile confidence of Americans. In part they lacked confidence in nature. "I am sure that not a wheelbarrow-load of stuff was ever taken from the find," wrote Schieffelin's partner Richard Gird, of the Graveyard mine: it was "the graveyard of our hopes." Morbid place-names also reflected a razor-thin confidence in the U.S. control over Apaches. Soldiers at Fort Huachuca had chuckled at Schieffelin's claim that he would discover something during his frequent forays into the hills along the San Pedro River. "Yes," laughed one, "you'll find your tombstone."[17]

The prediction seemed reasonable. The mines were far from Fort Huachuca, and many Apaches had simply refused to leave. When several ranchers moved nearby, "we all camped together for protection," Schieffelin recalled. To the east loomed the rugged Apache stronghold of the Dragoon Mountains: from there, Indians could see everything the interlopers did.[18] Ghosts of frontiers past also haunted Schieffelin and Gird. They camped at the Bronco House, a deserted building that had once belonged to Frederick Brunckow, one of Charles Poston's German associates at Tubac. Brunckow had opened a mine here in 1859 with friends from Pennsylvania and several Mexican miners. One of the owners returned one day from a supply trip to find that Mexicans had murdered his colleagues. Brunckow lay at the bottom of a shaft, run through with a rock drill. The tale must have chilled newcomers as they reclaimed this unsettled frontier, a place haunted by Apaches and German ghosts that had grown as wild — *bronco* — as the land itself.[19]

Finally in March 1878, the men struck it rich, finding silver cropping up in some places pure enough to "print a half-dollar into it," Schieffelin wrote. Joining forces with the Arizona governor, A. P. K. Safford, who used his eastern connections to raise money for a mill, they began to ship silver to Tucson in 1879. The road was soon packed with people and animals, "all bound for the new Eldorado." Tombstone was mapped onto the flats, and mining camps with names like Hog-em, Goug-em, and Stink-em sprouted up in the hills. Tombstone lay fifty miles south of the Southern Pacific, but this was close enough: eastern capitalists rushed in by the early 1880s, consolidating claims and industrializing the mining landscape in ways that Tubac operators had hardly imagined. Steam-powered hoists and Cornish pumps pulled out ore and dewatered mines at an unprecedented pace, and large quartz mills crushed ore at an equally large scale on the nearby San Pedro River, in the industrial mill towns of Millville, Charleston, and Contention City.[20]

The industrialization of Tombstone transformed a landscape whose population had been limited by nature, isolation, and warfare. In 1881, the town grew from under a thousand to more than seven thousand, putting it on a par with Tucson. By 1882, it was bursting at the seams, at between ten and fourteen thousand. Unlike Tubac, which had depended heavily on workers from Mexico, Tombstone tapped into a much larger pool of unemployed miners. Many moved south from Nevada's Comstock Lode, which was declining by the late 1870s, and others came from the oil fields of Pennsylvania. John A. Rockfellow noticed the large presence of transplanted Pennsylvanian entrepreneurs and workers in Tombstone. "These oil men took very naturally to a new mining camp; they were real speculators with plenty of nerve to back it," he recalled. "Many of the dollars that rolled on the gambling tables were oil region dollars."[21]

The Tombstone boom not only gave rise to an instant city, but also transformed the nearby countryside. The growing demand for cordwood—consumed by the hoisting machinery, mills, amalgamating pans, home fires, and cook-stoves—sent entire armies of woodcutters into a two-thousand-square-mile region around town. The Chiricahua and Huachuca mountains, east and southwest of Tombstone, respectively, provided mining timbers and lumber for houses, even after the railroad began to open the region to new competitive markets in California and Oregon timber. Tombstone also created a market for wild hay in the Sulphur Spring Valley to the east, whose savannas yielded harvests in the millions of tons for freighting and mining teams and for livestock headed for silver town butcher shops. On the west side of Tombstone, Mormon and Chinese farmers on the San Pedro River near St. David, Charleston, and Fairbank supplied an equally brisk urban market in fresh produce, milk, honey, and eggs.[22]

Tombstone fueled a revival of the livestock industry in southeastern Arizona. In the late 1870s most of Arizona's livestock were clustered along the Santa Cruz River, but after Chiricahua Apaches began to move to San Carlos, Mexicans, Texans, and Mormons brought herds to the San Pedro River. Ranches expanded as the population boomed, and by the 1880s Tombstone was the chief market for local cattle. Many cattle companies made their headquarters in the silver city. By 1885, some twenty thousand cattle were grazing along the San Pedro, greatly outnumbering their Mexican precursors, and ranchers also claimed springs, built corrals, fenced pastures, and drilled wells in the nearby Sulphur Spring Valley. Many assembled herds from animals purchased just across the border in Sonora, thereby pulling Tombstone's consuming population into a larger, transnational web of rural production.[23]

Ranching networks echoed other cross-border linkages. Tombstone lay twenty-five miles from Sonora, forty miles closer than Tucson, and was thus poised "to control the trade of the entire Sonora valley, and the mining country adjacent," one Tombstone entrepreneur claimed in 1882. Yet as in Tucson, early connections reflected dependence on rather than control over Sonora. Tombstone relied on Mexican farms and ranches on the San Pedro River in Sonora and in the San Luis Valley near Santa Cruz, in addition to Mexican ranches north of the border. The Tucson freighter Esteban Ochoa founded the town of Ochoaville on the San Pedro River, just north of the border, in the 1870s—and in 1880 he improved a road from Ochoaville south to the Sonora River to take advantage of new trade opportunities. The mill town of Charleston, north of Ochoaville, depended on this traffic, as did Tombstone, where much of the early trade, as in Tucson, was conducted in Mexican silver pesos.[24]

Mexican miners also profited from Tombstone's industrial orientation. The Arizona newcomer George Whitwell Parsons noted in 1881 that Mexicans with burros "laden with ore in sacks holding 200 to 250 lbs. to the animal" trekked into Tombstone from across the border, looking either to sell ore or negotiate for custom milling and amalgamation in the industrial works along the San Pedro. Miners shipped large amounts of ore north from such places as Cananea, which was controlled by ex-Governor Pesqueira. Pesqueira "draws most of his supplies from Tombstone and Charleston," a reporter noted in 1881. In 1882, Capt. Ignacio Corella came to Tombstone to stock up on provisions for Indian fighters stationed at Fronteras, agreeing to buy goods from the silver city from that point forward. If the conquest of the Apachería on the U.S. side had cleared the literal space for Tombstone, the ongoing fight against Apaches in Sonora helped fuel its commercial expansion.[25]

Commerce set other pathways in motion. "There is a constant tide of travel from Tombstone over the border, radiating in almost every direction," wrote a correspondent in 1882. A new four-horse stage service picked up travelers in Tombstone or Charleston and headed south along the San Pedro River to the border. Its first, obligatory stop was the San Pedro customshouse, just across the line, an official acknowledgment of the rising importance of transnational trade. From San Pedro, the stage took a circuitous path that led southwest through the mining district of Fronteras (which included the mines of Cananea), then south and east to the Sonora River villages of Bacoachi, Arizpe, and Las Delicias. The service helped Mexicans from this region do business in Tombstone, but it also lured U.S. entrepreneurs into Sonora. Many Americans began to see Tombstone not just as a destination, but also as a gateway into Mexico.[26]

These Tombstone border crossings laid early foundations of American mining in the copper centers of Cananea and Nacozari and in the surrounding country. The Tombstone rancher John Hohstadt was one of many who took up claims around Pesqueira's holdings at Cananea in the early 1880s. Gird, after helping open the Tombstone mines, organized the California Land and Cattle Company, which bought half a million acres in northern Sonora, including land on which the company town of Cananea would later be mapped. Also part of this new Tombstone–Sonora axis was Cornelius T. Cutler, a California entrepreneur who arrived on the scene in the 1860s as one of the promoters of the "monster mine" of copper at Nacozari. Cutler left Sonora in the mid-1860s when the French invaded, but he gradually worked his way back to Nacozari in the late 1870s by way of Tombstone.[27]

We catch glimpses of these Anglo-American border crossings in Parsons's diary entries. Parsons, who wandered from Tombstone to Sonora in 1881 in search of new economic opportunities, saw familiar faces everywhere he went. Hohstadt and Cutler were two men from Tombstone who helped him get his bearings. A third was George F. Woodward, a rancher who prospected briefly at Cananea before marrying into a prominent family at Moctezuma, below Nacozari. Like the Englishman John Hall, these men served as brokers between nations, teaching Parsons about "the country, laws, business, resources, boundaries, etc." But unlike Hall, who had traveled solo into Sonora, these men tended to move in packs, and their world centered on Tombstone. When the *Tombstone Daily Epitaph* arrived in camp, the "expatriates" gathered around to hear news from the silver town. It kept their mobile terrains of venture seeking pinned down: were it not for this paper, wrote Parsons, "all tracks of dates and days would be lost."[28]

This fugitive landscape was distinguished not only by isolation and mobility, but also by lawlessness. For not all border crossers sought respectable fortunes. In the early 1880s, a shifting group of outlaws and cattle thieves known as the cow-boys haunted the countryside around Tombstone. They included the Clanton family, based on the San Pedro near Charleston, and the McLaury brothers from the Sulphur Spring Valley. Most were Anglo immigrants from Texas whose "feelings towards Mexicans was so bitter that they had no compunction about stealing from them or shooting and robbing them," one local wrote. They stole cattle in Sonora and sold them in Arizona, and sometimes vice versa. The only Mexican customshouse was at San Pedro, and there were few mounted guards, so smuggling was easy. Selling the loot was also easy, whether to ranchers who "ask no questions," Tombstone butchers, or the government, who bought "out-law" beef to feed Apache "renegades" at the San Carlos Reservation.[29]

If the cow-boys echoed the racial hatred and disregard of Mexican sovereignty shown by Henry Crabb and William Ake in the 1850s, others did not share such sentiments. Most objected to the cow-boys because they disrupted trade with Mexico and harmed investors' confidence. In July 1881, the marauders robbed a Mexican caravan in Skeleton Canyon, just above the San Bernardino ranch, murdering eight. Weeks later, they ambushed Mexicans riding from Fronteras to Tombstone to buy supplies. Mexican and Opata militias from Bavispe, armed to fight Apache raiders, began trailing the cow-boys "and are disposed to take summary vengeance if they overtake them," one reporter noted. Two weeks later, Mexicans massacred a party of the invaders in Skeleton Canyon. In Tombstone many shrugged, saying the men had brought trouble onto themselves. Mexicans had "suffered greatly from the depredations of those outlaws," claimed one resident. "This killing business by the Mexicans," added Parsons, "in my mind was perfectly justifiable."[30]

Mexican officials were outraged. "Is it possible that within the boundaries of the best organized Government on the planet a few outlaws . . . can band together, defy the civil authorities, and while taking advantage of the security [U.S.] soil affords, reach out and paralyze the industries of a neighboring state?" asked Mexico's minister to the United States. Those with business in Sonora grew fearful. "Every merchant and courier who is sent up from here is waylaid and robbed or murdered," reported Eugene Hathaway of the St. Helena Gold Mine at Las Delicias. If the United States failed to do something, "property and lives of the many Americans in Sonora . . . will be endangered." Locals on both sides "organized for self-protection," but what Arizona really needed, insisted Gov. Frederick A. Tritle, was a "mounted border patrol" to finally bring outlaws finding "safety and refuge in the sparsely populated portions of Arizona and Sonora" under control.[31]

Locals also kept a watchful eye on the San Carlos Reservation. The state saw this as a place where wandering Indians could be domesticated—elevated, in General Crook's words, "beyond the state of vagabondage." Yet the hot climate, infighting among government elites, and intertribal tensions made Apaches restless. The borders of the reservation became as porous as the line between Sonora and Arizona. Victorio, Geronimo, and Nana were a few who slipped through in the early 1880s, fleeing with their bands to isolated refuges in the Sierra Madres. It was only after the United States and Mexico negotiated a series of reciprocal crossing treaties, starting in 1882, that the military tracked down and deported Geronimo and his fellow renegades in 1886. Until then, newcomers worried in-

Figure 5. Geronimo (*front row, third from right*) and other Chiricahua Apaches
after their surrender to U.S. troops in 1886. Courtesy of the Arizona Historical
Society/Tucson; Gatewood Collection, PC 52, AHS Photograph #19796.

cessantly about Apaches. Officials set up an "early warning" alarm system of mining whistles in Tombstone and nearby Bisbee, and residents frequently sought
refuge in the surface tunnels when Apaches were said to be in the vicinity.[32]

White outlaws and Apache refugees often blurred in the public mind. At
Tombstone's 1881 shootout at the O.K. Corral, the whistles of the hoisting works,
which usually signaled changing shifts, "sounded a shrill alarm," noted the Tombstone resident Clara Spalding Brown. "'The cowboys!' cried some, thinking that
a party of these desperadoes were 'taking the town.' 'The Indians!' cried a few of
the most excitable." Even law and lawlessness were hard to tell apart. After the
alarm, noted Brown, a "committee" of well-armed "citizens" appeared to control the situation. Such ad hoc practices destabilized state power, and they were
widespread: sheriffs crossed into Mexico after criminals in violation of rules of
extradition, and mobs gathered to fight Indians with little regard for treaty. Troops
saw one such mob, the Tombstone Rangers, marching on San Carlos in 1883.
Fortunately, their whiskey ran out and the band "died of thirst," wrote one officer, "to the gratification of the respectable inhabitants of the frontier."[33]

Such lack of authority vexed Parsons as he passed into northern Sonora in the
1880s. Roads were lined with graves, and the countryside echoed with rumors of

ongoing "barbarities." "The simple name 'Apache' is enough to scar [*sic*] the wits out of a Mexican," he wrote. "Revolutions" led by local *caudillos* also troubled him. "I am getting heartily sick of all this excitement and risk," he grumbled. "I wouldn't care if it would only pay." He soon found a job at Nacozari, running a company store for a small mining venture. Here, too, things were chronically unsettled. The company was always running short on food, and when an epidemic of yellow fever cut off access to the company's accounts, even money was scarce. "A very bad time . . . because there was no money to pay Mexican laborers with," he wrote one day. The miners surrounded the store "with clubs, shouting dinero, dinero, etc." Mexican merchants covered him with a loan at the last minute, but Parsons was done with Sonora. At his first chance, he returned to Tombstone.[34]

Yet Tombstone's future was anything but certain. In 1881, as miners dug deeper to sustain their industrial dreams, they broke through to a subterranean river. Managers had to invest in costly pumps to keep the mines from flooding, and smaller mines began to shut down owing not only to growing costs, but also to labor strikes and the general woes of a glutted silver market. A destructive fire and corporate struggles in 1886 only made things worse. By 1887, Tombstone was starting to live up to its name, as workers packed up and moved on, leaving nothing but ghosts in their wake. Yet if flooded mines, empty homes, and fire-gutted works commemorated the death of one mining empire, just miles to the south another was finding its feet. It was to the Mule Mountains, to the industrial future of Bisbee, Arizona, that borderland dreamers would now turn.[35]

In 1877, as Schieffelin scoured Apache lands along the San Pedro River, an army tracker stumbled across outcrops of lead in the Mule Mountains that suggested the presence of silver. Miners swarmed in, encouraged by discoveries in the Tombstone hills. They extracted lead near a place known as Mule Pass, but little silver. By 1880, the camp—renamed Bisbee, after a San Francisco lawyer— had shifted its attention to copper and to financial networks on the Pacific coast. The Tucson merchants Louis Zeckendorf and Albert Steinfeld relied on California investors to finance their Copper Queen Mining Company, and their first shipments in 1880 were sent by rail to San Francisco, loaded on ships, and sent to eastern refineries. By late 1880, Bisbee had a population of three hundred. It was a mere dwarf compared to Tombstone, but like its sister city, Bisbee had industrial bones. It already felt the pull of eastern markets and of capitalists who were turning to copper to lay the circuits of a modern nation.[36]

Unlike silver, which could be converted into the generalized wealth of currency, copper, and its alloy, brass, found their value in specific, usually industrial uses. Their malleability and resistance made them useful for many things:

sheathing for ships, pots and domestic utensils, fireboxes for locomotives, clocks, rivets, architectural decoration, and shell casings, to name a few. Although demand for these things was growing, there was sufficient supply of copper at competitive shipping points on the Upper Peninsula of Michigan. Capitalists had little incentive to invest in copper mines in a far-off region like Arizona. Only wartime markets (chiefly for shell casings) made it worth the effort: during the Civil War a few mines were opened but were then deserted after the fighting ended. It was generally not profitable—as it was for gold and silver—to haul copper long distances across isolated deserts to market.[37]

For those already in the transportation business, however, copper mining in Arizona could sometimes pay. As Tucson merchants, Zeckendorf and Steinfeld viewed Bisbee chiefly as a commercial venture: they sold supplies in the Mule Mountains and hauled copper back in the empty wagons. A similar logic held at the Longfellow mine of Clifton-Morenci, Arizona, founded by the Lesinsky brothers of New Mexico in the late 1870s. Clifton-Morenci was seven hundred miles from the nearest railhead at La Junta, Colorado. The Lesinskys could mine copper profitably because as merchants in nearby Silver City and Las Cruces, New Mexico, they already drove this distance with supply wagons. Their teams came south from La Junta with merchandise for their New Mexico stores and then crossed over to Clifton-Morenci, just west of Silver City, to unload more supplies and load copper for the return trip to La Junta. Only under such transportation advantages would copper yield profits.[38]

The railroad changed things, as did Thomas Edison's decision in 1882 to use copper as an electrical conductor. More than anything else, the rising need for refined copper to electrify America made Bisbee possible. Yet few could have predicted this in the early 1880s. The copper on the market at the time conducted electricity poorly because refining methods left arsenic, nickel, and iron impurities in the metal. The only way to make copper an effective conductor was through electrolytic refining, a process that required abundant, cheap electric power. Electricity needed electrolytic refineries, which needed electricity. Not surprisingly, the two had to evolve in tandem: it was not until 1891 that electrical generators using improved copper were themselves sufficiently improved to refine large quantities of quality copper at a cheap price. One has to consider this when thinking about Bisbee in the early 1880s, for the future of copper was not only uncertain, but also inconceivable to most Americans.[39]

Bisbee's future therefore lay not with nervy prospectors or frontier merchants, but rather with engineers and capitalists, people who could more clearly see the pieces of this evolving industrial puzzle. One such player was William E. Dodge Jr., who understood copper markets better than most. Another was a young engineer named James Douglas, who worked at an electrolytic refining plant on the east coast. They met at the offices of Phelps Dodge in 1881. Dodge sought advice about building a smelter on Long Island, but after he heard that Douglas was about to examine a mine at Bisbee, the conversation turned to Arizona. That very morning, Dodge explained, a man named William Church had asked for a loan to develop a copper property in Morenci. What could Douglas tell him about Morenci's mines? Douglas told him what he knew, elaborating with a description of Bisbee ores, which he had treated at his refinery. Intrigued, Dodge hired Douglas to visit Morenci after his inspection at Bisbee and report on what he saw.[40]

When Douglas returned with a positive report, Dodge gave Church his loan, but now he was growing curious about Bisbee. Soon afterward, Phelps Dodge was offered an option on a Bisbee claim called the Atlanta, adjoining the Copper Queen. Dodge sent Douglas back. He returned with a strong report but with concerns about borders: since it was so close to the Copper Queen, the Atlanta might become embroiled in future legal disputes over ownership of veins extending across property lines. Dodge decided it was a risk worth taking. In payment for his services, Douglas accepted a 10 percent share in the Atlanta and began developing it for Phelps Dodge. From this point on, the fortunes of Douglas, Phelps Dodge, and the borderlands would be tightly interwoven.[41]

For the first few years, these common fortunes were meager. By 1883, Douglas had been unable to come up with even a single carload of ore, and Dodge and his New York associates, having sunk almost sixty thousand dollars into the mine, had grown discouraged. They finally struck ore one year later, but as luck had it, it lay at the borders of the Atlanta and Copper Queen properties. Just as Douglas had predicted, the two companies were soon mired in litigation. The suit was resolved in 1885 when Phelps Dodge bought the Copper Queen and merged it with the Atlanta under the Copper Queen Consolidated Mining Company. Yet even then, declining copper prices and the high cost of mining copper so far from centers of supply continued to dilute the power of eastern financial connections into the late 1880s.[42]

As Phelps Dodge assessed its future at Bisbee, it also had to consider the ground on which it rested. The viability of a copper venture relies on two geochemical factors: the amount of copper in the ore, known as its grade, and how it is chemically bound up with other minerals. In most places, the grade decreases as miners descend into the ore body. This is true because miners tend to work higher-grade ores first, but also because groundwater often leaches metal from ore bodies, depositing it in higher concentrations just above, in what is called the zone of secondary enrichment. Miners typically begin with secondary-enriched ores and work down to lower-grade primary ores. This was true at Bisbee, where the grade dropped from 23 to 10 percent between 1880 and 1885. This made mining more expensive, for the simple reason that the energy used to turn ore into copper grows as the grade declines.[43]

Shifts in ore composition had a similar economic impact. Early on, Phelps Dodge found copper in a high-grade form of copper oxide, in which copper atoms are bound to oxygen atoms. This was "a condition of the highest advantage," Douglas recalled, since it was relatively easy to extract the copper through smelting. Copper takes another form, copper sulfide, in which copper atoms are bound to sulfur atoms. Usually associated with deep ore deposits, copper sulfides required smelting methods that were so costly at the time that we "imagined . . . that the day of doom for the copper interests of southern Arizona would date from the transition from oxidized to sulphide ore," he noted. It was a day that seemed near at hand, for Phelps Dodge hit copper sulfides soon after the mine was opened, further decreasing the ore that could be effectively treated.[44]

Officials soon sensed that the only way to save Bisbee was to increase the scale of its operations: to mine more ore (to compensate for its lower grade) and increase output of refined copper (to pay for expansion and new technologies, as they became available, for copper sulfides). Of course, saving Bisbee was not a foregone conclusion; the market was so bad that many were simply closing mines down. Douglas, good Scotsman that he was, looked to the market to save them. Economies of scale, he felt, would allow them to produce copper at a lower cost. He built a larger smelter and increased output, but copper prices kept falling, pulling the company deeper into debt. A different market logic saved Bisbee in the end. A group called the Secretan Syndicate tried (ultimately in vain) to corner the world metal-buying market in 1886, and began buying Bisbee copper. This turn of luck boosted capital and confidence and tided Phelps Dodge over until new discoveries of ore at Bisbee in 1887 finally put the company on a paying basis.[45]

It was a key turning point. Since Bisbee's natural value was declining, Phelps Dodge invested more heavily in the *transformation* of nature, which opened a Pandora's box of consequences. With its increased output and its growing appetite for technology, labor, and metallurgical agents such as coke, the Copper Queen's ties to the outside world became insufficient. In the early 1880s, eighteen- and twenty-mule teams hauled loads sixty-five miles north along the San Pedro River to the Southern Pacific at Benson. Managers dropped this to forty miles in 1885 by building a new road over Mule Pass to the Santa Fe railhead at Fairbank. But it was already clear that these wagons and drivers would soon be overwhelmed. Bisbee produced much more ore than Tombstone in 1885

Figure 6. Traction engine like that used in Bisbee in 1886. This one was used to
haul freight to Cananea in 1901. Courtesy of the Arizona Historical Society/Tucson;
Robert Torrance Photo Collection, PC 135, AHS Photograph #97347.

(it took more copper than silver to make a mine pay), and by 1888 it had qua-
drupled this output. At twenty thousand tons of copper a year (Tombstone measured its annual shipments in hundreds of bars, not thousands of tons), Phelps
Dodge realized that its days of mule-powered freighting were over.[46]

In 1886, managers bought a traction engine, a steam-powered compound engine on metal wheels that locals dubbed Geronimo, to replace its mules. If the
metal-and-steam Geronimo was named to celebrate the modern conquest of
space—for this was the same year that steam-powered trains had sent Geronimo
east into exile—it was an ironic symbol, for the contraption was poorly adapted
to the border landscape. "It could plow its way with difficulty through sand, but
after the lightest rain its wheels revolved and it became utterly powerless on a
muddy road," explained Douglas; "if a rainstorm occurred on a clayey stretch of
ground the engine came immediately to a standstill." It had to be repaired often,
and its constant need for water put it at a disadvantage on the arid wagon road
to Fairbank. Since the road lacked water stations, the company had to haul its
own, which cut into the traction engine's carrying capacity.[47]

Phelps Dodge finally yielded and built a railroad: a thirty-six-mile road that ran southwest from town, around the Mule Mountains, and north along the San Pedro River to Fairbank. It was incorporated in 1888 as the Arizona and South Eastern and finished in 1889. It was a large undertaking, especially for a company that thrived on copper, not traffic. It was one thing to build a light, narrow-gauge line, as mining corporations often did to connect mine and smelter, and another to build a standard-gauge road that would carry all kinds of goods, not only for the company but also for its neighbors. Despite the high cost of building and maintaining the road, its benefits were immediately apparent. It cut transportation costs to a sixth of what freighters had charged. With two engines, Phelps Dodge doubled the metal it sent to market, and it doubled its output again in the 1890s, after adding two more engines.[48]

As Bisbee expanded, rural workers began to reorient the wealth of nature toward the Copper Queen and her court. Timber companies in the Chiricahua Mountains began to send mining timbers to Bisbee in the early 1880s, and by the decade's end, sawmills in the Chiricahuas and Huachucas had shifted most of their production from Tombstone to Bisbee. Ranchers made similar decisions and likewise saw more of their profits flowing from Phelps Dodge coffers. By the late 1890s, many cattlemen made their headquarters and bought their supplies in Bisbee. In 1885, the Erie Cattle Company opened the Bisbee Butcher Shop, and as the copper camp boomed, so did their herds in the Sulphur Spring Valley. Like Tombstone, Bisbee relied on grain, fruit, hay, and vegetables from the San Pedro River, supplied by Anglo and Mexican ranchers, Mormon farmers at the village of St. David, and Chinese truck farmers who rode daily from their Fairbank and Charleston gardens to sell vegetables in town.[49]

As in Tombstone, too, demand for cordwood to heat homes and run steam-powered hoists and for charcoal burned in the early smelters had a dramatic impact on the nearby countryside. In the late 1870s, the Mule Mountains supported dense stands of juniper, piñon pine, and live oak; "the thick spreading branches of the mountain mahogany," wrote one traveler, would "excite the admiration of even the stolid and wearied miner." The brush was so thick that "we made frequent use of the axe," wrote a surveyor for the Atlanta mine in 1881. Yet these landscapes quickly became a distant memory. Mexican woodcutters and their burro teams had become an everyday feature of the hillsides and juniper flats around Bisbee by the early 1880s. Their output could hardly keep pace with the growing demand for wood to heat homes, shacks, and "rough little dugouts," not to mention the thousands of cords that steam-powered engines at the Copper Queen mines consumed annually during their first years of operation.[50]

The hum of wood-fired engines and the glow of home fires reflected a new industrial control of nature, but this control was selective and far from complete.

Figure 7. Phelps Dodge's El Paso and Southwestern Railroad after a flood. Courtesy of
the Arizona Historical Society/Tucson, AHS Photograph #20643.

Bisbee's demand for cordwood undermined efforts to domesticate the land. "In
the early days at Bisbee," Douglas later wrote, workers "stripped the hills of their
scanty growth of stunted wood" to feed the Copper Queen steam engines. By
the 1890s, many local woodcutters had become wood grubbers, excavating for
mesquite roots because there were no more trees left to cut down. If the demand
for wood skinned the Mule Mountains, it also had disastrous consequences for
the town itself. Bisbee was built in two converging valleys, Tombstone Canyon
and Brewery Gulch, and lay in the direct path of runoff from desert storms. After
the hills were denuded of timber, Douglas wrote, the water that tree roots had
once pulled into the ground ran off, "with the result that disastrous floods have
ever since almost annually deluged and damaged the town."[51]

Bisbee had a similar impact on the nearby San Pedro and Sulphur Spring
valleys. After the coming of the Southern Pacific, the Tombstone boom, and
the conquest of Apache communities, ranchers began importing cattle by the
tens of thousands. This reflected a general expansion of Texas livestock into Arizona, which seemed boundless in contrast to the heavily stocked ranchlands of
Texas. "In good seasons it did not seem possible to overstock the country," the
Tombstone rancher John Gray later recalled. "The winters were generally mild
and with grass in plenty cattle could winter out in the open without any losses
and during the '80's the open range cattle business thrived wonderfully." If these
ranchers saw a landscape of abundance, however, it was in a limited way: they
saw tall grass—often stirrup-high—and space that seemed "boundless" in the

sense that it lacked competing ranchers. It would take them only a few years to realize just how ephemeral both of these things were.[52]

By the time Bisbee replaced Tombstone as the chief headquarters and market for ranching in the 1890s, the foundations of this industry were crumbling. In places the grass had simply vanished. The Tombstone Stock Growers' Association warned that the ranges were becoming overstocked in the 1880s and offered to blaze a trail to Wyoming and Montana to move their cattle to other grasslands. When drought struck in the early 1890s, Tombstone and Bisbee ranches were destroyed, and in 1893 over half the cattle in southern Arizona died of thirst before the summer rains. Ranchers packed their starving assets onto railroad cars to move them away, but they were often too late. "Near almost every railroad station there were accumulated great stacks of bones hauled in from cattle ranges," Gray recalled. "Mother earth has been stripped of all grass covering," one San Pedro rancher noted in 1901. "The very roots have been trampled out by the hungry herds constantly wandering to and fro in search of enough food."[53]

The Phelps Dodge railroad relieved some of the pressure on local forests and grasslands by shifting the burden to distant landscapes. Merchants could now sell coal at competitive prices, providing an alternative to dwindling native cordwood. And when coal became scarce—as it often did in winter, when Bisbee competed with others on the southwestern rail system—suppliers could turn to more distant cordwood camps in the Chiricahuas. Markets, butchers, and restaurants could now buy beef from Kansas City and Chicago at competitive prices and tap into packinghouse markets as well. And merchants and consumers alike benefited from new connections to wholesale markets. Copper town residents saved at places like the Copper Queen store, where ham, flour, and sugar now sold for less than two-thirds of their former price. "Around the depot we see empty freight cars marked from nearly every railroad in the United States," observed a reporter. "These wanderers from home speak volumes of the trade carried on with Bisbee."[54]

As beneficial as these outside linkages were, they forced Phelps Dodge into new economic terrain, where control had to be negotiated with other corporate concerns. At first, this seemed to work to the company's favor. As the Copper Queen looked for new sources of timber beyond the Chiricahua and Huachuca mountains, a bidding war ensued between the Southern Pacific, which brought Oregon pine through Los Angeles, California, and the Santa Fe, which shipped timber from the Pacific Northwest via Guaymas. Since it drove prices down, this game seemed to favor Phelps Dodge. But because its road to Fairbank was tributary to the Santa Fe, the copper company played a vulnerable hand. In 1894, when the Southern Pacific underbid the Santa Fe for lumber, the Santa Fe re-

Figure 8. Burros carrying supplies into the mountains near Bisbee. As railroads replaced animals, freighters simply moved their business farther into the countryside. Courtesy of the Arizona Historical Society/Tucson; Opie Rundell Burgess Lea Collection, AHS Photograph #48263.

taliated by canceling the special rates it applied to Bisbee copper. Once again, Phelps Dodge had to lay track, for only by extending its line to Benson could it gain competitive access to both outside lines and thereby preserve its transportation advantages.[55]

Phelps Dodge expanded to compete, but also to keep from collapsing under its own weight. To treat more ore and address its changing chemical nature, managers had to keep enlarging the smelter. But Bisbee's narrow gulches, made narrower by a chaotic accretion of buildings, coal piles, lumberyards, people, animals, wagons and teams, slag heaps, tailings piles, and urban trash, were not places where a smelter could spread out. Owing to "congestion, dilapidation, and confusion," Douglas later recalled, "the expanded Bisbee works at times produced no more than 2,750,000 pounds per month." Managers also worried about an increasing scarcity of water in Bisbee. The vast cooling towers for the smelters, the hydraulic engines for the converters (machines added to liberate sulfur from copper sulfides), and the engines in the powerhouse drank hundreds of thousands of gallons daily that the Mule Mountains simply did not have in reserve.[56]

These were all essentially spatial problems. From a corporate perspective, space in Bisbee and southeastern Arizona was shrinking. On one hand, the material networks and energy flows that connected city and country—and breathed new life into each one—were withering. Cordwood supplies were dwindling, livestock was dying off, and wells were drying out in the face of an inexorable industrial thirst. On the other hand, space was shrinking in Bisbee's urban landscape: accoutrements of an industrial age cluttered the streets; the sounds of industry reverberated from hillside to hillside; floods and fires periodically ate away at the built environment; and fumes of liberated sulfur permeated everything, forcing Phelps Dodge to run gargantuan smelter pipes up the mountainsides to keep the town from suffocating.[57]

From the instant Phelps Dodge had first decided to enlarge its smelter, build a railroad, and replace mules with steel and fossil fuels, it had set this implosion of space in motion. And as copper markets boomed in the 1890s, the company took a second, more resolute step from the crowded streets of Bisbee into the world beyond. It began with the search for more room—to accommodate industrial expansion by moving the smelter away from the Mule Mountains—but this coincided with new journeys south across the border. In 1895, Douglas hired the Arizona mining engineer Louis D. Ricketts to investigate the copper resources of Sonora. His exploration would ultimately lead to the purchase of a new property at Nacozari, roughly a hundred miles southeast of Bisbee. This out-of-the-way mining camp gave men like William E. Dodge, Jr., and James Douglas more to think about. How might they reorganize the borderlands, not only to free up space in Arizona but also to incorporate new extractive landscapes to the south?

Such questions gave the border new meaning. If space was shrinking in Arizona, it seemed boundless in Mexico. This seemed to be a new frontier, where industry had yet to make resources scarce. Scarcity was a concern for many in the 1890s. In 1891, two years before the historian Frederick Jackson Turner pondered vanishing frontiers, Douglas had declared the end of U.S. mineral abundance. "For forty years a large army of active and sanguine men has been marching back and forth over very obstacle, and in every season, traversing the Rocky Mountains from east to west, and from north to south, in search of hidden treasure," he wrote. Their search had been exhaustive, he explained, for ever since the railroad came to Arizona, miners had found no new sources of metal and were therefore confined to older discoveries. The frontier in mining had closed. The future of copper, he argued, would be based on the search not for high-grade treasure, but for new technology to make known lower-grade deposits pay.[58]

Yet Douglas had forgotten about Mexico. As Phelps Dodge elites looked south to Nacozari in 1895, they found themselves at a familiar place, a place to which Matías Romero had led Dodge years before. To understand this new frontier, all they had to do was consult a map. "Mexico has the shape of a cornucopia,"

Romero wrote in a new guide for U.S. capitalists in 1898, as if geography said it all. Eighteen ninety-eight was a pivotal year to be thinking about expansion. The United States was fighting Spain in Cuba and the Philippines and gearing up for a new age of commercial influence abroad. Romero, as always, hoped to avert U.S. energies from conquest of territory and toward a shared conquest of nature. And in 1898, entrepreneurs and capitalists in Arizona began to take his vision seriously. In the copper boomtowns of Nacozari and Cananea, Sonora, they began to dream with their Mexican neighbors about a new, modern age. Gazing into the Mexican cornucopia, they learned, like James Douglas, to see the borderlands in a new way.[59]

4

THE MEXICAN CORNUCOPIA

As Phelps Dodge crossed into Mexico, it found itself taking a well-worn path. For over a decade, Sonora had been teeming with treasure seekers from beyond the northern pale, each pursuing so many apparitions of Mexico—whether ghosts of former golden ages or dreams of El Dorados yet to come—that it was hard to get one's bearings. How did one stop moving between dreams and ghosts, past and future, failure and promise, to strike a sustainable bargain with nature? How did one pin this fugitive landscape down? This was a riddle not only about Sonora, but also about empire: successive regimes had tried to domesticate this frontier and failed. But now the question was more complicated and more interesting. What happened when frontiers became borderlands? What happened when Mexican and American elites worked in tandem to solve their respective riddles of social and environmental control?

We might begin with the 1860s, when Mexicans and Americans began to visit the ghosts of Nacozari and Cananea together. As U.S. entrepreneurs grappled with their ill-starred reconquest of Tubac, Gov. Ignacio Pesqueira set his sights on the deserted mines of Cananea, near his family's ranch in Bacanuchi. Cananea had first appeared on the map of empire in the 1680s, after Spaniards discovered silver near Bacanuchi. Local ranchers such as the Perea, Munguía Villela, and Romo de Vivar families, hailing from a close-knit fraternity of Basques, moved their cattle north into nearby savannas to supply new mining markets for hides, tallow, and beef. Cananea was one of many Basque place-names that emerged on this ranching landscape, conjuring memories of lands thousands of miles away in the northern highlands of the Iberian Peninsula.[1]

By the late 1680s, Pima revolts and Apache incursions forced these early pioneers south, and Cananea became something of an imperial blind spot. This changed in 1760, after mining entrepreneurs stumbled upon something that earlier ranchers seem to have missed: vast deposits of silver. Hundreds flocked to Cananea. Ignaz Pfefferkorn asked his readers to "imagine a hall draped with tapestries interwoven with silver from top to bottom, so on all sides everything was streaked with silver." Apaches prevented large-scale development—and thus kept tales of this "lost" mine tall—until the Apache peace of the late eighteenth century. Not long after 1800, the Chihuahua merchant Francisco Elguea, who also owned the Santa Rita copper mines to the northeast, worked the mines on a large scale, and in the 1820s the local elites José Pérez and José María Arvallo operated a smelter at the foot of the Cananea Mountains. But with renewed Apache hostilities in the 1830s, Cananea fell once again into ruin.[2]

This fugitive past intrigued Pesqueira. In 1860, he hired the Sonora mining engineer Robert D'Aumaile to revisit Cananea. D'Aumaile wandered the ruins, reading them as a historian might read an ancient text. He sampled ores and sent his helpers to scour the slag heaps and dumps. The ore in the dumps, the scoria in the smelters, and the metal in the slag "would form a respectable fortune," he wrote. Yet the riddle he hoped to answer—what was this haunted land worth?— eluded him. He "consulted all the existing books," but they shed little light on Cananea. The wars of independence and subsequent battles had destroyed most of the local archives. Even nature resisted his gaze. The mines were "full of water to the brim" and "cannot be drained by a tunnel," he wrote: it would take steam-powered pumps to see what lay beneath. Only tales and nebulous traditions were there to guide him. Like the "missing records of the State of Sonora," he noted, Cananea had simply vanished in the fog of past generations.[3]

Soon afterward, the San Francisco promoter W. G. Moody made a similar visit to the abandoned mines of Nacozari. Like D'Aumaile, he noted how successfully Apaches had reclaimed the land. Their power was marked by a conspicuous absence of livestock and the decline of orchards and fields. Local mountains, once heavily grazed, were "covered with grass from base to summit," and trees that formerly succumbed to the axe formed a "perfect forest," interspersed with feral progeny of "peach, pomegranate, quince, and fig trees, with occasional grape vines." Apaches had made this a "waste," Moody observed, but they had also made nature abundant. Even the mines continued to yield up modest fortunes, for *gambusinos* from Cumpas, thirty miles to the south, made frequent forays north to supplement their harvests with silver. "The amount of rubbish thrown out upon the sides" and "immense heaps of slags in the neighborhood," he wrote, showed Nacozari to be an ongoing human venture.[4]

D'Aumaile and Moody also eyed the copper, a metal that frequently appeared with silver in nature, that early entrepreneurs had passed over. In Cananea, Pesqueira rebuilt the Pérez–Arvallo smelter to produce gold- and silver-bearing copper. Here, as in Arizona, copper mining was predicated on new transportation networks. Ocean-bound vessels carried mining machinery from San Francisco to Sonora and shipped copper to Swansea, Wales, for refining, but it was still incredibly expensive to move machines and ore between the eastern highlands and the coast. More than anything else, entrepreneurs in the 1860s were motivated by the promise of railroads. Boosters were always floating grand railroad schemes, and Pesqueira and his congress granted concessions, just in case. If Cananea and Nacozari would not yet pay, some opportunists were nevertheless satisfied to denounce claims and wait a few years for the iron horse to arrive.[5]

Of course it took more than a few years, and in the interim Pesqueira and others grew old and made do. D'Aumaile had envisioned Tubac as an outlet for Cananea ores, but when Tubac fell into ruins Pesqueira sent copper to Tombstone instead. Tombstone entrepreneurs joined Pesqueira at Cananea, but without railroads they were frustrated in the way that George Whitwell Parsons was at Nacozari in the 1880s. Many purchased or leased mines as purely speculative ventures, with little intent of actually taking ore from the ground. Cornelius T. Cutler, who promoted Nacozari in the early 1860s, operated in this fashion. James Douglas briefly considered a Cutler venture at Nacozari in 1881 but turned it down, probably because Cutler claimed it was oozing with virgin copper. In this climate, one had to be careful. Many dreamed of Mexico as a lost El Dorado, and for promoters, dreams, not mines, were often the real bonanzas.[6]

Such dreams both encouraged and worried border elites. After taking power in 1876, Porfirio Díaz tried to build the power of the state by promoting foreign investment and exerting control over a nation of relatively autonomous provinces. Replacing the power of *caudillos*, especially in the far north, was difficult. But in Sonora he found a coalition of notables that was sympathetic to his vision. Three of these—a military leader named Luis E. Torres, an *hacendado* named Rafael Izábal, and a political leader named Ramón Corral—forged close ties to Díaz and with his support held the governorship among themselves until 1911. This triumvirate shared Díaz's fervor for foreign investment. As governor in 1891, Corral was especially encouraged by the U.S. interest in Sonora's mines, and in the name of modernization he promoted Sonora as a land of plenty.[7]

What concerned him was the fact that investment was often based on the *idea* of Mexico's wealth rather than on the tangible product of its soil. Promises of railroads caused speculation to run wild, Corral wrote in 1891, and bloated mining prospectuses "abused the good faith of corporations." If U.S. promoters lacked restraint, U.S. managers lacked wisdom. They might have found greater returns if they had conducted their work "with judgment and prudence, but they have not done so," he noted. More than anything they lacked a desire to "make labor productive." "Many are the cases," he wrote, "in which it appears that the management of foreign mining ventures in the state has had as its chief aim its own ruin with fruitless expenditures, with a wasteful and useless administrative apparatus . . . such that one is led to believe that what they wanted was not to exploit mines and extract riches, but to enrich a staff of higher officials with fat salaries, and generate an ostentatious sense of wealth simply to speculate on the market."[8]

U.S. capital helped Sonora, Corral felt, but Americans often left much to be desired. Many had the means but lacked the restraint to build modern enterprises. They undermined the promise of foreign investment to state formation —to generate revenues, productive and satisfied citizens, and infrastructure for native enterprises—and they damaged Sonora's reputation by investing in reckless dreams rather than material wealth.[9]

Yet times were changing. In 1895, after a run of failed ventures at Nacozari, the Guggenheim family of New York purchased the famous Pilares mine near Nacozari. They "are wealthy and will enlarge operations," one local resident wrote, predicting that within a year the property would be "connected by rail with the Bisbee road." When he visited Nacozari for Phelps Dodge that year, Louis D. Ricketts was less buoyant. The Pilares mine impressed him, but the Guggenheims did not. They had capital and the restraint Corral wanted, but they lacked expertise. Copper mining was a large-scale, technology-intensive venture that demanded specialized expertise in mining, metallurgy, railroad construction, town building, and metal selling. The Guggenheims knew about large-scale operations, but not about copper, and they knew the distinction. When they "represented to Mr. Douglas that they were not copper miners and offered to turn the property over to him," Ricketts later explained, Douglas obliged.[10] In 1896, Phelps Dodge annexed the mine to its expanding empire of extraction.

Phelps Dodge would need more than expertise and reputation, however, to turn the Pilares into the kind of modern enterprise that Corral and Díaz wanted in Mexico. To "make labor productive," in Corral's words, they had to connect Nacozari to outside markets. This mining landscape, like Bisbee and Clifton-Morenci in the 1870s, had been profitable only to those already in the transportation business. E. G. "Lige" Clifford, a Mormon freighter between Fairbank and northern Sonora, had managed the Pilares mine before 1895, probably using Pilares ore as ballast for return trips to Arizona. He took the same road that Esteban Ochoa had improved in the 1870s, which followed the San Pedro south to a border crossing north of the customshouse in San Pedro, Sonora—known by the late 1890s as Naco—and then ran east to Fronteras and south across a "broken country" to Nacozari. The Pilares mine lay several more miles away, up a steep mountainside east of town.[11]

Phelps Dodge took this same road south, but lugging pieces of an industrial world that went beyond anything Nacozari had known. "The task of hauling hoisting machinery, air compressors, and mine cars through a mountainous country to the additional high altitude of the mine, was in itself a hard one," a reporter noted, "but how infinitely more difficult it was to haul thousands of tons of rail, ties, beams, engines, blowers, water jackets, converter vessels, crushers, and hundreds of other items." Freighters had as much trouble with these enormous loads as traction engines had had in the Mule Mountains a decade earlier. In all, it took two weeks to make the round-trip journey from Bisbee to Pilares: the time it took to cross the United States twice by train. And nature often made the passage longer still. In the rainy season, wrote the mining engineer Morris B. Parker, freighters were forced to make long detours into the foothills along the Fronteras valley, and even on this high road "wagons bogged axle deep in the black adobe soil, destroying the schedule completely."[12]

Yet the things Phelps Dodge brought with them into Mexico—and what they expected to build there—made all the difference. A freighter, Clifford had forged a loose relationship to Pilares, incorporating it into a heterogeneous, mobile world. Like their Mexican precursors, men such as Clifford mined on the fly, following ephemeral stringers and pockets of red metal when they paid, turning to different work when they vanished into barren rock. Copper came and went, but what mattered most was staying afloat, by staying in motion. For their part, the Phelps Dodge freighters were hauling the building blocks of a different kind of world. Engines, rails, crushers, water jackets, and converter vessels were technologies designed to pin space down. Phelps Dodge and Clifford both thought in terms of capital, but where Clifford followed capital, Phelps Dodge hoped to make capital out of a particular place. Their journey through the "black adobe soil" was a journey to finally domesticate Pilares and Nacozari.

And by journey's end, Phelps Dodge would anchor much more than a mining landscape. To become a full member of the regional mining guild, Nacozari, like Bisbee, needed a railroad. By 1898, workers had laid tracks from the Mule Mountains south into Naco and, after securing the necessary concession from the Mexican government, began to search for a path through the rugged countryside between Naco and Fronteras. Speculators began to stake out lots in Naco, which seemed an ideal Phelps Dodge crossroads. It was the jumping-off place for Mexican freighters, and it offered a solution to that other problem that had been plaguing mining elites: how to free up space in Bisbee. Naco was built on a plain that offered abundant space for the growing reduction works and had a vast aquifer to satisfy their incessant thirst. Topography and location made Naco naturally suited to support the growing transnational domain of Phelps Dodge.[13]

But nature was a fickle ally, and it proved uncooperative farther south. For two years, the chief engineer of the Arizona and South Eastern scoured the highlands between Naco and Nacozari for a railroad passage. Then one day, as

Douglas was taking the torturous stage road south, he saw the puzzle differently. Phelps Dodge had been hoping to build in Sonora, probably for good reasons: there was more potential mining traffic, and the concession was tied to Naco. Douglas thought: why not build east across Arizona to the Sulphur Spring Valley—a flatter route—and then south to Nacozari? An underground river in the valley offered water for a smelter and could be tapped by shallow wells at Whitewater Draw, where it crossed into Sonora. He sent surveyors into the field, and by early 1901 they had mapped the new border town of Douglas, Arizona. While Naco boosters watched in disbelief, crews began to build a new railroad extension from Bisbee to Douglas and south into Mexico.[14]

In the end, the railroad, more than nature, set the parameters for Phelps Dodge's regional empire. As long as Bisbee had been the sole Phelps Dodge town, the line from Benson to Bisbee was the best way to bring coke, fuel, food, and supplies to camp and to send copper to market. But as the Arizona and South Eastern stretched west to Douglas, these market pathways made less sense. It was an "economic absurdity," Douglas's son later explained, to haul freight from the east to Benson and then backhaul it fifty miles east to Douglas. Phelps Dodge asked Southern Pacific officials if they might build an extension to Douglas from their line in southern New Mexico. When they declined, Phelps Dodge built on, reaching El Paso in 1902 and renaming their road the El Paso and Southwestern Railroad. This road would ultimately structure Phelps Dodge's relationship to the borderlands in ways that would have surprised Douglas years before, when Mexico was a shadow at the edge of his corporate vision.[15]

By 1902, the El Paso and Southwestern had already begun to transform the region. The branch line from Douglas to Nacozari was still two years away from being finished, but the foundations for a new age of border crossings were falling into place. "From a few widely scattered tents," a visitor wrote, "Douglas has sprung into a city marvelous." Its new smelter for Bisbee ore and the El Paso and Southwestern shops made it the anchor of a vast industrial landscape. "If it maintains its present rate of growth," one enthusiast wrote, it would become "the chief city of Arizona." More important, it already served as a gateway to "one of the most richly mineralized regions of the American continent," the highlands of Sonora. Local entrepreneurs knew this region well, but the railroad was beginning to transform their field of vision. It was as if someone had telescoped space and time, allowing them to see Mexico's natural wealth—and its modern future—for the first time.[16]

Among those who began to see the borderlands anew was a Tombstone rancher named William Cornell Greene. As Phelps Dodge expanded south into Mexico, Greene was starting to assemble a transnational empire of his own, but his tale begins on a very different register. He was initially far removed from the stratosphere of Wall Street and the puzzles of mining, metallurgy, refining, and electricity that lured Douglas into Arizona. Greene came to Arizona as a young man in the 1870s. After drifting through the silver and gold fields of west-central Arizona, he came to Tombstone in 1883, where he fell in with an immigrant from California, Ed J. Roberts. In 1884, he married Roberts's sister, Ella, and helped her launch a livestock venture on San Pedro ranchlands near the village of Hereford, west of Bisbee and just north of Mexico. He also established a ranch for himself on the nearby San Rafael del Valle land grant, leasing land from the grantee, Juan Pedro Camou of Guaymas.[17]

The path Greene took into Arizona seemed hardly to signal his later fortune and power as copper baron of Cananea. He was a peripatetic entrepreneur who leaned heavily on the Roberts family. Ella had built up their herd from her own pocket, whereas his labor fell somewhat to the periphery of the Roberts family livestock enterprise. Until the 1890s, Greene spent much of his time growing beans and cutting hay for Bisbee and Fort Huachuca markets. It was respectable work and put him in touch with regional elites in southern Arizona, but it was relatively marginal for a land where money, status, and masculine identity gravitated toward herds and mines. His habit of shifting from job to job, frequently gambling what he earned, further destabilized these small-scale ventures. For most of the 1890s, noted the local cowboy Joseph "Mack" Axford, Greene spent his time with other adventurers in Sonora, "mining and trying to make up the loss of a large sum of money for a shipment of Mrs. Greene's cattle."[18]

Young Bill Greene was therefore anything but an independent man: networks of obligation and affiliation with local elites were the key to his success. One such elite was Burdette A. Packard, a Pennsylvania oilman who came to Tombstone after oil went bust. Packard dabbled in ranching and mining, raising cattle on the San Rafael del Valle grant with another Pennsylvania entrepreneur, John J. Vickers. In 1900, Packard and Vickers purchased the entire grant from the Camou family and made Greene a junior partner in their ranching game. Packard was a generous patron and lent Greene enough money in 1899 to show Cananea ores to Walter S. Logan on Wall Street. It was a lucky investment. Greene replaced Vickers as Packard's partner in 1901, a sign of his growing fortune below the border. He was suddenly becoming a powerful cattleman, but his rise had been anything but certain. And neighbors had made all the difference.[19]

Greene's entrepreneurial roots were also distinctive in other ways. He and other ranchers operated in a landscape of mobility and custom that was worlds apart from the more fixed industrial landscapes of Phelps Dodge. Although based in Arizona, Packard and Greene claimed water rights and leased land near Cananea and were listed in the census of 1890 as residents of Mexico. Either they had separate herds in Arizona and Sonora or maintained legal access to lands on both sides to accommodate their nomadic assets. The border was unfenced, "and American and Mexican cattle alike strayed back and forth between the two countries," recalled Axford, who worked with Packard and Greene. In the winter, cattle drifted south into Sonora, and part of a cowboy's job in spring was to join other ranchers on rides ranging fifty or more miles south of the line to round up strays. A strategy of leasing land and maintaining flexible residence may have simply been an effort to formalize these seasonal border crossings.[20]

The need to follow animals across boundaries had profound social consequences. During spring roundup, U.S. and Mexican ranchers gathered at the Elías Ranch, near the San Pedro customshouse. They began with horse races and other festivities to evoke the event's communal nature. "We had to be good neighbors," recalled John Gray. "If we fudged a little and put our brand on another fellow's calf, it would be discovered at the general round-up for it was a self-evident fact that your calf would not by rights suckle another fellow's cow." Gray's gendered metaphor was deliberate. It suggested a world in which nature trumped artificial distinctions: in which animals crossed borders and natural custom prevailed over the artificial laws of the state. By law, ranchers chasing strays had to pass customs and pay duty on their cattle. But "we did not know the exact location of the 'imaginary line' marking the boundary," Gray claimed. "We simply took the most direct method and avoided all unnecessary red tape."[21]

The rhetoric of custom—based on the idea that certain relationships predated the intervention of states—also resonated with regional Mexican elites, who drew on patron–client and kin relationships to manage economic exchanges and mobility. Custom was a byword for local relations of power, filtered through a ranching guild that had replaced older military guilds of Indian fighters. Ranch families like the Elíases, in fact, hailed from these military guilds: the language of custom was the language of their patriarchal power. And in a cross-border context, it became a lingua franca of enterprise because it benefited rural elites, but also because its grammar was familiar to both sides. U.S. and Mexican ranchers spoke similar dialects of patriarchy, privileged local over state power in similar ways, and often linked their patriarchal power to the same powerful symbol: fighting Indians. In a land where Anglo-Mexican violence ran deep, this shared rhetoric of custom had a surprising ability to transcend national divides.[22]

Custom prevailed, for instance, after the United States passed the McKinley Tariff in 1890, imposing high duties on cattle crossing north and forcing ranchers to answer to customs guards when crossing strays. "We are on Good terms with Mexican Ranches Where our Cattle is Strays," but "Wee have to pay $2 per head

Figure 9. John Slaughter (*right*) and Eduardo Gabilondo, posing here with their
wives at Slaughter's San Bernardino ranch east of Douglas, were two border
ranching entrepreneurs who forged intimate ties across the border. Courtesy of the
Arizona Historical Society/Tucson; Allen R. Erwin Collection, Slaughter Album,
AHS Photograph #17477.

Because they Crossed the Imaginary Line," wrote local ranchers. The Mexican
customs officer Juan Fenochio eventually met with the Arizona lawman John
Slaughter. "There was no Brussels carpet on the floor, champagn [*sic*] on ice,
private secretaries and red tape, but a good old frontier 'Hello Cap,' and 'Howdy
do John' and an adios," noted a reporter. These "diplomats of ordinary caliber"
were both regional entrepreneurs, both had fought Apaches, and this history reinforced their local authority. Fenochio agreed to let cowboys cross after their
cattle unhindered, thereby pragmatically subordinating the power of the state to
local economies of power dominated by frontier identities and fugitive spaces.[23]

It was this binational terrain of entrepreneurial alliance and local custom—
rather than large-scale convergences between Wall Street capital and the mod-
ernizing Porfirian state—that led Greene south to Cananea. When Governor
Pesqueira's widow, Doña Elena, put the family mines on the market in the 1890s,
Greene turned to locals such as William S. Cranz, a businessman in Nogales,
Sonora; Henry T. Caraway, a local rancher who had married Pesqueira's widow;
J. B. Storman, a Magdalena merchant; and Tadeo Yruretagoyena, a Spanish

millwright from Magdalena. In 1896, these locals pooled their resources and founded the Cananea Copper Company. With the "consent" of Caraway, Doña Elena leased Greene four properties she had purchased from her son, Alfredo. Yruretagoyena and Storman also added their own mines and savings to the mix. Alone, these entrepreneurs could hardly take on the colossal task of transforming Cananea, but jointly, they had a chance.[24]

Greene then turned to George Mitchell, a Welsh metallurgist in Jerome, Arizona, whom he had met during his days of wandering across west-central Arizona. With Greene's Mexican friends and Mitchell's expertise and ties to the Arizona mining fraternity, Greene proposed, Cananea was theirs for the taking. In 1899, the two men called on George A. Treadwell, a local mining engineer with a close friend in New York, a lawyer named Walter S. Logan. Logan was the linchpin, for when he liked what he saw, the playing field changed. He first guided the enterprise through the unfamiliar legal sea dividing the United States and Mexico. He created a Mexican corporation, the Cananea Consolidated Copper Company (CCCC), and then founded a U.S. holding company, the Greene Consolidated Copper Company, to control its operating stock. He then carried this new company across the Wall Street threshold as its chief promoter, organizing a stockholder base of "leading judges, lawyers, and business men."[25]

Local networks of friendship and acquaintance slowly gave way to metropolitan ties of corporate finance and management. To move Cananea from periphery to core, Logan replaced the rhetoric of custom with the rhetoric of confidence. Frontier enterprise had a reputation for being unstable, overblown, and treacherous for investors. But he had been cultivating a working relationship with the respected U.S. Geological Survey geologist Robert T. Hill with this problem in mind. In 1900, he sent Hill west to Cananea to assess its mines. When the geologist returned, Logan showed his cards. He wanted Hill's professional opinion on Cananea in print, and he offered him a commission on all stocks sold on his opinion. Hill was taken aback. As a scientist, it would "ruin my reputation" to take part in such a scheme, he told Logan. "My only capital . . . is the integrity which begets confidence and I hardly believe there is any fortune as yet in sight which would induce me to sell my integrity for a commission."[26]

Yet Logan pushed, and Hill finally agreed to meet with ambivalent directors and stockholders. "Tell them what you found in the Cananeas," Logan said. Later, after Hill gave Logan his written report, he was thunderstruck to discover excerpts printed in the popular press, stressing Hill's ties to the Geological Survey and to New York City's Cosmos Club. "The United States Geological Survey has a singularly clean record of not having its name mixed up with the promotion of any mining scheme" and "the Cosmos Club is an association of gentlemen,"

Figure 10. Mining and railroad capitalists paying a visit to William Cornell Greene's lands in Mexico. Courtesy of the Arizona Historical Society/Tucson; Robert Torrance Photo Collection, PC 135, AHS Photograph #97500.

Hill angrily wrote. Yet these were just the kinds of associations that Logan needed to twin capital with legitimacy and weave webs of confidence among "respectable" men who perhaps knew of William Cornell Greene's past. The world of frontier custom that gave Greene his foothold at Cananea now had to be selectively erased to satisfy the dreams of eastern capital.[27]

Cananea's transformation was well under way by 1901. That January a trainload of corporate directors pulled into Naco, which from a rural railhead in 1898 had become a border town of twelve hundred, almost wholly dependent on the Greene Consolidated Copper Company. The traffic flowing south from the El Paso and Southwestern station on the Arizona side was staggering. "We were surprised at the immense amount of freight handled by the Company," the directors reported. Up to nine hundred teams of animals moved across the savannas below Naco. For a world based on the machine-driven logic of railroads and industrial mines, this sea of hair, hooves, and sweat was overwhelming, even absurd, especially for those who had seen this scenario play itself out at Bisbee and Nacozari. The news that the company was grading a new road for traction engines may have raised a few eyebrows among old-timers, but the directors clearly knew little about local history, for they reported it as a sign of progress.[28]

After a "pleasant drive" of some five hours through a mostly unsettled land, the men approached the Cananea Mountains, which from a distance were shrouded in gray smoke. Reaching the edge of a mesa, the stagecoach suddenly pitched down. In a valley below, running up the mountains, was a buzzing industrial town, triple the size of Naco. "We were much surprised at the magnitude of the town; which has been entirely built within the past year," the passengers wrote. From their position on the lip of the mesa, they could view the massive smelter, "pouring out black volumes of smoke," long rows of wagons being relieved of supplies and reloaded with copper, masons and carpenters "busily engaged in erecting buildings," and a constant stream of teams hauling ore from the company's mines to the smelter bins on the edge of town.[29]

No less impressive were the industrial and urban lifelines connecting Cananea to the nearby countryside. Mountains of hay and barley, much of it harvested from the San Pedro valley, were set aside for the teams. Thousands of cords of oak were stacked near the smelter, and a hundred thousand feet of lumber lay in the sun nearby (the mines had even larger lumberyards) to feed mines, smelters, and workers' homes. Much of this was hauled from sawmills in Arizona and the Pacific Northwest, but the directors also noted the heavy growth of pine near the mines: thousands of trees had been "cut, peeled, and gulched" here for the narrow-gauge railroad to the smelter. Much of the timber harvested for Cananea, in fact, came from the Cananea Mountains and nearby Ajo Mountains, both on ranchlands controlled by Greene and his copper company.[30]

If the directors were amazed at Cananea's voracious appetite, they were similarly impressed with the organization of industrial consumption. At the smelting works, they watched workers turn ore into matte: mule teams dropped the ore into the smelter bins, from which it was later taken out in wheelbarrows, weighed, and dumped into the feed floors of the furnaces along with the appropriate amount of coke. During the smelting process, the matte was drawn off into pots, and the remaining slag was put into two-ton cars that were then drawn by mules to the edge of a nearby gulch and poured into the slag dump below. After it cooled, the matte was broken by mechanical crushers, then carried by an elevator to a bin where it was sacked, sampled, weighed, and numbered by sack. "We were much struck by the perfect system established," the directors claimed: "everything moved like clock work and every man in his place."[31]

A similar logic governed the flow of goods through the Cananea company store, the next stop on the visitors' itinerary. Here the directors crowded around to view how managers assembled and redistributed commodities from distant landscapes to support workers, bosses, and the service sectors of the copper camp. "Lack of time prevented us from examining the books thoroughly," they wrote. "But the committee took up five or six invoices, following them from the time the goods were purchased down to the date the receipts of the various bills therefore were filed. We made additions in journals and ledgers, went through the books of cost and selling prices and examined the work of the various book-keepers . . . including check books, files of vouchers, and other details necessary in a business of such magnitude."[32] Others were likewise amazed at the industrial reorganization of space. "Throughout the whole business everything is accounted for, even to the nails and bolts in every house and every piece of machinery," reported a group of stockholders a few weeks later; "we remarked at the perfect harmony of the working of the system."[33]

The transformation of Cananea underscored the growing transnational power of U.S. capital, technology, and expertise. "Twenty years ago as remote and inaccessible as Africa is today," Hill would write of the copper borderlands a few years later, "now by the magic of the desert conquering railway, American enterprise, and mining exploration, there is not a mountain but what has been scanned; not an acre that has not been surveyed; hardly a stone that has not been scrutinized."[34] Yet there was more to this picture than met the eye, for the reorganization of the borderlands was based on a complex and contingent set of negotiations between U.S. capitalists, Mexican statesmen, and local elites. Copper elites put a progressive spin on this development in hindsight, depicting the copper city as a natural product of U.S. capital and technology. But to put capital and technology to work, they had to do more. They also needed to accommodate parallel Mexican dreams.

U.S. and Mexican dreams were formally negotiated in the form of contracts, such as that which Greene signed with the State of Sonora in October 1899 to build a smelter. Contracts were crucial tools for both state and corporation because they spelled out the advantages to be gained by each side and established ground rules for development. In its 1899 smelter contract the CCCC sought permission to build a smelter, along with railroad, telegraph, and telephone lines to connect it to the mines. The state, for its part, pondered the same questions Corral had raised in 1891. Would the project bring something of lasting value to Sonora? Would it create revenues, orderly citizens, and infrastructure? Not surprisingly, the stipulations of the state had to do with the actual work of the smelter: the CCCC had to start building in three months and invest three hundred thousand pesos in a year and a half, meeting a production goal of two hundred tons of copper daily.[35]

Above all else, the state thought about revenues, and mining towns at the border created multiple revenue streams. The state taxed all goods brought across the line and applied export duties to silver and gold. It levied imposts on business transactions that involved bills of sale, contracts, checks, bills, and receipts.

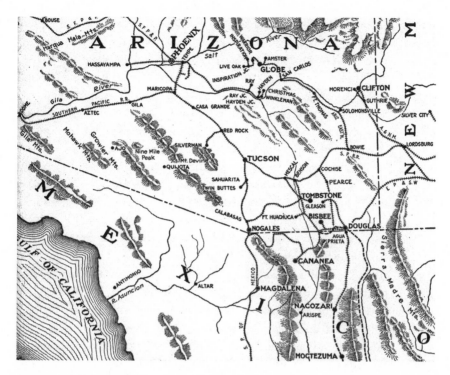

Figure 11. "The magic of the desert conquering railway." Networks of steel and copper began to knit southeastern Arizona and northeastern Sonora together at the turn of the century, laying the foundation for the copper borderlands. Note the contrast with the western Arizona–Sonora borderlands. The dotted lines signify booster dreams: railroad extensions that were never built. From *The Engineering and Mining Journal* (1916).

Ten pesos were charged each year on each mining claim, or *pertenencia*. Taxes on luxury items such as canned goods and nearly all goods manufactured abroad were high. Where mining companies saved was on the importation of mining machinery and supplies, which were taxed at a lower rate. Taxes on mine properties and improvements, land, and cattle were also lower than they were in the United States. "Foreigners obtain far greater privileges—almost without restriction here than in any other country," wrote one mining engineer at Cananea. Yet this also played into the hand of the Mexican state, for with such incentives, Mexico had more foreign entrepreneurs and corporations to tax.[36]

The Mexican state also used its contract with the CCCC to strengthen its political and legal control. The CCCC, a Mexican corporation, was considered a Mexican citizen and was subject to all laws. It had to have a properly authorized representative on call in Hermosillo, so the state could assess its compliance. Its

contract stipulated that it would take students from state schools as paid appren-
tices. State officials would choose the students and what work they would do at
Cananea. The CCCC also had to provide economic and statistical data to help
the state measure and manage its mining resources. Contractual relationships
thus supported a managerial vision of the state not unlike that associated with
the Bourbon-era Cuerpo de Minería. Finally, the CCCC agreed that as a Mexican citizen, it could never claim a foreign right in—nor could U.S. diplomatic
agents seek to control—anything related to the concession.[37]

The largest advantages to the CCCC, besides permission to build a smelter,
were tax breaks. Money used to build and maintain the smelter, railroad, and
telegraph lines (along with that invested in the mines) was exempted from state
and municipal taxes for twenty years. Also exempt was the capital tied up in
stocks and bonds and used to pay wages. Even the copper was exempt from taxes.
Exemptions also extended to salaried employees, who did not have to pay state
taxes. Those working for wages did pay state taxes but were exempted from military and municipal service. The company could also buy more land for development, and if it failed to reach an arrangement with the owner, its contract enabled
it to expropriate the land under Mexican law. In short, although the CCCC pre-
sumably had the same rights and responsibilities as other Mexican citizens, its
contract framed an important range of exceptions to this rule.[38]

Cananea had therefore been reorganized with more than dividends in mind.
The corporate landscape that directors saw in 1901 was a negotiated creation of
corporation and state, each trying to raise itself on the other's shoulders. There
was also more to this picture than contracts designed to build state and corporate power. Corporate directors had been astounded by a profoundly *modern*
landscape, characterized by the systematic transmutation of ore to copper, of
worker ants dumping and weighing and hauling and crushing, of carefully organized checkbooks and vouchers, of "the perfect harmony of the working of the
system." If Cananea once epitomized frontier disorder, it was now a machine in
the wilderness; a utopian crossroads of nature, technology, and labor. It was the
culmination of a modern conquest that J. Ross Browne described in its infancy
when he visited Tubac in 1864, where "the sound of the axe reverberated from
hill to hill," the "smoke of many charcoal pits filled the air."[39]

If Americans were hyperbolic about this modern landscape, Mexican elites
were more so. "Like the palaces and cities of the marvelous tales," Cananea
"emerged rapidly and grandly from barren fields and solitary mountains," wrote
Federico García y Alva in his account *México y sus progresos* (1907). This Porfirian booster tract narrated Sonora's transformation for a Mexican audience,
celebrating U.S. and Mexican entrepreneurs who helped bring modernity to a

land once "enshrouded in the shadows of the unknown." It was a motivational tract but also celebrated the *spectacle* of a new technological age. At night one could readily witness "the spectacle of fire" at the smelter: "From the wires that carry the current of the electric trains, at each instant escape stars of ephemeral but intense light; their blues and beautiful splendors rapidly envelop the columns of thick smoke of the gigantic chimneys . . . and from there, from the bottom of the smelter, from the magnificent and burning ovens, in a Dantesque procession, depart the electric trains with their cargo of burning slag [which] falls with a marvelous cascade of fire, that lights up the space, that lights up the immense settlement, and for an instant it seems as if the city is burning or that the sun has spilled out its rays in the middle of the night." In this manner, "while half of the city sleeps, the other continues working in the bottoms of the mines, and among the flames," he wrote, working "for the progress of Sonora and the nation."[40]

Few Mexicans would have taken García y Alva at face value, just as few believed everything they read in U.S. booster tracts. Yet for all their purple prose, these promoters spoke to the hopes of an age. Just as state and corporate officials found common ground in the transformation of the Mexican countryside, Mexican and U.S. elites found much to agree upon in their dreams of a new modern age. Contracts and dreams, however, were mere starting points. They pointed to Cananea's future, but from that point forward the world intervened. For much of what took place after the ink dried and the boosters left town had less to do with modernity than with the messy quotidian realities of border life. Behind the "spectacle of fire" and the "perfect harmony of the system," ordinary people were reorganizing space, trying to take control, and learning to cope with uneven results. In the dream it was "every man in his place," but in the real world it was harder than it seemed to constrain people and places.

"One begins to feel the power of the Cananea Consolidated Copper Company at Naco," wrote García y Alva. "The broad valleys and extensive hills along the sides of the railroad are populated by an uncountable number of fine cattle owned by Mr. Greene, who has managed not only to own many animals, but also to purify them so he has the luck of grazing only fine cattle on his vast lands." Visitors typically associated Cananea with the vast ranchlands that surrounded it. Both reflected the increasing monopolization of space by U.S. capital—and yet there was more to these connections. Whether his ultimate dream was purified copper or purified cattle, Greene gave his attention to both. The personification of an uneven frontier world that was constantly in motion, Greene moved forward pragmatically with his eyes trained on multiple landscapes and multiple opportunities.[41]

Indeed, one might very well ask what led a modest frontier businessman to think he might build and then hold on to a copper empire. Most men like Greene held on to their mines just long enough to sell them to those with greater means or expertise, just as Edward Schieffelin had done at Tombstone. For years, many assumed Greene would do the same: sell out to someone of Logan's stature or to an established robber baron, perhaps, if the price was right or else be pushed out into the cold. And eventually this is exactly what happened. Looking at Greene's entrepreneurial behavior, moreover, one has a hard time imagining he did not see such an end coming, for he seemed to be always hedging his bets. More than another opportunity, Greene's ranchlands were an insurance policy. For a man of his standing, it made perfect sense to move on multiple fronts, with one eye on the high-wire act of copper and the other on the rural safety nets that might catch him if he fell.

As soon as his mining profits made it possible, Greene consolidated his ranching interests. In April 1901, he joined up with Packard and the Roberts family to combine their lands in southern Arizona as the Greene Cattle Company. Included in the mix was the Palominas Ranch, which ran south from the San Rafael del Valle land grant to the border. One month later, Greene's representatives organized two new companies in Sonora: the Cananea Cattle Company and Turkey Track Cattle Company. Both were given generous privileges, including the right to buy, sell, and rent property of all kinds. The board of directors was made up of cronies from Greene's Tombstone days: the ranchers Packard, Egbert Gates, and Allen C. Bernard and Sheriff Scott White, who once helped Greene beat a murder rap after he killed a neighbor in cold blood.[42]

The new townsite of Cananea emerged, in part, from Greene's ranching business. Since the 1860s, settlement had centered on Cananea Vieja, where Pesqueira had built a smelter and garrison, and Ronquillo, an old mine at the base of the Cananea Mountains. Greene built his own smelter near Ronquillo, and it became the early core of his mining enterprise. Hoping to establish a new company town upwind from Ronquillo, Greene purchased 344,000 acres in and around the Cananeas in 1901. He bought the tract with funds from both the CCCC and the Cananea Cattle Company, thereby forging additional networks of corporate interdependence to strengthen his cattle company safety net. The Cananea Cattle Company probably bought the land on the mesa where the new town of Cananea was built, for in 1902, Greene and Bernard (a cattle company combination) organized the Cananea Realty Company to sell and rent town lots before later transferring the business to the CCCC Land Department.[43]

Greene relied not only on the Mexican state, but also on local Mexican elites to help in his borderlands balancing act. One such middleman was Bernard's nephew, Stephen Aguirre. His mother, the daughter of a U.S. merchant in the Santa Fe trade, had married Epifanio Aguirre, a Chihuahua trader who moved his business to the Arizona–Sonora borderlands in the 1860s. Stephen was born into this binational world, and his experience as a U.S. customs collector at Nogales prepared him for work with the CCCC, which he joined in 1901. Before the railroad arrived, he managed the freighters between Cananea and Naco: as the scion of a Mexican freighting family, he probably grew up with many of them. He also served as a cultural broker in other ways. He managed the CCCC customs department, and when Mexican authorities disagreed with copper elites (or with each other) about the rules of the transnational game, Greene turned to Aguirre and his knowledge of the region to sort things out.[44]

Two other key middlemen at Cananea were Tomás and Ignacio Macmanus, sons of a Santa Fe trader who married into a Mexican family in Chihuahua in the 1840s. The Macmanuses followed in their father's entrepreneurial footsteps, becoming bankers and surveyors. To build its transnational land market, Mexico passed laws in 1883 and 1894 that gave land surveyors the right to assess lands and release those lacking clear legal title into the public domain, keeping part for themselves. In the late 1880s, the Macmanuses traveled west and dispossessed lands between Cananea and Santa Cruz, much of it from the Elías family, and by 1901 this land had passed under the ownership of the Cananea Cattle Company. Greene owed a debt of some kind to the Macmanuses, for Ignacio became cashier of the Banco de Cananea, and Tomás became a political broker for the company in Mexico City. The Macmanuses had raided the frontier for the state, but also to their own local advantage — or rather to the mutual advantage of Mexican entrepreneurs and their U.S. corporate allies.[45]

Some elites worked hand in glove with Greene even as they yielded family lands to his growing empire. The rancher Antonio A. Martínez and his wife, Mariana Morales de Martínez, sold 37,140 hectares of land to the CCCC in 1901 and were compensated by more than the forty-six thousand pesos the company paid for the land. They bought an elegant hacienda on the Santa Cruz River, where Don Antonio raised wheat and alfalfa under contract to feed the thousands of mules and horses that hauled goods to Cananea. He held the contract for cordwood sold in camp and was one of several wealthy Mexicans who were given choice lots in the new townsite when it was still a grid in Greene's mind's eye. He was a pioneer of Cananea, García y Alva wrote, but others remembered him as part of a local Mexican clique that rode into town on Greene's coattails, monopolizing urban real estate "before the community could see what was happening, taking all of the best lands and leaving the rest with hardly any."[46]

In this way, the CCCC and its cohort reoriented the Mexican countryside bit

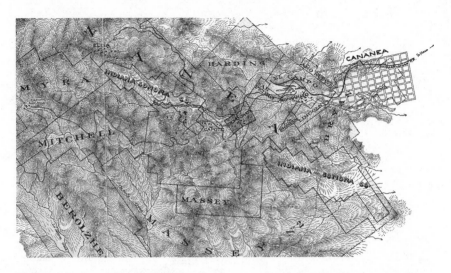

Figure 12. Industrial cartographies at Cananea. At the centers of Greene's enterprise
were colonial landscapes such as Ronquillo, San Pedro, and Capote, overlaid by new
corporate place-names and the new company town on the mesa. From Greene
Consolidated Copper Company, *Annual Report* (1902).

by bit, acre by acre, toward the orbit of copper mining. One could see the symbolic power of this world on a map of Cananea as early as 1899, as Americans
imposed their dreams over those of earlier generations. On the map were mining claims with irregular shapes and such names as San Pedro, Las Chivas, Pavo
Real, La Suerte, and Que Esperanzas, enduring fragments of a colonial landscape oriented around natural landmarks, spiritual geographies, and entrepreneurial dreams. These frontier cartographies and their lack of standardization
revealed a heterogeneous blend of local histories. To these were added El Logan,
El Chase, and La Myra. Named after corporate directors, investors, and members
of their families, they reflected a new rational order: each measured two hundred
pertenencias, echoing abstract systems of speculation, management, and rational taxation and visions of corporate obedience and domestication.[47]

Such maps lay a symbolic base for more tangible transformations. After securing titles to mines, ranches, and the new townsite, managers began to establish
the economic lifelines for a new population. To quench the thirst of workers and
smelters, they built a pumping plant and pipelines from the headwaters of the
Sonora River (known as the Ojo de Agua, or natural spring) on corporate ranchlands to the south. The government granted concessions for additional urban
utilities, including an electric light plant, telegraph and telephone lines, a sewer

system, an ice plant, and an electric railway, and by 1904 these were all in place. The company controlled not only public utilities, a manager told stockholders, but also extensive mercantile facilities, in this manner "supplying a large but scattered population with practically all the commodities they consume."[48]

Nothing did more to make this world of corporate control possible than new railroad linkages. Until 1901, the border town of Naco was a threshold between a steam-powered world and one powered by beasts and their drivers. These realms were knit together by transfer workers, who emptied cars of coke and supplies from the El Paso and Southwestern into animal-drawn wagons and refilled them with wagonloads of copper. Supplies for Cananea were rolled into warehouses to await the trip south. Mules and horses reflected abundant outlays of capital, work, and energy, but warehouses spoke to the limits of this world: it took days for teams to catch up with the load of a single train. And nature limited things even more. During the rainy season, teams might be trapped between Naco and Cananea for days, and between the smelter and the mines, rains often made the roads impassable, periodically forcing the smelter to shut down.[49]

In some ways, the shift from animal to machine power at Cananea was faster and more straightforward than it had been at Bisbee, since Phelps Dodge had already built a railroad to Naco. Yet all this railroad development also created new obstacles. Because Phelps Dodge had most of the regional railroad contractors tied up on the road between Douglas and El Paso in 1901, none could be enticed south into Sonora. When it began to build a railroad north that June, the CCCC had to organize its own labor, which led to uneven results. Competition for rails forced crews to wait for months, the railroad half-built, until a long-overdue second shipment finally arrived. Managers were anxious to finish the line, so "lesser details of construction were temporarily ignored," admitted the railroad manager, J. P. Hallihan. A great deal was spent to fix mistakes, and months after the narrow-gauge road to the mines was completed, the CCCC had to keep using animal teams because of "insufficient equipment."[50]

Yet in the end, technology seemed to triumph. With the completion of industrial connections to the outside, Cananea boomed. Corporate reports narrated these changes: they told of the enlargement of smelters, concentrators, and mills, the growing mileage of tracks, tunnels, telephone lines, and shortened pathways from mine to market. Balance sheets listed assets and investments (power plants, sawmills, quarries, kilns, hay camps, trails, roads); maps showed streets, railroads, and mines; and photos showed the visible reorganization of space. Juxtaposed with an 1899 photo of a lone freighting team and a row of tents in front of the Cananea Mountains, an image from 1904 depicted a densely packed city: smelter stacks, telephone wires, railroad tracks, multistory buildings, and throngs

Figure 13. Mexicans laying track to Cananea. Courtesy of the Arizona Historical Society/Tucson; Robert Torrance Photo Collection, PC 135, AHS Photograph #97348.

of workers dominate. Like Nacozari under Phelps Dodge, this was a landscape fixed in place. Anchored by electrical wires, steel rails, machinery, and paychecks, it calmed investors' fears about fugitive terrains and profits, lost somewhere in the blank spaces of unknown Mexico.[51]

Stockholders and directors also began to marvel at the reach of Greene's empire. What started as a series of small, diversified investments—a ranch here, a real estate venture there—became much more. By 1904, his Arizona ranchlands totaled 30,000 acres and covered the entire upper San Pedro and nearby San Rafael Valley, east of the old Mowry mine. Even more extensive were his 750,000 acres in Sonora, radiating in all directions from Cananea. These lands reached north to the border, where for fifty miles east to west a ribbon of barbed wire divided them from his Arizona ranches. "All this is one grand cattle range," wrote one observer, "where the cowboys employed could form a regiment of rough riders." The Cananea Cattle Company's slaughterhouse in Cananea literally carved up the wealth of these extensive savannas and foothills, in this way bringing the countryside to consumers in Sonora's largest industrial city.[52]

Yet all of this fell in the shadow of Greene's vast Sierra Madre holdings. In 1902, Greene created the Greene Gold-Silver Company to exploit mines in eastern Sonora and western Chihuahua. By 1905, he had bought dozens of mines in these states, 125,000 acres of timberlands, a concession to convert the rapids of the Aros River in eastern Sonora into hydroelectric power, and a sole right to mining claims on 2½ million acres. Greene also set his gaze on timberlands in Chihuahua. He purchased over a million acres from the land surveyor Telésforo García in 1904, and in 1905 he bought a million more from the Macmanus family for his newly formed Sierra Madre Land and Lumber Company. To connect these mines and forests to U.S. markets, he also bought the Rio Grande, Sierra Madre, and Pacific Railroad, which ran southwest from El Paso to Terrazas, Chihuahua, just north of his Chihuahua lands.[53]

If Greene saw profits and corporate safety nets in Chihuahua, he also seemed to be thinking about empire, or something like it. In 1905, he organized a team of scientists and explorers to evaluate and map his territory. The geologist Robert T. Hill led the team; with him were Edmund O. Hovey of the American Museum of Natural History, the mining engineer John Seward, and Frank H. Fayant, a magazine writer. Their assignment was to make an exhaustive study of Greene's holdings. Their enthusiasm for filling blank spaces on the map of empire would have warmed the heart of Alexander von Humboldt. They returned with topographical maps, a thousand glass-plate photos packed over miles of rugged terrain, and rocks and ores for display in the American Museum of Natural History. The jaunt was "full of incident and adventure," reported Hill, and "was a revelation to those scientific men who have learned something about the country down in Mexico that they never knew or dreamed of."[54]

For his part, Greene dreamed on a large scale. The previous owners of one of his Chihuahua mines had deserted it after hitting the water table. Greene proposed to drain the mine by boring a hole through the bottom of the mountain. He hoped to run barbed wire all around his million-acre timberlands and set up a "police and fire patrol" to keep them under his watchful eye. He planned to install two gargantuan sawmills capable of spitting out half a million board feet daily, to transform Chihuahua's forests into mining timbers and lumber for consumers at Cananea. Perhaps the most ambitious part of this dream of linking Chihuahua and Cananea was a proposed extension of the Rio Grande, Sierra Madre, and Pacific across the Sierra Madres—an indomitable land that had traditionally resisted all but the most modest ventures of mules and men.[55]

Such was the world of dreams. On the ground in Mexico, things were a different matter. For decades, Cananea's corporate elites struggled to exert the control suggested in corporate balance sheets, maps, photos, and corporate portfolios. It was easy enough to contract with the state for the right to buy land and negotiate with elites like the Macmanuses and the Martínezes to turn buying power into ownership. But not all land converted easily to the commodity-driven logic

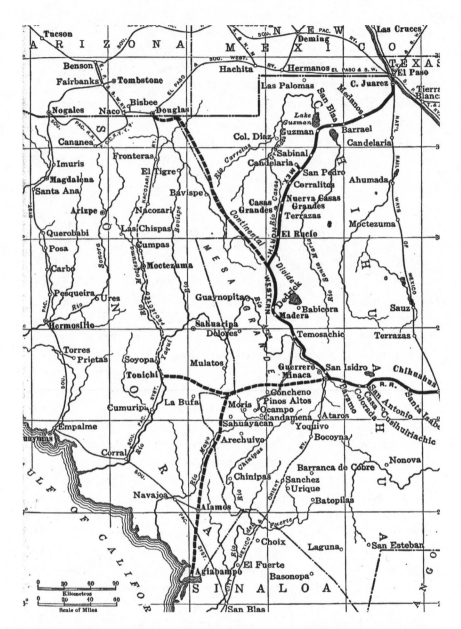

Figure 14. The Mexico Northwestern Railway system in Chihuahua, 1910. Much of this was previously owned by William Cornell Greene. Dotted lines show enduring dreams of laying track over the Sierra Madres into Sonora, north toward Douglas and south, via Ocampo, toward the Southern Pacific of Mexico at Tonichi and Alamos. From *The Engineering and Mining Journal* (1910).

of U.S. capital, as Greene and the CCCC found when they bought lands at the Ojo de Agua. This land had none of the simplicity of the Macmanus or Martínez tracts because its old owner, José María Arvallo, had passed it on to multiple heirs. To control it, copper elites had to deal with seven different owners, each with different demands.[56]

Two heirs, Secundino Ahumada and Ramón Díaz, refused to move and became a permanent thorn in the side of the copper company. What made these men especially troublesome—for together, they barely owned 6 percent of the grant—was the nature of the grant: heirs had inherited the lands in common. Under Mexican law, one could not divide common land into alienable holdings, which meant that although Ahumada and Díaz claimed only a very small fraction of the grant, there was no part of the CCCC's claims over which they did not exert some control. Decisions about how to use the land also had to be decided in common. Since they would not sell their rights, these men "have caused us a great deal of embarrassment in the matter of leasers, deeds, etc.," explained CCCC Secretary George Young. They consistently voted against CCCC efforts to lease its land, whether for railroad rights-of-way, grazing rights, or mineral survey rights.[57]

The feud was more than a contest between private and common rights, for the Ojo de Agua grant blended the two. Ahumada and Díaz fenced their lands, yet "this does not prevent their ranging cattle, cutting wood, etc. on all of the lands included in the Ojo de Agua grant," grumbled Young. They had a legal right, yet the fences tell us a great deal. Fences were costly, and they probably reflected a breakdown of customary authority for managing common lands. This may have predated the CCCC, but the copper company did not make things better: it wanted land without obligations. So owners built fences, and they picked fights. Ahumada leased lots in Catalina, a village on the grant, without CCCC approval. When the CCCC challenged him, he said he was retaliating against its own unapproved leases to the Cananea Cattle Company. Thus, the Ojo de Agua drifted out of control, into the contested terrain of a land feud. And despite its power, the CCCC seemed unable to do anything about it.[58]

The Ojo de Agua was just one of many fugitive landscapes that plagued Cananea officials. Another was the Exedencias de Cienega de Heredia, a ranch the CCCC and Cananea Cattle Company had purchased in tandem. The nomadic business of ranching was often marked by the trading of lands among ranchers, as owners sought to move or consolidate herds and ranch managers juggled spaces they needed for livestock: water sources, lowland savannas to fatten stock in the rainy season, highland valleys to shelter herds in winter. After making the purchase, the Cananea Cattle Company traded part of their Cienega de Heredia claims to Rafael Elías for rights in the San Pedro de Palominas Ranch, to the north. Once set in motion, the land kept moving. A fence had once divided the cattle and copper company pastures; Elías had rebuilt it, and it was only after consulting a map in their files that copper elites realized the new fence—and Elías's land—had drifted considerably toward their side.[59]

Elías offered to make up for his "mistake" by giving the company another part of his land, since under Mexican law the locations of borders within a shared grant did not matter as much as the acreage. Seen from the corporate offices in Cananea, the exchange may have seemed fair. By building the fence, Elías had fixed borders at his own expense; it was hard to see how the land would keep drifting. And acreage was acreage. But when Young drove to the ranch, he found something the company map had failed to reveal. "The piece of ground belonging to us which he took in when he moved his fence, includes quite a large tract of watered bottom-land, almost ideal for farming in this country," Young noted, "while the strip which he proposes to give in exchange for it is hilly upland on which one might have difficulty in raising an umbrella." He learned a valuable lesson about trying to see space from the corporate center. Elías "did not seem particularly glad to see us," Young noted. "I think he had hopes of making the exchange the way we used to trade jack-knives, 'unsight and unseen.'"[60]

Unsight and unseen. If the copper borderlands threatened to drift out of control, it was because corporate elites were assembling a landscape that required them not only to transform, but also to *see* space on a large scale. If Ahumada, Díaz, and Elías could resist corporate control and sustain alternative spaces, it was because they operated at the edges of the corporate vision. But they also exploited the gaps between state and corporate power. The CCCC acquiesced to Ahumada and Elías because the state had given citizens rights the company could not ignore. Although these laws unsettled corporate dreams—just as laws protecting *gambusinos* rankled previous entrepreneurs—U.S. corporate elites needed the law to keep investors confident and keep assets in place. No matter how much it appeared at odds with the market, the CCCC could not afford to challenge the Mexican state's legal vision. And this is what locals understood when they cleverly stretched the law to defend their own landed interests.

As the copper borderlands grew in the early twentieth century, the problems of seeing and controlling space at the edges of the corporate vision grew as well. In years to come, corporations would increase their power over land and life through expanding circuits of railroads, mines, banking, and trade. These market-driven pathways would link the copper borderlands to a larger, regional economy and amplify earlier ties to the centers of U.S. and Mexican power. Yet as corporations and states gained power, so too did ordinary people and landscapes. Networks of corporate and state power supported equally powerful shadow pathways oriented around the local lives of Mexican smelter workers, Yaqui miners, Chinese farmers, U.S. colonists, and others. These human webs kept the borderlands in motion, even as states and corporations bent their collective will to lashing this fugitive terrain to the managerial foundations of modern America.

5

Transnational Passages

Shadows are worlds in motion; to appreciate them, we must trace their passages. When the U.S. mining engineer Morris B. Parker came from Chihuahua to Sonora in 1900, he took a passage familiar to many miners in the colonial era, from the old trade center of Casas Grandes through the Púlpito Pass to the highlands of northeastern Sonora. Squeezing through this "rough, rocky bottle-neck" in a rickety buckboard, he paused at Colonia Oaxaca, a new Mormon colony on the Bavispe, before pushing on to his destination, the mining region below Nacozari. Four years later, a traveler like Parker would have taken a train north to El Paso, east to Douglas, and south into Sonora on the Phelps Dodge rail network. In May 1900, however, Douglas was still Whitewater Draw, a rural landmark beyond the industrial frontier. Púlpito Pass, open to mule and wagon, was the shortest way to Sonora. Except for the nearby Carretas Pass, the next road across the sierras lay a thousand miles to the south.[1]

Parker's journey was far from unusual. He was one of many mining engineers who shuttled back and forth between New Mexico, Chihuahua, Arizona, and Sonora at the turn of the century to sell his expertise to miners. He began his borderland odyssey as a teenager in the 1880s, when he moved with his family to White Oaks, a gold mining town in southern New Mexico. By the 1890s, he and his neighbors had begun to look to Mexico. "I was lured into that cornucopia in 1895," Parker later recalled, "and from then until 1932 a goodly portion of my time was spent below the border." In 1898, as William Cornell Greene was peddling mines on Wall Street, Parker became superintendent of the San Pedro mine, 125 miles southwest of El Paso near the Sierra Madres of Chihuahua. It was here that he was called west in 1900 to assess the wealth of Sonora.[2]

Parker's journey offers a snapshot of Sonora on the brink of a new industrial age. Two things that stand out in his diary are times and distances. From Colonia Morelos, he and his partner headed for Fronteras, twenty miles west as the crow flies, but seventy miles for mule and buckboard, which had to swing north to avoid one of Sonora's many mountain ranges. Driving "by ruts and gullies" through pastures, mescal ranches, and customs outposts, they finally hit Ochoa's wagon road between Naco and Nacozari. Suddenly the world spun into motion. At meal stations spaced to match the speed of freighters, they dined with captains of industry. Louis D. Ricketts breezed by en route to Nacozari, as did John P. Ramsey, manager of the Rio Grande, Sierra Madre, and Pacific Railroad. Like Parker, Ramsey was "looking over country" but with a bolder eye: he envisioned himself driving rails west across the sierras from Chihuahua and thus knitting together northern Mexico into a larger, industrial whole.[3]

With Phelps Dodge's machine dreams still "bogged axle deep in the black adobe soil" of Sonora, such talk must have seemed like idle chatter. This was still a profoundly local world, bound together by modest desires. North of Nacozari, "where we expected to get B'fast and didn't," Parker found Americans struggling to make ends meet with "a small rattle trap stamp mill." In Cumpas, south of Nacozari, he dined with a doctor who had found his way into Mexican society by marrying a local woman. In Moctezuma, he was the guest of the old-timer George F. Woodward and his Mexican wife, who was "very kind and feeds us *fine!*" His journey revealed a different sort of human landscape than that oriented around the industrial pace of Ochoa's wagon road. These rural pathways, structured by economic isolation, family ties, and local custom, had changed little since the 1820s, when Moctezuma and Cumpas residents guided Robert Hardy and Simon Bourne through the haunted remains of former empires.[4]

The road one took made all the difference, but so did the starting point. Another pilgrim in Sonora at the time was Maud Kenyon-Kingdon, the young wife of George Kingdon, a mining engineer of Parker's cohort. Kingdon had served his apprenticeship in Arizona and Mexico, prospecting and supervising mines, at times traveling, like Parker, to inspect properties. Maud met him in the Arizona copper town of Globe and joined him on a new path. "We unfurled our sails upon life's matrimonial sea and anchored across the Mexican border in one of the remotest, uncivilized little towns," she wrote of a move around 1903 to Pilares, where George found work as a superintendent. It was a "barren, desolate place," she wrote. Douglas was booming, and Phelps Dodge was laying tracks south, but not yet to Pilares. "Roads were forced to surrender to the rough and winding footpaths" winding up "precipitous slopes," she recalled of her new home, a "wild spot" she could hardly regard "without some trepidation."[5]

Above all, this was a world of men. "I was about the first American woman that had ever come to this place," she wrote. She pressed George to make her feel at home. Mexicans were "put to work with spades, pickaxes and dynamite" to excavate a garden, and "in the matureness of time we had a garden blooming in wondrous profusion," she wrote. Embellished with a new rosebush, a Madeira vine around the veranda, and rows of "thrifty cottonwoods" nearby, it made for "a most attractive setting—a veritable garden spot . . . and this was home." Yet Maud felt hemmed in. "Violent gales," she noted, "howled around our prem-ises in weird, uncanny sounds, portending, as it were, some dark omen, some hidden tragedy awaiting this unsuspecting land." A ravine opened behind their house, and here miners played cards at night. They "were a law-breaking gang of thieves," she feared, addicted to "a vile and poisonous beverage of their own distillation, and which would likely result in some terrible feud."[6]

For Maud, Pilares was both out of control—a nomadic land of unrestrained gangs and gales—and claustrophobic. The same Mexico that seemed boundless to white male entrepreneurs was, for her, a reduced, restricted world. It was the fugitive nature of the land that confined her the most. The only "diversion for the mind" was the "occasional visit of a Mexican circus" that performed on one of the few flat areas near town. But the male consumption of space interfered with even this small pleasure. One night, without warning, "an alarming crash inter-rupted the stillness." Rushing outside, Maud saw part of the mountain "calmly and majestically slip away into the black depths of the mine . . . taking with it that precious piece of circus ground." The only other dream of civilization was a Mexican dance hall they patronized until one of Maud's lawless denizens shot out one of the windows. "As far as we and our pleasure was concerned," she wrote, "that dance hall might as well have dropped into the abyss along with our circus ground."[7]

Yet in time the copper borderlands became more fixed and less confined for the likes of Kenyon-Kingdon. In 1913, after a hiatus in the States, George took a job in Cananea. "It was a violent shock" to think of returning to Mexico, Maud wrote, but Cananea was not what she expected. The streets were "wide and very well laid out," and "the homes for American people were attractively built." Their house had a manicured lawn, Chinese servants, and French doors opening onto "verandas, walks and sweet-scented flower gardens." Cananea was a larger town than Pilares, but in a decade the borderlands also had changed. Her "haven of refuge" in a land controlled by others had now become a cosmopolitan cross-roads, managed—or so it seemed—with her own dreams in mind. "It was so very civilized," she happily admitted. "An unruffled world, it seemed, stretched its length before us."[8]

Cananea's metropolitan intensity also attracted others. Coming to Cananea was like "entering another world," wrote Jesús Corral, who moved there as a child from the small mining town of La Dura in southern Sonora. Compared to La Dura, it seemed like a lost city of gold. "American and Mexican money flowed freely," Corral recalled. "The smell of luscious fruits and the din of silver dollars on the counter, as miners were being paid at the end of a week's work, made this place far different from the sleepy towns where [my] family had been before." Like Maud and George, Jesús saw the shift from hinterland to core as a migration from danger to safety, for southern Sonora in the early 1910s was beginning to spiral into a renewed cycle of ethnic violence among Yaqui Indians and Mexicans. "Fear of Yaqui raids was far from everybody's mind" in Cananea, he wrote. In terms of its economic promise for working families and its isolation from ethnic warfare, it was "a mecca for those desiring a better life."[9]

Yet fear and comfort were relative, as Corral knew well. If Kenyon-Kingdon gravitated toward an "unruffled world" among other Americans on Cananea's mesa, the Corral family also saw Cananea within the context of separate ethnic and class spheres. The men toiled in the Chivatera mine in the mountains, and the family lived in the working-class Mexican enclave of Chivatera Ridge, or, as Corral translated it, Billy Goat Hill. This world was anything but domesticated. "Cananea was a hell-raising town," Corral noted. "Miners were making money," and "music was always to be heard in the early morning hours as drunk young men serenaded their girls. Gun fights were common occurrences." As for Chivatera Ridge, it was a fugitive landscape of masculinity and risk. The earth constantly shook from dynamite blasts, which "scared the hell out of me," Corral recalled. Fathers and brothers prospered, but children played in abandoned tunnels rather than on lawns, and mothers worried, "for hardly a week went by that the mine ambulance was not seen racing toward the Chivatera mine to fetch an injured or dead miner."[10]

If Jesús Corral, Maud Kenyon-Kingdon, and Morris B. Parker took different roads into the borderlands, they had at least this in common: their worlds were in constant motion. Places like Nacozari and Cananea were stopping places on larger, transnational circuits that knit together local spaces: gardens and dance halls, meal stations and rural hosts, the refuge and quaking earth of Billy Goat Hill. The itinerary of the Corral family linked the contested countryside to a working-class mecca and eventually pointed farther north. After toiling under Chivatera Ridge, Jesús's brother, Emilio, frequented the male refuges of Cananea's pool halls. "It was there, where men gathered, that he heard that farmers in the United States were recruiting large families to help harvest cotton crops in Arizona and California," Corral wrote. "That announcement presented an alternative to the Corral family. We now had a choice." If Parker chased nature's bounty over hill and dale, and Kenyon-Kingdon settled for French doors in a wild land, the Corrals ultimately chose the "open fields" of Arizona as the final stop on their journey of toil.[11]

These roads were as diverse as those who took them, and they suggest a human side to the borderlands that we miss by perusing contracts, annual reports, and booster tracts. They also suggest the *range* of transnational tales: U.S. mining engineers stringing together disparate landscapes on a tenuous scientific thread; Yaqui and Mexican villagers working and fighting for traditional homelands; Chinese servants working to sustain a new life abroad; mining directors and railroad builders seeking to wring dividends from a rebellious land; *rancheros* and *mescaleros* chasing more modest dreams at the edges of the copper borderlands; immigrants passing through to the other side; worlds of women and men, their work, play, fantasies, and fears.

Such relationships approximated the modern electrical grid that Thomas Edison manufactured from copper in the late nineteenth century. Circuits of human energy led in all directions, yet each strand had its own logic and bundle of connections. Each was linked to discrete places, the human equivalent of transformers, insulators, pole lines, switchboards, and generators. It was a network that made connections and also created distinctions. Yet the analogy of electrical networks only goes so far, for unlike systems conceived by the Edison Electric Company and Westinghouse, these were anything but static fixtures. Spatial coordinates shifted over time as Mexicans, Americans, Yaquis, Chinese, and others migrated between spaces that corporate and state elites could see — smelters and mines, company towns, corporate reports, censuses — and "subterranean" spaces of ethnicity, culture, and family: regions of refuge from the official gaze. These unseen worlds burrowed beneath the more visible arteries of capital and state power to provide the essential human bedrock of the borderlands.

At a basic level, the rise of industrial mining mapped a modern world on frontier foundations. From a Mexican perspective, copper mining promised to help reorganize a landscape that was already generations old. As Mexican entrepreneurs entered the new corporate realms of Cananea and Nacozari, they sought to regenerate and improve upon older pathways with the help of outsiders. And yet there was more to the story than new immigrant pathways being mapped onto older Mexican foundations, for part of the story is also about Mexican migrations. If copper corporations required massive inputs of energy in the form of hoisting machinery, concentrators, mills, smelting furnaces, and railroads to carve up places like Pilares Mountain and the Cananeas and get their pieces to market, they also needed more human labor than the local countryside could provide. To transform the U.S.–Mexico borderlands, Phelps Dodge and the CCCC needed to remake the region's Mexican population.

This process began as early as 1902, when the El Paso and Southwestern Railroad began to ship carloads of Mexicans south into Sonora to build the Nacozari road and work in the mines and smelters of Pilares and Nacozari. Local accounts about the workers' origins are vague, but they probably came via El Paso from Chihuahua, Durango, and other states on the far side of the Sierra Madres. Unlike the Sonora Railway, which was not extended south of Sonora until 1907, the Mexican Central Railroad below El Paso tapped the entire central plateau of Mexico and its vast pool of labor. In 1903, additional workers came from Chihuahua to complete the Nacozari Railroad. The road's labor contractor, Enrique Rodríguez, also supplied crews around Naco, and many of his men, whom he assembled at El Paso, were newcomers even to Chihuahua. Many had traveled hundreds of miles from villages in southern Mexico to take advantage of new industrial wages at the Arizona–Sonora border.[12]

Cananea managers also had to reassemble "native" labor from afar. In 1903, CCCC officials noted that even though workers were arriving daily from all over Sonora, the company had also imported labor from Baja California. Like Phelps Dodge and its contractors, the CCCC manufactured mobility to pin their mining landscapes down. If this seemed paradoxical, it was a contradiction that workers willingly took advantage of. The Mexicans bound for the Lucky Tiger, a gold mine near Nacozari, benefited from the railroad journey but to the company's dismay kept moving. "No amount of herding would keep the gang intact," a reporter later noted. Some "skipped out" before the train reached the station. It was hard to keep these workers tied down, Greene acknowledged, "as they are never satisfied." In a climate of high demand for labor, they "work for a few days in one place and then go to another camp and so on," pursuing tales—and there were many—of higher wages elsewhere.[13]

If corporate elites grumbled about Mexican mobility and opportunism— much as their precursors had in Tubac years before—they also found that putting workers in place once they got to camp was anything but straightforward. For labor may have seemed to move as freely (and, indeed, as abstractly) as capital, but spatial and cultural distinctions mattered. In 1905, the CCCC imported miners from Aguascalientes and San Luis Potosí, Mexico, to the Cananea mining camp of Buenavista, only to find that local Sonorenses ridiculed their appearance, dress, and habits. The mining manager, Arthur S. Dwight, finally asked Cananea's chief of police, Pablo Rubio, to post a policeman near their new homes "until they have acclimated to their new surroundings and made the locals understand they're here to stay."[14]

Figure 15. Mexican miners waiting to be lowered underground at Cananea. By law, most of Cananea's miners were Mexican, even though most of their foremen hailed from north of the border. Courtesy of the Arizona Historical Society/Tucson; Robert Torrance Photo Collection, PC 135, AHS Photograph #97336.

In Sonora, by law, at least 70 percent of the workers in a given camp had to be Mexican citizens. Mexicans also flocked to Arizona camps, but here the geography of labor was often different. In camps such as Clifton and Morenci, Mexicans dominated underground, but Bisbee was considered a "white man's" mining camp, where higher-paid mining jobs were reserved to Anglo-Americans and immigrants from northern and western Europe. Mexicans worked for lower wages on the smelter floor, and after the smelter went to Douglas, so did many Mexicans. A Bisbee reporter assured Anglo readers that the loss of jobs to Douglas was "no cause for alarm," since smelting was a largely Mexican profession. "Bisbee's future is that of a mining town," he explained, with "an American population." Mexican neighborhoods such as Ragtown in Douglas and Bajo, a *barrio* in Agua Prieta, just south of the Douglas smelter, reflected this segregation of mining and smelting labor between the Mule Mountains and Whitewater Draw.[15]

In reality, the white man's camp of Bisbee was anything but. Although they were excluded underground, Mexicans found plenty of work on the surface, even if it was work that others didn't want. Many worked in the transfer business, taking goods up Bisbee's steep hills from the train depot. "If we cannot go to the house with a wagon," noted one company, "we deliver the load at the foot of the nearest trail, when Mexicans are employed to pack it to its destination." Mexicans were also put to work after storms; in the 1902 monsoon season, a Mexican gang cleared Bisbee's tracks after "several loads of dirt washed down the ravine from the mountain side." In 1904, a contractor brought Mexicans from El Paso to build a subway to control urban flooding, and when it filled with debris "an army of Mexican laborers" cleaned up the mess. After one devastating flood, Mexicans even had to muck Anglo homes—even if, as one witness observed, their own shacks "built of grass and tin cans" survived the storm unscathed.[16]

Not all Bisbee's Mexicans lived in homes of "grass and tin cans," but their ethnic enclaves, like their work, were worlds apart. The largest Mexican neighborhood was on Chihuahua Hill, likely named after the homeland of the many Mexican workers that El Paso and Southwestern contractors pulled north through El Paso. Two other Mexican barrios were Zacatecas Canyon—where the main Bisbee thoroughfare of Brewery Gulch ran up into the Mule Mountains—and Tintown, a neighborhood underneath the El Paso and Southwestern tracks where the houses were built of corrugated iron and "patched with five-gallon kerosene cans." Such place-names speak volumes about the pragmatic, often transitory nature of these communities. Places like Chihuahua Hill were landscapes of poverty, risk, and disease: fires swept through the tightly packed shacks, scavengers' wagons were unable to reach many of the homes, allowing garbage to pile up, and many homes "for sanitary reasons should be burned,"

Figure 16. American picnickers at Cananea. Courtesy of the Arizona Historical
Society/Tucson, AHS Photograph #63814.

proposed a local doctor. Yet they were also regions of refuge, where one could
evade scrutiny and find common cultural terrain in a foreign land. Police chasing
"stray Mexicans" frequently lost them in this dense ethnic enclave, where family
ties and fiestas kept the *patria* (fatherland) close at hand.[17]

Ethnicity, class, and nationality also inflected urban divides in Sonora. Entering Cananea by train, one passed through the town on the mesa, upwind from
the smelter. Here Kenyon-Kingdon and her cohort had their French doors, Chinese servants, and lawns. "Life in a Mexican mining town for an American
group is rather like an Army outpost in that they adhere as far as possible to
their own customs, and life is not so different from that of the United States," recalled Mildred Young Wallace, the daughter of CCCC Secretary George Young.
"There were breakfasts, luncheons, numerous afternoon and evening . . . parties,
tennis, dances at the American Club, horseback rides and moonlight picnics."
Mexico entered this world, but in a selective fashion. The center of town was
the plaza, where Wallace remembered "listening to the band concert and watching the slowly-moving throng" and admiring "the gaily dressed *señoritas*, with
their *dueñas* or chaperones." Here Americans encountered Mexico, but not the
Mexico that most Mexicans saw when they came to Cananea.[18]

To get to this Mexico, one had to continue to the edge of the mesa and wander down into working-class Ronquillo or climb to mountain barrios such as Chivatera. Like Chihuahua Hill and Tintown, these were regions of refuge. This was especially true for the camp of Buenavista, a nerve center of Cananea's labor movement. Like Chihuahua Hill, mining camps and smelter-side homes were perilous places, as Jesús Corral's mother knew well. Pneumonia killed in Chivatera, "where the accommodations for the miners are of a primitive character" but also near the smelter. "When anyone living in the vicinity of the smelter is afflicted with the disease," a resident wrote, "it is almost certain that death will follow" since "fumes of sulphur prevent the curing of the lungs." This was far from the Mexico where Mildred Young lived. "My wife and daughters go about the streets at will unattended," George Young bragged. For his family and others, Mexican Cananea lay beyond the pale: a mere shadow of the familiar and domesticated landscapes of Anglo-American Mexico.[19]

These borders were especially clear in Pilares, where an artificial terrace halfway up the mountain divided the camp in two halves. "The Mexican town swarmed up to it and covered it," wrote the mining engineer Ralph Ingersoll in the 1920s, "but above, the odd hundred feet before the topography came to a sharp point at the top, was reserved for the American quarter." Here were "attractive" houses on a "fashionable thoroughfare," each with a garden, "where the almost-green grass and peach- and fig-trees were neatly fenced off from the roving burro." Each had "a Mexican girl to help out, and every modern convenience included in a realtor's paean of praise—electric lights, hot and cold water, and two minutes' run (down-hill) to work. In the morning the vegetable man, a withered old Chinaman, came along with a string of burros loaded with fresh vegetables, and the wife stood at her gate and selected what she wished, and argued with the huckster, in the six or eight Spanish phrases she had picked up."

Ingersoll likened Pilares to white settler enclaves of the British Empire. "I have read of Englishmen who go into the wilderness and, living there, dress for dinner, play cards in the evening, and build golf-courses on Sunday," he wrote, but Anglos at Pilares played another game. Most "came from Main Street towns," where "they had not amounted to much socially," he wrote, "but when they journeyed into a foreign land . . . there was not the slightest doubt that they were all used to much better things, much more exclusive friends, and in general an entirely different (and higher) rung of the social ladder." Here in the American colony, transnational dreams became imperial fantasies.[20]

One day, curious to learn how the "other half" lived, Ingersoll traveled downhill to the "Mexican Town." He encountered one of the company's contractors, Angel Solis, "smoking his evening cigarette as calmly as possible, still arrayed in his uniform of toil." One of the highest-paid Mexican contractors, "he should have a model home," Ingersoll mused. Instead he found a "little adobe building roofed over with what were evidently ancient iron fire-doors from the mine." Its chimney "consisted of half a dozen coffee cans telescoped one in another," it had a single room with a "dissolute-looking iron bed" and a "battered wash-stand," and children, dogs, and pigs inhabited the same interior space. "If the wealthy Angel lived like this, in what kind of shack did my poor Salomon exist, who lives solely on the dollar and a half?" Ingersoll wondered. He found Salomon in a similar home, different only in that he "shared his castle with another family, and everything—children, wives, and dirt—was doubled."[21]

When Ingersoll published his exposé, U.S. residents of Pilares rebutted his stark dichotomies. He gave readers "the wrong impression," wrote one. "He fails to mention the homes of such men as Don Pastor Valenzuela, with flowers in the yard, and window boxes, which are spotlessly clean." And although families often did crowd single rooms, "living conditions for Mexican laborers are infinitely better than the majority of Mexican towns." Yet perhaps because they lived in such a segregated camp, there was much the Anglo critics simply didn't know about their neighbors. Mexicans rented mostly single-room adobes or shacks without plumbing. They had dirt floors, and often "the level of the floor was considerably below the door sill, due to sweeping," noted an official. "The Mexican house situation is quite bad up there [in Pilares]," wrote another, "and from all I hear the men are altogether too crowded."[22]

Phelps Dodge tried to solve the problem in the 1920s by building "model homes" that Mexicans could buy and make their own, yet even these were a far cry from those in the American colony up the hill. Company blueprints showed homes with two rooms, each 140 feet square, with a tiny window and safety flue. Walls were adobe, roofs were corrugated iron, floors were dirt, and four anchor bolts pinned the house down onto its foundation. "No door is to be provided in the partition, no wooden floors or ceilings are to be provided, and no plastering is to be done on the adobe walls," specifications read. Each house cost $556 to build. The owner "would have the privilege of adding lean-tos, etc. on the house and making it larger," one Phelps Dodge elite noted. What he failed to explain was that such additions would be necessary, at least for an outdoor kitchen, because managers hoped to fit up to four families into these two-room homes.[23]

Things uphill were different, even for Phelps Dodge's "cheap" American homes. These were prefabricated in Los Angeles and sent by rail to Nacozari. Initially as cheap as their adobe counterparts, shipping and assembly more than doubled their price. And when lighting, plumbing, and fencing were factored in, four homes cost $7,794, or three and a half times more than the Mexican homes (up to fourteen times more, if calculated by family). This was the cheap plan.

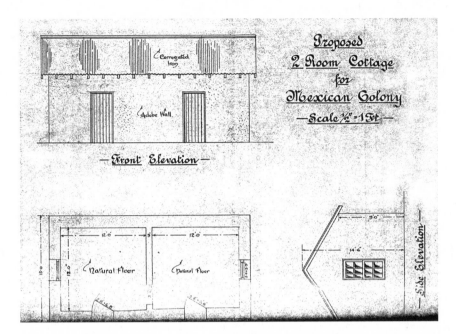

Figure 17. House plan for Mexican colony in Pilares (1920).
Phelps Dodge Corporation Archives, Phoenix, Arizona.

More typical was a request to build two houses in Anglo Pilares at $4,450 each. These were balloon-frame homes with drop siding on the outside, plasterboard on the inside, and floors of wood. Each had a kitchen, dining room, living room, bathroom, and two bedrooms—which by themselves covered a space equal to that of the entire Mexican cottage—as well as three porches, cupboards, closets, bookshelves, and cabinets. Covering an area of 1,150 square feet, each could contain three Mexican cottages or twelve Mexican families. Doors divided the interiors, and everything was painted "a suitable color." From the uphill perspective, these were unremarkable spaces. But from downhill they loomed as ostentatious signs of another world.[24]

It is hard not to see these Anglo houses—prefabricated abroad, designed for a life on the interior—as a metaphor for the U.S. transnational experience. This was a world of refuge, patrolled by the paternalism of corporate capital. Phelps Dodge even prepared a guide to help new U.S. employees navigate Pilares. It introduced newcomers to special American rentals, hotels offering board, a market selling beef from the company's ranch, the company store, the Chinese peddlers selling produce door to door, how to get home deliveries of wood and milk.

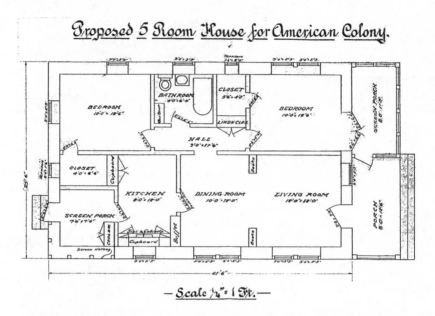

Figure 18. House plan for American colony in Pilares (1918).
Phelps Dodge Corporation Archives, Phoenix, Arizona.

One could remain completely inside, like Maud Kenyon-Kingdon and the U.S. wives in Ingersoll's portrait. Phelps Dodge also managed mobility with special railroad passes, available at its local office. The Nacozari Country Club and Nacozari Book Club offered other refuges bounded by class, culture, and language. The paternalism of company towns was familiar to mining engineers, but in Mexico it had an additional purpose: to keep them from getting lost in a foreign land.[25]

Mexican spaces were less contained and less managed. Held together by culture and family ties, they were also supported by pathways that wandered off the corporate map. Like Anglo enclaves, Mexican barrios served as refuges: not because corporations sheltered them, but because they pushed them to the margins. Mexicans moved in and out of focus, tracing shadow circuits that met in Zacatecas Canyon, Tintown, Buenavista, and Chivatera Ridge. These pathways ran through the male spaces of the mines, smelters, and pool halls and the domestic spaces of the company homes, where extended families came together for work, fiestas, or casual visits. For those from Chihuahua and beyond, these circuits were often far-reaching and attenuated. In Sonora, they formed sinews of a regional community that ran south along the Yaqui, Sonora, and San Miguel valleys, a community that had changed little in its geographical contours since Mexican and Opata grandparents had cycled in and out of Tubac.[26]

One saw these regional lifelines in Huépac, an Opata–Mexican outpost one hundred miles south of Cananea and Nacozari. Huépac's fields, pastures, and orchards fed a few local mining ventures, but workers and products also took a longer road to the copper mines. Unsettled conditions often triggered migrations: floods in 1914 and 1926, for instance, washed away much of Huépac's land, pushing farmers to become miners. Conversely, the periodic reduction of workforces in Cananea and Nacozari could push miners south toward rural safety nets. The roads between city and country were in constant motion, and mobility just as often reflected good times. When conditions were flush in Cananea and Nacozari, the roads teemed with livestock, cheese, meat, and agricultural surpluses heading north from Huépac and nearby villages to feed miners. The children of farmers thereby consumed the fruits of their families' lands as industrial workers, while sending wages south to help keep the other half of the regional community alive.[27]

If copper mines anchored regional communities in place, so did their mercantile adjuncts. Howard Carroll Groton, a sales representative of the Phelps Dodge Mercantile in Nacozari, learned about these commercial ties in the 1920s. He saw them from the tail end of the Nacozari railroad, where trains unloaded carloads of corn, flour, coffee, and lard from the United States, fine thread from Glasgow, and every ten months or so a full carload of cigarette papers from Italy. The Phelps Dodge wholesale trade in Sonora was enormous. At any given time, "thirty or forty pack animals" were in line behind the warehouse from villages to the south, Groton recalled. Freighters "always had a certain amount of trading to do as soon as they hit camp." They peddled *panocha* (brown sugar cakes), *carne seca* (dried meat), cheese, oranges, squash, tobacco, molasses, and chickens, most of it ending up at the company store for resale. They then loaded up green coffee, sugar, lard, flour, rice, cigarette papers, candles, plows, dynamite, fuse and caps, roofing iron, kerosene, lace, thread, and cloth before returning south.[28]

Since rural capital was locked up in the fields most of the year, merchants bought on credit, as they had in the colonial era. Groton made frequent trips south to collect for prior shipments and take future orders. The contrast with the scale and organization of trade at Nacozari was noteworthy. Cash was "stashed in everything from an old boot to a twelve-quart water pail." Often they used the gold and silver that customers hauled in from local mines. It was like stepping back in time into a cash-poor frontier. "There was a lot of swapping where no cash was available," Groton wrote: "A little girl came in and placed one egg on the counter and said, 'Darme cinco de tabaco' [give me five cents' worth of tobacco]. Another egg was good for 'Cinco de petróleo' [five cents' worth of oil], for which she produced a pop bottle. A third egg was good for 'cinco de papel' (cigarette paper)." This "frontierish" realm was also disconcerting, for it lay miles from Groton's corporate refuge. On the road back to Nacozari, "how easy it would have been for some *bandido* to roll a small boulder into the road," he remembered. "I was never absolutely relieved until, on arrival at the company store, we would arouse the *velador* (watchman), carry the strongbox into the store, and put it in the vault."[29]

Yaqui Indians also wove the mines and smelters of Cananea and Nacozari into broader transnational circuits, migrating from lowland villages in the Yaqui River delta of southern Sonora to copper towns along both sides of the border to supplement the annual harvests. Their migration from lowland to *sierra*, from farm to mine, built on a colonial strategy of moving between their Jesuit mission towns on the Yaqui River delta and mines in the Opata and Pima highlands. Unlike the Opatas, who married *mestizos* and ultimately became *mestizo* to survive, Yaquis migrated to preserve their autonomy. Famous for their technical skills underground, miners sought them out, whereas Jesuits needed their labor in the fields to keep the mission economy alive. This gave Yaquis a competitive edge, which allowed them to dictate the terms of their relationship to the colonial world.[30]

Yaquis moved between village and mine well into the nineteenth century, but their relationship to Mexico became increasingly volatile. They resisted efforts to open up their homeland to development, and by the twentieth century, battles for the Yaqui homeland raged as *broncos*, or "hostile" Yaquis, launched raids from the mountains to defend their lands while *pacíficos*, "peaceful" Yaquis, worked in mines and haciendas. They drifted not only between village and wage work, but also between imposed categories of *bronco* and *pacífico*. "The tamer ones always aided, concealed and furnished information to the wild ones," claimed one Anglo correspondent. "Sometimes they would slip out at night and do their devilment and be back before morning looking as peaceful and as innocent as lambs." Whether or not this was true, it put Sonora in a bind. Officials saw Yaquis as enemies of the state, but it was one thing to brand them as outlaws and another to defeat them, especially when a modern Mexico valued their labor more than ever.[31]

Yaqui mobility and resistance led to pathways that resembled the roads taken by Mexicans and Opatas but that were harder for outsiders to pin down. In every respect, this was fugitive terrain: it was based on relations of mobility, it was invisible to most Americans and Mexicans, it drew on shifty categories, and it often harbored fugitives from the law. As a land of shadows, it also provided refuge and power. Morris B. Parker snatched glimpses of this autonomous realm at Pilares, whose Yaqui workers "were quick to learn and, after a short period of training made excellent miners, the best in Mexico." Mine managers paid a premium for this labor, for twice a year, during the planting and harvesting seasons, Yaquis "simply stopped work and went home." All managers could do was anticipate the exodus and cope. Before they left, the company had Yaquis break up as much ore as possible, so that in their absence others could carry out the less skilled work of shoveling the broken ore and bringing it to the surface.[32]

These migrations made it hard not only to manage time, but also to police space, for unless managers were careful, fragments of the mining landscape also flowed south. One year Parker found some of the canvas hose that ran air into the shafts was missing. When Yaqui workers returned from the harvest, they were wearing canvas pants, "stiff, uniform in circumference, baggy, and wearing quality to last a lifetime." When accused of pilfering, "the only reply was a mischievous grin — '*Muy buenos pantalones, señor*' — the Yaquis considered their trousers a big joke." During these migrations, drill steel also ran low. Yaquis allegedly used the steel for planting sticks, but that was not all: "Yaqui blacksmiths forged this steel into weapons of war, knives, machetes, spear and arrow points," Parker wrote, "many of which were among the weapons used by the Yaquis in their revolt against the state and federal troops." Technologies of development from one borderland were thereby used to resist capital and state power in another.[33]

Yaquis also converted their industrial wages into weapons of resistance. "Every one of them who comes to Arizona and works, goes back to Sonora with either a rifle or ammunition," claimed one mining entrepreneur. Yaquis working in Douglas bought guns from U.S. merchants, and most probably came from the Copper Queen Mercantile. This commerce, proposed President Díaz in 1906, contributed greatly to the prolongation of Yaqui campaigns, causing the unnecessary deaths of both Mexicans and Americans. Yet when the Díaz regime began to deport Yaquis to the Yucatán peninsula later that same year, many U.S. entrepreneurs pointed the finger at Mexico. Hunger forced the Yaquis "to the trails and roads to plunder," insisted one: "they cannot work in the mines or on the ranches; they cannot cultivate their lands or raise cattle." Consigned to the shadows, "they must either rob or die of starvation."[34]

As Yaquis were driven underground by Mexican efforts to make them outlaws in their own land, many crossed the border into Arizona. Refugee pathways to the north, which built on previous networks between U.S. mines and fields and Yaqui villages in the Yaqui River delta, eventually gave rise to new communities north of the border, such as Pascua Village and Barrio Libre in Tucson and

Guadalupe in Phoenix. From these "expatriate" communities, Yaqui migrants sustained cultural, religious, and family ties to villages in Sonora. Like many of their Mexican and Anglo-American neighbors, they were relatively free to cross the border well into the twentieth century, and many would continue to do so to their advantage.[35]

By contrast, the Chinese, another group that lived in the shadow of the copper borderlands, found themselves much more constrained. Anti-Chinese sentiment began to rise in the western United States during the 1870s, and the Chinese Exclusion Act of 1882 barred all but a few specific classes of Chinese from immigrating to the States. Already a destination for Chinese entrepreneurs by the late nineteenth century, the borderlands of Arizona and Sonora became a new backdoor for immigration into the United States. Some of these Chinese—especially merchants and other "select" classes—immigrated legally, whereas others migrated to Sonora and Arizona with little intent of crossing borders. But the copper borderlands, in particular, also became a fugitive landscape of smuggling rings, border crossings, and border patrols, places where transnational relationships frequently coincided with illegal practices.[36]

The first Chinese immigrants to Arizona came in the early 1870s, but large-scale immigration came with the railroad. Hundreds of Chinese were among those who built the Southern Pacific into Tucson in 1880, and soon afterward they began to put down roots of a regional border community in the Mexican barrios of Tucson and along the nearby Santa Cruz River. Most found work as launderers, but some worked as cooks and farmers, and by the early twentieth century, many had become merchants, restaurant managers, clerks, and hotel-keepers. Others followed the rails east, settling in railroad towns and mining camps like Benson and Tombstone, where they moved into similar jobs. Tombstone had a Chinese colony of almost five hundred, many of them launderers, housekeepers, and cooks. Some moved to the nearby countryside, a number establishing truck farms on the San Pedro River near Hereford, Fairbank, and Charleston, where they raised produce for the urban markets of Tombstone, Bisbee, and their satellite communities.[37]

Chinese charted a different path into Sonora. Some Chinese associated with the Manila trade came to New Spain in the colonial era, but their numbers were small until the late nineteenth century. Thinking about labor shortages in the 1870s, Matías Romero pointed to "the great population of that vast empire" and "the relatively low wages they earn." Mexico and China signed a Treaty of Amity and Commerce in 1899 to promote trade and immigration, but by then Mexico was becoming an alternative destination for Chinese barred from the United

States by the exclusion act. By the time steamship lines from China opened for business in 1902, the most popular Mexican destination for Chinese was Sonora: the attractions were its relative proximity to Asian labor streams, its mining and railroad development, and, for those looking farther north, its border with the United States. From the 1890s until the early 1930s — when Sonora passed its own anti-Chinese laws — the Chinese were the first or second largest foreign group in the state.[38]

Many gravitated toward new frontiers of development, finding work as small merchants, cooks, houseboys, and launderers in railroad towns like Magdalena and mining towns like Cananea and Nacozari. Here would-be merchants, in particular, did not have to compete against as many established mercantile houses as in Guaymas and Hermosillo, although some firms, Juan Lung Tain of Magdalena and Hermosillo and Siu Fo Chon of Guaymas, for instance, found niches in even these cities as manufacturers of cheap shoes and clothing. By 1903, Cananea had the largest Chinese colony in the state. Just as William Cornell Greene had mapped a new city onto lands declared vacant by Mexican land surveyors, Chinese immigrants mapped new entrepreneurial networks of grocery stores, meat markets, pawnshops, and restaurants onto a place that formerly lay beyond the reach of regional commercial networks.[39]

Americans would later recall that Chinese controlled Cananea's restaurants and stores. This assumption also fueled anti-Chinese sentiment among Mexicans seeking to control these businesses, which were at the top of the ladder for most independent entrepreneurs in this company town. Yet according to a 1906 census things were more complicated. Chinese dominated restaurants and groceries but were an adjunct to a Mexican majority in general stores, butcher shops, and fruit stands. Theirs was, more than anything else, a grocer's world. Americans also saw an entrepreneurial world the census taker missed, made up of Chinese domestic cooks, houseboys, and handymen. The CCCC manager Tindall Evans had a Chinese gardener, houseboy, and cook, and his colleague, George Young, hired a series of Chinese cooks who frequently doubled as domestics. "They knew how to make themselves indispensable," recalled Young's daughter, Mildred. Anti-Chinese sentiment in Sonora bolstered Anglo-Chinese ties, especially in the refuge of the Anglo home. "They got along better with the Americans, who were also, in a very real sense, strangers in a strange land," Wallace observed, "and there was even trust and affection between them and their white employers."[40]

If Chinese entrepreneurs forged patron-client relationships in the intimate heart of the Anglo-American borderlands, they also mapped connections from the kitchens, restaurants, and groceries of Cananea into the nearby countryside. At the Ojo de Agua, one resident noted, an "almost unbroken line of Chinese

Juan Lung Tain y Compañía.

En la plaza de San Francisco, el punto mas céntrico de la población, sorprende á la vista el edificio que presentamos en esta parte de nuestra obra, por ser el que cuadra mejor al objeto á que está destinado.

Esta, por lo que respecta al exterior; que, en cuanto á la parte de adentro, es superior aún.

La tienda y escritorio ocupan una gran extensión á lo largo para ambos lados, en el ángulo que forma la esquina, dejando un espacio amplísimo entre las puertas de entrada y los mostradores, que son cómodos y de buen gusto.

A continuación de la Tienda, por el lado de mayor longitud, hay enormes salones dedicados á la fabricación de calzado, que ocupa un número considerable de operarios.

Bodegas extensísimas, distribuidas convenientemente, contienen toda clase de telas de lana, de algodón y lino; sombrillas, chales, rebozos; perfumería fina y corriente; artículos de mercería y lencería; calzado de todos tamaños y calidad variada; sombreros y corbatas, etc., y cuanto abarca el ramo de abarrotes.

Los Sres. Lung Tain y Compañía, propietarios de esta Casa Comercial, estableciéronse el año de 1896, desarrollando una labor constante, basada en la mejor buena fé; y sus negocios han prosperado de manera

tal, que traspasando los límites de este Distrito fueron á establecer sucursales á las importantes plazas de Hermosillo y Cananea.

En la de Hermosillo, situada en la calle de Don Luis,

Exterior de la Casa.

frente al Seminario Conciliar, fundaron una fábrica de calzado y otra de ropa, cuyos productos alcanzan gran demanda por sus precios y calidad razonables.

La Sucursal de Cananea gira bajo la razón social de Juan Chon y Cía. y está situada en la Comisaría del Ronquillo.

En esta misma población han ensanchado sus ventas en diferentes barrios, por medio de dos sucursales (No. 3 y No. 4) que se hallan en las calles de San Lorenzo y Principal, respectivamente.

Los escaparates y aparadores de este importante centro industrial y de comercio, presentan constantemente las últimas novedades en todo gérnero de mercancías Extranjeras y del País, atrayendo al público por la comodidad de sus precios. Sus importaciones son directas.

Interior de la Casa.

Figure 19. Advertisement for Chinese merchant house of Juan Lung Tain y Compañía in Magdalena with branch stores in Hermosillo and Cananea. From Federico García y Alva, *México y sus progresos* (1907).

gardeners" leased CCCC lands and watched over "miniature farms, tending the growing plants and keeping the burros away." Each morning at daybreak a wagon with vegetables left these farms for the mesa, and by nine o'clock, wrote Mildred Young Wallace, "a Chinaman carrying a long pole over his back with a basket suspended from each end would dog-trot into the yard, pull off the wet gunnysack coverings, and announce his arrival." These baskets were truly Mexican cornucopias, added Maud Kenyon-Kingdon, for they spilled forth "the most luscious of strawberries, asparagus, tomatoes, cauliflower, cabbage, peas, beans and various other sorts of the vegetable kingdom."[41]

Looking at a map, one is struck by the proximity of these farms to their Chinese counterparts across the line, some thirty miles to the north, on the San Pedro River near Bisbee. Strung roughly twenty miles between Fairbank, Charleston, Lewis Springs, and Hereford, these truck farms took root in the 1880s and were referred by some as Bisbee's "Chinese quarter." Farther south on the San Pedro, Chinese also farmed the Las Nutrias ranch of the Cananea Cattle Company in Sonora, another node in what seemed to be an unbroken transnational chain of Chinese fields. Yet these spaces were also worlds apart. The Sonora farms were tied to one of the most powerful Chinese urban networks in the borderlands, in Cananea, whereas those in Arizona were pushed to the margins of urban life. A farmer named Hop Sing hauled truck to Bisbee, but according to an "unwritten law" had to leave by sunset. A farmer on the San Bernardino ranch, Charley, was the only Chinese allowed in Douglas, and in Naco a simple "nod of a head, in the direction of Benson or towards El Paso," told Chinese to keep moving.[42]

Given the informal exclusion of Chinese from Bisbee, Douglas, and Naco, as well as the formal exclusion of entire classes of Chinese from Arizona by the Exclusion Act of 1882, it is harder to flesh out these shadow landscapes along the San Pedro than it is on the Ojo de Agua, which were clearly tied to the Chinese colony of Cananea. Were men like Charley and Hop Sing simply lone entrepreneurs working in relative isolation from urban Chinese enclaves in northern Sonora or southern Arizona? And if not, which way did their local worlds point? Were their farms outliers of Tucson's Chinese barrio or of the smaller Chinese quarter of Tombstone, were they tied to the Chinese colony of Cananea (much closer than Tucson, for instance, but a nation apart), or all three? Because these immigrants, more so than their Yaqui and Mexican neighbors, were forced off the public stage, their lives remain largely hidden from view. But even the most fleeting glimpses are suggestive.

In August 1903, a Chinese inspector named Charles T. Connell got off the train from Douglas at Charleston, where with a deputy he "doubled back to the Chinese colony," on the San Pedro. Entering the house of Hop Sing, they found

Lee Quong, the man they were looking for. Hop Sing had given Lee Quong a room as an office, and here Connell and his deputy found telegraph blanks, books with names of Chinese, and addresses of Chinese firms in San Francisco, Los Angeles, and El Paso. This evidence confirmed their suspicion that Lee Quong was "the king pin of the smugglers," a regional broker "in the traffic of smuggling Chinamen into the United States." Their hunch—that this seemingly isolated San Pedro enclave was actually a crossroads for illegal migration north— seemed further supported after two border crossers, Gin Wo and Wah Kee, were arrested near Fairbank later that year. In 1905, Connell found proof that these fugitives were part of a smuggling ring run by Yee Yin, "a Cananea Chink, who has a mountain hiding place for the Chinese."[43]

Chinese inspectors left many pieces unexplained. The fact that migrants passed along the San Pedro—a thoroughfare in the colonial era, and the high road for Sonora before the railroad—does not mean the Chinese of Cananea and Bisbee were part of the same regional community. Take Wong Took Lung, a rancher on the San Pedro near Fairbank. In 1903, he visited his family in China, and several weeks later sailed to San Francisco. On reentry, he posed as a laborer going to Mexico. He had his photograph taken and boarded a train to Sonora. "It was easy for him to get back to his ranch," noted a reporter, "and he once more assumed the role of a San Pedro truck raiser." Perhaps Wong Took Lung knew Chinese in Sonora, or perhaps he simply paid the right people to get him home: Mexico may have been the same blank space for him as Chinese Arizona was for most outsiders. From such fragmentary evidence, we cannot know what these border crossings meant.[44]

In 1913, however, law officers confiscated a message in Chinese characters from a sojourner that provided a compelling snapshot of a shrouded passage— an underground railroad—that jumped the gap between Chinese Sonora and Arizona. As the interpreter deciphered the message, a ghost landscape appeared. "Starting from Cananea to Naco, go to the Jew Hing Store and inquire of a man named Wong Ah Yot, and give him a little money as fees for guiding you out to the road," it read:

> On the left side of the road there is a railroad. Follow this until you come to two houses. You must pass by the back of those houses. Continue on the railroad until you come to a cattle ranch. It is surrounded by a fence, and it is neces- sary to jump over this fence. Follow the railroad until you come to a railroad station house. Near the station is located a water tank. Continue on the rail- road you will come to a place having ten or more houses. You must walk down to the ditch and cross over until you come to a station house located near the

railroad. That is the Fairbank Station. Walk on the left side you will find the Town of Fairbank. It has a Chinese laundry having some Chinese writings in front, named Wo Hing conducted by Yee Jung Hung. You can go to his place and he may direct you where to take a train to Tombstone. In Tombstone there is a laundry conducted by Woo and Yee Sack. You can go to their place and stay for a little while. There is a train going to Pearce and there change cars for Willcox. While you are traveling, should you meet any Chinese people who ask you if you have a certificate of residence, you must answer in the affirmative. You must be very careful while traveling.[45]

This vernacular map—revealing a network of human nodes in the shadow of the copper borderlands—no doubt had counterparts among Yaquis, Mexicans, and even Americans. Passed by word of mouth or on rare documents such as these, these networks had vanished from formal maps, even if they depended on similar signs: a cattle ranch here, a railroad there, stations, ditches, a prominent display of Chinese characters that travelers saw but rarely registered. It was the same visible world, a vast transnational document available to all, but encoded throughout with fugitive scripts.

In this world, even the dominant dialect trailed off into the shadows. Americans remade their lives with power and privilege in Cananea and Nacozari, but in the copper hinterlands, beyond the pull of copper and steel, gravity weakened. Here one found an exile community of immigrants who crossed borders—like the Chinese—as refugees from worlds of exclusion. In 1882, weeks before voting to exclude Chinese, the U.S. Congress passed the Edmunds Act, outlawing polygamy. In 1884, federal marshals began making arrests in Utah, Idaho, and Arizona, where Mormons practiced plural marriage as one of the cardinal Mormon doctrines. As marshals swept through Mormon country to impose new domestic laws at home, many Mormons, like their Chinese neighbors, began to take their families and households abroad.[46]

William Carroll McClellan was among these refugees. A resident of the Mormon enclave of Pleasanton, New Mexico, he was in constant fear of Indians, since "Geronimo and his renegades were on the rampage." But U.S. marshals were also "invading remote frontiers, bent on arresting every man having more than one wife." Ironically, McClellan soon took a path familiar to Geronimo, leading south into the Sierra Madres. Here, church officials hoped, polygamists might find "a place of refuge under a foreign government." Starting at the Mormon town of St. David—along the San Pedro near Tombstone—a party left for Chihuahua in 1885, camping near Casas Grandes. After gaining permission from the Díaz regime, church officials bought land on the Casas Grandes and Piedras Verdes rivers and in the nearby highlands, where they created six new colonies: Colonias Díaz, Juárez, Pacheco, Dublán, García, and Chuhuichupa.[47]

In 1892, Mormons expanded into Sonora after colonists bought two hundred square miles of land on the Bavispe River from the customs officers and land-owners Juan Fenochio and Emilio Kosterlitzky. They founded Colonia Oaxaca at the mouth of Púlpito Pass in 1893, followed by Colonia Morelos, established just to the north in 1900. Both places appealed to the exiles precisely because they were so isolated. As one resident later recalled, they wanted "a place where they wouldn't be mixed up with outside or other people; where they would have a place to raise up their own." Unlike their Chihuahua sister colonies, which lay near Greene's Rio Grande, Sierra Madre, and Pacific Railroad, Colonias Oaxaca and Morelos lay off the industrial grid, as Morris B. Parker noted when he and his buckboard rattled through in 1900. This suited residents, many of whom had served prison sentences in the States as polygamists. Theirs was a new fugitive terrain, far from the prying eyes of the American state.[48]

One could measure its isolation by Parker's grueling trip from Colonia Oaxaca to Nacozari or the equally long journey to the nearest railhead, across the Púl-pito Pass into Chihuahua. This was "a pioneer road," wrote one Mormon: "It was solid rock for miles and in places it was like a staircase." One point, called The Squeeze, was nightmarish for wagons. "I could only take one wagon at a time, taking it to the top of the mountain, leaving it, and going back after the next," explained another resident. "High mountains capped with snow, dark canyons where wild beasts made their lair," and "wild" Indians encircled this dis-tant realm, embellished another writer. And a wild, disorienting land it seemed. Mesquite, catclaw, and "other varieties of trees and brush" surrounded Colonia Morelos, giving it "the appearance of a jungle," recalled the colonist Thomas Romney. The land was "so densely wooded," he explained, "that my wife at-tached a sheep bell to the neck of our eldest child" so he would not wander like a wild beast.[49]

Yet, for exiles who wanted "a place where they wouldn't be mixed up with [the] outside," these newcomers were remarkably well connected to the world around them. Connections started at home: the trademark brick buildings of Colonia Morelos, whose facades were made of local clay fired in local kilns, were sup-ported by frames harvested in the pine forests of Chihuahua. Their doors, win-dow frames, porch pillars, and lathed ornamental dowels came from workshops in Colonia Juárez, across Púlpito Pass, roofs were topped with pine shingles from the towering Sierra Madres, and plaster was made from gypsum from moun-tains in southwestern New Mexico. Compared to the Anglo-American homes of

Figure 20. Mormons harvesting wheat at Colonia Morelos, 1914. The wheat was
ground at a local mill owned by the Lillywhite family and sold to miners at nearby
El Tigre and Pilares de Teras. Most Mormons fled after revolutionaries took the
colony in 1912, but some returned intermittently to work fields for years afterward.
Courtesy of the Arizona Historical Society/Tucson; Burns/Naylor Collection,
AHS Photograph #54557.

Pilares, prefabricated in California, these were local spaces—but not nearly as
local as Mexican adobes farther south along the Bavispe, in the Opata–Mexican
villages of Bavispe, Bacerac, and Huachinera.[50]

Mormons were also tied to the outside world by their labor. Miners struck it
rich at Pilares de Teras, near Colonia Oaxaca, in the 1890s, following up with
the spectacular discovery of gold at El Tigre, in the nearby Tigre Mountains, in
1900. "These mines were a benefit to the colony because they were markets for
our farm produce," noted the Mormon resident Estelle Webb Thomas. "Whatever else a man did, he had fields, an orchard and vineyards, cattle, and poultry,"
all finding their way to nearby mining camps. Most of the fruit in their orchards
and vegetables from their fields were packed over the hills to the El Tigre and
Pilares de Teras mines. Miners lived on Mormon corn, melons, grapes, sweet
potatoes, eggs, and peanuts; their animals ate Mormon hay and corn. A hundred
mules hauled wheat to the mines weekly, while others took the longer road to
Cananea, Nacozari, and Cumpas. "Fields of golden, waving grain could be seen

for miles on both sides of the Bavispe," recalled one resident. "It was a promising time."[51]

Not all Mormons were blessed with the capital to build mills on the river. Many had few belongings and, with no jobs or fields waiting, were quickly reduced to poverty. Houses had dirt floors, mattresses were stuffed with cornhusks, and chairs were "slabs with wooden pegs for legs," noted one. Miles P. Romney's new home consisted of "four posts driven into the ground with burlap sacks sewed together to form the walls on two sides and a wagon box and brush on the other sides." Despite dreams of living in divine isolation, many had to work on the outside to survive. Mormon men and boys turned to an asset they brought with them—wagons and teams—and the rise of mining in Nacozari and Cananea gave these rural assets new value. It "changed life for many that couldn't make it dry farming," recalled the colonist Alvah Fenn. His father "rigged up some freight outfits," moved his family to Naco, and joined other colonists in the business of hauling coke and machinery south and metal north. When the Cananea–Naco railroad was built in 1902, they moved to Nacozari; and when the Nacozari railroad was done, they moved south, to connect more distant mines to the new Phelps Dodge railhead.[52]

If Maud Kenyon-Kingdon and her world moved toward the centers of the copper borderlands, Alvah Fenn, James Wilford Ray, and Lucien Mormon Mecham migrated to its edges, facilitating its expansion. The nomadic business of living in tents and working day after day with six-horse teams and wagons was difficult, recalled Laura Ann Hardy Mecham. When a loaded wagon ran over and mangled Ray's leg, he had to ride a hundred miles for help. Even on good days, hauling from Nacozari to Cumpas and from there to more distant mines was simply "hard work," noted Alvah Fenn. The road crossed the creek sixty-eight times in the first twelve miles, and "there was always water." Tailings from Nacozari washed downstream, making a dangerous mess of these passages. One had to keep moving, for "if you stopped, the wheels would stick tight." Meanwhile, women and daughters shouldered the burden at home, whether planting or harvesting, canning crops, or, as Frances Godfrey Jarvis did, holding down a family store while her husband and boys kept in motion between country and city.[53]

In the end, these nomadic pathways were not much different from those taken by Chinese, Yaqui, Mexican, and Opatas. As difficult as it could be, this was also a world of possibilities. Mormons such as the Haymores gravitated to rural work, moving from the Turkey Track Ranch of Sonora to the Empire Ranch of Arizona to the Ojitos Ranch in Chihuahua. William Claude Huish, Isaac Alldredge, and David Alvin McClellan cycled through mines and smelters in Sonora, and in Chihuahua they hauled goods, cut trees, and laid track for Greene's mining

and timber empire. It was an uneven world, one in which, like freighters crossing Nacozari Creek, one had to keep moving. Men like David Alma Stevens
could hardly stop to breathe. He started out as a freighter in Chihuahua, shifted
to railroad construction, and then hit the Cananea–Nacozari freighting boom.
After that, he returned to Chihuahua, where he farmed, freighted, and raised
cattle, barely making ends meet. In 1905, he hauled supplies for the Kansas City,
Mexico, and Orient Railroad in Chihuahua and then crossed the Sierra Madres
to do the same work for the Southern Pacific. The intense heat finally drove
him back across the *sierras*, where he finally came to rest on a farm near Casas
Grandes.[54]

As he drifted, Stevens covered terrain that would have been familiar to Morris B. Parker, Maud Kenyon-Kingdon, Jesús Corral, Hop Sing, the Yaqui Indians
of Pilares, and countless others who came to call the borderlands home at the
turn of the century. Yet even though they had landmarks in common, each of
these travelers charted different journeys, set off from the others by culture, class,
ethnicity, nationality, and any number of individual idiosyncrasies. What they
had in common was the nature of their traffic: these were all people in motion,
turning border space to their own ends and stirring up endless clouds of human
sediment that both nurtured and obscured transnational space. It nurtured this
space through dreams, labor, and cultural exchanges that motivated and under-
wrote economic development, but it obscured this space because at the end of
the journey, the local worlds made more human sense than the expanding networks of rails, mines, capital, and contracts that connected nations to each other.

Many things set these worlds apart. Borders often emerged from the uneven
and unequal relationships of development: some people moved to the centers
of power, and others were pushed to the margins; some anchored their lives in
smelters and cities, and others toiled at the rural frontiers. Yet even the ragged
edges of the copper borderlands had ways of empowering people by creating regions of refuge, autonomy, and mobility that allowed people to inhabit the region on their own terms. Mormons followed their own path by moving between
mines, roads, and utopian villages on the Bavispe; Yaquis took similar journeys to
preserve autonomy and power vis-à-vis the Mexican state; rural and urban Chinese entrepreneurs found ways to maintain both legal and illegal webs of commerce and migration; and Mexicans, Opatas, Yaquis, and even Mormons frequently left the industrial borderlands during planting and harvesting seasons to
sustain safety nets for an unstable modern world in which jobs and wages came
and went. Indeed, as it had for generations, mobility offered the best means for
living in a world at the margins of state, entrepreneurial, and corporate power.

Ultimately, these separate seen and unseen worlds underscored the gap that still persisted between corporate and state dreams of pinning the borderlands down, and the complicated, messy, and ever-shifting worlds that people called home. The more power corporate and state elites tried to exert over the region—the more space their rails, mines, and smelters consumed—the more it slipped from their grasp. The lustrous dream of the modern world cast a series of long shadows, and these shadows, some feared, seemed to be taking on fugitive lives of their own.

Part III

CONTESTED TERRAIN

6

DEVELOPMENT AND DISORDER

In the end, perhaps the hardest thing to pin down was modernity itself. Most found it easier to gaze backward and evaluate the modern borderlands in contrast to the unmade frontier and its familiar grammar of wildness, barbarism, and disorder. The measure of modernity at Cananea, wrote one Mexican, was its sudden rise as a "flourishing city where not many years before was a barren desert devastated by the depredations of the murderous Apache." The mining geologist Robert T. Hill viewed the copper borderlands through a similar lens. "Today the home of the Apache is the site of a prosperity not often witnessed," he observed in 1902. "From the top of Huachuca Mountain, whence Geronimo sent up his signal smokes, you can see three of the most profitable mining camps in the Southwest [that is, Bisbee, Globe, and Cananea], and where he hid in Bisbee Canyon you can sit in a club, read the latest literature, and eat and drink all that the world affords."[1]

In these frontier mythologies, civilization replaced barbarism, but the real world was more complicated. Hill had visited Cananea in the late 1890s and found "armed litigants" posted at the mines. The mining engineer Ignacio Bonillas found things in greater disarray in 1900 when making a government inspection. Managers told him that rogue shareholders were trying to take over the mines—and when a local judge came to take possession of the mines for the outsiders, Bonillas witnessed "the most unedifying spectacle." William Cornell Greene's men, reinforced by others from Arizona, met the judge with "gun in hand." They rode in like "bandits of the worst reputation, as if they were 'cowboys,' to pose armed resistance," he wrote, evoking memories of days when Tombstone cattle rustlers terrorized northern Sonora. He watched in disbelief as these modernizing elites fortified the company store with "sacks of flour and smelter dust" and prepared for a showdown against rival entrepreneurs, the local judge, and his small police force.[2]

Such disorderly behavior hardly seemed appropriate for corporate elites. When Arizona reporters covered the conflict, they emphasized lawsuits, not armed invasions. The local press hoped to generate confidence in Cananea, tributary as it was to Arizona, and stories of showdowns by cowboy capitalists would only feed eastern stereotypes of frontier backwardness. More ink was spent on the affair south of the border. Sonora elites shared Arizona's view of economic progress, but for years they had worried about the staying power of U.S. entrepreneurs. U.S. mining ventures were often as ephemeral as the ghost landscapes they proposed to remake. Officials had sent Bonillas to Cananea with this in mind—to ensure the company was actually producing as agreed in its contract with the state—and his report probably confirmed their worst fears about the fugitive terrains of U.S. frontier capitalism.[3]

Curiously, given the outrage of various officials, we have little record of how the state responded. Not only had Cananea's managerial elite supported an armed invasion of Sonora, but, as Bonillas found, it also failed to meet its agreed-upon production quota. By contract, the CCCC had to renounce five thousand pesos it had deposited with the state. But the next year, after bringing production to the agreed-upon level—a year too late—the CCCC asked for and received its deposit. How did the company avoid being punished for its invasion of Mexican territory on one hand, and its failure to fulfill its contract on the other? And how, generally, did the state deal with the basic contradiction between corporate goals of progress and order and the disorderly practices that Bonillas witnessed at Cananea? How did elites on both sides of the border tolerate the persistence of frontierish traits that seemed so profoundly at odds with their visions of modernity?[4]

Sam King, one of the "invaders" from Arizona, recalled that things were resolved after Greene telegraphed Gov. Ramón Corral (actually, Celedonio Ortíz, not Corral, was governor) from New York City, asking him to intervene on his behalf. The *Tombstone Epitaph* reported that Greene "resisted" through his Mexican attorneys, and a Nogales reporter emphasized the "undivided support" Greene's faction received from Governor Ortíz, the Sonora elite Corral, and "the state authorities of Sonora." And yet another version emerged later, when Lt. Col. Emilio Kosterlitzky of the Gendarmería Fiscal (customs guards) at Magdalena, Sonora, claimed he had ridden into town with his fellow mounted officers just in time to prevent a battle from breaking out—and so "saved one of the bloodiest pages in the history of Sonora from being written."[5]

In the end, the protagonists mattered less than the stories, which all boiled down to the same thing. Personal and informal relationships prevented illegal practices from spinning out of control, whether it was Kosterlitzy riding into town to rescue his old friend Greene or Ortíz, Corral, and other statesmen buying Greene time to mount a legal counteroffensive. Greene's lawyers finally secured an annulment of the district court's order, thus "disarming further interference." And what about the unfulfilled contract and the five-thousand-peso deposit? This perhaps owed something as well to informal arrangements that served the state and not just corporate elites. One finds a tantalizing clue in the letter that Stephen Aguirre, Greene's representative, wrote to request a return of the deposit. The company was finally producing copper, Aguirre wrote. As "previously agreed upon," he added, the company donated the five thousand pesos "for the benefit of public education."[6]

Memories of the "cow-boy" invasion faded, but fears that copper elites acted as a law unto themselves, taking advantage of informal relationships with the state, lingered. The CCCC exerted what many saw as an unfair monopoly over community space, using its own police force to enforce this monopoly. Problems emerged as corporate and state elites set out to reorganize residential space. As operations at Cananea began to take off in 1900, a settlement rose around the smelter. People built small houses of wood and adobe on company lands with the understanding, according to a state official, "that the land would be vacated when it became necessary." By late spring 1902, the population had reached twelve thousand, all "settled in the same place." Deciding the time had come to move the population to a site with better hygienic conditions and room to grow, the company began to map out its new town on the mesa.[7]

Part of the problem lay with the new town. Usually the formal center of a village or town, known as its *fundo legal*, was constituted on land granted by the nation (before this, the Spanish Crown), and although it contained private lots, it was the symbolic and legal core of the community at large. It was the essence of the *pueblo*. Cananea's *fundo legal* was different because it arose on company lands. The new municipal government, organized in 1902, could neither afford to pay for these lands at their new market value nor legally demand their expropriation. As a compromise, the Mexican government allowed the copper company to build the new town on its own ranchlands, after which the CCCC donated a fixed number of the lots to the municipal government to use for its public buildings—and in some cases, to rent or sell on its own behalf. The company then kept the remaining lots as its private property.[8]

The ad hoc, hybrid nature of this landscape gave rise to countless complaints. Residents complained that a foreign corporation, not representatives of the nation, controlled the selling of lots. The best lots, one state official observed, were "assigned to people closest to the employees in charge of giving them out." Worse, the CCCC began to enclose public space. It has "put wire fences in every direction obstructing streets and avenues," complained petitioners in 1902, "leaving hundreds of thousands of souls with no means of communicating, or entering or exiting their own homes." Police patrolled the fences, forcing residents to humiliate themselves—in the words of several petitioners, "transforming ourselves into reptiles, in order to crawl under the wires," for which they were fined and even jailed. "Is not our condition worse than if we were beasts owned by the company?" the petitioners inquired: "Why do Mexicans tolerate to be treated like beasts and expelled from their own land as if they were foreigners?"[9]

If residents in some places faced fences, others faced eviction. The merchant Angel L. Coronado bought a shack in 1902 on a lot within the *fundo legal* and established a small store there. In 1903, he received a notice from the CCCC for his immediate eviction. His neighbor, Bonifacio Romero Rubio, had built a shack on the land in early 1900, before it became the *fundo legal*. Romero likewise found himself on one of the private lots and received a similar notice. Because the government had let the company donate the town site lands without restrictions and keep part for itself, he now lay "at the mercy and whim of a foreign company." Likewise, those living in tents, houses, or other buildings near the smelter at the bottom of the mesa were told to move "just outside of the Company Line." The same forces that pulled workers to these spaces now pushed them away, for to keep up with its growth, the CCCC now had to clear the ground not only for the expansion of its smelter, but also to build its electric light plant, ice plant, and urban trolley line.[10]

From the corporate view, these were squatters. When the CCCC mapped its new town, Greene urged officials to be flexible in imposing a corporate grid over local moral geographies. "The few people scattered around on the west line of the town site, so that they keep out of our way, will not make very much difference," he told one: "Remember we are foreigners." Yet the company's patience soon wore thin. Allen C. Bernard asked Antonio Martínez to create a list of squatters on company land in 1902, so Chief of Police Pablo Rubio could "put them off at once." When the CCCC fenced its lands and patrolled its fences, it criminalized those refusing to move. In just this way it justified the removal of an entire community at its Cobre Grande mine—shut down in 1902—by tagging residents as "strangers" who sold mescal and housed "women of ill repute." Thus corporate managers and their hired guns divided Cananea into fixed and fugitive halves, to justify—even naturalize—their visions of industrial order.[11]

The bulk of the dispossessed did not even bother to lodge formal complaints, but those of independent means, notably small-scale merchants, did. Many merchants saw their own evictions and the fencing of public space as efforts to prevent the traffic of goods in the streets of Cananea and force out those competing with the company store. And they were not completely wrong, for those policing the company fences were given specific orders to prevent the flow of merchandise through "squatter" lines. The "mean spirited ambition" of the CCCC and "hateful offices of the Mexicans that work for the company wove this infamous plot to uproot their competitors," disgruntled members of this small merchant class argued. The copper company and its "mandarins" had thus transformed Cananea residents "into much less than a flock of sheep or a herd of beasts of burden on its own exclusive property."[12]

The despotic rule of corporate strongmen, locals argued, also prevailed in the butchering, selling, and buying of beef. By 1906, the company had established a local monopoly over the slaughter and sale of beef in Cananea, Ronquillo, and surrounding mining camps. Beef at the company stores was so expensive, miners noted, that all they could afford to buy was neck meat, back meat, and heel bones, "while the best pieces are reserved for sale to the Americans." Some bought beef slaughtered by individuals in the countryside, but the copper company tried to prevent its passage into camp. And when mining camp residents came to buy cheaper or better-quality beef in Cananea, police or customs guards often intercepted them on their return up the mountain, forcing them to return the meat or throw it away before proceeding. "This serious and transcendental evil," as one rancher called it, evoked a world beyond the fringes of modern Mexico, where cowboy capitalists and their hired guns continued to hold sway.[13]

In reality, the enclosing of public space and the policing of beef were both part of a new, "modernizing" world in which the state looked to foreign companies to carry out its functions at the periphery. The Sonora government's 1906 contract with the Cananea Cattle Company helps explain why butchers and residents were in arms. In its contract, the cattle company took responsibility for slaughtering cattle in Cananea and was given the exclusive right to do so. The contract also obliged municipal authorities to apprehend anyone found taking part in "clandestine" slaughter and traffic of beef. The state profited by transferring to the cattle company the responsibilities of inspecting cattle, maintaining inspection corrals, and gathering taxes. The company could keep the taxes it gathered but had to pay a flat monthly fee in their stead. The municipal authorities set rules for hygiene and safety, but the company had to enforce them.[14]

In other words, copper elites gained unprecedented power—and gained power to do things that were usually reserved for states—but in return they had to shoulder local financial and administrative burdens of state making. What many saw as an extension of frontier justice and disorder into the modern era was a creative fusing of informal and formal practices to exert control over a landscape that remained awkwardly suspended between modern and frontier worlds. The problem facing corporate and state elites was how these relations of power would be performed, juggled, and justified in years to come. For in these complex, ad hoc relationships, the tenuous balance between national and transnational dreams would ultimately be preserved or lost.

By 1905, the CCCC had transformed a frontier outpost of nine hundred people into an industrial city of twenty thousand. Memories of armed invasions and corporate hired guns soon faded before the supposed order of copper markets and time clocks. But order was always fragile, and pockets of frontier disorder persisted, often adapting to the modern world. In the 1890s, when the so-called Apache Kid raided ranches and towns from the Sierra Madres, the U.S. Army signed a new reciprocal crossing treaty with Mexico and worked with Mexican soldiers to pursue this new public enemy. Industrial mining, with its rising concentrations of wealth, also gave rise to new outlaws such as Billy Stiles, a lawman-turned-train-robber who haunted the region around Cananea for years. Border elites could hardly dispel the gnawing fear that border banditry, instead of vanishing before the modern era, was beginning to forge profitable new relationships with it.[15]

"What we need," proposed Gov. Nathan Murphy of Arizona, "is a hard riding, sure shooting outfit something like the Texas Rangers or the Mexican Rurales." In 1901, the territorial legislature created the Arizona Rangers, a force the governor could deploy in case of "public emergency." Just what constituted a public emergency was up to the governor. This resonated with the regional rhetoric of custom, but it also appealed to corporations such as the CCCC and Phelps Dodge, who could more easily get the ear of governors than those of distant bureaucrats or military officers in their effort to keep the borderlands safe for investors. Tellingly, the first headquarters of the Arizona Rangers was in Bisbee. The first captain, Burt Mossman, was a local ranching entrepreneur and was selected for the position by "influential friends and poker-playing cronies" such as William Cornell Greene of Cananea and Epes Randolph, a Southern Pacific official who controlled the road between Cananea and Naco.[16]

Throughout their brief existence (1901–09) the Arizona Rangers were posted in the copper borderlands. They moved to Douglas in 1902 and to Naco in 1907. From here, they combed the countryside for bandits, outlaws, and rustlers, also helping to suppress strikes and other copper town "emergencies." South of the border, Mexico supported its own police, including the *rurales*, a rural force that answered directly to President Porfirio Díaz. To generate confidence in Mexican modernity, *rurales* paraded at world's fairs and diplomatic functions in Mexico City. Even if their practices of violent suppression were far from enlightened, the state and capitalists saw them as a handmaiden to order and progress. Also playing a key role in policing the border was the Gendarmería Fiscal, the Department of Treasury customs guard, which patrolled points of entry into the United States and the vast spaces in between for contraband. Along with the Arizona Rangers, *rurales* and *gendarmes* sought to make the borderlands safe for investment.[17]

No Mexican evoked the police power of the state more famously than Lieutenant Colonel Kosterlitzky. Born in Moscow, the young Emil Kosterlitzky had deserted from a naval training vessel in Venezuela as a teenager and made his way north to Mexico. Changing his name to Emilio, he enlisted as a private of cavalry in the Mexican army and began to move up the ranks. In roughly a year, he became sergeant and major general of Sonora's military colonies—founded in the late Spanish and early Mexican era to populate and defend Sonora against Apaches—and in 1885 he joined the Gendarmería Fiscal, while continuing to rise through the ranks of the army, earning the rank of lieutenant colonel in 1890.[18]

Kosterlitzky was still a relatively low-ranking officer in the 1880s, but Americans were irresistibly drawn to him. Possibly it was the sight of a Russian cavalryman riding across the equally romanticized Mexican countryside. The idea of the Cossack as a free and wild hero had widespread currency: many equated this Old World horseman with the western cowboy. Visitors to Sonora may have read Jules Verne's recently published popular novel *Michael Strogoff*, featuring a rugged "courier to the Czar" who, although Siberian, was assimilated to the romantic icon of the Cossack. Kosterlitzky also drew attention for practical reasons. He was a master linguist—he reportedly spoke Russian, German, Spanish, French, Polish, Italian, Danish, Swedish, and English—and this made him valuable to many Americans, who were classically at a loss for words in Mexico. If Americans saw him as exotic, they also turned to him as a native informant, someone who might translate Mexico for them.[19]

Yet what endeared Kosterlitzky most to those on both sides of the border was his role in the Apache wars. In the 1880s he fought Apaches under Col. Angel Elías, scion of a colonial Indian-fighting family, and gained notoriety for his service in the Moctezuma district, a contested ethnic borderland between the Apache-controlled Sierra Madres and Mexican Sonora. These were christening ceremonies through which he earned the right to call himself not only a Mexican patriot and citizen, but also a frontiersman. Families of northeastern Sonora, especially those who profited from the Apache conquest, made much of Indian-fighting pedigrees. Kosterlitzky's ability to claim military kinship with these families eased his passage through this frontier region, where authority and power remained a matter of local negotiation.[20]

Kosterlitzky's Indian-fighting past also boosted his standing north of the line. He helped soldiers capture Geronimo and his followers in 1886, and when several of these prisoners escaped back to Mexico, he led Mexican efforts to track them down. He was "a favorite with all the boys in blue," an American recalled. Kosterlitzky's own memories of these days were more tempered; in 1885 he defended the village of Huásabas against Apache scouts in the U.S. Army, who were harassing their Mexican and Opata enemies. If this put him at odds with U.S. military elites, it drew him closer to Anglo-Americans in Arizona, who also distrusted the army's Apache scouts and felt the government had put border communities in danger by using them. Kosterlitzky would later agree with many locals in Arizona that leaders like Gen. George Crook had been "unfitted" to "deal with savages" and had coddled Apaches when they should have been avenging the deaths of Arizona and Sonora "pioneers."[21]

Americans and Mexicans on the border shared more than fighting Indians and distrusting central authorities. Both sides also placed great stock in pioneer rhetoric and identities. Sonorans had fought Indians, taken native lands, and argued with distant state authorities for much longer, and Anglo "pioneering" had also been based on hating and taking land from Mexicans, but these practices of frontier self-fashioning nevertheless reinforced early cross-border alliances. As in Sonora, these ties were frequently resolved within a kinship of Indian fighting. Many of Kosterlitzky's friends in Arizona, among them John Slaughter, Burdette A. Packard, Allen C. Bernard, James Kirk, and William Cornell Greene, claimed to be veterans of the Apache wars. The fact that they fought as frontier citizens, not as soldiers, only improved their reputation in Sonora, where militias had long compensated for a weak federal military.[22]

Entrepreneurial ties thus joined with frontier rhetoric to map out a "progressive" border geography that emphasized transnational connections alongside national and local identities. When Kosterlitzky took a position under Col. Juan Fenochio of the Third Zone of the Gendarmería Fiscal in 1885, he would further develop his complex and ambivalent relationship to the United States and Mexico. As a customs guard, he patrolled a national boundary, but he also managed the flow of people, goods, and capital across borders. As an employee of the state, he formalized border crossings, but as an adopted "frontier citizen" he relied on local, often informal alliances that complicated efforts to control the borderlands from the center.

Locality and informality dominated Kosterlitzky's relationships with the Ari-

Figure 21. Emilio Kosterlitzky (*far left*) and his *gendarmes*. Courtesy of the
Arizona Historical Society/Tucson, AHS Photograph #45754.

zona Rangers. Like their precursors, Rangers and *gendarmes* negotiated reciprocal crossings, but they were based on local arrangements, not on formal treaties.
Lt. John Foster of the Rangers told reporters how his men often crossed into
Sonora to help Kosterlitzky and his *gendarmes* catch thieves. "In the past much
time has been lost on account of our having to stop at the boundary line when we
were close on the trail of men wanted for crimes in Arizona," he noted. "We can
now go into Mexico whenever necessary." When Ranger John Brooks captured
a man wanted in Mexico, rather than arrange a formal extradition, he simply
dropped him off at the line for Kosterlitzky. When Brooks crossed the border
with a posse to recover horses and Mexican horse thieves, they turned their prisoners over to local Mexican authorities without a second thought. Kosterlitzky
later wrote Brooks to let him know that the men "had been disposed of."[23]

How could these men cross the border with such disregard for international
law? The historian Bill O'Neal explains that the Rangers would simply request a
leave of absence from the force so "technicalities of Mexican law would be satisfied." These relationships also seem to have been grounded in years of tradition.
Kosterlitzky helped military and civilian officers, all friends, "subdue Bandits &
outlaws" in Sonora as early as the 1880s, and informal ties of friendship and trust
continued to anchor these crossings after 1900. These relations of law and order
also gave rise to new forms of outlawry. Ranger Joe H. Pearce later recalled that
Kosterlitzky's men wore .44 Winchesters and Colt .45s, fruits of covert trade. "For
after the monthly confiscation of guns in the tough joints or the tough towns," he
wrote, "Rangers were not averse to making a not too dishonest dollar, even though
of Mexican coinage." That he viewed this traffic as "not too dishonest" speaks to
the enduring authority of informal arrangements in this contested land.[24]

If the modern age invoked the specter of frontier disorder and informality, it also inherited unresolved frontier conflicts. Into the twentieth century, Mexican villagers in far eastern Sonora continued to live in fear of refugee Apaches in the Sierra Madres and raided their strongholds as late as the 1930s. And there was the enduring battle between Mexicans and Yaquis, which intensified as modernizing elites sought to open the Yaqui homeland to development. This struggle was complicated because Yaquis were valued as miners and had widespread support from U.S. employers, even as they resisted the modernizing state. Many "peaceful" Yaquis who worked in the mines used their wages to buy arms and ammunition for *bronco* ("wild") relatives. Capitalists and state elites increasingly turned to men like Kosterlitzky to mark out and police the blurry line between productive and dangerous Indians.[25]

Like the collaborations between Rangers and *gendarmes*, this work transcended boundaries. Kosterlitzky frequently met journalists at the border to calm fears that the violence of the Yaqui–Mexican conflict might reach north into the copper borderlands. Many newspaper articles were "fakes manufactured out of whole cloth," Kosterlitzky claimed. He grew exasperated at having to fight off "fantastic stories." Risk was hardly unique to Sonora, he grumbled—weren't holdups and murders also common in U.S. cities? Kosterlitzky countered tales of violence to promote confidence in Sonora, as an agent of a modernizing state and as an entrepreneur in his own right. Yet his defensiveness also revealed a frustration with the U.S. habit of associating Mexico with disorder: it offended his patriotic sensibilities. Kosterlitzky patrolled the line to promote U.S. investment and development, but he also did so with his adopted nation centrally in mind.[26]

Tensions were amplified in late 1905, when the U.S. consul Albert Morawitz told his superiors that Sonora had no real desire to put down the Yaqui rebellion; that the ruling triumvirate of Rafael Izábal, Luis E. Torres, and Ramón Corral were making millions on what the Mexican government sent for rations and military supplies. If anything, they had made this struggle even worse by forcing peaceful Yaquis at work in Sonora mines and haciendas, "by means of the most barbarous tortures," to confess to crimes they had not committed. Some were hanged, and others were deported to the Yucatán peninsula in southeastern Mexico. This "increased the number of rebellious Indians," Morawitz explained, "as many of the peaceful ones preferred to join the hostiles, rather than suffer torture, banishment from their homes, or death." [27]

These allegations incensed Mexican authorities. At the end of 1905, Díaz ordered a moratorium on U.S. purchases of mines in Sonora. Americans brought this on themselves, explained the Mexican statesman Guillermo B. Puga, "owing to complaints that they do not enjoy security and protection." Local entrepreneurs and capitalists tried to distance themselves from the critics. The Moctezuma elite George F. Woodward argued that journalists had spread tales "without foundation"; that *bronco* Yaquis were nowhere in the vicinity. The complaints leading to the moratorium, another wrote, were "brought on by dishonest wildcat mining fakirs" who needed excuses for their failure to generate dividends. "They raised a howl that their stockholders were suffering because the Yaqui troubles prevented them from developing their properties," to "square themselves" with outside investors who knew little about the conditions of northern Sonora.[28]

The person most disturbed at allegations that Mexican authorities were trying to prolong the Yaqui war was Governor Izábal. In late January 1906, Izábal wrote a letter to "the leading mining and industrial concerns owned by foreigners" in Sonora to assess the validity of recent U.S. complaints. This letter was a thinly disguised call for formal apologies; like Kosterlitzky, Izábal seems to have been offended by the U.S. habit of equating Mexico with disorder, but more than Kosterlitzky, he had the means to hit Americans where it hurt. Until Americans set this record straight, they would have to put their dreams on hold. "Yourself as well as all other *bona fide* foreigners . . . are well aware of the falsity and malice of such charges," he wrote. To "dispel the unfavorable impression" that some had made, he urged local U.S. entrepreneurs and corporations to speak out against these allegations of Mexican disorder and thereby renew confidence in the Porfirian state.[29]

Given their own interest in making Sonora appear safe for investment, it is hardly surprising that U.S. capitalists backed Izábal. "I will say without hesitation that foreigners here are on an equal footing with those of any other civilized country," declared an official of the Cananea Cattle Company, "and with respect to protection to our persons and property, I believe that we have it to a greater extent than we would anywhere else." R. S. Vickers, a banker and merchant in Moctezuma, insisted that all the "wild and wooly Yaqui stories" were "lies, pure and simple." Although several non-Yaqui "renegades" haunted nearby mountain ranges, the area was "as safe to travel through and prospect in as it ever was." If anything, others argued, government officials went out of their way to protect U.S. interests. "I remember that last year you kindly offered me an escort to accompany me to a mine I own, for which I thank you," the British vice consul in Sonora wrote Izábal. "As a general rule," added J. C. Townsend of R. G. Dun and Company in Guaymas, "foreigners living in Mexico enjoy greater considerations than the natives themselves."[30]

Not all responses were so positive. Two companies near Hermosillo agreed that they had not suffered direct losses, but "fear experienced by people who cut wood in the forests causes fuel to be scarce and dear." R. I. Horitt, a doctor, said he had lost business because of "difficulty of a communication with the small towns in the interior." Ambivalent reports tended to come from the area below Moctezuma. They varied widely, ranging from those who saw Indians everywhere to those who declared investments absolutely safe; but the farther south one went from the copper borderlands, the more common rumors of disorder grew. This geography of risk and confidence, marked by distance from the U.S. border, played to the favor of Cananea and Nacozari. Moctezuma "is the furthest east or north they have been," one witness insisted: "Everything is perfectly safe all east and west of the Nacozari railhead and all along the line."[31]

Izábal published the responses in early 1906 in *El Diario Oficial*, the government newspaper, to formally dismiss "the calumnious charges" against Sonora's government elite.[32] However true the complaints may have been, the moratorium on investment, the solicitation of friendly American testimony, and the subsequent dissemination of the results underscored the extent to which disorder was as much a product of negotiations between state and corporate elites as it was a useful descriptor of actual ethnic contests. And although the responses were formally solicited and published in the official record, they also reflected more local, informal relationships. For power in the borderlands was still as informal as it was formal and as transnational as it was national. Increasingly, it relied on the ability of state and corporate elites to keep all of these relationships in motion as they marched in tandem toward an ambivalent modern future.

The intricacies and tensions of this juggling act came into sharp relief in 1906, when Mexican miners went on strike in Cananea. Things started peacefully enough: Mexican workers walked off the job early on the first of June, demanding to be paid and promoted like their U.S. counterparts and calling for an eight-hour workday.[33] As worker representatives met with company and municipal officials, the strikers began marching through town, calling on others to join them. When they reached the company lumberyard on the mesa above town, events took an unfortunate turn. The manager, George Metcalf, perhaps reacting to wild rumors that the workers were conspiring to dynamite company property and kill all Americans, shut the gate to the lumberyard and opened a high-pressure fire hose on the crowd. As outraged strikers threw themselves at the gate, gunfire filled the air, and within minutes several men on both sides lay dead or wounded on the ground.[34]

According to Mexican reports, the Americans shot first. Most Mexican witnesses pointed their finger at Metcalf, who was said to have killed two Mexicans before they could open the lumberyard gate. Metcalf then took refuge with his brother William in the office of the lumberyard, from which he continued to fire on workers through an open window. The Metcalf brothers were eventually forced out after the strikers set fire to the lumberyard offices and nearby lumber and grain warehouses. They tried to escape but were caught by the crowd, disarmed, and killed. Not surprisingly, U.S. witnesses claimed that Mexicans had shot first and in most cases portrayed the Metcalf brothers as innocent victims. George Metcalf faced the strikers with his gun in hand, but he was struck down before he could fire it, one witness claimed. "The mob was upon him in an instant," and before Metcalf could get back on his feet, "a dozen knives and candlesticks had pierced his lungs and heart."[35]

With men lying dead in the street and the lumberyard in flames, the residents of Cananea began to lose control. After hearing about the violence at the lumberyard, corporate elites began deputizing U.S. employees with the blessing of Cananea's desperate chief of police. Greene telephoned other company officials, saying that strikers were moving toward the center of the town to loot the bank and company store. Armed managers and employees moved to intercept them—Greene and his fellow old-timer James Kirk driving their new modern automobiles "50 miles an hour through the thick crowds, scattering strikers in all directions." Near Greene's mansion on the mesa, Mexicans and U.S. employees clashed another time, the better-armed Americans taking the upper hand. When the air cleared, half a dozen more Mexicans lay dead. Meanwhile, police in the center of town engaged panicked strikers who were starting to loot pawnshops for guns to defend themselves against equally panicked authorities.[36]

Corporate and municipal elites sent a volley of alarming messages to officials in both nations. Greene wired Governor Izábal to come quickly with troops. The U.S. consular agent W. J. Galbraith wired his superiors in Washington, claiming that strikers had murdered U.S. citizens and dynamited their property. For their part, municipal officials painted a picture of unrestrained cowboy capitalists roaming the streets. Judge F. López Linares wired Izábal that Greene and other prominent company officials were riding through town ordering Americans to kill Mexicans. Smoke from the lumberyard fire could be seen in Arizona, and rumors spread that Cananea was burning and that Mexicans were dynamiting homes and killing Americans. "Crowds thronged both telegraph offices" in Douglas, and "the telephone office was in a continuous furor," a reporter wrote. "Men with rifles, revolvers and ammunition congregated on the streets, waiting for word that their services were required."[37]

After receiving the news, Governor Izábal boarded a train north with a guard of twenty *rurales*. In Magdalena he ordered Kosterlitzky to ride as fast as he could to Cananea with his *gendarmes*, and in nearby Imuris he told his *rurales* to do the same, to avoid the problem of crossing Mexican police into U.S. territory. He reached Nogales after midnight. The fastest way to Cananea was east through

Arizona to Naco, and then south by train to Cananea. Izábal made the trip with Vice Consul Albert W. Brickwood, Jr., who had been receiving frantic news from Cananea all day, and they probably fed each other's fears along the way. They arrived in Naco around six that morning and found a group of Americans with rifles and shotguns, led by Arizona Ranger Thomas Rynning. Rynning and Phelps Dodge officials in Bisbee had assembled the "volunteers" the night before, but they had been denied entry into Mexico. When Izábal arrived, Rynning tried again, asking if he and his men could accompany him to Cananea.[38]

Izábal refused, but after making a telephone call to Greene he changed his mind. Conditions were serious, Greene claimed: strikers "intended to blow up the company with dynamite." He urged Izábal to travel south with an escort. When Izábal asked for help in Naco, Sonora, he later wrote, he "was presented with only four ancient insomniacs." Yet there were risks in letting Americans make up the deficit. Izábal later said they were doctors, lawyers, and other "professionals," but Rynning was closer to the truth. They were, he recalled, "cowpunchers, miners who'd seen service in Cuba and the Philippines, some of my rangers, and the usual scattering of outlaws." Many tied the "liberation" of Cananea to a mix of older frontier models—where posses took matters into their own hands—and new models of U.S. militarism abroad. And there was an even larger problem: just as Izábal could not cross *rurales* into Arizona, Rynning could not lead armed men south—and Territorial Governor Joseph H. Kibbey had, in fact, warned him to stay in Arizona.[39]

Izábal and Rynning then made a judgment that would forever haunt the region. Rynning told his men to "break ranks and string across the line as civilians," and as they did, Izábal made them Mexican volunteers. "I told them that they had to be exclusively under my orders and therefore under the authority of the laws of Mexico," Izábal wrote in his most candid report of the incident. They boarded the train "amid cries of 'Viva el Gobiernor [*sic*]!' 'Viva la Cananea!' 'Viva Yzabal!,'" explained one of the men: "The Bisbee boys had already learned the language and were doing the thing up brown." When the train reached Cananea the volunteers disembarked and marched through Ronquillo, around the concentrators and smelters. The Americans "overawed the rioters, for they very soon dispersed," Rynning recalled. They then stood by as Izábal and Greene made speeches to the workers.[40]

Perhaps because corporate and state officials had strayed so far from their own prescriptions of order and progress, their performance held little sway. Such breaches of proper official behavior, explains James C. Scott, "disrupt or desacralize the ceremonial reverence" of performances of power, and so it seemed at Cananea. Greene noted that the miners seemed to pay little attention to Izábal—

Figure 22. The Cananea strike of 1906. William Cornell Greene (*center, pointing*) addresses striking workers from the front seat of his automobile; at his side is Governor Rafael Izábal. Behind them, armed U.S. "volunteers" form a barrier to protect the company store. Courtesy of the Arizona Historical Society/Tucson, AHS Photograph #4355.

and some even threatened to kill him. "The situation was very much strained a number of times," he recalled, "and it was only by the exercise of the greatest forbearance on the part of our boys that another collision was averted." Izábal was "frequently interrupted by young men," confirmed another witness, who wrote that Greene was ridiculed as well. The arrival of Izábal's *rurales* made things worse: that afternoon, following a "drinking spree," residents again traded gunfire on the street, generating fresh casualties on both sides. Izábal and his men could do nothing, claimed Cananea mayor Filiberto Barroso, "since between the Mexicans and Americans, there were more than three thousand men, many of them armed."[41]

According to most accounts, it was Kosterlitzky's arrival before sundown that resolved this awkward situation. "Kosterlitzky's name was on everybody's lips and there was a feeling of security that had not existed since the hostilities commenced," one participant observed. Yet if Americans expected Kosterlitzky to champion their view of transnational order, they were disappointed. To undo Izábal's damage, Kosterlitzky had to reassert the official performance of power

Figure 23. Rangers and *gendarmes* posing after the Cananea strike of 1906, including Thomas Rynning (*center, to left of yucca plant*) and Emilio Kosterlitzky (*on white horse*). Courtesy of the Arizona Historical Society/Tucson, AHS Photograph #4362.

and remove from the public stage all informalities that challenged the state's official claim to authority. Kosterlitzky normally drew on informal relationships to police the borderlands, but he knew what Izábal had forgotten: one had to disguise such relationships. They needed to remain offstage. He began by reproaching the invading army. "I have known you . . . for a long time, and we have always settled our little affairs peacefully," he said to Rynning. "I wish you would order your men to immediately board your train and return to the border."[42]

Rynning played his part as well. He ordered the volunteers to board the train, which left Cananea without incident. Soon after this public performance but before the train left Kosterlitzky and Rynning posed offstage for a photograph (fig. 23). The photo depicts three Rangers facing three *gendarmes* on a desolate plain. A yucca plant divides warriors with cowboy hats from those sporting sombreros. The yucca seems to evoke wild nature, or the border itself. Perhaps it represents problems bringing the men together or a prickly line dividing them. The back of the photograph reads, "Rangers & Rurale [*sic*] leaders suppressing Cananea War, 1906." From this side, the meaning is less vague: heroes celebrate the state's triumph over frontier disorder. Indeed, Kosterlitzky soon restored the official veneer. "No one was allowed on the streets, under penalty of death," a reporter noted. Some were "stood against an adobe wall the next morning and shot," added a resident. Authorities buried bodies all night, wrote another, "to keep the people from knowing how many were killed."[43]

Whether or not Kosterlitzky shot untold dozens, the idea that he *could* have only amplified his mystique. Many celebrated his armed intervention at Cananea as an extension of his work as a warrior for civilization—even if Cananea's strikers, unlike Apaches and Yaquis, also became heroes. And yet despite his effort to preserve the national order, the event transformed him more than ever into a *transnational* warrior. The government placed a permanent garrison at Cananea, and U.S. residents successfully lobbied to have the Russian-Mexican stay on as its commanding officer. The CCCC also began to employ *gendarmes* through Kosterlitzky, who served as a *patrón*, or labor broker, to extend its police power into the nearby countryside. Not only did Kosterlitzky disburse wages for these men, but he also used personal connections to Cananea's corporate elites to secure other jobs for his subordinates, building on informal connections that had served him for decades as a warrior of the state.[44]

These customary ties proved less advantageous to William Cornell Greene after the 1906 strike. His frontier persona, central to his rise in the 1890s, now seemed a liability to Cananea's modern development. Greene "seems to find his mining operations in New York quite as strenuous as they were in the southwest in the days of the Apaches and the cowboy 'rustlers,'" wrote a correspondent as early as 1904. "It is questionable whether his southwestern tactics are altogether suited to this field of action." Violence in the streets of Cananea in 1906, where industrial cowboys shot it out with Mexican strikers, only seemed to confirm these fears. Later that year, owing partly to declining stockholder confidence in the CCCC affairs after the strike, but also to the saturation of the securities market in the months leading up to the Panic of 1907, the sale of Greene Consolidated Copper Company stocks and securities took a nosedive. Greene seemed to be spiraling, ever more deliberately, out of control.[45]

Desperate for more capital to sustain his overextended empire, Greene sold some of its properties to the Cananea Central Copper Company, a small venture organized in 1906 by John D. Ryan and Thomas F. Cole. Ryan and Cole, who had cut their teeth in the Lake Superior copper mining region of Michigan and who were associated with the well-funded Amalgamated Copper Company, founded this new enterprise with Greene and capitalists from Minnesota and Montana. Greene sold them their land in return for two million dollars in Cananea Central Copper Company stock. This will be an "asset of great value," Greene assured stockholders, not only because their stock was strong and promised to pay dividends, but also because the "installation of new machinery and the opening up of another property by another strong Company" in Cananea promised to increase confidence in the mining camp.[46]

By late 1906, it was becoming clear that fresh infusions of capital and confidence were insufficient to keep the CCCC in the black. Corporate directors met and proposed merging the CCCC with the Cananea Central by establishing a new holding company in Duluth, Minnesota, the Greene Cananea Copper Company, which would take over the stock of both companies. The plan was to essentially transfer the enterprise to the control of the capital-rich Cole–Ryan combination. In December, directors submitted the plan to stockholders, and by year's end the merger was complete. "Colonel Greene is still identified with the company," explained a reporter, "but the management of the mines which he developed has passed out of his hands." With this power shift, added another, with a newfound confidence, "there can be no doubt that Cananea will soon be the largest copper camp on earth."[47]

The management of Cananea passed on to the mining engineer Louis D. Ricketts, the guiding light behind Phelps Dodge's purchase of the Pilares mine in the 1890s. As early as 1903, Ricketts, then a consulting engineer at Cananea, had been shocked by Greene's appetite: he felt the Tombstone rancher had created an oversized beast that could not be properly domesticated. When he took over at Cananea in 1907 he found things had only gotten worse. "The mines were underdeveloped and required a great deal of planning and a great deal of money," he noted, and "the smelter was an impossible structure and . . . had to be completely re-constructed." He set out to reorganize, remove dead weight, and rein in Greene's untamed imperial vision to focus the enterprise more efficiently on the bottom line: the production and sale of copper.[48]

As the Panic of 1907 set in, mining officials took advantage of hard times to close Cananea down and reorganize the industrial landscape. "Cananea has begun to curtail and the general atmosphere of the camp is very blue," a reporter noted, as troops began to march toward the camp to manage the exodus of workers. Local managers canceled seventy-four thousand dollars of supplies, and to defend against local retaliation against the company they added a hundred thousand dollars to their fire insurance. In October some five thousand men were laid off, and most of Buenavista, Ronquillo, and Cananea Vieja as well as the Anglo town on the mesa were deserted. Workers drifted to mining camps in Magdalena, Moctezuma, Nacozari, Cumpas, and Arizona or toward the new Southern Pacific extension below Guaymas, where capitalists and workers alike tracked economic opportunity south.[49]

By the following summer, Cananea's metamorphosis was complete; its doors

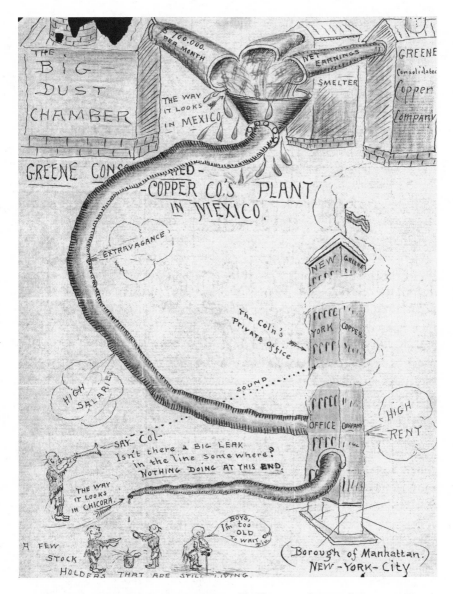

Figure 24. Cartoon drawn by CCCC stockholder, complaining about excessive spending and mismanagement of Greene's Mexican enterprise. It was this lack of investor confidence that directors hoped to address when reorganizing the company in 1907. Courtesy of the Arizona Historical Society/Tucson; Cananea Consolidated Copper Company Collection, MS 1032/f.41.

had opened again by July 1908. Visitors were amazed by the changes. "Since the shut-down at Cananea practically everything but the concentrator has been changed," one reporter explained, adding that the mining community had in less than a year "evolved from a 12-cent copper camp to a 7-center." Among the changes was a shift from coal and coke to fuel oil in the furnace and powerhouse, made possible by new technologies, contracts with the El Paso–based Texas Oil Company to deliver oil from producers in Texas and Oklahoma, and agreements with the Mexican government, in which it granted remission of duties on fuel oil for the company for an undisclosed period. The company's previous smelting furnaces had been replaced, and the concentrator facilities had been completely overhauled, reflecting the most current technological innovations.[50]

Managers retooled Cananea with an eye toward both natural and social control. Among the most celebrated features of the new reduction works was the increased level of mechanization—a measure that many saw as a response to the 1906 strike. With a new conveyor belt system in the concentrator, one writer noted, "the handling of the ore is a matter really of little moment, because it is done automatically and there is little danger of a lot of Mexicans failing to show up some morning." The *Engineering and Mining Journal* made this point visually. It compared a photo of an interior landscape of debris and disorder—which read "Converter Department in July, 1906, just after the riots, when labor was scarce and inefficient"—to a photo of a carefully swept interior with two well-dressed Mexicans posing near two modern smelting furnaces, titled "The new furnaces from the feed floor, showing feeding device which eliminates hand labor."[51]

By early 1908, the reassertion of corporate and state power was all but complete. The strike of 1906 and the Panic of 1907 had unsettled life at Cananea, but with the new garrison under Kosterlitzky and the ouster of the industrial cowboy Greene, things seemed to be looking up—even for Greene. By late 1907, a correspondent wrote that Greene had decided to shift the bulk of his attention east to Chihuahua, where his Greene Gold-Silver and Sierra Madre Land and Lumber companies seemed to be doing better than ever. The safety nets he had woven over time to soften his fall from Cananea seem to have done their job. Yet with the social and economic crises of the previous two years, conditions in Mexico were less settled than ever. And nowhere was the ground shifting more than among the high crags of the Sierra Madres.

In 1907, William Cornell Greene hardly skipped a beat as he packed his bags for Chihuahua. As early as 1905, he had begun to realize his dream of connecting his vast timberlands in Chihuahua to Cananea and nearby mining camps.

That summer he had erected a band saw mill with a capacity of eighty thousand feet at the new mill town of Dedrick, later renamed Madera. Soon he began to turn out lumber not only for his mining camps in Chihuahua, but also for his Chihuahua railroads. By 1907, the CCCC signed a contract with the Sierra Madre Land and Lumber Company to buy a million dollars of lumber annually for twenty-five years. "The forests of Texas and Louisiana are being rapidly depleted," Greene told stockholders in 1906, and "the only source of supply will be Puget Sound, with the price of lumber constantly increasing." It was only natural, he concluded, that the CCCC should seek a controlling interest in the "heaviest pine timber there is on this continent."[52]

The most ambitious part of Greene's dream to link Cananea and Chihuahua was the sinews to hold them together. His larger goal was to join his Sierra Madre Land and Lumber lands with his Greene Gold-Silver mines, along his private railroad, the Rio Grande, Sierra Madre, and Pacific. He began by building a wagon road to connect the mines of Concheño and Ocampo to the railhead of Temosachic, which in itself was an audacious venture. "For the first 60 miles along the fairly uniform plateau, construction was normal," recalled Morris B. Parker, "but from there on were continuous gradings, cut in solid rock, and bridges to erect." The road cost $350,000 to build, and most of the money covered the last few miles into Ocampo, where the road suddenly pitched thirty-five hundred feet down into the valley below. "The resulting road was a suspended scratch line with horizontal trenches along the bluff," etched with dynamite as if to illustrate to the town below Greene's technological prowess.[53]

By May 1906, the road had been completed most of the way to Ocampo. Greene decided to test it with a party of corporate elites in his twenty-four-horsepower Panhard and two Pope-Toledo automobiles. Winthrop Scarritt, one of the participants, gazed in wonder at this feat of engineering, which seemed oddly out of place in this land of burro trains and steep mountain trails. "In many places it was blasted out of the precipitous side of the mountain and these places not infrequently on a sharp curve," Scarritt marveled: "the skidding of the car for thirty-six inches meant a sheer drop of a thousand feet and a disaster too horrible to contemplate." The drivers drove to the end of the road, where they switched to mules and took the trail the last fifteen miles to Ocampo. Here Scarritt described a world that was in stark contrast with that of fast-paced cars and capitalists. Greene's backcountry mining camps, he wrote, stood testament to centuries of harder labor, where Mexicans had dug ore "by the most primitive methods," bringing it up "chicken ladders" on their backs.[54]

Scarritt was impressed by the way that "American genius, American brains, and American scientific up-to-date methods" were transforming this landscape.

Greene had carved out a new mining empire in this "sparsely settled country where the inhabitants were living as did Abraham on the plains beyond Hebron, and where the peasants were using oxen and a crooked stick for a plow." Along a particularly rough stretch of road, Scarritt worried that he might damage his car. "If you do, we have a big machine shop," Greene replied. "We will repair the damage and go on." "This is the spirit of the man," Scarritt wrote. "Big, broad, brainy, far-seeing, fearless whatever may betide, whatever obstacles may be met, whether it be a criminal mob in Cananea or a no less criminal mob in Wall Street, this unconquerable American will repair the damage and go on."[55]

Such engineering feats, awesome as they must have seemed, hid a more somber reality. By May 1907, as Greene turned to Chihuahua, the CCCC began to gradually disassociate itself from this Mexican white elephant. It closed down its Temosachic branch of the Banco de Cananea and severed its contract with the Sierra Madre Land and Lumber Company as part of its broader cost-cutting strategy during the economic downswing. Owing to Greene's outstanding debts to the copper company, Ricketts informed stockholders, "this onerous contract was cancelled, and a new contract made which obligates the Lumber Company to supply us the lumber we require at the market price." Rumors began to circulate that the Greene Gold-Silver Company was also sliding toward bankruptcy. By August 1908, Greene's sawmills and mines began to lay off workers and shut down, bringing an end to his short-lived Chihuahua adventure.[56]

That summer, the mining engineer Mark R. Lamb rode through Greene's empire on horseback. He took the same road that Greene had driven with Scarritt and other capitalists in the summer of 1906. But his experience was considerably less enthusiastic. He passed heavily loaded wagons drawn by huge Norman horses, which, like so many features of Greene's venture, carried a large price tag and were only marginally effective. Their importation, like the experiments in bringing traction engines to Bisbee and Cananea, was ultimately a failure. "What can they expect such elephants to do on mountain roads?" laughed one driver in disgust. Compared to mules and burros, born and raised at high altitudes, these draft animals were completely out of their element. "They have all they can do to drag their own big feet up these grades, much less can they negotiate the big loads piled up on us!," the driver told Lamb. "I've been driving for three months for this company and at least one of these poor fellows has died on every trip."[57]

Lamb found more problems in the mining camp of Concheño. It was congested, and a "good natured mill man insisted on kicking a couple of puppies off the last cot in town, for me," he recalled. The resources for the overcrowded population were no less encouraging. His horse found "complimentary grass-hay worth about 100 pesos per ton and was on a very short ration of corn, that ne-

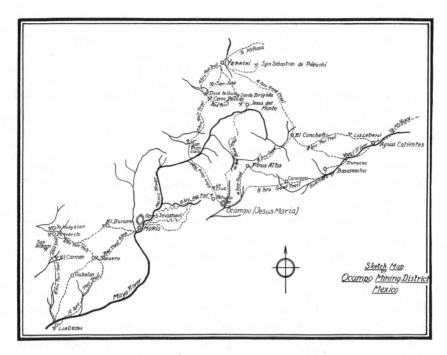

Figure 25. Vernacular geographies beyond the corporate pale. Trail systems
connecting the highland mining camps near Ocampo and Concheño, Chihuahua,
before Greene built his road to Ocampo. The local knowledge used to construct this
map had its roots in the colonial era and endured long after Greene's empire failed.
From *The Engineering and Mining Journal* (1904).

cessity being almost unattainable for man or beast." The stamp mill was being
rebuilt, and it hardly seemed worth the effort. The stamps were "old and rickety,"
Lamb noted, and seemed inappropriate to the proposed scale of production.
Framing for an additional forty stamps had been built but then had been dis-
assembled to build a carpenter shop. "The whole plant is so old and tumbled-
down," he wrote in disgust, "that the company should ensure and burn it."[58]

The mining engineer Morris B. Parker told a similar tale of excess and failure. Not very long after the 1906 "journey of the nabobs" by automobile to
Ocampo, he recalled, "one of those torrential thunderstorms with cloudburst at-
tachments occurred, and in about an hour the Concheño–Ocampo portion of
the road was back where it was before the third of a million dollars was spent;
it was non-existent." Although the company continued to carry freight to Concheño "by means of heavy wagons and big American mules," Parker continued, it
soon became clear that the freighters could transport goods more efficiently and

cheaply by pack mule. "Small Mexican mules" soon replaced Greene's ostentatious American mules, and "the pack mule and arriero were back on the job to stay."[59]

However the tale was told, the moral was the same: Greene's enormous appetite for the fruits of the Mexican cornucopia had led him to ruin. By October 1908, both of his Chihuahua ventures were bankrupt. "The wages of the Mexicans have been settled in full, but there are still large sums due Americans and other foreigners," explained one reporter. When a receiver appointed for one of Greene's creditors went to Chihuahua to recover what assets were remaining at his former camps, he found $1.48 cash in the bank and "an assortment of old furniture." As Greene's "hopelessly bankrupt" ventures passed on to other owners, the Colonel retreated to his large ranch near Cananea. In a moment of lucidity he had transferred the ranchlands to his wife, thus protecting them from his creditors. In this way his Mexican journey—supposedly initiated to make up a sum of money he owed his wife—came full circle.[60]

As William Cornell Greene's empire came undone in Chihuahua, the clouds of a more powerful storm were dark on the horizon. Border people had seen warning signs in 1906 and 1907, when social turmoil and hard times created fresh stress fractures in the façade of corporate power. For some, dreams of a modern world had come to an abrupt end. Once one is awake, it is hard to return to the same dream. And thus, the clouds of discontent gathered. Prophets of a utopian future seemed oddly silent, and as President Porfirio Díaz assumed the mantle of power again in 1910, some began to wonder about the modern world he had helped weave. It had become worn and threadbare, revealing an unsettlingly familiar terrain just beneath. For those who could remember, there was nothing strange about this. For the insurgent landscape of northern Mexico had always carried in its contested ground the seeds of its own unmaking.

7

INSURGENT LANDSCAPES

When the winds of the Mexican Revolution reached Sonora, few were taken by complete surprise. Frustrations with the Díaz regime and its preferential treatment of U.S. interests in Mexico were rampant, and rumors of insurgency had grown chronic in the borderlands. The strike at Cananea in 1906 had inspired anti-Díaz groups on both sides of the border, many of them tied to the Flores Magón brothers, who published and distributed their anti-Díaz newspaper, *La Regeneración*, from exile in St. Louis, Missouri. Magonista intellectuals had, in fact, already established a clear presence at Douglas and Cananea by the time of the strike, and even though workers had been guided by mostly local grievances, Magonistas drew fresh inspiration from the worker movement. As the Mexican independence celebrations approached in September 1906, rumors circulated that Cananea and other border towns were preparing to rise against the Díaz regime and U.S. residents of Mexico.[1]

Much as they did to counter fears of Yaqui uprisings, border elites denied these rumors. But they could hardly dispel the larger clouds of social and political discontent gathering above Mexico. Agents of law and order on both sides of the border began to monitor the activities of suspected revolutionaries. A dragnet snared Abrán Salcido, a well-known labor organizer in Clifton-Morenci and Cananea, and ten others who were reportedly planning to "march into Sonora and raise the flag of insurrection." Witnesses claimed they had hoped to raid the Copper Queen store in Douglas for arms and ammunition, tear up the railroad, cut telegraph wires, and then march on Cananea. U.S. immigration officials said they had found a trunk of letters to the men from Ricardo Flores Magón in a Douglas rooming house. One letter reminded them of the "massacre" in Cananea, a symbol of revolutionary work left undone.[2]

Owing partly to heightened surveillance, revolution was forestalled. On Sep-

tember 13, just in time to build confidence for Mexican independence day, Salcido was deported to the notorious Juan de Ulúa prison at Veracruz, where he
joined the "martyrs" of the Cananea strike. On September 16, the "junta pa-
triótica" of Douglas visited the home of Consul Antonio Maza with a crowd of
Mexican locals. "Both the American and Mexican flags were displayed," one witness wrote, "and those present sang the Mexican national hymn and afterwards
the band played America." Likewise, residents of Nacozari and Moctezuma engaged in harmonious binational celebration, or so correspondents said, and the
only discord in Cananea was "a mixup between a pig, his driver, and a bicycle
rider" (*rurales* "rushed up and pinched the pig, causing him to squeal in protest,"
joked one reporter). Otherwise, Cananea was "more than normally quiet," and
the presence of Gen. Luis E. Torres helped create "absolute confidence."[3]

Such displays simply pushed anxieties underground, however. Four years later,
as opposition to Díaz mounted before the election of 1910, border residents cast
a nervous eye once again to the "revolutionary hotbed" of Cananea. Hardware
stores in Bisbee and Douglas reported an increased sale of ammunition to Mexicans, and in June, police and *gendarmes* began to arrest men in town and in the
nearby hills, seizing rifles and ammunition. Many suspected a secret alliance between Mexicans in Cananea and the shadowy Mexican demimonde of Arizona's
copper towns. On June 21, *gendarmes* prepared for a rumored two-pronged attack on Naco from Cananea and Bisbee's ethnic enclave Tintown. Naco chief
of police Adrián Cubillas, who had held the line against the Bisbee "volunteers"
in 1906, crossed to the U.S. side and bought all the rifles and bullets in the Copper Queen store to prepare himself and a few hastily deputized locals against the
coming invasion.[4]

This time when rumors led to nothing, the borderlands remained on edge.
Off the public stage, U.S. Secret Service and Bureau of Investigation (pre-FBI)
agents began to join U.S. marshals, immigration officials, and customs officers
on both sides to monitor suspected revolutionaries. That summer Emilio Kosterlitzky kept in touch with informants on the streets of Cananea and sent *gendarmes* to comb the nearby San José Mountains for arms caches. Antonio F.
Sierra, a U.S. immigration officer, infiltrated revolutionary circles in Douglas,
where he learned of a local plan to invade Sonora. Kosterlitzky heard the equally
troubling news that Bisbee merchants were arming insurrectionists. When Francisco I. Madero called for revolution in November 1910, Kosterlitzky strength-
ened his cordon between Agua Prieta and Nogales, indicating that he took the
looming threat from the north seriously. Indeed, revolutionary sentiment seemed
especially strong in Arizona's mining camps: in Clifton-Morenci, for instance,

over a thousand Mexicans were said to be packing their belongings and returning south to fight.[5]

Yet when revolution came to Sonora, it came not from the urban working class
—as many had feared—but from the nearby countryside. It crept unseen along
half-forgotten pathways, from former Apache and outlaw haunts in the Sierra
Madres. A charismatic backcountry freighter named Pascual Orozco led the way.
With Pancho Villa and a few others, Orozco monopolized freighting contracts
in the Ocampo and Rayón districts of William Cornell Greene's Chihuahua
mining empire. "Every trail and settlement, nook or hideout was to them about
as familiar as their own backyard," noted the mining engineer Morris B. Parker.
Orozco joined Madero's 1910 revolt for a profoundly local reason: to liberate the
sierras from his competitor, a *cacique* named Joaquín Chávez. His followers included muleteers, *vaqueros*, farmers, miners, and woodcutters: men with a thousand different motivations. By 1911, they were masters of a vast insurgent terrain,
a highland refuge that many knew as intimately as the Apaches did before them.[6]

Calling them desperados and bandits, Díaz sent reinforcements north and
drove Orozco and his men into the sierras. From here they carried their battle
west across high mountain passes into Sonora. By early 1911, leaders such as José
de la Luz Blanco rode out of the mountains with hundreds of well-mounted and
well-armed rebels into the Bavispe River valley, where they descended on villages and made demands of money and food. In early March they reached the
El Tigre gold camp, where they overpowered the police and secured arms, ammunition, and recruits. At Colonia Morelos, Blanco "replenished his commis-
sary" from Mormon fields. Rumors of another band in the countryside south of
Cananea sent the mining town into a dither. Residents threw up breastworks,
raised fortifications, and strategically positioned machine guns around camp.
"The talk about town," wrote the Cananea Cattle Company manager and consular agent George A. Wiswall, "is, that the railroad will be cut and the water-
works blown up."[7]

Rebels stayed out of sight, however, until April 13, when a local *vaquero*-turned-
outlaw named Red López jumped a train from Nacozari with his men, rode
it north to Agua Prieta, and captured the town. "The first thing the Federales
knew of it," recalled the Nacozari resident Inez Horton, "was when the 'passengers' began firing as they poured off the train into the Agua Prieta streets." U.S.
troops posted along the border since the Mexican Revolution had broken out in
late 1910 tried to keep things calm in Douglas, "a very difficult task," wrote one
official, since hundreds "rushed to the line to see the fighting." Phones rang off
the hook in Bisbee, "and every automobile in the place was immediately pre-

pared for a run to Douglas." After López took the town, foreigners tried valiantly
to show their neutrality. "Over one store was the flag of Japan, over several the
American and the stores of the Chinese were closed, with no flags above them,"
one witness wrote. Others dispensed with national symbols altogether: crossing
the border, they simply left Mexico behind.[8]

Although bullets crossed the line, wounding two Americans and killing another, Douglas residents looked on as if the battle were somehow unreal. They
gawked from rooftops and from the streets, some standing nonchalantly within
fifteen or twenty feet of the battle. Maybe it seemed unreal to those taking the
town, too, but reality sank in soon enough. A few days later as federal reinforcements closed in, the resistance collapsed as suddenly as it had begun. Early in the
morning of April 18, hours before sunrise, rebels quietly emptied their trenches
and faded into the countryside. Some retreated to local highland refuges such as
the Ajo Mountains near Cananea—a favorite Apache stronghold in years past—
and others spirited themselves across the border into Arizona. By dawn, "there
was not a rebel to be seen."[9]

Some blamed the strange disappearance on the machines of war. A ragtag
band with no formal organization, one Douglas resident surmised, López's men
had to count on whatever weapons they could get their hands on. Unlike federal
troops, who could rely on bulk purchases of standard rifles and ammunition, distributed by rail to military command centers, the rebels inhabited a fugitive terrain where "it was impossible to get ammunition for all." Weeks later, a Douglas
doctor collecting spent cartridges from the battle was amazed to find as many as
twenty-eight different varieties, ranging from long, sharp bullet shells, .22 caliber rifle shells, and shotgun shells. This local heterogeneity was also reflected in
the saddles the rebels left behind when they left town. These "included every
kind of make and shape," one witness observed, "from the fine cowboy type to
the homemade tree without trimming."[10]

It was as if the veneer of the modern world had been ruptured, to reveal an
unfixed universe lurking just beneath. Although *federales* restored order to Agua
Prieta, it was this fresh breach between worlds, between "modern" present and
"frontier" past, that troubled locals most. Equally disconcerting was the ease
with which López and his army vanished. Rumor said they went toward Cananea, but when they failed to turn up there, others guessed they had crossed into
the Douglas *barrio* of Ragtown, where they became invisible to outsiders. A forest ranger saw Mexicans moving north from Agua Prieta along the San Simon
valley, in the shadow of the Chiricahua Mountains, perhaps toward regions of
refuge in Clifton-Morenci. Someone even said he saw López drifting toward El
Paso, his eye on Chihuahua. These fugitive pathways recast the borderlands in

an unsettling light: they revealed a vast insurgent terrain that modernizing elites had too willingly forgotten in their quest for order and progress.[11]

By May 1911, what outsiders saw as a confusing blend of local revolts and bandit invasions took more definite shape in Chihuahua, after forces fighting for Madero won a decisive victory over federal troops in Ciudad Juárez. By now Díaz was facing setbacks throughout Mexico. On May 25, he signed the Treaty of Ciudad Júarez, passing his authority to a provisional president, Francisco León de la Barra, who ruled until elections could be held that October. Despite new political divisions, Mexicans would elect Madero by an overwhelming majority. Some optimists began to believe that the brief revolution for control of Mexico had run its course.[12]

The transition was surprisingly seamless in the copper borderlands. Residents of Douglas awoke on May 10, two weeks before Díaz's formal resignation, to learn that all federal troops had left at daybreak. Soon afterward, Madero's provisional government in Ciudad Juárez named Agua Prieta the new capital of Sonora, with the *hacendado* José M. Maytorena as governor. On May 12, Juan Cabral, a local *revoltoso* who had studied at the University of Arizona and worked for the CCCC, demanded Cananea's surrender. After brief negotiations with corporate and municipal authorities, Cabral and his men marched into town without a fight. Cananea celebrated into the night, "and cries of 'Viva Cabral' and 'Viva Madero' filled the air." Embraced as a local hero, Cabral was "almost dragged from his horse by his admirers and wreaths of flowers were hung around his neck." From the corporate perspective, the takeover took place "in the most orderly and lawful way."[13]

If Madero, Maytorena, and Cabral seemed ready to bring peace and order to the region and restore stockholder confidence, the view on the ground was less comforting. Five months of fighting had devastated the countryside. "Most of the wheat crop in the state has been destroyed, the people have not planted their crops of beans and squashes nor prepared the ground for the planting of the corn crop," noted U.S. Consul Alexander Dye. Many of the men who usually worked in the fields were in the army. Mexicans on the Bavispe River were "almost to the starvation point," reported one Mormon colonist. They "are eating weeds and many of them have had nothing more substantial for days." In Nacozari, the company had to send abroad for food that was normally grown locally. "Well, if we must we will get along with less," a farmer noted. Their sons would soon come home, and if they did not return to the fields they might at least work in the mines, "so instead of what we gathered in the past we will have to buy."[14]

Yet many of the mines that would have helped local sons smooth out the hard

spots had either curtailed operations or shut down completely. They had to re-
negotiate contracts, get machines back up and running, and restock the camps
with the necessities of life. This all took time. Once the new regime came to
power, managers had to rush to beat the rainy season. "Orders were telegraphed
to the different bases of supplies and every available pack animal in the country
was put on the trails to the mines," wrote the mining engineer W. D. Pearce—but
in some places it was too late. Once the rains came, remote camps were sealed
off for months. Rains also meant fewer workers, for hundreds were now at home
planting corn, and some, "having had a taste of the more or less romantic life
of the undisciplined revolutionist, will not be content to return." Yet capital also
took to the road. For even with the onset of peace, many smaller mines never
reopened, thus tearing down one more safety net for locals, who took to wandering not so much for its romance but out of sheer necessity.[15]

If U.S. managers misread Mexican motivations, they also misread Mexico.
Many imagined revolution had ended with the overthrow of Díaz and the election of Madero. Few fully understood the Pandora's box Madero had opened.
The new regime did promise a more liberal political process and opportunities
for those Mexican elites who had failed to curry favor with Díaz, but it offered
little for workers or *campesinos,* many of whom felt ignored by Madero, a son
of a wealthy landowning family. Among those who spoke out against Madero's
weak reformist platform was Pascual Orozco, who also had a bone to pick because he felt Madero had never properly repaid him for his role in overthrowing
Díaz. As U.S. mining entrepreneurs lulled themselves into a false sense of security in Sonora, Orozco began organizing a new uprising in Chihuahua.[16]

Orozco's revolt, launched in early 1912, was short-lived. *Federales* and irregular
forces under Villa tore the Orozquistas apart in a series of skirmishes, eventually
forcing them back into their highland strongholds. But then Orozco's lieuten-
ants looked west and with increased vigor began to descend into Sonora along
former Apache trails, looking for supplies, support, and renewal. Although many
residents of Sonora saw this as an invasion, their compatriots in Arizona seemed
to think otherwise. In early August, supporters left Douglas for strongholds in
the Ajo Mountains, and over a hundred were said to be on the road south from
Chihuahua Hill and Tintown. As winds of war rushed in, U.S. entrepreneurs
moved property across the line. Mexican refugees from villages in the shadow
of the Sierra Madres followed them north, as did Mormons from colonies at the
foot of Púlpito Pass, the main *insurrecto* thoroughfare from Chihuahua.[17]

Compared to the Madero revolt, this one was far more violent and more destructive. Orozquistas fell on the Transvaal Mining Company near Cumpas, loot-
ing their stores and taking horses, saddles, guns, and ammunition. Their next

victim was the Mexican–Opata village of Aconchi, which they shelled with dynamite. When citizens rallied to defend their town, a fierce battle ensued, leaving the town in ruins. The rebel leader Emilio Campa rode into Santa Cruz on the railroad from Nogales to Cananea and ordered the local railroad crews to soak the bridges on both sides of town with "coal oil" (kerosene) and set them on fire. They hit the Cananea Cattle Company ranchlands, destroying property, butchering cattle, and taking everything from visitors, "even to the cigarette papers." Meanwhile, rebels under Antonio Rojas approached Nacozari, cut telegraph and telephone wires, burned bridges, and left the town—as one alarmed Douglas correspondent put it—"completely marooned from the outside world."[18]

Reporters were not the only ones to panic. When a courier reached Douglas with the disturbing news that Rojas was planning to "kill and burn everything" in Nacozari, President Walter Douglas of Phelps Dodge assured the U.S. secretary of state that it would be impossible to restrain "forces now being organized" at Douglas. Word on the street was that a "filibustering outfit" was preparing to ride to Nacozari, yet when authorities came to investigate, locals denied it. A few said local cowboys had floated the scheme before thinking the better of it. An undercover Bureau of Investigation agent, however, stumbled across something more sinister after watching men drive a suspicious load of rifles and ammunition to the back of the Copper Queen store. Lurking in the shadows, he watched as Walter Douglas's brother, James S. "Rawhide Jimmy" Douglas, took the boxes into the cellar. "If anything was said about the shipment," he heard Douglas say, "somebody would lose a job."[19]

That evening the agent heard Douglas offer a local man named Pete Thompson money "to go with a bunch of men that he, Douglas, was hireing [sic] to go to Nacozari, Mexico, to help protect the Phelps-Dodge Co.'s property there." Thompson declined, so Douglas asked another local named Bob Hilburn. Hilburn also hesitated when he learned that Douglas lacked a permit. Hilburn later claimed that Douglas told him not to worry, that he would "stand between him and the law." Douglas approached a third man, who refused the offer on the same grounds, that he and his friends "did not want to be outlawed by their own country and take chances of the rebels catching them, too." Frustrated, Douglas approached "a large number of cowboys," who agreed but then changed their mind. In the end, the plan failed. Reports said "Jim Douglas [then] telephoned to Nacozari, to the manager, to buy the rebels off." According to the undercover agent, Douglas was said "to have told the manager to pay most any price to save the town."[20]

In the end, Rojas never invaded Nacozari, and the Phelps Dodge filibuster never materialized. All trace of the conspiracy was buried deep in Washington,

D.C., with the field report of an unnamed Bureau of Investigation spy. One might almost have written off the idea of a U.S. invasion of Mexico altogether were it not for the fact that one week later, in the wee hours of the morning, some three hundred "young men mostly cowboys" crossed the border, reportedly to protect "the property of friends and other Americans." "The movement is not upheld by the people of Douglas," one local reporter hastened to add. "It was organized by men who came in here from the outside and kept their scheme so well under cover that even citizens who are wide-awake and watching every movement of strangers could not get next to it."[21]

Just as one could easily write off such fugitive movements to cowboys, who had a reputation for taking violence across the border since the 1880s, "strangers" also made perfect fall guys. Yet one did not have to look far afield to explain their behavior. Ever since Campa, Rojas, and others had crossed the sierras that summer, Arizonans had feared a Mexican invasion. The local sheriff and former Arizona Ranger Harry Wheeler responded by creating local "home guards" in Douglas and other communities, "so as to have a force that could be quickly called in case of necessity," should a rebel band "herd too close to the line." If the Orozquista invasion of Sonora motivated their formation, the 1906 strike at Cananea was also a powerful reference point. In 1906, when the "lives of Americans were threatened," hundreds of Americans from Bisbee and Douglas had crossed to Cananea "without any red tape," explained one reporter. Wheeler's plan, he added, built on this local tradition: "The feeling among the Americans along the Arizona border today is just as warm for their friends in the mining camps as it was when the Cananea incident occurred."[22]

If men such as Harry Wheeler and Rawhide Jimmy Douglas looked to an older, frontier heritage of home guards and so-called volunteers to allay fears and defend space, Mexicans did the same. To combat the Orozquista invasion, state officials in Sonora formed irregular troops to supplement the regular army. Such irregulars, explains the historian Alan Knight, were "a traditional feature of northern, frontier society." The most famous of these was a battalion recruited by Álvaro Obregón, the mayor of Huatabampo in southern Sonora, who would later rise through the ranks to become president of Mexico. His successes against the Orozquistas was popular not so much because Sonora was a hotbed of revolutionary sentiment—Sonora was, in fact, relatively conservative—but because the offensive evoked memories of prior Apache and bandit invasions. Like their neighbors to the north, the Sonora elite looked back to a not-so-distant frontier past when outsiders had unsettled hearth and home.[23]

Nobody embodied the connections between frontier past and insurgent present better than the former Indian fighter Emilio Kosterlitzky. Almost sixty, he had just retired, but now, as Chihuahuenses spilled across mountain passes into Sonora, he changed his mind. He asked permission to organize a special body of the Gendarmería Fiscal with "frontier service," including veterans of the Yaqui wars. "Let them come," he declared. "I want nothing more to complete my career [than] to drive this invading horde from the state." Kosterlitzky saw things through the spectacles of his Apache-fighting days, but this was a different battle. The "invading horde" included former Apache fighters from Chihuahua, and although some of Kosterlitzky's men could remember Geronimo, most were of a newer generation that had battled Yaquis, not Apaches. Moreover, many of the defenders of Sonora *were* Yaquis. It was, in a sense, a nostalgic effort to assimilate new crises to old times, a last stand for men like Kosterlitzky.[24]

What was most intriguing about this rhetoric was its transnational scope: people on both sides saw the borderlands slipping out from underneath them, into the abyss of the colonial past. When Wheeler established the same sort of home guards that had defended Tombstone and Bisbee in the age of cowboys and Indians, when Douglas tried to send arms and volunteers across the border as Bisbee elites had done in Cananea in 1906, and when Kosterlitzky heaved himself back in the saddle to clean the countryside of Orozco's "rebels, looters, cattle thieves, and smugglers," they seemed profoundly anxious about the modern world. Perhaps they feared that the real fugitive terrain was modernity itself, and not the frontier it had replaced. For this world seemed to be coming undone, and "invading hordes" from beyond the pale were merely the first of many ghosts of frontiers past.

For many, the battle for Sonora really began in 1913, when the nation fell apart a second time in Mexico City. In early February, counterrevolutionaries launched a coup against the Madero regime, and after days of bloody fighting in the capital city, Gen. Victoriano Huerta took over the presidency. When Huerta's sudden and violent rise to power was followed by the murders of President Madero and Vice President José María Pino Suárez, Mexico plunged into a new cycle of revolutionary violence. On February 21, hours before Madero and Pino Suárez were shot, Cananea's City Council voted to oppose Huerta. And once the news of the assassinations reached the state, the rest of Sonora followed suit. Formerly a refuge from the winds of revolt, Sonora became insurgent terrain.[25]

This was not a working-class, urban rebellion; neither was it a rural revolt to restore confiscated land or a nationalistic uprising to combat foreign domination — even if labor, land, and the power of capital weighed heavily on many local minds. This was a revolt against the violent overthrow of Madero, whose moderate vision of political reform had resonated in Sonora. It was a revolt to restore the constitutionally elected government, with a pinch of traditional federalism stirred in. Under Madero, many Sonora elites had assumed political offices that had been denied them by the centralist Porfirian clique of Ramón Corral, Rafael Izábal, and Luis E. Torres. When Sonora's leaders rose against Huerta in 1913, they rallied to defend political gains at the provincial level. They sought to pre-serve rather than challenge the status quo.[26]

If provincial concerns drove the Sonora revolt, they also presented new ob-stacles. In the absence of a strong national presence, locals fell back on an older frontier tradition of lining up behind charismatic *caudillos*. Many turned to Gov-ernor Maytorena, Sonora's highest elected official, but when he took a leave of absence to Arizona, some turned to Acting Governor Ignacio P. Pesqueira in-stead. Others allied themselves with a military clique that had emerged as local heroes against the Orozquista invasion: Álvaro Obregón, Benjamin Hill, Plu-tarco Elías Calles, Juan Cabral, and others. This group took the most decisive action in March 1913, when it seized trains on the Sonora Railway, moved troops north and south, and began to systematically eject Huerta loyalists from the state. Later that month, the state cast its lot with the Constitutionalist movement, led by Venustiano Carranza. A wealthy landowner from the north, Carranza had two goals in common with Sonora's leaders: to overthrow Huerta and to return Mexico to a moderate constitutional order.[27]

If a coalition with Carranza enhanced Sonora's revolutionary power, faction-alism continued to rip the state apart. As Carranza and Obregón marched south toward Mexico City in 1914 to overthrow Huerta, Obregón's second in Sonora, Calles, began to feud with Maytorena. And by the time the Constitutionalists ousted Huerta and took Mexico City that August, conditions in Sonora were spinning out of control. Maytorena had gathered his own personal troops—many of them Yaqui Indians who worked on his family's haciendas—and had driven Calles and his troops north to the border. He then began to forge an alliance with Villa, another northerner who was increasingly at odds with the Constitutional-ists. In September 1914, Maytorena and Villa withdrew recognition of Carranza, and Maytorena then sent his troops north to the border town of Naco, where Calles and his troops were posted, to force a showdown. By October 1914, the copper borderlands were once again in flames.[28]

Like previous border battles, this was one in which Americans quickly became involved. Before attacking on October 2, Maytorena urged all civilians to take refuge in Arizona, and Sheriff Wheeler took charge of moving noncombatants on the U.S. side out of the line of fire. To keep insurgent and noninsurgent land-scapes separated, a series of boundary markers were also used. "By use of long trains of freight cars loaded with coal on the railroad close to the international line," the U.S. commanding officer at Naco explained, "there is only one narrow means of egress from Naco, Sonora, to Naco, Arizona, which enables the troops to comply with the orders enforcing neutrality laws." To limit accidents and "misunderstandings," he added, the line was also "marked very distinctly with United States flags."[29]

These barriers were more symbolic than real. One contingent of Yaquis claimed to have crossed the line and attacked from the north, despite the presence of U.S. troops. When the battle was on, nobody was allowed into Naco, Arizona, but sightseer caravans from Bisbee often got around the official cordon. Authorities patrolled the line, but selectively. Each night most of the Callista women and children came to the U.S. side to sleep, "and the town is filled with refugees who claim they will return to Mexico as soon as the fight is over," wrote an immigration authority. Even the U.S. Army, posted to ensure that the rule of a distant state trumped local custom, supported these informal border crossings by establishing a special sanctuary for Mexican women and children in the opera house of Naco, Arizona. Gendered relations of power thus inflected a local moral economy of war — in which a select Mexican few could seek refuge on U.S. soil — that confused as much as it reinforced larger distinctions between nations.[30]

More often it was local law officers, not federal troops, who subverted the state's efforts to cordon off revolutionary Mexico. One such officer was Sheriff Wheeler, who claimed the U.S. Army was preventing Mexicans from entering Arizona for medical help and "protection from Yaquis." "Arizona sentiment regards this policy as unchristian and at variance with spirit of modern civilization," protested the Arizona governor George W. P. Hunt, but behind the mask of Christian charity lurked the specter of frontier self-rule. Wheeler and Hunt were worried less about Sonorenses than about their own power. One Naco official said Hunt was prepared to call out the local militia because he felt U.S. troops were not really defending Arizona. "The feeling among Americans about Naco is intense, and may well lead to rash or lawless measures if Maytorena's troops continue to fire into the American town," he wrote. Locals also focused their fears on the "half civilized" Yaquis fighting for Maytorena, "over whom control is uncertain."[31]

These were deliberate images: Mexican women and children seeking the help of white American men, "alien" aggressors who created a need for "home guards," and the threat of "barbaric" Indians, a familiar foil for the expansion of U.S. "civilization." They tied insurgent Sonora to an epic frontier struggle and called for frontier justice. More to the point, they naturalized local power, that of paternalistic corporations and their masculine cowboys, over that of a distant state. "I was attempting to protect my people," Wheeler recalled of his efforts at Naco. Again he turned to gendered imagery to make his point. One day a rebel fired a machine gun into an office window of the Hotel Naco, on the U.S. side. "There was a girl in the office; a young girl I had known from babyhood," Wheeler noted, "and [the bullet] entered her piano. I heard her scream and I ran into [the] office and found her face slightly bleeding from broken glass." This random act of violence, he said, "made me believe that the thing had to end one way or another."[32]

Wheeler confronted one of Maytorena's agents about the gunner, but he refused to listen. Infuriated, Wheeler said that if someone did not take care of him, "I would call a posse as sheriff of that county and enfilade his trenches and drive [him] out myself." He then told the U.S. commanding officer of his plans. The officer informed Wheeler that "if I did it would be his painful duty, as much as he regretted it, to arrest me and my posse. I said, 'There is no martial law, no declaration of war; it is my belief that I am the supreme authority here.' He said: 'My orders as a soldier will compel me to take the action I have indicated to you,' and tears came in the old gentleman's eyes when he told me." It was only to avoid causing "embarrassment" to this "gentleman," Wheeler said, that he eventually backed down. "I could not understand it," he remarked. For "had a ranch been attacked a mile east or west of this town by bandits I would have proceeded there and protected that ranch."[33]

It is hard to tell if Sheriff Wheeler genuinely felt the modern world was spiraling into the abyss of the wild west past, if he saw this as an opportunity to regenerate his own masculinity and local prestige, or if he was a shrewd rhetorician with an interest in preserving conservative, local forms of power, whether corporate, state, or otherwise. It is likely that all of these aspects came into play in some way. Whatever his deeper motivations, Wheeler was far from unusual for his place and time. As the Mexican Revolution raged below the border and as the United States moved toward World War I, fears of unmade landscapes—of threatened invasions of a landscape created through the prior invasion of others —consumed Americans as they never had before.

By early 1915, when Maytorena called in his troops and left Naco, Sonora was in ruins. In August 1914, facing "lawless conditions" resulting from the Maytorena–Calles feud, the CCCC had closed down, throwing four thousand Mexicans and two hundred Americans out of work. It was just one of many times in the decade that corporate elites emptied Cananea and fled to Arizona. Only ten Americans and forty Mexicans were left to guard the property. Mexicans who had once been shipped to Cananea to make up for labor deficits were now shipped out by military and civil officers, many headed for the revolutionary rank and file. So many were out of work, one American noted, that those finding arms and ammunition "go to the hills in small bands and commit depredations on the adjacent ranches and small towns." Even soldiers posted at Cananea had to steal to survive, and on a daily basis Americans received complaints from Chinese merchants that "stores had been entered by armed soldiers and merchandise forcibly taken."[34]

Yet as they had for centuries, Mexicans fell back on local safety nets. When the CCCC suspended operations, wrote the consular agent Charles Montague, few "had made provision for such a contingency." Thousands of residents "have been eking out a bare existence since then washing placer gold, hunting, hauling wood, etc., while others have joined the various armies passing through." Few could support themselves, much less their families, in this way, and "during the past few months," he wrote, "I have seen evidence of more suffering in Cananea than I have ever witnessed before." Even rural merchants, who normally had large stocks of necessary staples such as corn, beans, lard, sugar, rice, flour, and coffee, had little to sell because authorities had commandeered the stock for the various soldiers passing through town.[35]

A classic Mexican safety net was farming, but conditions were just as bad in the Sonora River valley to the south. Roaming bands of Callistas and Maytorenistas had devastated corn, wheat, and bean fields, and floods had washed away the best lands. "Farmers inform me that, even if they wanted to plant crops, they could not do so as they have no farming land left," Montague claimed. In normal times, such shortages could be relieved by shipping food by rail from the west coast states of Sinaloa and Jalisco, but these states were now shut off to the Sonora trade. Revolutionary factions also confiscated the work stock of farmers and ranchers, Montague explained, and "after the horses have served a short time in the cavalry they are unfit for use." On a recent march from Chihuahua to Cananea, he noted, over twelve hundred horses had died, "and of those that did arrive here, many died, and the balance could scarcely walk."[36]

The situation was even worse farther south. U.S. Consul Frederick Simpich found the region around Guaymas at a standstill owing to floods and fear of Yaqui Indians, who had gained enormous mobility and power as soldiers. "So many Mexican men have been killed by the Yaquis, and so many women have been violated and carried away," he reported, "that the people in many regions of southern Sonora have abandoned their farms and moved into the towns, failing thus to plant their usual crops." There had been an almost total loss in wheat, corn, and garbanzo crops. The cost of goods was driven up because most were paid in revolutionary currency, worth a tenth of its former value. "If it were not for the fact that the peon can subsist on so little, and is comfortable and happy even when clad only in a ten-cent straw hat, a 25-cent shirt and a 50-cent pair of overalls," Simpich concluded, "he would be starving to death now, instead of being merely hungry, and unusually ragged."[37]

Yet with so many safety nets falling out beneath them, even a thrifty and flexible population—or, particularly such a population—had to look elsewhere to survive. U.S. Immigration Inspector Frank W. Berkshire found as many as ten thousand people huddled just across the border in Agua Prieta. Some were "fortunate enough to be provided with tents," but many were living in boxcars. News had it that Maytorena and his Yaquis would soon attack, and indeed, Douglas residents could see the smoke from their campfires at night. But this was not the only fear Berkshire had. "If starvation eventually faces the present occupants, a break for the United States may naturally be expected," he wrote, assuring his superiors that he would "exert all proper effort to keep out the inadmissible aliens."[38]

The immigration inspector Frank W. Heath saw a similar storm brewing. Lands near the Nacozari Railroad and south toward Cumpas and Moctezuma, he wrote, had been "continuously harassed with frequent and intermittent sanguinary conflicts." Refugees told him that after taking a town, soldiers would often "rape, pillage, and execute" those thought to side with the opposing faction. They plundered freely and destroyed crops, compelling many "to leave the country and seek a livelihood elsewhere." "It can readily be understood that there are a large number of Mexicans coming to the Border who are being forced out of their own country, as only an imaginary line separates that country from the United States," he noted. "It is a very easy matter for those who desire to do so to cross into the United States, mingle with the Mexicans on this side of the international line and thus lose their identity." If pushed by fear or desperation, he insisted, the entire population of Agua Prieta "will stampede to the United States."[39]

Thus the unmaking of the Mexican countryside, and the movement of refugees north, only added to the fears of Mexican "invasion" on the American side of the copper borderlands. These fears took on an added sense of urgency as 1915 unfolded, for in the nearby state of Texas, local raids on ranches, railroads, and irrigation works by Mexicans and Mexican-Americans all along the border began to stir up widespread anxiety. The raids seemed to fulfill a manifesto that had surfaced earlier that year, the so-called Plan de San Diego. The manifesto called for a "liberating army" made up of Mexicans—but also blacks and Indians—to reclaim the lands in the U.S. Southwest that the United States had formerly taken from Mexico. The freed lands would first become an independent nation but would later, perhaps, rejoin Mexico. Fueled by fears of invasion, Texas Rangers and local vigilantes led counterraids and violent suppression that would

last throughout the year and intermittently, in fact, until the end of the first decade of the Mexican Revolution.[40]

Arizona residents fretted when similar raids broke out along the Sonora border. By September 1915, "bands of Mexicans" were crossing the line, stealing
horses, cattle, and other goods, even automobiles. "Driven by necessity raiders
[are] growing bolder and obviously civil authorities, lacking numbers and organization, cannot keep raiders out of Arizona or protect American property," noted
local officials. "Unless immediate adequate military action is taken possibly a
situation may develop not unlike that now existing at [the] Texas border." The
sheriff of Santa Cruz County, north of Nogales, said he would organize a "civilian
body" if the army failed to do its job. Fears about Plan de San Diego–like uprisings reached as far north as Tucson. Locals there worried about the "large numbers of strange Mexicans" in town, and rumors of demonstrations to be staged
on September 16. "In view of the disturbed conditions in Texas," several wrote,
"the moral effect of a few American regular troops on that day would be all that
would be required."[41]

Rumors of invasions saturated Sonora as well. In early 1915, Douglas residents
heard that Pancho Villa was preparing to lead an expedition west into Sonora,
along the same pathways that earlier rebels had taken through the Sierra Madres.
Curiously, U.S. Army officers in Douglas had only vaguely heard of these east-
west passages and had to learn about them locally, for they did not appear on official maps of the region. New railroad networks, leading north-to-south and skirt-
ing the sierras on the U.S. side of the border, dominated the landscape and made
these older pathways invisible to outsiders. They were certainly "not indicated on
the map in this office," one officer wrote, after gaining information on the roads
from ranchers "familiar with the country." And if forgotten spaces only slowly became legible to these agents of the state, the Villistas themselves took even longer
to materialize: phantom hordes haunted the countryside for months to come.[42]

Yet by late summer 1915, the rumors seemed to be yielding something more
solid. Earlier that year, Villa had been one of the most potent leaders in Mexico,
holding most of the far north. But by summer he had suffered a series of military
setbacks against the Constitutionalists under Obregón, and soon Villista morale
began to falter, even in his home state of Chihuahua. As the Villista offensive
shifted from conventional to guerrilla status, Villa plotted a new counteroffensive to the west. He planned to cross the sierras, join with Maytorena's forces,
and take Agua Prieta. Then, the combined (and hopefully renewed) Villista force
would move down the west coast, eventually taking Mexico City. By October 4,
upon hearing the news that flesh-and-blood Villistas were marching through the
high mountain passes, many Sonorenses began flooding the U.S. immigration

Figure 26. U.S. soldier and Mexican revolutionary, battle of Agua Prieta (1915).
This was one of many picture postcards produced at the border at the time that visually
reinforced a growing distinction in the U.S. mind between a heroic, progressive
United States and barbarous, unsettled Mexico. Courtesy of the Arizona
Historical Society/Tucson, AHS Photograph #58732.

offices in Agua Prieta, once again renewing fears of a refugee "rush to the American side."[43]

Ranchers began to herd their cattle across the border, and Americans again shut down the mines at Cananea and Nacozari. By now it was well known on the U.S. side that the United States had agreed to let Carranza cross troops on U.S. soil from El Paso to Agua Prieta, where Calles was posted, and U.S. interests in Sonora worried about the repercussions. There was little support for Villa in Sonora—just as there had been little support for the Orozquista invaders in 1912. "No one here wants Villa in Sonora," wrote the U.S. commanding officer in Nogales, Arizona. "They fear him personally and feel that he will strip the country of all that remains of any value and destroy what he cannot use." Refugees spilled north and anxieties mounted, especially after Villa heard about the U.S. support of Carranza. "Villa was very indignant and reported to have stated that he was through with any dealings with the United States," reported the journalist who had broken the news to Villa. It was said he "would attack Agua Prieta and also Americans if necessary."[44]

Villa had the advantage of numbers, but Calles had plenty of other advantages, including the historical animosity of Sonorenses toward invaders, the U.S. agreement to bring Carrancistas to Agua Prieta, and an impregnable system of trenches and barbed wire entanglements south of Agua Prieta. But probably the most important advantage Calles had was the element of surprise: Villa attacked on November 1, expecting to take the town in an hour, and yet met unexpected defeat. Those who had been paralyzed by a fear of Villa were amazed when Villa's men, exhausted and starved from the trek through the sierras, began to desert. Villa veered to the south, slashing his way across Sonora to Hermosillo, but he lost battle after battle. He was eventually forced to take the remnants of his army back across the snow-packed passes of the sierras. With his disastrous Sonora campaign over, the skies began to clear above the copper borderlands, and many began to imagine a return to business as usual.[45]

But it would take years for U.S. mining capitalists to fully overcome the collapse of investor confidence and for Sonora's economy to recover from three years of almost constant turmoil. It would take even longer for Americans to shake the fear of invasion that had haunted them. Villa's raid on Columbus, New Mexico, in 1916 did not help, nor did the new fears of German–Mexican conspiracy associated with the so-called Zimmerman Telegram in 1917. Among other things, this intercepted message proposed a wartime alliance in which Germany might help Mexico take back part of the U.S. Southwest, generating uncanny echoes of the Plan de San Diego manifesto of 1915. And then there was World War I. A war that fueled new efforts to patrol the boundaries of both the

body politic and of political identities in general, World War I simply amplified many of the anxieties brought on by the Mexican Revolution in southern
Arizona.[46]

These various elements converged in Bisbee in June 1917, when thousands
walked off the job at the Copper Queen and neighboring mines. The strike,
which lasted for weeks, brought the production of copper to a near standstill.
Mining officials, town elites, and even the national press considered the strike
unpatriotic for several reasons. Bisbee copper was being used for the wartime
effort; each bullet included a quarter of an ounce of the red metal. And Americans had increasingly associated one of the leading unions behind the strike—
the Industrial Workers of the World, or IWW—with the fervent socialism that
seemed to be driving their new enemies in Europe. Two groups organized against
the strike: the Citizens' Protective League, an association of local business interests, and the Workmen's Loyalty League, made up of nonstriking workers. Both
agreed that striking workers were disloyal because they were frustrating the war
effort, and that the strike desperately needed to be suppressed.[47]

On the morning of July 12, 1917, two thousand members of both groups banded
together. Along with hundreds of local private detectives and Phelps Dodge president Walter Douglas, they joined Sheriff Harry Wheeler, who deputized them,
marked them with white armbands, and sent them to round up workers. Some
twelve hundred were placed under an armed guard at the baseball field and
were then marched at gunpoint to waiting El Paso and Southwestern cars. Then,
like Chiricahua Apaches a generation earlier, they were deported. They were
dumped in the desert town of Hermanas, New Mexico, near Columbus, and
told never to return. For weeks the Loyalty League guarded Bisbee to make sure
their "popular" mandate was carried out. Outsiders explained the episode as a
case of wartime patriotism gone awry, and many locals said they believed German saboteurs were behind the strike. Indeed, eastern and southern Europeans
were prominent among the deportees.

What is generally forgotten is that the largest foreign group that was dumped in
the desert that day was from Mexico. Americans thinking about wartime patriotism—not to mention subsequent historians—were quick to forget the larger
transnational context, that another war was raging south of the border. Indeed,
for Wheeler, the Mexican Revolution was critical. In testimony he later gave to
U.S. authorities, he argued that Mexicans had dominated the strike. Many, he
said, were Villistas who had forced mines to close down in Cananea. Wheeler
may have been looking for a foreign scapegoat, but he was not alone in his fears,
for indeed local newspapers at the time were filled with reports of armed Villistas
roaming the countryside near Cananea. "I heard through Mexican sources that

Figure 27. The Bisbee Deportation of 1917. Appealing to patriotism, fears of
Mexican rebels, and frontier justice, "volunteers" rounded up and deported striking
workers in cattle cars, just as their forebears had done to Geronimo and his fellow
Apaches a generation earlier. Courtesy of the Arizona Historical Society/Tucson,
AHS Photograph #43181.

some of these Villistas had rifles all cached in the [Ajo] Mountains," he added,
"and that when the opportunity presented itself that they would secure these
rifles."[48]

In later testimony to Senator Albert Bacon Fall on matters related to the Mexican Revolution, Wheeler elaborated. Before the Bisbee strike, Mexicans "ran the
Americans out of Cananea," he said. Later he heard a Mexican tell an American, "We run you out of Cananea a short while ago; we will run you out of here."
"Did you ever hear of the Plan of San Diego?" Fall asked. "I heard of it in various
places," Wheeler replied: "The time I remember best of all was in Tombstone,
near Bisbee. I heard a Mexican . . . say that the time would soon arrive when this
county would be restored to Mexico." Fall nodded. "That was the first time you
heard of the Plan of San Diego?" "I don't know that it was the first time," Wheeler
said, "it was the time most distinct in my memory; I remember the Mexican and
his looks; he was a stranger in town."[49]

Within the context of the European war, however, most Americans were thinking about other enemies, and Bisbee's "strange Mexicans" remained forgotten in
the shadows. As time went by, the Mexican context of the Bisbee Deportation
was forgotten. Forgotten, too, were fears of invasion and inversion—of a modern world consumed by its frontier past—that had haunted the borderlands in

the years leading up to the deportation. And yet these age-old anxieties permeated the deportation to its very core. Bisbee's Loyalty League, Wheeler noted in passing, consisted of the remnants of an older group he had organized in 1912, when the Orozquista invasion of Sonora was at its height. "We formed a military organization here and in Douglas, and in all the little towns in this County," he noted, "for the purpose of resisting an invasion from Mexico, which was threatening." These were, in fact, the so-called home guards that were formed to "be quickly called in case of necessity"—ad hoc bodies that predated the patriotic fervor of World War I.[50]

But the roots ran even deeper. In 1912, Arizonans viewed the home guards against the backdrop of the 1906 strike in Cananea, in which locals had crossed south to protect friends "without any red tape." But the idea of reinforcing friends and transcending state-imposed barriers to customary practices also recalls the meeting of Juan Fenochio and John Slaughter, "two diplomats of ordinary caliber," whose local negotiations had prevailed over the letter of the law in 1890. And the idea of local vigilance groups at the border, of course, was as old as the border itself, reflected in the Crabb filibuster, the Sonoita Massacre, and the "committee" of well-armed "citizens" who materialized from side alleys to respond to Tombstone's shootout at the O.K. Corral. It hardly seems accidental that the distress signal used to call together the Loyalty League in 1917 was sounded by shift-change whistles at the Copper Queen mine hoist: the same signal deployed in the 1880s to mobilize citizen groups against Apache Indians.

The Apache Wars, Cananea strike, Mexican Revolution, and Bisbee Deportation thus found common terrain not only in the same transnational landscape, but also in symbolic webs associated with the frontier. In all of these contexts, the frontier became a useful ideological weapon in the effort to rally border "citizens" behind corporate and state visions of power and control, by anchoring the policing of space to a timeless, naturalized defense of civilization. Yet these relationships were anything but timeless. In the end, the Mexican Revolution also served as a key turning point in the history of frontiers and borderlands. Before the Mexican Revolution, Mexicans and Americans claimed transnational kinships as Indian fighters and pioneers. Frontier imagery underpinned shared ideas of progress and shared journeys into a modern future. But for Americans, frontier imagery during the revolution began to articulate *differences* between Mexicans and Americans. Emerging from this insurgent terrain, U.S. border residents imagined themselves as persisting frontier heroes, and these new heroes held the line against barbaric Mexicans.

For Mexicans, too, the violent onset of the Mexican Revolution marked a crucial juncture in borders and border crossings. Although copper corporations began to slowly reassemble their working populations, bringing themselves back to the forefront of many migrant lives, the unmaking of the countryside in Sonora and periodic closure of mines between 1911 and 1917 had set people into even greater motion. If Americans began to patrol borders in new ways after 1917, Mexicans were beginning to cross them more frequently than ever, increasingly pulled—as Jesús Corral and his family were in the 1920s—by new labor markets in the U.S. Southwest. With mobility came new dreams: of worker pathways leading beyond—not simply through—the shadows of frontiers past. The borderlands were once again on the move. And as copper elites began to rebuild their transnational realm, they would find its shifting foundations harder than ever to control.

Epilogue

REMAPPING THE BORDERLANDS

As much as revolution had unsettled the borderlands, forcing corporations to close their doors, pushing Mexicans into exile, and conjuring ghosts of frontier barbarism, it hardly spelled an end to the copper borderlands. The CCCC and Phelps Dodge emerged on the other side stronger than ever. With the help of bilingual lawyers and new government allies who translated the legal and political landscapes of postrevolutionary Mexico, they forged ties to the state that were in some ways more privileged and exclusive than ever. Most important for copper managers, the Mexican leaders who controlled Mexico in the 1920s—Álvaro Obregón and Plutarco Calles—hailed from Sonora. Like their nineteenth-century precursors in the north, they embraced ideas of development, modernity, and progress and carried these ideas to the nation's center. Mexico had "emerged from out the dark shadows," observed Maud Kenyon-Kingdon in 1925, "and brighter days were predicted for this unhappy but beautiful land."[1]

Such prophecies—reminiscent of the 1850s, when newcomers predicted the rise of a new American empire from the Spanish ashes—inspired a new generation of dreamers willing to turn a blind eye to history. With the coming of peace under Obregón in the early 1920s, U.S. Department of Commerce officials proposed that northern Mexico was again pioneer territory. The Southern Pacific was rebuilding its west coast line, and corporations were investing in new agricultural markets in Sonora and Sinaloa. Despite a postwar slump in metal markets, mining entrepreneurs were also encouraged. "There could scarcely be a more favorable time than the present to revive old enterprises and to create new ones," observed one. "Pioneers will find obstacles, but hope of reward will attract adventurous men, whether they risk their money or use their brains and strength."[2]

But the copper borderlands would never be the same. A land transformed by the captains of transnational industry passed increasingly under the shadow of the Mexican state. Elected officials came to power by promising to deliver on Mexico's revolutionary promise, whether to curb the excesses of foreign development, support labor reforms, or rebuild the economy without excluding the majority from the good life. More than ever, corporate officials had to negotiate with the state to square demands of stockholders and directors with those of citizens and elected officials. Large corporations, having the money and time to negotiate, adapted. But new mining, labor, and indemnity laws made things harder than ever for smaller ventures. Sonora's top mining companies "can be counted on the fingers of one hand," claimed one American in the late 1920s, "as a mine operator may get up any morning and find that on account of some new regulation his costs have been increased to such a degree that he is left no margin of profit."[3]

If the state began to assert itself in new ways by adding new bureaucratic layers to earlier contractual and policing relationships, it rarely overshadowed the local control of corporations. In many ways, state *power* was as spotty as ever. In the 1920s, Sonora's government elite often asked copper companies for loans, and Phelps Dodge officials in Nacozari complained that rural police paid to keep the peace, protect mines and ranches against theft, and prevent manufacture of illegal mescal in the nearby countryside did nothing. Meanwhile, political candidates frequently denounced the company. "All this tends to create ill-feeling," claimed the manager at Nacozari, Herman Horton, "making it most difficult to obtain the cooperation of our workmen." For if such efforts to assert political and state power in the copper borderlands did anything, Horton suggested, they tipped the balance of power away from states and corporations and in the favor of workers, by encouraging them to live and work on their own terms.[4]

Yet if workers found increased autonomy and power in the 1920s, this was owing less to postrevolutionary concessions than to new transnational labor markets. The Phelps Dodge official P. G. Beckett wrote that Nacozari and Pilares were losing workers by 1923, not only to mining and railroad camps in the southwestern United States, but also to employers in the East. "Pilares is a stopping-off place for transient labor," he claimed; "when there is a demand at higher wage prices from other points, they leave us." As early as 1918, the company tried to stem this emigration by improving conditions in camp. Better houses, plazas, and sanitary conditions would reduce the exodus of miners, felt President Walter Douglas: "We want our operations to be a model of everything that is fair and generous in the treatment by American capital of Mexican employees." Managers patched leaky roofs, improved libraries, set up soda fountains, and opened theaters in an effort to turn a company town into their paternalistic idea of a better home.[5]

In a sense, copper companies sought to redeem a landscape they had helped unmake. Driven by dividends and dependent on copper markets, Phelps Dodge and the CCCC had repeatedly left Mexico during the Mexican Revolution, leaving workers to their own devices and reinforcing a negative stereotype of Cananea and Nacozari as unsettled terrains. This pattern continued through the early 1920s, when Cananea and Nacozari closed down again during the economic depression following World War I. When operations resumed, Phelps Dodge and the CCCC had to repopulate their copper ghost towns with green workers from nearby villages. These workers, usually farmers, lacked experience and industrial discipline, were prone to accidents, and purportedly dissipated their wages on mescal brewed in the countryside. Local agrarian revolts in the 1920s made conditions even more uneven, as many of these same workers were conscripted into the Mexican army.[6]

Green workers, rural drinking, and agrarian uprisings fed the nagging suspicion that the countryside had become more than a refuge: it now threatened, as it had during the Mexican Revolution, to destabilize corporate power at its industrial core. Managers remapped and reformed Nacozari and Pilares to keep these rural shadows at bay. Had they known their history, they might have been disconcerted by how much they shared with their precursors in the 1850s, who grumbled at the "irregular" schedules that rural workers kept, their poor familiarity with modern metallurgical practices, the mescal and "endless games of monte" after payday, and the worrisome specter of rural revolt. More than anything, this history might have shaken their new, progressive assumptions about social planning and transnational progress.[7]

Yet managers ultimately faced more than the ghosts of frontiers past. They were also haunted by the fugitive nature of the modern world. They had to work harder than ever to pin down labor, sending agents down the coast and over the sierras with photos and propaganda describing the "favorable working conditions" in Nacozari, Pilares, and Cananea. In Hermosillo, the labor agent Simón Russek saw many men like himself. "Some have large placards at the corners," he explained, "others have men walking through the streets using megaphones saying what they pay their workmen and what the working conditions are." He competed with sugar plantations, tomato growers, and the railroad, which was on the march south. The same "pioneer" conditions that lured capital across the border in the 1920s offered workers endless opportunities. The best Russek could do was to hawk photos of new churches, schools, picture shows, and handball courts: icons of a modern mining landscape produced as much for labor as for capital.[8]

And workers were not the only ones to benefit. As in decades past, corporations depended on local elites to help carry out their industrial transformations. As corporate scouts headed into the river valleys below Nacozari and Pilares to find workers in 1924, they leaned on local officials who served as labor agents, or *patrones*. Meanwhile, regional Mexican elites took advantage of the difficulties in disciplining labor by hiring on as contractors, managing their countrymen to their own economic advantage. Copper companies emerged on the other side of the Mexican Revolution more powerful than ever, but they still had to reconcile dreams of control with local networks of power, rooted beyond the managerial gaze of state or corporation. The basic issue of who gained and who lost in this transnational world—of who would ultimately domesticate this fugitive terrain, and to what greater good—remained unresolved.[9]

The enduring uncertainties of the borderlands were perhaps best reflected in the different paths that Nacozari and Cananea took in the 1930s. Efforts to rebuild Nacozari after the postwar depression masked persisting economic difficulties. In the late 1920s, Wall Street financiers kept copper prices stable, but the Great Depression sent this fragile scaffolding crashing down. Copper companies retreated and reconsolidated, just as they had in the Panic of 1907. In 1931, one generation after James Douglas first gazed into the Mexican cornucopia, Phelps Dodge shut its doors in Nacozari and Pilares, withdrawing to Arizona for what many assumed to be the last time. Hundreds headed for the border, and thousands traveled south "to primitive villages where either they or their ancestors had lived," one refugee recalled. Wagons with furniture, firewood, corrugated iron, and windows and doors scavenged from company homes rattled over the hills, deserting the ghosts of one frontier for the shadowy dreams of the next.[10]

These multiple retreats—the corporate retreat to the United States, the retreat of workers to the countryside—reflected a larger expulsion of border workers from the wage economy in the 1930s. In villages such as Huépac, sons of farmers drifted home from the mines to become farmers once again. But the decline of capitalist markets—much like their rise—was uneven, owing as much to local conditions as to global trends. Initially, things looked just as grim in Cananea: by the 1920s, ore reserves were "dwindling rapidly and the end of operations was almost in sight," recalled the son of a corporate manager. But then something unexpected happened. In 1926, workers stumbled across a body of high-grade ore that had eluded discovery for years: it turned out to be one of the richest ore bodies on the continent. It paid dividends into the 1940s, leading the CCCC down a very different path. As miners left Nacozari and Pilares, Cananea found a second wind, sustaining corporate ties across the border until the 1970s.[11]

These two journeys help remind us that neither nations nor transnational capi-

tal, by themselves, can fully contain or explain the past. Local conditions matter as much as state and corporate power in shaping borderlands history. And
yet we should not fully discount larger turning points, for even though transnational linkages endured, the way people made sense of these connections was
changing in profound ways. For some, the watershed was the Mexican Revolution, when new specters of fear and exclusion had sharpened national divides.
Others imagined a return to business as usual in the 1920s, but borders became
increasingly hard to ignore. In 1924, the U.S. border patrol replaced earlier military patrols, and efforts to "repatriate" Mexicans in the early 1930s revived on a
national scale the xenophobia witnessed in Bisbee in 1917. The deportation of
Chinese from Sonora in 1931 reinforced these bordered lands, where efforts to
fix national space dovetailed with new desires to "purify" the body politic.[12]

The 1930s were also a turning point in another way, for during this decade
Mexicans and Americans began to rethink history in the borderlands. The U.S.
historian Herbert Eugene Bolton brought the field of Spanish Borderlands history to the center of the U.S. imagination at this time, piggybacking on New
Deal programs that sought to reinvigorate the nation by integrating alternative
cultural traditions into the mainstream of American identity. Bolton and New
Deal planners celebrated Hispanic traditions but paid scant attention to cultural
ties between the United States and Mexico after 1821. Borderlands history, in
this context, became a romantic precursor to an east-to-west master narrative in
which the United States replaced Mexico and relegated its history to the margins. Transnational tales of frontier progress and modernization, central to the
borderlands at the turn of the century, were eventually lost in the shadows and
forgotten.[13]

Memory also faded in Mexico in the 1930s as government elites set out to
rewrite Mexican history. In the 1920s, artists such as Diego Rivera had celebrated the revolution as a national movement that sought to overturn the excesses of the Porfirian epoch, and by the 1930s, political leaders and national text-
books were disseminating a new vision of Mexican history, one in which Mexico
moved from the dark ages of the Porfiriato into the light of the postrevolutionary era. Like their New Deal counterparts in the United States, government
agents combed the countryside for folk traditions to reinvigorate national identity. They recorded Indian and mestizo folktales, transcribed *corridos* and plays,
and turned rural revolutionaries such as Emiliano Zapata into national heroes.
Thus, as Sonora's political elite moved to the nation's center, so too did the nation's histories, crafted around a new cultural core of mestizo roots, a shared
revolutionary inheritance, and stories of progress that faced inward, obscuring
connections to the outside world.[14]

This erasure of the borderlands from historical memory has endured, despite the rise of border crossings in the late twentieth and early twenty-first centuries. And in the copper borderlands, other shifts have reinforced this historical myopia. In the late 1940s, the CCCC began to send blister copper to refineries in Mexico City, thereby severing one of its most essential lifelines to southern Arizona. A decade later, Mexico initiated a new process of nationalization in northeastern Sonora, starting with the expropriation of the Greene family's vast ranchlands in 1958 and concluding with the Mexican government's takeover of the CCCC in 1971. If half of the copper borderlands thus gradually detached itself from the regional web of transnational connections, the other half simply vanished. In 1975, Phelps Dodge shut down its mines at Bisbee, turning this industrial outpost into a ghost town. When it closed its Douglas smelter a decade later, the blank spaces on the map grew: this former crossroads now felt more remote than ever.

This feeling of isolation and distance permeates the copper borderlands today. It is hard to imagine the social tissue that once knit Cananea and Bisbee together. Cananea remains an industrial city, controlled by one of the most powerful companies in Mexico and sustained by legions of sweating, toiling Mexicans. Bisbee, by contrast, is a quintessential "western" ghost town, where mostly white tourists from all across the United States come to play. Some will buy Native American or western paraphernalia in gift shops before driving north to watch Wyatt Earp fight "cow-boys" in the streets of nearby Tombstone. Few will take the old highway south to Cananea, and fewer still will guess that Mexico still lives on in Bisbee. Merchants gave me dull stares when I asked about Zacatecas Canyon, but two Mexican-Americans in a brown Buick at the end of Brewery Gulch, where my map ended, didn't. They told me to hop in, handed me a beer, and drove me through their childhood home, a long-forgotten shadow of Arizona's favorite ghost town.

Other fugitive landscapes persist here as well. As in decades past, the San Pedro River remains a transportation corridor for those seeking less visible border crossings at the periphery of the state's vision. In recent years, this former high road for Tombstone prospectors, Apache raiders, and Chinese smugglers has become one of the most heavily traveled routes for undocumented workers seeking access to the United States. And if empty water bottles, cut fences, and footprints fuel concerns of border invasions to rival those of the Mexican Revolution era, "volunteer" groups such as Ranch Rescue, American Border Patrol, and the Minuteman Project evoke familiar specters of American posses and "cow-boy" justice. Whether one sees this unsettled land from north or south, what is most apparent is its uncanny persistence, its failure to submit to dreams of order, domestication, and civility after all these years.

Above all else, these enduring terrains reflect what is most easily forgotten about the borderlands. In the wake of NAFTA and 9/11, we often see the border-lands in terms of competing models of authority and power. Some imagine a new world order led by transnational markets, corporations, and cultures, beyond the national pale, while others see a future of border patrols and increased homeland security, where nations and states matter more than ever. In the borderlands, history moves us beyond such dichotomies, for here market and state operated in tandem for years, tacking back and forth between national and transnational co-ordinates. Even more important, it reveals the persisting failures of market and state actors, for neither controlled their worlds as expected. Their tangled tales remind us to look beyond abstract forces, to keep our eyes on the quotidian and the local. For often it is the smallest things—the fugitive shadows at the edges of our historical vision—that haunt us most deeply in the end.

NOTES

PROLOGUE. HIDDEN HISTORIES

1. Walter S. Logan and Matías Romero, *A Mexican Night: The Toasts and Responses at a Complimentary Dinner Given by Walter S. Logan, at the Democratic Club, New York City, December 16th, 1891, to Señor Don Matías Romero, Mexican Minister to the United States* (New York: Albert B. King, 1892); Matías Romero, *Artículos sobre México publicados en los Estados Unidos de América por Matías Romero en 1891–1892* (México: Oficina Impresora de Estampillas, 1892), 180–203; and Walter S. Logan and John Nichol Irwin, *Arizona and Some of Her Friends: The Toasts and Responses at a Complimentary Dinner Given by Walter S. Logan, at the Marine and Field Club, Bath Beach, N.Y., Tuesday, July 28th, 1891, to Hon. John N. Irwin, Governor of Arizona, and Herbert H. Logan, of Phoenix, Arizona* (New York: Albert King, 1891). For Logan, see New York Bar Association, *Proceedings of the Thirtieth Annual Meeting* (Albany: Argus, 1907), 344–48; and Lewis Wilder Hicks, comp., *The Biographical Record of the Class of 1870, Yale College, 1870–1911* (Boston: Thomas Todd, 1912), 159–63.

2. Walter S. Logan, "The Nation-Maker," in *A Mexican Night*, 13; Frederick J. Turner, "The Significance of the Frontier in American History," in *Annual Report of the American Historical Association for the Year 1893* (Washington: GPO, 1894), 199–227; and Ray Allen Billington, *The Genesis of the Frontier Thesis: A Study in Historical Creativity* (San Marino, Calif.: Huntington Library, 1971), 147–77. For Turner and Buffalo Bill, see Richard White, "Frederick Jackson Turner and Buffalo Bill," in *The Frontier in American Culture: An Exhibition at the Newberry Library, August 26, 1994–January 7, 1995*, ed. James R. Grossman (Chicago: Newberry Library; Berkeley: University of California Press, 1994), 7–65.

3. Romero, *Artículos*, 181–83.

4. Matías Romero, "The Future of Mexico and Its Relations with the United States," in *A Mexican Night*, 17, and Matías Romero, *Mexico and the United States: A Study of Subjects Affecting their Political, Commercial, and Social Relations, Made with a View to their Promotion* (New York: G. P. Putnam, 1898), ix. For Romero's career,

see Thomas Schoonover, "Dollars over Dominion: United States Economic Interests in Mexico, 1861–1867," *Pacific Historical Review* 45 (February 1976), 23–45; and David M. Pletcher, "Mexico Opens the Door to American Capital, 1877–1880," *The Americas* 16 (July 1959), 1–14. For ideas of progress in the age of Díaz, see Charles A. Hale, *The Transformation of Liberalism in Late Nineteenth-Century Mexico* (Princeton: Princeton University Press, 1989).

5. For Logan's borderland enterprises, see Walter S. Logan, *Mining for Profit* (New York: W. S. Logan, 1891); Walter S. Logan, *Irrigation for Profit* (New York: Albert B. King, n.d.); and Walter S. Logan, *Yaqui: The Land of Sunshine and Health; What I Saw in Mexico* (New York: Albert B. King, 1894). See William Cronon, *Nature's Metropolis: Chicago and the Great West* (New York: W. W. Norton, 1991), 36, for the doctrine of natural advantages.

6. Anthony DePalma, *Here: A Biography of the New American Continent* (New York: PublicAffairs, 2001), 7.

7. Susan Zakin, "The Hunters and the Hunted: The Arizona–Mexico Border Turns into the 21st Century Frontier," *High Country News*, October 9, 2000.

8. D. W. Meinig, *The Shaping of America: A Geographical Perspective on Five Hundred Years of History*, vol. 3, *Transcontinental America, 1850–1915* (New Haven: Yale University Press, 1998), 152–57.

9. Here I build on the lessons of James C. Scott's seminal study of states and power, *Seeing Like a State: How Certain Schemes to Improve the Human Condition Have Failed* (New Haven: Yale University Press, 1998), but this is also a central insight of environmental history. See, for instance, Richard White, *The Organic Machine: The Remaking of the Columbia River* (New York: Hill and Wang, 1995).

10. For more in-depth discussion of these multiple historiographical strands, see Samuel Truett and Elliott Young, "Making Transnational History: Nations, Regions, and Borderlands," in *Continental Crossroads: Remapping U.S.–Mexico Borderlands History*, ed. Samuel Truett and Elliott Young (Durham: Duke University Press, 2004), 1–32.

11. Michiel Baud and Willem Van Schendel, "Toward a Comparative History of Borderlands," *Journal of World History* 8 (Fall 1997), 211–42.

1. GHOSTS OF EMPIRES PAST

1. For Bartlett's journey, see John Russell Bartlett, *Personal Narrative of Explorations and Incidents in Texas, New Mexico, California, Sonora, and Chihuahua*, 2 vols. (New York: D. Appleton, 1854); but also see Robert V. Hine, *Bartlett's West: Drawing the Mexican Boundary* (New Haven: Yale University Press, 1968).

2. Bartlett, *Personal Narrative*, 1:35, 138, 248, 2:562–63, 1:247.

3. Ibid., 1:25–28, 41–43, 44–45.

4. Ibid., 1:255–56, 383, 397.

5. Ibid., 1:273, 282–83, 414.

6. William H. Emory, *Report on the United States and Mexican Boundary Survey: Made Under the Direction of the Secretary of the Interior*, 2 vols. (Washington: A.O.P. Nichol-

son, 1857–59), vol. 1, part 1, 94–95; and T. Robinson Warren, *Dust and Foam, or Three Oceans and Two Continents* (New York: Charles Scribner, 1859), 216–17.

7. Bartlett, *Personal Narrative*, 2:10.

8. Rolena Adorno and Patrick Charles Pautz, *Álvar Núñez Cabeza de Vaca: His Account, His Life, and the Expedition of Pánfilo de Narváez* (Lincoln: University of Nebraska Press, 1999), 3:341–59, 370–72.

9. Ibid., 1:245, 2:359–60.

10. Ibid., 1:139–41, 229–31.

11. Ibid., 1:231.

12. Herbert Eugene Bolton, *Coronado on the Turquoise Trail: Knight of Pueblos and Plains* (Albuquerque: University of New Mexico Press, 1949); and George P. Hammond and Agapito Rey, eds., *Narratives of the Coronado Expedition, 1540–1542* (Albuquerque: University of New Mexico Press, 1940).

13. For Zacatecas and the expansion of mining, see Peter J. Bakewell, *Silver Mining and Society in Colonial Mexico: Zacatecas, 1546–1700* (Cambridge: Cambridge University Press, 1971); and Oakah L. Jones, Jr., *Nueva Vizcaya: Heartland of the Spanish Frontier* (Albuquerque: University of New Mexico Press, 1988).

14. Bakewell, *Silver Mining*, 27–29; and J. Lloyd Mecham, *Francisco de Ibarra and Nueva Vizcaya* (Durham: Duke University Press, 1927). For Ibarra in Sonora, see George P. Hammond and Agapito Rey, eds., *Obregón's History of Sixteenth Century Explorations in Western America* (Los Angeles: Wetzel, 1928). Quotes are from page 161.

15. See, for example, in Robert C. West, *The Mining Community in Northern New Spain: The Parral Mining District*, Ibero-Americana 30 (Berkeley: University of California Press, 1949).

16. For the colonization of Sonora, see Cynthia Radding, *Wandering Peoples: Colonialism, Ethnic Spaces, and Ecological Frontiers in Northwestern Mexico, 1700–1850* (Durham: Duke University Press, 1997); Robert C. West, *Sonora: Its Geographical Personality* (Austin: University of Texas Press, 1993); Peter Gerhard, *The North Frontier of New Spain*, rev. ed. (Norman: University of Oklahoma Press, 1993), 276–77, 281–83; and Oakah L. Jones, Jr., *Los Paisanos: Spanish Settlers on the Northern Frontier of New Spain* (Norman: University of Oklahoma Press, 1979), 177–95. For the Jesuit entrada, also see John Francis Bannon, *The Mission Frontier in Sonora, 1620–1687* (New York: United States Catholic Historical Society, 1955). For native communities, see Edward H. Spicer, *Cycles of Conquest: The Impact of Spain, Mexico, and the United States on the Indians of the Southwest, 1533–1960* (Tucson: University of Arizona Press, 1962).

17. Bernard L. Fontana, "Pima and Papago: Introduction" and "History of the Papago," and Paul H. Ezell, "History of the Pima," in *Handbook of North American Indians*, ed. William C. Sturtevant, vol. 10, *Southwest*, ed., Alfonso Ortiz (Washington: Smithsonian Institution Press, 1983), 125–60; and Spicer, *Cycles*, 118–28.

18. Juan Matheo Mange, *Luz de tierra incógnita en la América septentrional y diario de las exploraciones en Sonora*, Publicaciones del Archivo General de la Nación (Mexico City: Talleres Gráficos de la Nación, 1926), 10:339–41; West, *Sonora*, 45–46, 83–90; West, *Parral Mining District*, 47–52; and Susan M. Deeds, *Defiance and Deference*

in Mexico's Colonial North: Indians under Spanish Rule in Nueva Vizcaya (Austin: University of Texas Press, 2003), 61. Parral is in southern Chihuahua, near the Durango border.

19. Thomas H. Naylor and Charles W. Polzer, eds., *The Presidio and Militia on the Northern Frontier of New Spain: A Documentary History*, vol. 1, *1570–1700* (Tucson: University of Arizona Press, 1986), 16–21; and Max L. Moorhead, *The Presidio: Bastion of the Spanish Borderlands* (Norman: University of Oklahoma Press, 1975).

20. Bolton, *Coronado*, 317–25; Hammond and Rey, *Obregón's History*, 162–74.

21. Hammond and Rey, *Obregón's History*, 173–74, 205–08; and Juan Nentvig, *Rudo Ensayo: A Description of Sonora and Arizona in 1764*, trans. Alberto Francisco Pradeau and Robert R. Rasmussen (Tucson: University of Arizona Press, 1980), 125.

22. For Casas Grandes and Sonora, see Curtis F. Schaafsma and Carroll L. Riley, eds., *The Casas Grandes World* (Salt Lake City: University of Utah Press, 1999). Edward Spicer treats early Opata migrations in *Cycles*, 86–87. The archaeologist Richard A. Pailes thinks remains of larger sixteenth-century settlements may be under the plazas of present-day towns, evading scrutiny. Richard A. Pailes, "An Archaeological Perspective on the Sonoran Entrada," in *The Coronado Expedition to Tierra Nueva: The 1540–1542 Route Across the Southwest*, ed. Richard Flint and Shirley Cushing Flint (Niwot: University Press of Colorado, 1997), 180–89.

23. For disease in Sonora, see Daniel T. Reff, *Disease, Depopulation, and Culture Change in Northwestern New Spain, 1518–1764* (Salt Lake City: University of Utah Press, 1991), 132–225.

24. Radding, *Wandering Peoples*, esp. 47–65, 142–50; for place-names, see Nentvig, *Rudo Ensayo*, 94–95; and Ignaz Pfefferkorn, *Sonora: A Description of the Province*, ed. Theodore E. Treutlein (Albuquerque: University of Arizona Press, 1949), 236–38.

25. Philipp Segesser, "The Relation of Philipp Segesser," ed. Theodore Treutlein, *Mid-America* 27 (July 1945), 144, 149, 160, 161; Pfefferkorn, *Sonora*, 273–75; Radding, *Wandering Peoples*, 66–99; and Theodore E. Treutlein, "The Economic Regime of the Jesuit Missions in Eighteenth Century Sonora," *Pacific Historical Review* 8 (1939), 289–300.

26. Pfefferkorn, *Sonora*, 205; and Nentvig, *Rudo Ensayo*, 69, for Indian farming practices. For the incorporation of domestic animals, see Nentvig, *Rudo Ensayo*, 56; Pfefferkorn, *Sonora*, 98; Segesser, "Relation," 151; and West, *Sonora*, 38.

27. Segesser, "Relation," 179, 181; and Joseph Och, *Missionary in Sonora: The Travel Reports of Joseph Och, S.J., 1755–1767*, ed. and trans. Theodore E. Treutlein (San Francisco: California Historical Society, 1965), 170.

28. Pfefferkorn, *Sonora*, 175, 96–97, 174, 241–42.

29. Ibid., 273, 43–44.

30. Ibid., 272, 46; and Segesser, "Relation," 149.

31. Pfefferkorn, *Sonora*, 288.

32. For incorporation of native foodways, see Pfefferkorn, *Sonora*, 46–59, 70–78; Nentvig, *Rudo Ensayo*, 36–43; and Segesser, "Relation," 179–82; for native medicinal plants, see Pfefferkorn, *Sonora*, 60–69; Segesser, "Relation," 179–82; Och, *Mission-*

ary, 170–75; and Nentvig, *Rudo Ensayo*, 43–53. Quote is from Nentvig, *Rudo Ensayo*, 43–44.

33. West, *Parral Mining District*, 2–13, 39–76; Gerhard, *Northern Frontier*, 244–77, 285; West, *Sonora*, 46–48, 51–59; Radding, *Wandering Peoples*, 66–99; and Ana María Atondo Rodríguez and Martha Ortega Soto, "Entrada de colonos españoles en Sonora durante el siglo XVII," and Martha Ortega Soto, "La colonización española en la primera mitad del siglo XVIII," in *Tres siglos de historia sonorense (1530–1830)*, coord. Sergio Ortega Noriega and Ignacio del Río (Mexico City: Universidad Nacional Autónoma de México, 1993), 97–136, 189–245.

34. Pfefferkorn, *Sonora*, 100; West, *Sonora*, 51; and West, *Parral Mining District*, 41, 23, 39–42.

35. West, *Sonora*, 51, 55–56; West, *Parral Mining District*, 79–81; Michael M. Swann, "Migration, Mobility, and the Mining Towns of Colonial Northern Mexico," in *Migration in Colonial Spanish America*, ed. David J. Robinson (Cambridge: Cambridge University Press, 1990), 143–81; and *Statement of Don Juan A. Robinson*, Bancroft Library, Mexican Manuscript 375, 1–4.

36. Och, *Missionary*, 147, 149; Segesser, "Relation," 185; and Pfefferkorn, *Sonora*, 42.

37. Segesser, "Relation," 184–85; Nentvig, *Rudo Ensayo*, 118; and Pfefferkorn, *Sonora*, 91–92. For *vagabundaje* (mobility) among miners, see Patricia Escandón, "Economía y sociedad en Sonora, 1767–1821," in *Tres siglos*, 365–69; and Peter Stern and Robert Jackson, "*Vagabundaje* and Settlement Patterns in Colonial Northern Sonora," *The Americas* 44 (April 1988), 461–81. For a broader discussion of mobility, see Radding, *Wandering Peoples*.

38. For Apaches and rising Apache–Spanish hostilities, see Donald E. Worcester, "The Beginnings of the Apache Menace of the Southwest," *New Mexico Historical Review* 16 (January 1941), 1–14; and Spicer, *Cycles*, 229–44. Historians have yet to write a history of Apaches in colonial Sonora, but see William B. Griffen, *Apaches at War and Peace: The Janos Presidio, 1750–1858* (Albuquerque: University of New Mexico Press, 1988). For the late colonial and early national era, see Edwin R. Sweeney, *Mangas Coloradas: Chief of the Chiricahua Apaches* (Norman: University of Oklahoma Press, 1998).

39. Letter of February 6, 1683, from Don Pedro García de Almazán, Don Juan de Escalante, Pedro de Peralta, Joseph Romo de Vivar, and Francisco de Mendoza to the Viceroy, in Charles Wilson Hackett, ed., *Historical Documents Relating to New Mexico, Nueva Vizcaya, and Approaches Thereto, to 1773*, 3 vols. (Washington: Carnegie Institution of Washington, 1923–37), 2:291–97; Nentvig, *Rudo Ensayo*, 90, 94–95, 135; and report of August 13, 1735, of Juan Bautista de Anza, in Polzer and Sheridan, *Presidio and Militia*, 306–07.

40. Pfefferkorn, *Sonora*, 290, 94–96; and West, *Sonora*, 58–59.

41. Segesser, "Relation," 186–87, 157; and Pfefferkorn, *Sonora*, 101, 97.

42. Pfefferkorn, *Sonora*, 97, 44–45.

43. Charles W. Polzer and Thomas E. Sheridan, eds., *The Presidio and the Militia on the Northern Frontier of New Spain: A Documentary History*, vol. 2, part 1, *The Californias*

and Sinaloa–Sonora, 1700–1765 (Tucson: University of Arizona Press, 1997), 254–55; Jones, *Los Paisanos*, 178; Moorhead, *The Presidio*, 19–26; and "Petition by the Settlers of Nacozari, 1718," in Polzer and Sheridan, *Californias and Sinaloa–Sonora*, 278–81.

44. Moorhead, *Presidio*, 48–110; David J. Weber, *The Spanish Frontier in North America* (New Haven: Yale University Press, 1992), 204–35; James E. Officer, *Hispanic Arizona, 1536–1856* (Tucson: University of Arizona Press, 1987), 53–96; Radding, *Wandering Peoples*, 171–263; and Ignacio del Río, "El noroeste novohispano y la nueva política imperial española," and Edgardo López Mañón and Ignacio del Río, "La reforma institucional borbónica," in *Tres siglos*, 249–86, 289–325. In 1835, Ignacio Zúñiga reported at least fifty *rancherías de paz* between Janos and Tucson, all of which helped fight against "wild" Apaches. Ignacio Zúñiga, *Rapida ojeada al estado de Sonora, dirigida y dedicada al supremo gobierno de la nación* (Mexico City: Juan Ojedo, 1835), 14. Ironically, as administrators set out to fix space they unsettled it even more by constantly moving presidios to create whatever line they deemed appropriate for the time. This was true for Tubac, Fronteras, and Terrenate.

45. Zúñiga, *Rapida ojeada*, 14–15; Ray H. Mattison, "Early Spanish and Mexican Settlements in Arizona," *New Mexico Historical Review* 21 (October 1946), 285–86; and Cynthia Radding, "Las reformas borbónicas en la Provincia de Sonora: El régimen de propiedad en la sociedad colonial," *Noroeste de México* 10 (1991), 51–57. For frontier family networks, see Officer, *Hispanic Arizona*, 40–42; Armando Elías Chomina, *Compendio de datos históricos de la familia Elías* (Hermosillo, 1986); and Héctor Alfredo Pesqueira P., *Parentescos Extendidos de Sonora S.A.* (Morelia: H. A. Pesqueira P., 1998).

46. For frontier elites, see Officer, *Hispanic Arizona*, and Stuart Voss, *On the Periphery of Nineteenth-Century Mexico: Sonora and Sinaloa, 1810–1877* (Tucson: University of Arizona Press, 1982); for the Elías family, see Elías Chomina, *Compendio*. For Bourbon visions and frontier identities, also see Daniel Nugent, *Spent Cartridges of Revolution: An Anthropological History of Namiquipa, Chihuahua* (Chicago: University of Chicago Press, 1993), 39–56.

47. *Exposición hecha al supremo gobierno de la unión por los representantes de los estados de Chihuahua, Sonora, Durango, y Territorio del Nuevo-Mejico, con motivo de los desastres que sufren por la guerra de los bárbaros* (Mexico City: Imprenta de Galvan, á cargo de Mariano Arévalo, 1832), 1–2. Also see Edwin R. Sweeney, *Cochise: Chiricahua Apache Chief* (Norman: University of Oklahoma Press, 1991), 15–98; and Sweeney, *Mangas Coloradas*, 37–158.

48. For battles in Sonora, see Voss, *Periphery*, 33–120; for a regional view, see David J. Weber, *The Mexican Frontier, 1821–1846: The American Southwest Under Mexico* (Albuquerque: University of New Mexico Press, 1982); and Andrés Reséndez, *Changing National Identities at the Frontier: Texas and New Mexico, 1800–1850* (Cambridge: Cambridge University Press, 2005).

49. José de Aguilar, Gobernador de Sonora, *Memoria en que el gobierno del estado libre de Sonora, da cuenta de los ramos de su administración al congreso del mismo estado, con arreglo a lo dispuesto en el artículo 27 de La Constitución* (Ures: Imprenta del Go-

bierno del Estado, a cargo de Jesús P. Siquieros, 1850), 4, 6–7, and appendix 2 for abandoned communities. For Aguilar, see Francisco R. Almada, *Diccionario de historia, geografía, y biografía sonorenses*, 3d ed. (Hermosillo: Instituto Sonorense de Cultura, 1990), 13–15. For Apache–Mexican tensions in the 1850s, see José Francisco Velasco, *Noticias estadísticas del estado de Sonora* (Mexico City: Imprenta de Ignacio Cumplido, 1850).

50. Bartlett, *Personal Narrative*, 1:398–401.

51. Ibid., 1:268–70. Regulations for dress were laid out in royal regulations of 1772; see Sidney B. Brinckerhoff and Odie B. Faulk, trans. and eds., *Lancers for the King: A Study of the Frontier Military System of Northern New Spain, With a Translation of the Royal Regulations of 1772* (Phoenix: Arizona Historical Foundation, 1965), 19–21; and Weber, *Spanish Frontier*, 217.

52. Walter Howe, *The Mining Guild of New Spain and Its Tribunal General, 1770–1821* (Cambridge: Harvard University Press, 1949); José Luis Peset, "The Reception of Modern Scientific Mining in an Enlightened Mexico," in *In Quest of Mineral Wealth: Aboriginal and Colonial Mining and Metallurgy in Spanish America*, vol. 33, *Geoscience and Man*, ed. Alan K. Craig and Robert C. West (Baton Rouge: Geoscience Publications, 1994), 233–51; and Alexander von Humboldt, *Political Essay on the Kingdom of New Spain*, trans. John Black (London: Longman, Hurst, Rees, Orme, and Brown, 1811), esp. 3:118–19, 151–52, 323–25. The most enduring aspect of these mining reforms was the royal ordinances for mining, first published in 1783. See *Reales ordenanzas para la dirección régimen y gobierno del importante cuerpo de la minería de Nueva-España, y de su Real Tribunal General* (Madrid: Ibarra, 1783).

53. Cincinnati and Sonora Mining Association, *Geological Report and Map of the San Juan del Rio Ranche, in Sonora, Mexico* (Cincinnati: Wrightson, 1866), 15, 23; and Sylvester Mowry, *Arizona and Sonora: The Geography, History, and Resources of the Silver Region of North America*, 3d ed. (New York: Harper and Brothers, 1864), 126–27, 131. For liberal attempts to revive Bourbon mining reforms, see Charles A. Hale, *Mexican Liberalism in the Age of Mora, 1821–1853* (New Haven: Yale University Press, 1968), 267–71.

54. John Denton Hall, *Travels and Adventures in Sonora; Containing a Description of Its Mining and Agricultural Resources and Narrative of a Residence of Fifteen Years* (Chicago: J. M. W. Jones, 1881), 44–45.

55. *Reales ordenanzas*, 95.

56. Cincinnati and Sonora Mining Association, *Geological Report*, 31; but also see Mowry, *Arizona and Sonora*, 129–30; Cincinnati and Sonora Mining Association, *Geological Report*, 24, 26, 29, 38; and Hall, *Travels and Adventures*, 157, 160, 172.

2. BORDERLAND DREAMS

1. Douglas Botting, *Humboldt and the Cosmos* (New York: Harper and Row, 1973), 22–65; Mary Louise Pratt, *Imperial Eyes: Travel Writing and Transculturation* (London: Routledge, 1992); 111–20; Mary Maples Dunn, "Introduction," in Alexander von

Humboldt, *Political Essay on the Kingdom of New Spain,* abridged edition (1972; reprint, Norman: University of Oklahoma Press, 1988), 4–13; and Robert Fischer, "Humboldt in New Spain," *Américas* 26 (February 1974), 25–31.

2. Alexander von Humboldt, *Political Essay on the Kingdom of New Spain,* trans. John Black (London: Longman, Hurst, Rees, Orme, and Brown, 1811), 1:ii–ix.

3. J. Fred Rippy, "Latin America and the British Investment 'Boom' of the 1820s," *Journal of Modern History* 19 (March–December 1947), 122–29; Robert W. Randall, *Real del Monte: A British Mining Venture in Mexico* (Austin: University of Texas Press, 1972); and N. Ray Gilmore, "Henry George Ward, British Publicist for Mexican Mines," *Pacific Historical Review* 32 (February 1963), 35–47.

4. For Guaymas and the Pacific, see Stuart Voss, *On the Periphery of Nineteenth-Century Mexico: Sonora and Sinaloa, 1810–1877* (Tucson: University of Arizona Press, 1982); and Gregorio Mora Torres, "Los comerciantes de Guaymas y el desarrollo económico de Sonora, 1825–1910," in *Memoria: VII Simposio de historia de Sonora* (Hermosillo: Instituto de Investigaciones Históricas, 1984), 213–16. For Sonora and the Santa Fe trade, see Lieutenant R. W. H. Hardy, *Travels in the Interior of Mexico, in 1825, 1826, 1827, and 1828* (London: Henry Colburn and Richard Bentley, 1829), 458–59.

5. Simon Bourne, "Notes on the State of Sonora and Cinaloa," in Henry G. Ward, *Mexico in 1827,* 2 vols. (London: Henry Colburn, 1828), 1:559, 563, 568.

6. Hardy, *Travels,* 95–96; and Bourne, "Notes," 1:575.

7. Bourne, "Notes," 1:577.

8. My copy of Ward's *Mexico in 1827* was marked up in this fashion. Since I borrowed the volume from the Stanford University library, it is likely that these are the jottings of a turn-of-the-century mining engineer who later donated books (and perhaps funds) to Leland Stanford Junior College.

9. For renewed Apache raids, see Edwin R. Sweeney, *Mangas Coloradas: Chief of the Chiricahua Apaches* (Norman: University of Oklahoma Press, 1998), 39–43. New peace treaties and subsidies temporarily improved relations but fell apart by 1831. For the British in Mexican trade, see Hilarie J. Heath, "British Merchant Houses in Mexico, 1821–1860: Conforming Business Practices and Ethics," *Hispanic American Historical Review* 73 (May 1993), 261–90.

10. Juan M. Riesgo y Antonio J. Valdez, *Memoria estadística del estado de Occidente* (Guadalajara: C. E. Alatorre, 1828), 34–37; and Ignacio Zúñiga, *Rapida ojeada al estado de Sonora, dirigida y dedicada al supremo gobierno de la nación* (Mexico City: Juan Ojedo, 1835), 16–18. Also see Mora Torres, "Los comerciantes," for discussion of these visions. For a broader Pacific coast context, see Edgar O. Gutiérrez, "Comerciantes marítimos del noroeste de México, 1810–1835," *Siglo XIX* 13 (September–December 1995), 49–62.

11. See Max L. Moorhead, *New Mexico's Royal Road: Trade and Travel on the Chihuahua Trail* (Norman: University of Oklahoma Press, 1958) for the Santa Fe trade. For general networks between Mexico and the U.S., see also David J. Weber, *The Mexican Frontier, 1821–1846: The American Southwest Under Mexico* (Albuquerque: University of New Mexico Press, 1982); and Andrés Reséndez, *Changing National Identities at the Frontier: Texas and New Mexico, 1800–1850* (Cambridge: Cambridge University

Press, 2005). For Robinson, see *Statement of Don Juan A. Robinson*, Bancroft Library, Mexican Manuscript 375, 1–4.

12. Ralph Adam Smith, *Borderlander: The Life of James Kirker, 1793–1852* (Norman: University of Oklahoma Press, 1999); Rex W. Strickland, "Robert McKnight," in LeRoy R. Hafen, ed., *The Mountain Men and the Fur Trade of the Far West* (Glendale, Calif.: Arthur H. Clark, 1965–72), 9:260–66; Rex W. Strickland, "The Birth and Death of a Legend: The Johnson 'Massacre' of 1837," *Arizona and the West* 18 (Autumn 1976), 268–69; and Sweeney, *Mangas Coloradas*, 44–87.

13. Philip St. George Cooke, *The Conquest of New Mexico and California* (Oakland: Biobooks, 1952), 66–90; Forbes Parkhill, "Antoine Leroux," in Hafen, ed., *Mountain Men* 4:175–77; and William Cochran McGaw, *Savage Scene: The Life and Times of James Kirker, Frontier King* (New York: Hastings House, 1972), 97–104. For Apache testimony, see William H. Emory, *Lieutenant Emory Reports: A Reprint of Lieutenant W. H. Emory's Notes of a Military Reconnaissance*, ed. Ross Calvin (Albuquerque: University of New Mexico Press, 1951), 100.

14. Odie B. Faulk, *Destiny Road: The Gila Trail and the Opening of the Southwest* (New York: Oxford University Press, 1973); Patricia A. Etter, *To California on the Southern Route, 1849: A History and Annotated Bibliography* (Spokane: Arthur H. Clark, 1998); James E. Officer, *Hispanic Arizona, 1536–1856* (Tucson: University of Arizona Press, 1987), 218–44; and James E. Officer, "Yanqui Forty-Niners in Hispanic Arizona: Interethnic Relations on the Sonoran Frontier," *Journal of Arizona History* 28 (Summer 1987), 101–34.

15. Sonora Exploring and Mining Company, *First Annual Report of the Sonora Exploring and Mining Company, Made to the Stockholders, March 16, 1857* (Cincinnati: Railroad Record Print, 1857), 1.

16. Transcript from Poston journal in J. Ross Browne, *Adventures in the Apache Country: A Tour Through Arizona and Sonora* (New York: Harper and Brothers, 1869), 237–38. For Ehrenberg, see introduction in Diane M. T. North, ed., *Samuel Peter Heintzelman and the Sonora Exploring and Mining Company* (Tucson: University of Arizona Press, 1980), 20; and *Arizona Weekly Star*, February 26, 1880.

17. Charles D. Poston, *Building a State in Apache Land: The Story of Arizona's Founding Told by Arizona's Founder*, ed. John Myers Myers (Tempe: Aztec Press, 1963), 41–46. By "Arizunea," Poston was referring to Arizonac, the location of a famous discovery in 1736 of chunks of silver near Nogales, Sonora. Francisco R. Almada, *Diccionario de historia, geografía, y biografía sonorenses*, 3d ed. (Hermosillo: Instituto Sonorense de Cultura, 1990), 65–67.

18. Browne, *Apache Country*, 238–52. For the Texas Western Railroad Company survey, see Andrew B. Gray, *Southern Pacific Railroad: Survey of a Route for the Southern Pacific R.R. on the 32nd Parallel, by A.B. Gray, for the Texas Western R.R. Company* (Cincinnati: Railroad Record Print, 1856), 81.

19. Byrd Howell Granger, "Southwest Chronicle: The Journal of Charles D. Poston, 1850–1899," parts 1–3, *Arizona Quarterly* 13 (1957), 254–55; Poston, *Building A State*, 61–64; Thomas Butler King, *First Annual Report to the Board of Directors of the Southern Pacific Railroad Company* (New York: American Railroad Journal Office,

1856), 3; Sonora Exploring and Mining Company, *Sonora and the Value of its Silver Mines. Report of the Sonora Exploring and Mining Co., Made to the Stockholders. December 1856* (Cincinnati: Railroad Record Print, 1856), 5; Sonora Exploring and Mining Company, *First Annual Report,* 1; Sonora Exploring and Mining Company, *Possessions and Prospects of the Sonora Silver Mining Co. Report of the Sonora Exploring & Mining Co., Made to the Stockholders, September 1857* (Cincinnati: Railroad Record Print, 1857), 305; and North, ed., *Heintzelman,* 14–15, 21–22. Apart from Walker, another common denominator between the Sonora Exploring and Mining Company and the Texas Western Railroad was the Cincinnati capitalist Edgar Conkling, who helped organize the former company and was agent for both companies. Gerald E. Thompson, ed., "Railroads and Mines in Arizona: The Cram Memoir of 1858," *Arizona and the West* 10:4 (Winter 1968), 364.

20. Poston, *Building a State,* 64–71; and Sonora Exploring and Mining Company, *First Annual Report,* 1.

21. Henry F. Dobyns, *Tubac Through Four Centuries: An Historical Resume and Analysis* (Phoenix: Arizona State Parks Board, 1959), 170–410; Officer, *Hispanic Arizona,* 36–50; and Diana Hadley and Thomas E. Sheridan, *Land Use History of the San Rafael Valley, Arizona (1540–1960)* (Fort Collins, Colo.: U.S. Department of Agriculture, U.S. Forest Service, Rocky Mountain Forest and Range Experiment Station, 1995), 18–21.

22. Dobyns, *Tubac,* 410–533; Officer, *Hispanic Arizona,* 50–114; and Hadley and Sheridan, *Land Use,* 21–22.

23. Dobyns, *Tubac,* 533–643; and Officer, *Hispanic Arizona,* 134–283.

24. Poston, *Building a State,* 71–72, 83–84; Granger, ed., "Southwest Chronicle," 255; and Raphael Pumpelly, *Across America and Asia: Notes of a Five Years' Journey Around the World and of Residence in Arizona, Japan, and China* (New York: Leypoldt and Holt, 1870), 15. For the Arivaca grant, see Ray H. Mattison, "Early Spanish and Mexican Settlements in Arizona," *New Mexico Historical Review* 21 (October 1946), 306–09.

25. Poston, *Building a State,* 66–67; John Denton Hall, *Travels and Adventures in Sonora: Containing a Description of its Mining and Agricultural Resources and Narrative of a Residence of Fifteen Years* (Chicago: J. M. W. Jones, 1881), 144–45, 201; Sweeney, *Mangas Coloradas,* 331–32; and Joseph F. Park, "The Apaches in Mexican-Indian Relations, 1848–1861: A Footnote to the Gadsden Treaty," *Arizona and the West* 3 (Summer 1961), 139–41.

26. Poston, *Building a State,* 73; Bernard L. Fontana, "Calabazas of the Río Rico," *The Smoke Signal* 24 (Fall 1971), 80–84; Sonora Exploring and Mining Company, *First Annual Report,* 1; Rasey Biven, "Letter from Hermosillo," *Daily Alta California,* May 2, 1857; and John Coleman Reid, *Reid's Tramp, or a Journal of the Incidents of Ten Months Travel Through Texas, New Mexico, Arizona, Sonora, and California* (Selma: John Hardy, 1858), 194. Poston was later called the Father of Arizona and was a founder of the Arizona Pioneers' Historical Society; it is through this lens that he saw much of his earlier time in Arizona.

27. Fontana, "Calabazas," 81–82; William B. Roods to Marvin Wheat, December 30, 1856, in William B. Roods biographical file in Hayden Arizona Pioneer Biographies

Collection, Arizona Collection, Department of Archives and Manuscripts, Arizona State University Library; Hall, *Travels and Adventures*, 135–38; Mike Bell, "Felix Grundy Ake: Arizona Pioneer, 1855–1861," Felix Grundy Ake biographical file and Jefferson Ake biographical file, Hayden Arizona Pioneers Collection; Virginia Culin Roberts, *With Their Own Blood: A Saga of Southwestern Pioneers* (Fort Worth: Texas Christian University Press, 1992), 39–40; and Elias Green Pennington biographical file in Hayden Arizona Pioneers Collection.

28. Sonora Exploring and Mining Company, *First Annual Report*, 1; Sonora Exploring and Mining Company, *Second Annual Report of the Sonora Exploring and Mining Co., Made to the Stockholders, March 29, 1858* (Cincinnati: Railroad Record Print, 1858), 4–6; Sonora Exploring and Mining Company, *Possessions*, 6, 10–11; and Sonora Exploring and Mining Company, *Report of Frederick Brunckow, Geologist, Mineralogist, and Mining Engineer, to a Committee of the Stockholders of the Sonora Exploring and Mining Co. upon the History, Resources, and Prospects of the Company in Arizona* (Cincinnati: Railroad Record Print, 1859), 12–13.

29. Phocion R. Way, "Overland Via 'Jackass Mail' in 1858: The Dairy of Phocion R. Way," ed. and annot. William A. Duffen, *Arizona and the West* 2 (Summer 1960), 147–64, (Autumn 1960), 279–92, and (Winter 1960), 353–70; Pumpelly, *Across America*; and Report of F. Biertu, Metallurgist and Mining Engineer, February 1861, in Mowry, *Arizona and Sonora*, 79, for the Santa Rita Mining Company. For the Patagonia and Mowry mines, see Biertu in Mowry, *Arizona and Sonora*, 75–76; but also see Mowry, *Arizona and Sonora*, 61–64; Frank C. Schrader, *Mineral Deposits of the Santa Rita and Patagonia Mountains, Arizona*, U.S. Geological Survey Bulletin 582 (Washington: GPO, 1915), 296; Browne, *Apache Country*, 203; and Joseph Pratt Allyn, *The Arizona of Joseph Pratt Allyn: Letters from a Pioneer Judge: Observations and Travels, 1863–1866*, ed. John Nicholson (Tucson: University of Arizona Press, 1974), 190.

30. Browne, *Apache Country*, 169, 191; Hall, *Travels and Adventures*, 38, 133; Sonora Exploring and Mining Company, *Report of Frederick Brunckow*, 19; Sonora Exploring and Mining Company, *Third Annual Report of the Sonora Exploring and Mining Co., Made to the Stockholders, March, 1859* (New York: W. Minns, 1859), 9; North, ed., *Heintzelman*, 100, 112, 129; Mowry, *Arizona and Sonora: The Geography, History, and Resources of the Silver Region of North America*, 3d ed. (New York: Harper and Brothers, 1864), 3; and Col. B. L. E. Bonneville to Lt. Col. L. Thomas, U.S. War Department *Report of the Secretary of War for 1859* (Washington: George W. Bowman, 1860), 2:305.

31. Census data, Joe Park Collection, Box 1, Arizona Historical Society. For colonial connections, see Dobyns, *Tubac*. For Opatas, see North, ed., *Heintzelman*, 160; and Mowry, *Arizona and Sonora*, 94. In 1860, a hundred or more Tohono O'odham, many from Sonora, were camped near town. Pumpelly, *Across America*, 7; and 2nd Lt. R. S. C. Lord to Capt. R. S. Ewell, February 17, 1859 in Thirty-Sixth Congress, First Session, House of Representatives, Ex. Doc., *Message from the President of the United States in the Two Houses of Congress at the Commencement of the First Session of the Thirty-Sixth Congress* (Washington: George W. Bowman, 1860), 2:292.

32. Mowry, *Arizona and Sonora*, 65, 94; Pumpelly, *Across America*, 32; Poston, *Build-*

ing a State, 81–82; and Sonora Exploring and Mining Company, *Report of Frederick Brunckow*, 17; but see Cincinnati and Sonora Mining Association, *Geological Report and Map of the San Juan del Rio Ranche, in Sonora, Mexico* (Cincinnati: Wrightson, 1866), 49; and Way, "Jackass Mail," 280–81, for depictions of cheap and docile Mexican and Indian labor. Poston justified the *boleta* system by saying it was used in Mexico. See also discussion in Miguel Tinker Salas, *In the Shadow of the Eagles: Sonora and the Transformation of the Border during the Porfiriato* (Berkeley: University of California Press, 1997), 187. Debt peonage existed in northern Mexico but was weakened by wage labor in the mines (and later by U.S. labor markets). Friedrich Katz, "Labor Conditions on Haciendas in Porfirian Mexico: Some Trends and Tendencies," *Hispanic American Historical Review* 54 (February 1974), 1–47; and Hall, *Travels and Adventures*, 269–72.

33. For Padrés, see Mowry, *Arizona and Sonora*, 60; North, ed., *Heintzelman*, 129; and Roberts, *With Their Own Blood*, 44–45. For merchants at Cucurpe and the Gila gold rush, see Hall, *Travels and Adventures*, 209.

34. Browne, *Apache Country*, 203, 169, 191; and Pumpelly, *Across America*, 13.

35. Browne, *Apache Country*, 258; Santa Rita Silver Mining Company, *Second Annual Report of the Santa Rita Silver Mining Company, Made to the Stockholders, March 18, 1860* (Cincinnati: Railroad Record Print, 1860), 11; and North, ed., *Heintzelman*, 90.

36. Way, "Overland Via 'Jackass' Mail," 359, 361; and North, ed., *Heintzelman*, 119, 121–22, 157.

37. Sonora Exploring and Mining Company, *Third Annual Report*, 7–8, 20; North, ed., *Heintzelman*, 58; and Mowry, *Arizona and Sonora*, 166. For ore complexity, silver reduction technologies, and their limits, see Rodman Wilson Paul, *Mining Frontiers of the Far West, 1848–1880*, rev. ed. (Albuquerque: University of New Mexico Press, 2001), 98–100.

38. See Browne, *Apache Country*, 205; North, ed., *Heintzelman*, 62–68, 92–93, 155, 151; and Mowry, *Arizona and Sonora*, 38–39. By seeing the fiesta at Magdalena largely as an event that disrupted industrial discipline, Heintzelman failed to realize how important the event was for enterprise. "Parties are met with from all parts of [Sonora]" at this annual event, noted John Hall, and "a great deal of business" took place. Hall, *Travels and Adventures*, 43.

39. North, ed., *Heintzelman*, 33; Robert H. Forbes, *Crabb's Filibustering Expedition into Sonora, 1857* (Tucson: Arizona Silhouettes, 1952); Rodolfo Acuña, *Sonoran Strongman: Ignacio Pesqueira and His Times* (Tucson: University of Arizona Press, 1974), 29–37; Sonora Exploring and Mining Company, *Report of Frederick Brunckow*, 7; and Poston, *Building a State*, 91. For examples of expansionist rhetoric at this time, see Mowry, *Arizona and Sonora*, 16–17, 35, 53; Robert Anderson Wilson, *Mexico: Its Peasants and Its Priests; or Adventures and Historical Researches in Mexico and Its Silver Mines During Parts of the Years 1851-52-53-54* (New York: Harper, 1856), 389; and T. Robinson Warren, *Dust and Foam; or, Three Oceans and Two Continents* (New York: Charles Scribners, 1859), 202, 216.

40. Hall, *Travels and Adventures*, 185–87; *Weekly Arizonian*, May 12, 1859; *Weekly Alta California*, May 28, 1859; Roberts, *With Their Own Blood*, 66–67; and Joseph F. Park,

"The History of Mexican Labor in Arizona during the Territorial Period" (MA thesis, University of Arizona, 1961), 74–75.

41. *Weekly Arizonian*, May 16, 1859; Hall, *Travels and Adventures*, 187–89; Park, "Mexican Labor," 75; and Roberts, *With Their Own Blood*, 68–69.

42. *New York Daily Tribune*, June 9, 1859; *Weekly Arizonian*, May 19, 1859; and Hall, *Travels and Adventures*, 189–91.

43. *Weekly Arizonian*, May 19, 1859, June 2, 1859; Park, "Mexican Labor," 75–76; and Roberts, *With Their Own Blood*, 71–75.

44. Hall, *Travels and Adventures*, 199–200.

45. Poston, *Building a State*, 93–96; and Brevet Lieutenant Colonel J. V. D. Reeve to Lieutenant J. D. Wilkins, *Secretary of War 1859*, 2:323–24.

46. Emory, *Lt. Emory Reports*, 100; and Edwin R. Sweeney, *Cochise: Chiricahua Apache Chief* (Norman: University of Oklahoma Press, 1991), 94–117.

47. Sweeney, *Cochise*, 99–110; and Thomas Edwin Farish, *History of Arizona*, 8 vols. (San Francisco: Filmer Brothers, 1915–18), 2:30.

48. Reeve to Wilkins, *Secretary of War 1859*, 2:324; Poston, *Building a State*, 96–99; Pumpelly, *Across America*, 16–17; Robert M. Utley, "The Bascom Affair: A Reconstruction," *Arizona and the West* 3 (Spring 1961), 59–68; Benjamin H. Sacks, "New Evidence on the Bascom Affair," *Arizona and the West* 4 (Autumn 1962), 261–78; Sweeney, *Cochise*, 142–65; and Dan L. Thrapp, *The Conquest of Apacheria* (Norman: University of Oklahoma Press, 1967), 18.

49. *Report of the Postmaster General for 1861* (Washington: GPO, 1862), 560–61; "An Act Making Appropriations for the Service of the Post Office Department during the Fiscal Year ending the Thirtieth of June, 1862," *Congressional Globe*, Thirty-Sixth Congress, Second Session, Appendix (1861), 335–36; Poston, *Building a State*, 100–01; and Sweeney, *Cochise*, 173–77.

50. Poston, *Building a State*, 101; Pumpelly, *Across America*, 17, 22–28.

51. Poston, *Building a State*, 104; Pumpelly, *Across America*, 26; Browne, *Apache Country*, 147, 268.

52. Browne, *Apache Country*, 147, 266.

53. Poston, *Building a State*, 105.

54. Browne, *Apache Country*, 149; Pumpelly, *Across America*, 30.

3. INDUSTRIAL FRONTIERS

1. Matías Romero, *Mexican Lobby: Matías Romero in Washington, 1861–1867*, ed. Thomas D. Schoonover (Lexington: University Press of Kentucky, 1986), ix–xviii, and Robert Ryal Miller, "Matias Romero: Mexican Minister to the United States during the Juárez-Maximilian Era," *Hispanic American Historical Review* 45 (May 1965), 228–45.

2. *Gran Banquete dado en Nueva York al Ministro de la República Mejicana* (New York, 1864), 15, and "Speech of the Honorable Matías Romero, Envoy Extraordinary and Minister Plenipotentiary of the Republic of Mexico to the United States of America, at a Dinner Given in his Honor by Distinguished Citizens of New-York, on the Twenty-

Ninth Day of March, 1864," in *Proceedings of a Meeting of Citizens of New York to Express Sympathy and Respect for the Mexican Republican Exiles* (New York: John A. Gray and Green, 1865), 52.

3. For William E. Dodge and the early history of Phelps, Dodge, and Company, see Richard Lowitt, *A Merchant Prince of the Nineteenth Century, William E. Dodge* (New York: Columbia University Press, 1954); Robert Glass Cleland, *A History of Phelps Dodge, 1834–1950* (New York: Alfred A. Knopf, 1952), 3–74; and Carlos A. Schwantes, *Vision and Enterprise: Exploring the History of Phelps Dodge Corporation* (Tucson: University of Arizona Press, 2000), 25–49. For Dodge and Romero, see Matías Romero, *Diario personal (1855–1865)*, ed. Emma Cosío Villegas (Mexico City: Colegio de México, 1960), 567, 620–21; letters from William E. Dodge, Jr. to Matías Romero in U.S. House of Representatives, Fortieth Congress, First Session, *Executive Document no. 33* (Washington: GPO, 1867), 33; Philip L. White, *The Beekmans of New York in Politics and Commerce, 1647–1877* (New York: New-York Historical Society, 1956), 624–26; and Lowitt, *Merchant Prince*, 153–57. For the Nacozari mine, see W. G. Moody, *A Comparison of the Northern and Southern Mines in Mexico: With a Description of Two of the Mining Districts in North-Eastern Sonora* (San Francisco: Towne and Bacon, 1863); and U.S. Department of State, *Commercial Relations of the United States with Foreign Countries* (hereafter referred to as *Commercial Relations*) (Washington: GPO, 1864), 720.

4. Thomas D. Schoonover, "Dollars over Dominion: United States Economic Interests in Mexico, 1861–1867," *Pacific Historical Review* 45 (February 1976), 26; and David M. Pletcher, *The Diplomacy of Trade and Investment: American Economic Expansion in the Hemisphere, 1865–1900* (Columbia: University of Missouri Press, 1998), 77–113. The quote is from U.S. Secretary of State William E. Seward.

5. *Commercial Relations* (1868), 647, and (1864), 719; Charles P. Stone, *Notes on the State of Sonora* (Washington: Henry Polkinhorn Printer, 1861), 8–9; Sylvester Mowry, *Arizona and Sonora: The Geography, History, and Resources of the Silver Region of North America*, 3d ed. (New York: Harper and Brothers, 1864), 92; and reports from Guaymas in *Commercial Relations* (1864–68).

6. John Spring, *John Spring's Arizona*, ed. A. M. Gustafson (Tucson: University of Arizona Press, 1966), 189, 46, 73–79; Darlis A. Miller, *Soldiers and Sutlers: Military Supply in the Southwest, 1861–1885* (Albuquerque: University of New Mexico Press, 1989), 289–94; and Joseph F. Park, "The History of Mexican Labor in Arizona during the Territorial Period" (MA thesis, University of Arizona, 1961), 117–40. For freighting links between southern Arizona and Sonora, see Henry Pickering Walker, "Freighting from Guaymas to Tucson, 1850–1880," *Western Historical Quarterly* 1 (July 1970), 291–304.

7. John Gregory Bourke, *On the Border with Crook* (New York: Charles Scribners' Sons, 1891), 59; and John A. Rockfellow, *Log of an Arizona Trial Blazer* (Tucson: Acme Printing, 1933; repr., Tucson: Arizona Silhouettes, 1955), 30.

8. *Commercial Relations* (1868), 647; Ramón Corral, *Obras históricas* (Hermosillo, 1959), 84; and Edwin R. Sweeney, *Cochise: Chiricahua Apache Chief* (Norman: University of Oklahoma Press, 1991), 248–54, 364–97.

9. Stuart Daggett, *Chapters on the History of the Southern Pacific* (New York: Ronald Press, 1922), 120–39; David F. Myrick, *Railroads of Arizona*, vol. 1, *The Southern Roads* (Berkeley: Howell-North Books, 1975), 15–61; and Neill C. Wilson and Frank J. Taylor, *Southern Pacific: The Roaring Story of a Fighting Railroad* (New York: McGraw-Hill, 1952), 59–66.

10. *Commercial Relations* (1877), 727–28, (1879), 430–32, and (1878), 950–52; and Report of Governor John C. Frémont, Governor of Arizona Territory, U.S. Department of Interior, *Annual Report of the Secretary of the Interior, 1879* (Washington: GPO, 1879), 406–07.

11. Sonora Exploring and Mining Company, *Possessions and Prospects of the Sonora Silver Mining Co. Report of the Sonora Exploring and Mining Co., Made to the Stockholders. September 1857* (Cincinnati: Railroad Record Print, 1857), 15; Andrew B. Gray, *Southern Pacific Railroad: Survey of a Route for the Southern Pacific R.R. on the 32nd Parallel, by A. B. Gray, for the Texas Western R.R. Company* (Cincinnati: Railroad Record Print, 1856), 81, 86; Captain T. J. Cram, *Memoir Showing How to Bring the Lead, Copper, Silver and Gold of Arizona into the Marts of the World, and Project of a Rail Road Through Sonora, to Connect With the Pacific Rail Road in Arizona* (Troy, N.Y.: R. V. Wilson, 1858), 3–5; and James Eldredge, *A Short Description of the Frontier State of Sonora, One of the States of the Republic of Mexico: With Some Notices on its Climate, Soil, and Productions, and of its Future Commercial Importance, From its Immediate Proximity to the United States of America, and its Proposed Railway from Guaymas in the Gulf of California to Tucson in the Territory of Arizona* (London, 1872), 3–4, 11–12.

12. *Commercial Relations* (1872), 687; Ignacio Pesqueira to the Mexican National Congress, reprinted in *Commercial Relations* (1877), 729; 1874 memorial from Sonora mayors to the Mexican National Congress, *Commercial Relations* (1874), 846; General G. Sánchez Ochoa to the Minister of War, November 1, 1877, and Antonio Moreno, in response to the report of General G. Sánchez Ochoa, in U.S. Congress, *Papers Relating to the Foreign Relations of the United States, 1879* (Washington: GPO, 1879), 828–33; and editorials in *La Estrella de Occidente*, cited in David M. Pletcher, "The Development of Railroads in Sonora," *Inter-American Economic Affairs* 1 (March 1948), 14.

13. U.S. Congress, *Papers Relating to Foreign Relations* (1879), 778, 826–33, and (1880), 719–22; U.S. Department of State, *Commercial Relations of the United States: Reports from the Consuls of the United States on the Commerce, Manufactures, etc., of their Consular Districts* (hereafter referred to as *Consular Reports*) (Washington: GPO, 1880), October 1880, 43–44; *El Fronterizo*, February 15, 1880; and *Tombstone Epitaph*, October 28, 1882. See also David M. Pletcher, "Mexico Opens the Door to American Capital, 1877–1880," *The Americas* 16 (July 1959), 8–11; Miguel Tinker Salas, *In the Shadow of the Eagles: Sonora and the Transformation of the Border during the Porfiriato* (Berkeley: University of California Press, 1997), 131–32; and Consuelo Boyd, "Twenty Years to Nogales: The Building of the Guaymas–Nogales Railroad," *Journal of Arizona History* 22 (Autumn 1981), 305–24.

14. *Consular Reports* (March 1882), 443, and (November 1882), 45; *Commercial Rela-*

tions (1882–83), 229–30; *Annual Report of the Board of Directors of the Atchison, Topeka and Santa Fe Railroad Co. to the Stockholders for the Year Ending December 31, 1883* (Boston: Geo. H. Ellis, 1884), 17; *Annual Report of the Board of Directors of the Atchison, Topeka, and Santa Fe Railroad Co. to the Stockholders for the Year Ending December 31, 1885* (Boston: Geo. H. Ellis, 1886), 17; *Annual Report of the Board of Directors of the Atchison, Topeka, and Santa Fe Railroad Co. to the Stockholders for the Year Ending December 31, 1888* (Boston: Geo. H. Ellis, 1889), 102–05; Bryant, *History*, 82; and Signor and Kirchner, *Southern Pacific*, 17–23.

15. *Arizona Citizen*, December 7, 1872; A. P. K. Safford et al., *Resources of Arizona Territory, with a Description of the Indian Tribes; Ancient Ruins; Cochise, Apache Chief; Antonio, Pima Chief; Stage and Wagon Roads; Trade and Commerce, etc.* (San Francisco: Francis and Valentine, 1871), 15; and C. C. C. Carr, "The Days of the Empire— Arizona, 1866–1869," *Journal of the United States Cavalry Association* 2 (March 1889), 14. For U.S.–Apache relations, see Sweeney, *Cochise*, 166–320.

16. Sweeney, *Cochise*, 318–97, and Dan Thrapp, *The Conquest of Apachería* (Norman: University of Oklahoma Press, 1967), 95–161.

17. Lonnie E. Underhill, ed., "The Tombstone Discovery: The Recollections of Ed Shieffelin and Richard Gird," *Arizona and the West* 21 (Spring 1979), 45–47; and Richard Gird, "True Story of the Discovery of Tombstone," *Out West* (July 1907), 45.

18. In the 1850s, Mangas Coloradas told John Russell Bartlett how Chiricahua Apaches often kept watch on outsiders, unnoticed, and as late as the 1930s the last remaining Apaches in the Sierra Madres talked of watching Mexicans from high mountain camps in the same way. John Russell Bartlett, *Personal Narrative of Explorations and Incidents in Texas, New Mexico, California, Sonora, and Chihuahua*, 2 vols. (New York: D. Appleton, 1854), 1:300, and Grenville Goodwin and Neil Goodwin, *The Apache Dairies: A Father–Son Journey* (Lincoln: University of Nebraska Press, 2000).

19. Underhill, ed., "Tombstone," 48–49; Gird, "Discovery," 41–42; Frederick Brunckow biographical file in Hayden Arizona Pioneer Biographies Collection, Arizona Collection, Department of Archives and Manuscripts, Arizona State University Library; Diane M. T. North, *Samuel Peter Heintzelman and the Sonora Exploring Company* (Tucson: University of Arizona Press, 1980), 25; and Thompson M. Turner, *Latest from Arizona! The Hesperian Letters, 1859–1861*, ed. Constance Wynn Altshuler (Tucson: Arizona Pioneers' Historical Society, 1969), 107–08.

20. Underhill, ed., "Tombstone," 58–64; *Arizona Daily Star*, October 29, 1879; Lynn R. Bailey, *Tombstone, Arizona, "Too Tough to Die": The Rise, Fall, and Resurrection of a Silver Camp, 1878 to 1990* (Tucson: Westernlore Press, 2004), 1–52; Odie B. Faulk, *Tombstone: Myth and Reality* (New York: Oxford University Press, 1972), 47–101; William B. Shillingberg, *Tombstone, A.T.: A History of Early Mining, Milling, and Mayhem* (Spokane: Arthur H. Clark, 1999), 43–59; and Richard W. Fulton, "Millville-Charleston, Cochise County, 1878–1889," *Journal of Arizona History* 7 (1966), 9–22.

21. Faulk, *Tombstone*, 87, 98, 60; and Rockfellow, *Arizona Trail Blazer*, 50.

22. For timber, see *Arizona Quarterly Illustrated*, July 1880; *Tombstone Daily Epitaph*, September 23, 1880; *Tombstone Epitaph*, July 3, 1881; Conrad J. Bahre and Charles F. Hutchison, "The Impact of Historic Fuelwood Cutting on the Semidesert Woodlands

of Southeastern Arizona," *Journal of Forest History* 29 (October 1985), 175–86; and Conrad Joseph Bahre, *A Legacy of Change: Historic Human Impact on Vegetation in the Arizona Borderlands* (Tucson: University of Arizona Press, 1991), 146–54. For use of timber and water in milling and amalgamating in Charleston, see W. Lawrence Austin, "Silver Milling in Arizona," *Transactions of the American Institute of Mining Engineers* 11 (1883), 91–106. For hay and farming hinterlands, see *Tombstone Epitaph*, September 17, 1881; *Tombstone Daily Nugget*, October 4, 1881; Conrad J. Bahre, "Wild Hay Harvesting in Southern Arizona: A Casualty of the March of Progress," *Journal of Arizona History* 28 (Spring 1987), 69–78; Bahre, *Legacy of Change*, 172–75; and S. C. Bartlett, "Arizona Development," *The Golden Era* 38 (June 1889), 245–47; for Mormon suppliers of Tombstone, see Olive Kimball B. Mitchell, *Life is a Fulfilling: The Story of a Mormon Pioneer Woman—Sarah Diantha Gardner Curtis and her Part in the Colonization of the San Pedro Valley in Southern Arizona, the Homeland of the Powerful, Antagonistic Apache* (Provo: Brigham Young University Press, 1967), 94–95.

23. J. Jay Wagoner, *History of the Cattle Industry in Southern Arizona, 1540–1940*, University of Arizona Social Science Bulletin no. 20 (Tucson: University of Arizona Press, 1952), 37–44; William M. Rodgers, "Historical Land Occupance of the Upper San Pedro River Valley Since 1870" (MA thesis, University of Arizona, 1965), 42–74; and Lynn R. Bailey, *"We'll All Wear Silk Hats": The Erie and Chiricahua Cattle Companies and the Rise of Corporate Ranching in the Sulphur Spring Valley of Arizona, 1883–1909* (Tucson: Westernlore Press, 1994), 14–48.

24. *Tombstone Daily Epitaph*, October 7, 1882; *Tombstone Weekly Epitaph*, May 1, 1880; *Arizona Daily Star*, September 11, 1879; and George Whitwell Parsons, *A Tenderfoot in Tombstone: The Private Journal of George Whitwell Parsons: The Turbulent Years, 1880–82*, ed. Lynn R. Bailey (Tucson: Westernlore Press, 1996), 67, 85.

25. Parsons, *Tenderfoot*, 176; and *Tombstone Daily Epitaph*, August 13, 1881, September 29, 1881, March 16, 1882.

26. *Tombstone Daily Epitaph*, January 11, 1882, February 13, 1882; and *Tombstone Weekly Epitaph*, October 7, 1882.

27. Parsons, *Tenderfoot*, 216–18; Faulk, *Tombstone*, 189; George Whitwell Parsons, *The Devil Has Foreclosed: The Private Journal of George Whitwell Parsons: The Concluding Arizona Years, 1882–87*, ed. Lynn R. Bailey (Tucson: Westernlore Press, 1997), 9; Moody, *Comparison*, 32–34; *Arizona Weekly Star*, July 21, 1879, September 26, 1878, July 21, 1879, December 25, 1879; and *Tombstone Daily Epitaph*, February 22, 1882.

28. Parsons, *Devil*, 1, 4, 9, 27, 11, 15; *Tombstone Daily Epitaph*, September 22, 1880; *Douglas Daily International*, Annual Number 1905, section 3; Bailey, *Silk Hats*, 48; and Lynn R. Bailey and Don Chaput, *Cochise County Stalwarts: A Who's Who of the Territorial Years*, vol. 2, L–Z (Tucson: Westernlore Press, 2000), 196.

29. William M. Breakenridge, *Helldorado: Bringing the Law to the Mesquite* (Boston: Houghton Mifflin, 1928), 102–19; John P. Clum, *Apache Days and Tombstone Nights: John Clum's Autobiography, 1877–1887*, ed. Neil B. Carmony (Silver City, N.M.: High Lonesome Books, 1997), 45, 55–59; Fred Dodge, *Under Cover for Wells Fargo: The Unvarnished Recollections of Fred Dodge*, ed. Carolyn Lake (Boston: Houghton Mifflin, 1969), 12–19; Matías Romero to Frederick Frelinghuysen, June 23, 1882, *Papers*

Relating to the Foreign Relations of the United States, December 4, 1882 (Washington: GPO, 1883); and *Tombstone Daily Epitaph*, August 18, 1881.

30. For the Skeleton Canyon (or Guadalupe Canyon) "massacre" and related events, see *Tombstone Daily Epitaph*, August 5, 1881; Clara Spalding Brown, *Tombstone from a Woman's Point of View: The Correspondence of Clara Spalding Brown, July 7, 1880, to November 14, 1882*, ed. Lynn R. Bailey (Tucson: Westernlore Press, 1998), 39–40; Parsons, *Tenderfoot*, 167; Breakenridge, *Helldorado*, 11; and Bailey, *Silk Hats*, 34.

31. Mexican Minister Manuel de Zamacona to U.S. Secretary of State James G. Blaine, April 13, 1881, and Eugene H. Hathaway to the Secretary of the Interior, August 30, 1881, *Letters Received Relating to Disturbances Along the Mexican Border, December 13, 1878–January 25, 1884*, Interior Department Territorial Papers, Arizona, 1868–1913, microcopy no. 429, roll 3 (Washington, 1963); and Arizona Governor Frederick Tritle, Governor of Arizona Territory, U.S. Department of Interior, *Annual Report of the Secretary of the Interior. Report of the Governor of Arizona Territory* (Washington: GPO, 1884), 530.

32. Report of Brigadier-General Crook, September 9, 1885, in U.S. War Department, *Report of the Secretary of War* (Washington: GPO, 1885), 169–78. For Apaches in the early 1880s, and cooperation among Mexicans and Americans, see John Gregory Bourke, *An Apache Campaign in the Sierra Madre* (New York: Charles Scribner's Sons, 1886), 13–14; but also see Eve Ball, *Indeh: An Apache Odyssey* (Norman: University of Oklahoma Press, 1988); and Shelley Ann Bowen Hatfield, *Chasing Shadows: Indians along the United States–Mexico Border, 1876–1911* (Albuquerque: University of New Mexico Press, 1998). For "Apache drills" at Bisbee, see Howard Barkell, "History of Schools in Bisbee," in Frank L. Wentworth, *Bisbee and the Big B* (Iowa City: Mercer, 1938), 191–93.

33. Brown, *Correspondence*, 42; M. de Zamacona, Mexican Minister to the United States, to James G. Blaine, U.S. Secretary of State, August 2, 1881, *Disturbances Along Mexican Border*; and Bourke, *Apache Campaign*, 13–14. For the Tombstone Rangers, see Lynn R. Bailey, *The Valiants: The Tombstone Rangers and Apache War Frivolities* (Tucson: Westernlore Press, 1999). For militias, see Arizona Governor Frederick Tritle, Governor of Arizona Territory, U.S. Department of Interior, *Annual Report of the Secretary of the Interior, 1883* (Washington: DPO, 1883), 513–14; and Frederick Frelinghuysen to Matías Romero, June 23, 1882, and Matías Romero to Frederick Frelinghuysen, June 23, 1882, *Papers Relating to the Foreign Relations.*

34. Parsons, *Devil*, 12, 19–20, 21, 113, 120.

35. Shillingberg, *Tombstone, A.T.*, 323–44; Bailey, *Too Tough to Die*, 173–215; and Eric L. Clements, *After the Boom in Tombstone and Jerome, Arizona: Decline in Western Resource Towns* (Reno: University of Nevada Press, 2003).

36. *Tombstone Epitaph*, September 1, 1880, November 30, 1880; James Douglas, "Notes on the Development of Phelps, Dodge & Co.'s Copper and Railroad Interests," January 1906, and James Douglas, "The Story of the Copper Queen Mines," n.d. [1908], Phelps Dodge Corporation Archives; *Engineering and Mining Journal* 87 (February 20, 1909), 409; and F. L. Ransome, "Copper Deposits of Bisbee, Ariz.," in *Contributions to Economic Geology, 1902*, U.S. Geological Survey, Bulletin no. 213 (Washington: GPO, 1903), 152.

37. R. Chadwick, "New Extraction Processes for Metals," in *A History of Technology*, ed. Charles Singer et al., vol. 5, *The Late Nineteenth Century c1850 to c1900* (Oxford: Clarendon Press, 1958), 83–84; and Thomas R. Navin, *Copper Mining and Management* (Tucson: University of Arizona Press, 1978), 5–6, 9–13. For Arizona copper mining in the Civil War era, see Robert Lester Spude, "Mineral Frontier in Transition: Copper Mining in Arizona, 1880–1885" (MA thesis, Arizona State University, 1976), 27–97.

38. Albert Steinfeld, "Copper Queen History as told by A. Steinfeld," recollections in the form of clip books, Arizona Historical Society; James Colquhoun, *The History of the Clifton-Morenci District* (London: John Murray, 1924); Richard J. Hinton, *The Hand-book to Arizona: Its Resources, History, Towns, Mines, Ruins, and Scenery* (San Francisco: Payot, Upham; New York: American News Co., 1878), 81–84; *Engineering and Mining Journal* 19 (January 16, 1875), 38, and 34 (September 2, 1882), 121–22; and James Douglas et al., "The Copper Queen Mines and Works, Arizona, U.S.A.," *Transactions of the Institution of Mining and Metallurgy* 22 (1913), 532–33.

39. For copper, electricity, and electrolytic refining, see Chadwick, "New Extraction," 84–86; and Nevin, *Copper Mining*, 13.

40. Douglas, "Notes," 11–12.

41. Ibid., 15–16; Douglas et al., "Copper Queen Mines," 534–35.

42. Douglas, "Notes," 16–23; Douglas et al., "Copper Queen Mines," 535–36.

43. Chadwick, "Extraction Processes," 73; and Brian J. Skinner, "Copper Resources," in Robert B. Gordon et al., *Toward a New Iron Age?: Quantitative Modeling of Resource Exhaustion* (Cambridge: Harvard University Press, 1987), 25, for ore grade and secondary enrichment; quote is from Skinner, "Copper Resources," 27. For Bisbee, see "Description of Property," 7; and *Copper Queen Copper Mine and Smelting Works [1881]*, and 1882 *Stockholder's Report of the Copper Queen Mining Company*, in James Douglas Papers, Arizona Historical Society, box 3, file 29; James Douglas, *The Cupola Smelting of Copper in Arizona*, Department of the Interior, U.S. Geological Survey (Washington: GPO, 1885), 401–05; James Douglas, "Conservation of Natural Resources," *Transactions of the American Institute of Mining Engineers* 40 (1910), 422; and James Douglas, "The Copper Queen Mine, Arizona," *Transactions of the American Institute of Mining Engineers* 29 (1899), 513–14.

44. Douglas, "Conservation," 422–23.

45. Douglas, "Notes," 19–21; Douglas, "Story," 14–17; and Douglas et al., "Copper Queen Mines," 533.

46. "Description of Property of the Copper Queen Mining Company . . . Bisbee, Cachise [sic] County, Arizona," 8–9 (1881 report in James Douglas Papers, box 3, file 29); *Tombstone Daily Epitaph*, August 7, 1881, September 1, 1880, October 21, 1880, October 6, 1881; Douglas, "Notes," 26; Douglas, *Cupola Smelting*, 402–03; and James Douglas, "Notes on the Operation of a Light Mineral Railroad," *Transactions of the American Institute of Mining Engineers* 28 (1899), 600–04. At its peak, the Contention Consolidated Company mined twenty-five thousand tons of *ore* a year (632 bars of silver), compared to twenty thousand tons of *copper* at Bisbee in 1888. Faulk, *Tombstone*, 59.

47. Douglas, "Mineral Railroad," 601.

48. Ibid., 600–03; Douglas, "Notes," 26–27; *Tombstone Weekly Epitaph*, April 14, 1888; and Myrick, *Southern Roads*, 179.

49. For timber supplies, see Douglas, "Notes"; and *Tombstone Epitaph*, September 15, 1895. For Bisbee's growth, see *Tombstone Daily Epitaph*, August 10, 1880, October 26, 1880, November 6, 1880, November 30, 1880. For ranching and Bisbee, see Bailey, *Silk Hats*, 81–83; and *Tombstone Daily Epitaph*, June 27, 1889, July 23, 1890, March 22, 1891. For Mormons, see Mitchell, *Fulfilling*, 87–95; and Bartlett, "Arizona's Development," 245–47. For Chinese, see *Tombstone Epitaph*, June 12, 1898. For haying, see *Tombstone Epitaph*, September 20, 1893, September 15, 1895.

50. *Arizona Weekly Star*, September 19, 1878, November 14, 1878, August 15, 1878; *Tombstone Daily Epitaph*, September 22, 1880; Arthur Laing to William E. Dodge, Jr., July 18, 1881 and July 17, 1881, James Douglas Papers, box 3, file 27. For woodcutters, see Wm. (Bill) Liggett, Sr., *My Seventy-five Years Along the Mexican Border* (New York: Exposition Press, 1964), 18; *Tombstone Daily Epitaph*, October 26, 1880; and Douglas, "Conservation," 429; for charcoal burning, see *Cochise Review*, January 26, 1901.

51. Douglas, "Conservation," 429; and *Bisbee Daily Review*, January 29, 1903.

52. John Pleasant Gray, "When All Roads Led to Tombstone," 1940 manuscript, Arizona Historical Society, 104–05.

53. *Tombstone Daily Epitaph*, May 5, 1887; *Tombstone Weekly Epitaph*, October 11, 1891; Gray, "All Roads," 129–32; and C. H. Bayless in David Griffiths, "Range Improvement in Arizona," U.S. Department of Agriculture, Bureau of Plant Industry, Bulletin no. 4 (Washington: GPO, 1901). Also see Rodgers, "Land Occupance," 42–66; Wagoner, *Cattle Industry*, 44–53; and Bailey, *Silk Hats*, 127–37.

54. Douglas, "Story," 17; *Bisbee Daily Review*, December 14, 1905, February 16, 1902, March 20, 1902, July 24, 1904, February 13, 1902; and *Tombstone Epitaph*, November 20, 1897.

55. Douglas, "Notes," 27–28; autobiographical notes, James Douglas Papers, box 1, file 6, 24–25.

56. Douglas, "Notes," 28–29; and *Tombstone Daily Epitaph*, September 22, 1880, October 21, 1880, October 26, 1881. For Copper Queen smelter water use, see *Engineering and Mining Journal* 82 (August 11, 1906).

57. For Bisbee's smelter smoke, fires, and floods, see *Tombstone Epitaph*, September 15, 1895; and Tom Vaughan, "Bisbee's Transition Years: 1899–1918," *Cochise Quarterly* 14 (Winter 1984), 3–42.

58. Douglas, "Copper-Resources," 697.

59. Matías Romero, *Mexico and the United States: A Study of Subjects Affecting their Political, Commercial, and Social Relations, Made with a View to their Promotion* (New York: G. P. Putnam, 1898), 1:8–9.

4. THE MEXICAN CORNUCOPIA

1. Diana Hadley and Thomas E. Sheridan, *Land Use History of the San Rafael Valley, Arizona (1540–1960)* (Fort Collins, Colo.: U.S. Department of Agriculture, U.S. For-

est Service, Rocky Mountain Forest and Range Experiment Station, 1995), 18–19; and Donald T. Garate, *Juan Bautista de Anza: Basque Explorer in the New World* (Reno: University of Nevada Press, 2003), 138. Garate notes that Cananea was a common name from the vicinity of Karrantza (Carranza) in the Basque province of Bizkaia (Vizcaya).

2. Hadley and Sheridan, *Land Use*, 19; Francisco R. Almada, *Diccionario de historia, geografía, y biografía sonorenses*, 3d ed. (Hermosillo: Instituto Sonorense de Cultura, 1990), 122; Ignaz Pfefferkorn, *Sonora: A Description of the Province*, trans. Theodore Treutlein (Tucson: University of Arizona Press, 1989), 89; and Juan Nentvig, *Rudo Ensayo: A Description of Sonora and Arizona in 1764*, trans. Alberto Francisco Pradeau and Robert R. Rasmussen (Tucson: University of Arizona Press, 1980), 126. For Elguea, Pérez, and Arvallo, see Almada, *Diccionario*, 122; Report of Robert L. D'Aumaile, in Sylvester Mowry, *Arizona and Sonora: The Geography, History, and Resources of the Silver Region of North America*, 3d ed. (New York: Harper and Brothers, 1864), 103–04; *Arizona Weekly Star*, November 21, 1878; *Tombstone Daily Record-Epitaph*, September 22, 1885; and Ray H. Mattison, "Early Spanish and Mexican Settlements in Arizona," *New Mexico Historical Review* 21 (October 1946), 310–13. Elguea used the Santa Rita mines to supply the government with copper for coins; he may have done the same at Cananea. Thomas William Lawson, *Report on the Property of the Santa Rita Mining Company* (Boston: T. W. Lawson, 1909), 1–2.

3. Mowry, *Arizona and Sonora*, 103–06.

4. W. G. Moody, *A Comparison of the Northern and Southern Mines in Mexico: With a Description of Two of the Mining Districts in North-Eastern Sonora* (San Francisco: Towne and Bacon, 1863), 24–34.

5. Moody, *Comparison*; *Arizona Weekly Star*, November 21, 1878; *Tombstone Daily Record-Epitaph*, September 22, 1885; George Young, "Greene Cananea Copper Company and Subsidiaries; Historical Sketch (August 1920; updated March 9, 1921)," 24, 13, Greene Cananea Copper Company Collection, box 1, folder 1; Robert F. Torrance, "A Brief History of Cananea," 2, Documentación Procedente de la Compañía Minera de Cananea, Centro INAH Sonora, Instituto Nacional de Antropología e Historia (hereafter referred to as CMC), microfilm 73/147, folder 4; and Mowry, *Arizona and Sonora*, 92.

6. For U.S. entrepreneurs at Cananea, see Young, "Historical Sketch"; Torrance, "Brief History"; S. F. Emmons, "Cananea Mining District of Sonora, Mexico," *Economic Geology* 5 (1910), 316; *Tombstone Daily Record-Epitaph*, September 22, 1885; and Edward Titcomb, "A Yankee Odyssey: Edward Titcomb's Adventures in Mexico and the Southwest," *Journal of Arizona History* 30 (Spring 1989), 83. For Nacozari, see *Arizona Weekly Star*, September 26, 1878, July 21, 1879, December 25, 1879; *Tombstone Daily Epitaph*, February 22, 1882; and *Tombstone Weekly Epitaph*, April 20, 1887, March 20, 1887. For Cutler option to Douglas, see September 22, 1881, letter from Arthur Laing to James Douglas, and report titled the "Union Village Mine," James Douglas Papers, folder 27, box 3, Arizona Historical Society.

7. Ramón Corral, *Memoria de la administración pública del estado de Sonora* (Guaymas: E. Gaxiola, 1891), 1:249–50.

8. Ibid., 1:250–51.

9. What frustrated Corral the most was how overblown U.S. portrayals of Sonora threatened to decrease its value in world markets. Corral, *Memoria*, 251.

10. *Tombstone Weekly Epitaph*, January 13, 1895; "Louis D. Ricketts: An Interview," in T. A. Rickard, *Interviews with Mining Engineers* (San Francisco: Mining and Scientific Press, 1922), 435–36; and James Douglas, "Notes on the Development of Phelps, Dodge & Co.'s Copper and Railroad Interests," January 1906, Phelps Dodge Corporation Archives.

11. *Tombstone Weekly Epitaph*, January 13, 1895; Lynn R. Bailey and Don Chaput, *Cochise County Stalwarts: A Who's Who of the Territorial Years*, vol. 1, A–K (Tucson: Westernlore Press, 2000), 67.

12. James Douglas, "The Story of the Copper Queen Mines," n.d. [1908], Phelps Dodge Corporation Archives, 25; Douglas, "Notes," 29; *Engineering and Mining Journal* 69 (June 9, 1900), 678–79, (June 16, 1900), 707, and 77 (March 3, 1904), 359; and Morris B. Parker, *Mules, Mines, and Me in Mexico, 1895–1932* (Tucson: University of Arizona Press, 1979), 77.

13. *Tombstone Weekly Epitaph*, June 26, 1898.

14. Douglas, "Notes," 29; and autobiographical notes, James Douglas Papers, box 1, file 6 (hereafter "Autobiographical Notes"), 26–27, Arizona Historical Society.

15. Douglas, "Transportation"; "Autobiographical Notes," 28–29; and Myrick, *Southern Roads*, 196–99. Phelps Dodge elites owned all of the stock of the El Paso and Southwestern, and the two companies shared officers and offices. The reason that James Douglas later gave for making the El Paso and Southwestern a separate corporation (up to then, Phelps Dodge had owned and managed its railroads) was legislation "which forbade any industrial enterprise controlling its own transportation facilities — if these facilities were organized as a public railroad company." James Douglas et al., "The Copper Queen Mines and Works, Arizona, U.S.A.," *Transactions of the Institution of Mining and Metallurgy* 22 (1913), 542. The corporate division was largely a fiction.

16. *Bisbee Daily Review*, May 17, 1903; and Edward N. Buck, *Douglas: Its Resources and Development* (Douglas: Nacozari Railroad, 1904), 2–17.

17. C. L. Sonnichsen, *Colonel Greene and the Copper Skyrocket* (Tucson: University of Arizona Press, 1974), 8–27; Joseph "Mack" Axford, *Around Western Campfires* (Tucson: University of Arizona Press, 1969), 13–14, 19–20; H. G. Howe, *Map of Cochise County, Arizona Territory*, map #2149, case 3, drawer 8, folder 2, and *San Rafael del Valle Private Land Claim*, 1891 map, Arizona Historical Society. For the San Rafael Land Grant and the Camou family, see William M. Rodgers, "Historical Land Occupance of the Upper San Pedro River Valley Since 1870" (MA thesis, University of Arizona, 1965), 47, 74; and Ray H. Mattison, "Early Spanish and Mexican Settlements in Arizona," *New Mexico Historical Review* 21:4 (October 1946), 317–18.

18. Sonnichsen, *Copper Skyrocket*, 25; *Arizona Daily Star*, September 29, 1886; and Axford, *Western Campfires*, 19–20.

19. Lynn R. Bailey and Don Chaput, *Cochise County Stalwarts: A Who's Who of the Territorial Years*, vol. 2, L–Z, 52–53; Howe, *Map of Cochise County*; Axford, *Western*

Campfires, 5–6; *Tombstone Epitaph*, April 1, 1894; *San Rafael del Valle*, 1891 map; and *Arizona Daily Orb*, January 24, 1900. Vickers probably left to work lands in the Sulphur Spring Valley. Greene and Packard were together by 1900. *Arizona Daily Orb*, December 22, 1900. By 1902, the "Greene-Packard franchise" ran for miles in all directions from Naco. *Bisbee Daily Review*, February 18, 1902. For Packard's loan to Greene, see Dane Coolidge, *Fighting Men of the West* (New York: C. P. Dutton, 1932), 202.

20. William C. Greene to George Mitchell, August 21, 1901, CMC, microfilm 69/147, folder 14; *Tombstone Epitaph*, October 15, 1899; Winifred G. Meskus, "Some Cochise County Pioneers: As Seen by One of Them," *Cochise Quarterly* 15 (Spring 1985), 18–19; Howe, *Map of Cochise County*; and Corral, *Memoria*, 501. For cattle and borders, see Axford, *Western Campfires*, 10; and John Pleasant Gray, "When All Roads Led to Tombstone," 1940 manuscript, Arizona Historical Society, 133–34.

21. Axford, *Western Campfires*, 14; and Gray, "All Roads," 128–29, 135; but also see U.S. Consul Delos H. Smith to Assistant Secretary of State William F. Wharton, April 25, 1890, U.S. Department of State, *Despatches from United States Consuls in Nogales, 1889–1906* (hereafter DUSC-N), microfilm T-323, roll 1, volume 1 (Washington: National Archives, 1959).

22. For the Elías family, see Armando Elías Chomina, *Compendio de datos históricos de la familia Elías* (Hermosillo, 1986).

23. R. A. and W. J. Key to U.S. Consul Delos H. Smith, May 12, 1891, Juan Fenochio to Alexander Willard, December 30, 1890, and Alexander Willard to John Slaughter, December 30, 1890, DUSC-N; and *Tombstone Epitaph*, January 4, 1891.

24. For the Cananea Copper Company's pooling of assets, see "Testimonio de la escritura de protocolización de la acta de la primera asemblea general de accionistas de 'The Cananea Consolidated Copper Company,' Sociedad Anónima," transcribed by Bernardo Cabrera, November 28, 1907, tomo 2218, expediente 2, Archivo General de Notarías del Estado de Sonora (hereafter referred to as AGNES); and Young, "Greene Cananea," 7–8. Yruretagoyena was listed as a "mecánico," in Magdalena in 1890; Greene may have hoped to enlist his expertise, together with his capital and land. Corral, *Memoria*, 501. For Yruretagoyena in Hermosillo, where he managed the "Hermosillense" mill, see Federico García y Alva, *"México y sus progresos": Álbum-Directorio del Estado de Sonora* (Hermosillo: Antonio B. Monteverde, 1905–07), n.p.

25. "Testimonio de la escritura de protocolización"; Sonnichsen, *Copper Skyrocket*, 46–59; *Report of the Directors of the Greene Consolidated Copper Company* (January 1901), 6, William P. Blake Collection, Yale University; J. S. Douglas, "Facts About the Verde and Copper, But Not Romantic," *Mining and Metallurgy* (June 1935), 258–59; Walter Logan to Greene Consolidated Copper Company stockholders, August 2, 1900, CMC, microfilm 70/147, folder 19; and Greene Consolidated Copper Company advertisement in *Cochise Review*, December 29, 1900.

26. November 24, 1893, invitation to Delmonico's, Walter S. Logan to Robert T. Hill, October 16, 1900, and Robert T. Hill to Walter S. Logan, October 17, 1900, box 4, folder 88, Robert T. Hill Papers, DeGolyer Library, Southern Methodist University. Hill's worries were reasonable, for it was illegal for USGS geologists to have personal

interest in mining property. S. F. Emmons, "The Mining Work of the United States Geological Survey," *Transactions of the American Institute of Mining Engineers* 10 (1882), 423.

27. Walter S. Logan to Robert T. Hill, October 24, 1900, and Robert T. Hill to Walter S. Logan, November 16, 1900, box 4, folder 88, Hill Papers. For Hill, the compelling logic of capital would ultimately prevail, as he became one of Cananea's chief prophets. See *Engineering and Mining Journal* 76 (December 31, 1903), 1000; *The Mining World* 27 (October 12, 1907), 589; and Robert T. Hill, "The Wonders of the American Desert," *World's Work* 3 (March 1902), 1830.

28. *Report of the Stockholders of the Greene Consolidated Copper Co.* (January 1901), William P. Blake Collection, Yale University; *Tombstone Weekly Epitaph*, September 11, 1898; and *Report of Directors* (1901), 4.

29. *Report of Directors* (1901), 4–5.

30. Ibid., 6, 8–15; and list of cars and commodities, Anson W. Burchard to Walter Douglas, May 2, 1902, CMC, microfilm 73/147, folder 11. For San Pedro farm and ranch lands and their ties to copper markets, see Governor Alexander O. Brodie to E. A. Hitchcock, Secretary of the Interior, *Annual Report of the Governor of Arizona to the Secretary of the Interior, 1902* (Washington: GPO, 1902), 301. There were several sawmills in the Cananea and nearby Ajo Mountains, the most economical source for timber when trees of appropriate quality could be found. *Annual Report of the Greene Consolidated Copper Company, for the Year Ending July Thirty-First, 1902* (hereafter *Annual Report*) (New York, 1902), 23. For sawmills in the Ajo Mountains (just east of Cananea), see George Mitchell to Mr. Rankin, March 24, 1902, CMC, microfilm 73/147, folder 11. For timber harvesting in the Cananea Mountains, see *Cananea Herald*, April 4, 1903.

31. *Report of Directors* (1901), 5–6.

32. Ibid., 7.

33. *Report of Stockholders* (1901), 3.

34. *Mining World* 27 (October 12, 1907), 589.

35. Contract between the State of Sonora and the Cananea Consolidated Copper Company for the establishment of a smelter at Cananea, October 4, 1899, tomo 1584, expediente 2, Archivo General del Estado de Sonora (hereafter referred to as AGES).

36. *Cananea Herald*, April 4, 1903. The *pertenencia*, or mining claim, was a square, one hundred meters to each side, a complete hectare, or a little less than two and a half acres. J. R. Southworth, *Las Minas de México: Historia–Geología–Antigua Minería–y Descripción General de los Estados Mineros de la República Mexicana* (Liverpool: Blake and Mackenzie, 1905), 54.

37. October 1899 Cananea smelter contract.

38. Ibid.

39. J. Ross Browne, *Adventures in the Apache Country: A Tour Through Arizona and Sonora* (New York: Harper and Brothers, 1869), 203, 169, 191.

40. García y Alva, *México y sus progresos*, n.p.

41. Ibid.

42. Sonnichsen, *Copper Skyrocket*, 102, 235; Isidro Castañedo, Libro de Protocolo (1901), Número 24 (pp. 33–37), and Número 25 (pp. 37–42), and Isidro Castañedo, Apéndice de Protocolo (1901), AGNES, 1901, caja 48, tomos 384 and 385 (District of Magdalena, Municipality of Nogales), Hermosillo, Sonora. Greene murdered his neighbor Jim Burnett because he had blown up a dam on the San Pedro above his ranch, drowning his daughter. Sonnichsen, *Copper Skyrocket*, 28–38.

43. *Cananea Herald*, September 21, 1902, September 28, 1902, October 5, 1902; William C. Greene to Stockholders of the Greene Consolidated Copper Company, June 19, 1901, William P. Blake Collection, Yale University; *San Francisco Call*, April 29, 1901; "1902 Escritura constitutiva de la Cananea Realty Company," in Manuel J. Aguirre, ed., *Cananea: Las garras del imperialismo en las entrañas de México* (Mexico City: Libro Mex, 1958), 35–42; *Annual Report, 1902*, 8; and *Cananea Herald*, September 21, 1902. The Cananea Cattle Company and CCCC bought the California Land and Cattle Company tract together, later negotiating a division of interests. Presidente Municipal, Cananea, to Prefect of Arizpe, February 26, 1912, tomo 2777, expediente 1, AGES; and George Young, "Memorandum Respecting Mining Titles, Land Deeds, etc.," CMC, microfilm 71/147, folder 15. Greene was probably trying to create a long-term beef franchise with the CCCC to fall back on if he lost his hold on the copper company. There was no need for a copper company to own this much ranch land, especially with railroad ties to outside markets. Investors complained that Greene's investments were extravagant. H. Block to George Mitchell, November 15, 1901, CMC, microfilm 69/147, folder 14.

44. *Report of Directors* (1901), 4; S. M. Aguirre to George Mitchell, August 12, 1901, Robert F. Torrance Papers, box 1, folder 1, Arizona Historical Society; *Cochise Review*, January 12, 1901, January 19, 1901. For the Aguirres and Bernards, see "Mrs. Epifanio (Mary Bernard) Aguirre," Bio File, Arizona Historical Society, Tucson; Mamie Bernard Aguirre, "Spanish Trader's Bride," *Westport Historical Quarterly* 4 (December 1968), 5–22; and "Mrs. Mary (Bernard) Aguirre," in *Portrait and Biographical Record of Arizona* (Chicago: Chapman, 1901), 341–43, 349–50.

45. For the 1887 survey, see Robert H. Holden, *Mexico and the Survey of Public Lands: The Management of Modernization, 1976–1911* (DeKalb: Northern Illinois Press, 1994), 102–03, 154; and *Tombstone Weekly Epitaph*, April 20, 1887. For the 1889 map of Sonora, see H. G. Howe, *Map of Cochise County, Arizona Territory*, map #2149, case 3, drawer 8, folder 2, Arizona Historical Society. A CCCC memorandum says the Cananea Cattle Company bought these lands from the Macmanuses. See Young, "Memorandum Respecting Mining Titles." For Francis Macmanus, the father of Ignacio and Tomás, see Max Moorhead, *New Mexico's Royal Road: Trade and Travel on the Chihuahua Trail* (Norman: University of Oklahoma Press, 1958), 156–57, 157 n. 11, 162–65, 172–77, 180–81. For Tomás Macmanus's role as a Mexico City broker, see George Young to L. D. Ricketts, September 8, 1908, CMC, microfilm 69/147, folder 8; and *Bisbee Daily Review*, June 9, 1905. Ignacio Macmanus was cashier of the P. Sandoval and Co. Bank of Nogales in the 1890s and may have met Greene through Nogales circles. "Ignacio Macmanus," in *Portrait and Biographical Record*, 887.

46. Isidro Castañedo, Libro de Protocolo (1901), AGNES, caja 48, tomo 384, número 62 (pp. 106–10); García y Alva, *México y sus progresos*, n.p.; and Rafael Castro to Governor of Sonora, February 8, 1912, tomo 2777, expediente 1, AGES.

47. George A. Treadwell, "Report on the Cananea Mines," November 14, 1899, William H. Brown Collection, Yale University. The Spanish names here translate to St. Peter, the goats, peacock, luck, and "what hope!" "Peacock" is probably a reference to the coloring of the rock.

48. *Annual Report, 1902*, 11, 31; *Annual Report, 1903*, 16; *Annual Report, 1904*, 9, 16; and *Engineering and Mining Journal* 77 (June 30, 1904), 1045.

49. *Report of Stockholders* (1901); *Report of Directors* (1901), 3, 7; and *Cochise Review*, February 9, 1901.

50. *Report of Directors* (1901), 4; and *Report of Directors* (July 1901), 2. For Cananea's experiment with traction engines, see letters in CMC, microfilm 69/147, folder 4.

51. *Report of Directors* (1901), 4; and *Annual Report, 1905*, 31; but also see annual reports for the preceding three years.

52. *Bisbee Daily Review*, June 8, 1904; *Cananea Herald*, November 23, 1902; and Alden Richard Longwell, "The Cananea Ejidos: From Private Ranch to Collective in Sonora" (PhD diss., University of Nebraska, 1974), 56–171.

53. *Greene Gold-Silver Company* (New York, 1905), 5–15, 20–29; *Mining World* 27 (October 26, 1907), 711; *Bisbee Daily Review*, September 30, 1904, November 4, 1904, November 23, 1904, January 7, 1905; *Douglas Daily International*, November 14, 1904, February 11, 1905; George Young to L. D. Ricketts, February 2, 1907, CMC, microfilm 72/147, folder 1; and *Engineering and Mining Journal* 87 (April 3, 1909), 712–13.

54. *Douglas Daily International*, February 11, 1905; and *Bisbee Daily Review*, April 7, 1905.

55. *Greene Gold-Silver*, 17–23; *Mining World* 21 (December 10, 1904), 581–82; and *Bisbee Daily Review*, September 8, 1905, September 20, 1905.

56. Copper elites were never quite sure how many heirs they were dealing with. When he began to cobble together the lands, the CCCC lawyer Pedro Robles assumed Arvallo had seven heirs, whereas family members later said there were six. George Young to James H. Kirk, December 23, 1910, CMC, microfilm 72/147, folder 3. Much of this land was bought from Anselmo R. Sicre; see Isidro Castañedo, Libro de Protocolo (1901), Número 60 (pp. 102–05), AGNES, caja 48, tomo 384.

57. Young, "Memorandum Respecting Mining Titles."

58. Ibid.

59. Ibid.; George Young to David Cole, September 24, 1909; and George Young to L. D. Ricketts, May 17, 1909, CMC, microfilm 72/147, folder 3.

60. Young to Cole, September 24, 1909; but also see Young to Ricketts, May 17, 1909.

5. TRANSNATIONAL PASSAGES

1. Morris B. Parker, *Mules, Mines, and Me in Mexico, 1895–1932*, ed. James M. Day (Tucson: University of Arizona Press, 1979), 48–51; and Morris B. Parker, Diary for

1900–01, n.p., box 3, diary 4, Morris B. Parker Papers, Huntington Library, San Marino, California.

2. Parker, *Mules*, 3–48. For an overview of U.S. mining development in Chihuahua and Sonora, see Marvin D. Bernstein, *The Mexican Mining Industry, 1890–1950: A Study of the Interaction of Politics, Economics, and Technology* (Albany: State University of New York Press, 1964), 17–77.

3. Parker Diary, n.p.; and Parker, *Mules*, 51.

4. Parker Diary, n.p.

5. Maud Kenyon-Kingdon, *From Out the Dark Shadows* (San Diego: Frye and Smith, 1925), 16–18. It is not clear when Kenyon-Kingdon first went to Mexico, but George Kingdon was working with the Moctezuma Copper Company by 1903. Horace J. Stevens, *The Copper Handbook: A Manual of the Copper Industry of the World* (Houghton, Mich.: Horace J. Stevens, 1904), 4:509.

6. Kenyon-Kingdon, *Dark Shadows*, 27.

7. Ibid., 19–20, 26–27.

8. Ibid., 70–74.

9. Jesus C. Corral, *Caro Amigo: The Autobiography of Jesus C. Corral* (Tucson: Westernlore Press, 1984), 40–46.

10. Ibid., 42–48.

11. Ibid., 49.

12. *Bisbee Daily Review*, January 8, 1902, June 2, 1903, and July 16, 1903; but also see H. T. Hamilton to P. G. Beckett, December 22, 1922, Moctezuma Copper Company Papers (hereafter referred to as MCC Papers), Labor Disputes and Strikes, Phelps Dodge Corporation Archives.

13. *Bisbee Daily Review*, July 14, 1903, June 28, 1903, May 9, 1903.

14. A. S. Dwight to Pablo Rubio, January 30, 1905, Documentación Procedente de la Compañía Minera de Cananea, Centro INAH Sonora, Instituto Nacional de Antropología e Historia (hereafter referred to as CMC), microfilm 71/147, folder 14.

15. *Bisbee Daily Review*, August 27, 1902, February 6, 1902, January 7, 1905, September 14, 1905; and *Douglas Daily International*, October 29, 1906. For Douglas neighborhoods, see Diana Hadley, "Border Boom Town—Douglas, Arizona, 1900–1920," *Cochise Quarterly* 17 (Fall 1987), 3–47; for Bisbee, see Katherine A. Benton, "What about Women in the 'White Man's Camp'?: Gender, Nation, and the Redefinition of Race in Cochise County, Arizona, 1853–1941" (PhD diss., University of Wisconsin-Madison, 2002). "Bajo" in Agua Prieta may translate as "below" or "underneath" (the smelter), but it may also refer to the low-lying ground of Whitewater Draw, just south of the smelter.

16. *Bisbee Daily Review*, July 15, 1902, August 26, 1902, May 4, 1904, August 7, 1904; and *Douglas Daily International*, July 25, 1910.

17. For El Paso ties in Bisbee, see *Bisbee Daily Review*, June 17, 1905, July 26, 1905. For El Paso and Southwestern shipments of laborers in 1903, see *Bisbee Daily Review*, June 12, 1903. For Tintown, see Bisbee Mining and Historical Museum mss., Anonymous, "Cousin Jacks" (n.p., n.d.), 9–10; and Christina E. M. Dickson and Robert Henry Dickson, *Dickson Saga: Story of Our Married Life* (Sun City, Ariz.: Robert H.

Dickson, 1970), 18. For Chihuahua Hill as a landscape of risk, see *Bisbee Daily Review*, March 20, 1902, May 20, 1902, August 2, 1902, April 19, 1905. For Chihuahua Hill as region of refuge, see *Bisbee Daily Review*, October 13, 1904, June 17, 1905, September 17, 1902.

18. *Bisbee Daily Review*, September 6, 1902; and Mildred Young Wallace, *We Three: Papa's Ladies* (San Antonio: Naylor, 1957), 73, 126, 160.

19. William A. Evans, *Two Generations in the Southwest* (Phoenix: Sims, 1971), 15; Municipal President Filiberto Barroso to the Second Judge of the First Instance, Cananea, June 1, 1906, Manuel González Ramírez, *La huelga de Cananea*, vol. 3, *Fuentes para la historia de la Revolución Mexicana* (Mexico City: Fondo de Cultura Económica, 1956), 31; *Bisbee Daily Review*, February 11, 1903; and George Young to Luis E. Torres, May 25, 1910, CMC, microfilm 69/147, folder 12.

20. Ralph McA. Ingersoll, *In and Under Mexico* (New York: Century, 1924), 25, 134–38. Ingersoll was writing in the 1920s, but my research suggests that his general description holds for the early twentieth century as well.

21. Ibid., 112–15.

22. *Engineering and Mining Journal* 118 (August 2, 1924), 183; T. H. O'Brien to P. G. Beckett, April 26, 1920, and P. G. Beckett to Walter Douglas, January 30, 1920, MCC Papers, Dwelling Houses and Quarters, 1918.

23. H. T. Hamilton to P. G. Beckett, March 12, 1920, T. H. O'Brien to P. G. Beckett, April 26, 1920, and P. G. Beckett to Walter Douglas, January 30, 1920, MCC Papers, Dwelling Houses and Quarters, 1918.

24. Statement from 1918 (?) of estimated cost of four new dwellings for Pilares; and D. D. Irwin to P. G. Beckett, August 19, 1920, MCC Papers, Dwelling Houses and Quarters, 1918.

25. Untitled document from mid-1920s, MCC Papers, Industrial Relations.

26. More research remains to be done on these networks, but one can get a sense from the interviews in Josiah McC. Heyman, *Life and Labor on the Border: Working People of Northeastern Sonora, Mexico, 1886–1986* (Tucson: University of Arizona Press, 1991), 47–49, 54, 66–67; but also see Corral, *Caro Amigo*, 50. For the concept of the regional community, see Sarah Deutsch, *No Separate Refuge: Culture, Class, and Gender on an Anglo-Hispanic Frontier in the American Southwest, 1880–1940* (New York: Oxford University Press, 1987).

27. Leslie Hewes, "Huepac: An Agricultural Village of Sonora, Mexico," *Economic Geography* 11 (July 1935), 284–92. In 1904, the anthropologist Ales Hrdlicka observed that "small numbers of pure-blood Opatas" could still be found in Huépac and other villages in the Opata homeland, and in Tuape, on the San Miguel River, "pure Opatas are still in large majority." Ales Hrdlicka, "Notes on the Indians of Sonora, Mexico," *American Anthropologist* 6 (1904), 71–72. Cynthia Radding has argued that Opatas endured, despite a pragmatic decision to pass as mestizo. Cynthia Radding, *Wandering Peoples: Colonialism, Ethnic Spaces, and Ecological Frontiers in Northwestern Mexico, 1700–1850* (Durham: Duke University Press, 1997), 158–68. For enduring Opata practices, see also Roger C. Owen, *Marobavi: A Study of an Assimilated Group in Northern Sonora*, vol. 3, *Anthropological Papers of the University of Ari-*

zona (Tucson: University of Arizona Press, 1959); and Thomas B. Hinton, *A Survey of Indian Assimilation in Eastern Sonora*, vol. 4, *Anthropological Papers of the University of Arizona* (Tucson: University of Arizona Press, 1959), 12–25.

28. Howard Carroll Groton, "Riding the Flying Tortilla: Recollections of a Gringo Store-keeper in Mexico," *Journal of Arizona History* 32 (Summer 1990), 198–200.

29. Ibid., 200–03.

30. Evelyn Hu-DeHart, *Missionaries, Miners, and Indians: Spanish Contact with the Yaqui Nation of Northwestern New Spain, 1533–1820* (Tucson: University of Arizona Press, 1981); Evelyn Hu-DeHart, *Yaqui Resistance and Survival: The Struggle for Land and Autonomy, 1821–1910* (Madison: University of Wisconsin Press, 1984), 3–17; and Edward H. Spicer, *The Yaquis: A Cultural History* (Tucson: University of Arizona Press, 1980), 3–57, 119–30.

31. Hu-DeHart, *Yaqui Resistance*, 18–154; Spicer, *Yaquis*, 145–61; and *Douglas Daily International*, February 5, 1906.

32. Parker, *Mules*, 74–75.

33. Ibid., 75–77.

34. *Bisbee Daily Review*, June 12, 1902; *Douglas Daily International*, April 9, 1906; Ambassador David E. Thompson to Acting Secretary of State Robert Bacon, July 18, 1906, July 21, 1906, July 24, 1906, U.S. Department of State, *Despatches from United States Ministers to Mexico, 1823–1906*, microfilm roll 178, vol. 183, National Archives, National Archives and Records Service, General Services Administration (Washington, 1955); and *Douglas Daily International*, January 9, 1907.

35. For Yaqui communities in Arizona, see Edward Spicer, *Pascua: A Yaqui Village in Arizona* (Tucson: University of Arizona Press, 1967); but for border crossings into the twentieth century, also see Rosalio Moisés, *A Yaqui Life: The Personal Chronicle of a Yaqui Indian*, ed. Jane Holden Kelley and William Curry Holden (Lincoln: University of Nebraska Press, 1977).

36. For the Chinese Exclusion Act and border crossings, see Erika Lee, *At America's Gates: Chinese Immigration During the Exclusion Era, 1882–1943* (Chapel Hill: University of North Carolina Press, 2003); and Grace Peña Delgado, "At Exclusion's Southern Gate: Changing Categories of Race and Class among Chinese *Fronterizos*, 1882–1904," in *Continental Crossroads: Remapping U.S.–Mexico Borderlands History*, ed. Samuel Truett and Elliott Young (Durham: Duke University Press, 2004), 183–207.

37. For Chinese in Arizona, see Lawrence Michael Fong, "Sojourners and Settlers: The Chinese Experience in Arizona," *Journal of Arizona History* 21 (Autumn 1980), 227–55; Florence C. Lister and Robert H. Lister, *The Chinese of Early Tucson: Historic Archaeology from the Tucson Urban Renewal Project* (Tucson: University of Arizona Press, 1989); and Wensheng Wang, "The First Chinese in Tucson: New Evidence on a Puzzling Question," *Journal of Arizona History* 43 (Winter 2002), 369–80; but also see Thomas E. Sheridan, *Los Tucsonenses: The Mexican Community in Tucson, 1854–1941* (Tucson: University of Arizona Press, 1986), 83–85; and Odie B. Faulk, *Tombstone: Myth and Reality* (New York: Oxford University Press, 1972), 197–99.

38. Kennett Cott, "Mexican Diplomacy and the Chinese Issue, 1876–1910," *Hispanic*

American Historical Review 67 (February 1987), 64–69; Evelyn Hu-DeHart, "Immigrants to a Developing Society: The Chinese in Northern Mexico, 1875–1932," *Journal of Arizona History* 21 (Autumn 1980), 276–77; and Lee, *At America's Gates*, 157–60.

39. Hu-DeHart, "Immigrants," 277–79; Leo Michael Dambourges Jacques, "The Anti-Chinese Campaigns in Sonora, Mexico, 1900–1931" (PhD diss., University of Arizona, 1974), 43–50; census data in Ramón Corral, *Memoria de la administración pública del estado de Sonora, Corral,* (Guaymas: E. Gaxiola, 1891), 1:n.p.; and Rafael Izábal, *Memoria de la administración pública del Estado de Sonora, 1903–1907* (Hermosillo: Antonio Monteverde, 1907), n.p.

40. Izábal, *Memoria,* n.p.; Kenyon-Kingdon, *Dark Shadows,* 79–80, 73; Evans, *Two Generations,* 11; and Mildred Young Wallace, "I Remember Chung," *Journal of Arizona History* 20 (Spring 1979), 35–36. Roughly 60 percent of the Chinese merchants in Cananea were grocers, and roughly the same percentage of grocers were Chinese. Historians see Mexican anti-Chinese sentiment in the light of job competition between Chinese and Mexican entrepreneurs, but census data in Cananea suggest a more complicated story. Mexicans and Chinese were the main competitors for groceries (Americans owned only three groceries, or 2.77 percent of the total), but Chinese and Americans were competitors for restaurants (Mexicans owned only three restaurants, or 8.11 percent of the total), and in terms of general stores and butcher shops, Americans competed more with Mexicans than the Chinese did.

41. *Douglas Daily International,* May 5, 1909; Wallace, *We Three,* 61–62; and Kenyon-Kingdon, *Dark Shadows,* 80–81. For similar relations in Pilares and Nacozari, see Estelle Webb Thomas, *Uncertain Sanctuary: A Story of Mormon Pioneering in Mexico* (Salt Lake City: Westwater Press, 1980), 74–75; and Ingersoll, *Under Mexico,* 122, 137.

42. *Bisbee Daily Review* April 14, 1904, May 24, 1904, August 13, 1904, December 5, 1903, September 30, 1902, August 1, 1903, July 31, 1903; and *Douglas Daily International,* September 16, 1910, August 13, 1910. Also see Richard Stokes, "Bisbee, No Good for Chinaman," *Cochise Quarterly* 3 (December 1973), 6–9. For Chinese farmers on the Las Nutrias ranch, see Charles E. Wiswall to U.S. Consul Alexander V. Dye, September 14, 1912, *Records of the Department of State Relating to Internal Affairs of Mexico, 1910–29,* National Archives Microfilm Publications, microcopy no. 274 (Washington: National Archives and Records Service, 1959), roll 20, 812.00/5058.

43. *Bisbee Daily Review,* August 18, 1903, August 19, 1903, October 2, 1903; and *Douglas Daily International,* March 30, 1905. See also Delgado, "Exclusion's Southern Gate," 198–202. Delgado argues that this was part of a larger network that originated in Guaymas and ran north via Hermosillo, Cananea, Magdalena, and Naco into Arizona.

44. *Bisbee Daily Review,* July 8, 1904.

45. Typescript translation in Tombstone Courthouse State Historic Park, Law Office Annex, Research Cabinet 97003, Jeff Milton file. Quoted (but not cited) in Melissa Keane, A. E. Rogge, and Bradford Luckingham, *The Chinese in Arizona, 1870–1950: A Component of the Arizona Historic Preservation Plan* (Phoenix: Arizona State His-

toric Preservation Office, 1992), 30–31. I am grateful to Melissa Keane, Gene Rogge, and Art Austin for helping me track this down.

46. See Thomas Cottam Romney, *The Mormon Colonies in Mexico* (Salt Lake City: Deseret Book Company, 1938); F. LaMond Tullis, *Mormons in Mexico: The Dynamics of Faith and Culture* (Logan: Utah State University Press, 1987); Barney T. Burns and Thomas H. Naylor, "Colonia Morelos: A Short History of a Mormon Colony in Sonora, Mexico," *The Smoke Signal* 27 (Spring 1973), 142–80; and Thomas H. Naylor, "The Mormons Colonize Sonora: Early Trials at Colonia Oaxaca," *Arizona and the West* 20 (Winter 1978), 325–42.

47. "William Carroll McClellan," in *Stalwarts South of the Border*, comp. and ed. Nelle Spilsbury Hatch and B. Carmon Hardy (El Paso: Ernestine Hatch, 1985), 442; Jesse Nathaniel Smith, *The Journal of Jesse Nathaniel Smith: Six Decades in the Early West, Diaries and Papers of a Mormon Pioneer, 1834–1906*, ed. Oliver R. Smith (Provo: Jesse N. Smith Family Association, 1970), 303; Romney, *Mormon Colonies*, 49–66; and Burns and Naylor, "Colonia Morelos," 143. The Mexican Colonization and Agricultural Company, a Mormon corporation, purchased most of these lands with liberal concessions similar to those granted mining companies. Charles W. Kendrick, "The Mormons in Mexico," *American Monthly Review of Reviews* 19 (June 1899), 703; Romney, *Mormon Colonies*, 703; and Millard Haymore, "A Letter to a Niece," *Cochise Quarterly* 22 (Winter 1993), 4–5.

48. Naylor, "Mormons Colonize," 325–33; Burns and Naylor, "Colonia Morelos," 143–47; and Romney, *Mormon Colonies*, 66–67, 115–23. Quote from Layne Lillywhite interview, in Burns and Naylor, "Colonia Morelos," 147. Colin Cameron was a contemporary of Burdette A. Packard and William Cornell Greene. In 1904, he sold Greene his San Rafael Ranch, located on the San Rafael de la Zanja grant near the Patagonia mountains. Jane Wayland Brewster, "The San Rafael Cattle Company: A Pennsylvania Enterprise in Arizona," *Arizona and the West* 8 (Summer 1966), 133–56.

49. Parker Diary, n.p.; "Robert Chestnut Beecroft," *Stalwarts*, 27; Kendrick, "Mormons in Mexico," 703; and Romney, *Mormon Colonies*, 123.

50. For built landscapes at Colonia Morelos, see Burns and Naylor, "Colonia Morelos," 158–59. I make assumptions about Mexican homes at Bavispe, Bacerac, and Huachinera from Leslie Hewes's description of the Mexican–Opata village of Huépac, which was, if anything, more connected to the outside world. Hewes, "Huepac," 285–86.

51. Thomas, *Uncertain Sanctuary*, 68; Alward Forster Fenn, *A House by the Side of the Road; Memoirs: The Story of Alvah and Carmen Forster Fenn* (Phoenix: Image Printers, 1974), 23; Burns and Naylor, "Colonia Morelos," 163–65; "Edward Elsey Bradshaw," *Stalwarts*, 60; Romney, *Mormon Colonies*, 119; and "Joseph Lillywhite, Jr.," *Stalwarts*, 399–402; quote from page 401. For the Pilares de Teras region, see *Engineering and Mining Journal* 63 (March 27, 1897), 315; for gold mining in the Tigre Mountains, see *Engineering and Mining Journal* 75 (April 18, 1903), 607.

52. "Philip Hurst," *Stalwarts*, 293; "Laura Ann Hardy Mecham," *Stalwarts*, 477–78; Thomas Cottam Romney, *Life Story of Miles P. Romney* (Independence: Zion, 1948), 181; Fenn, *House*, 14–30; "John Fenn," *Stalwarts*, 191–92; and Burns and Naylor,

"Colonia Morelos," 167–68, for Mormon freighters. For poverty, see R. Carmon Hardy, "Cultural 'Encystment' as a Cause of the Mormon Exodus from Mexico in 1912," *Pacific Historical Review* 34 (1965), 442–43.

53. "Laura Ann Hardy Mecham," *Stalwarts*, 477–78; "James Wilford Ray," *Stalwarts*, 557; Fenn, *House by the Side*, 30; and "Samuel Walter Jarvis," *Stalwarts*, 332.

54. Haymore, "Letter to a Niece," 5; "William Claude Huish," *Stalwarts*, 287; "Isaac Alldredge, Sr.," *Stalwarts*, 12; "David Alvin McClellan," *Stalwarts*, 428; "Austin Martindale Farnsworth," *Stalwarts*, 164–65; "Jesse Nathaniel Smith, Jr.," *Stalwarts*, 623; Fenn, *House*, 12, 59–62; "John Amasa Whetten," *Stalwarts*, 747; "Edward Franklin Turley," *Stalwarts*, 714; "James Andrew Jesperson," *Stalwarts*, 335–36; and "David Alma Stevens," *Stalwarts*, 636–38; but also see Burns and Naylor, "Colonia Morelos," 167–68.

6. DEVELOPMENT AND DISORDER

1. Robert T. Hill, "The Wonders of the American Desert," *World's Work* 3 (March 1902), 1830; and *La Constitución*, August 11, 1911.

2. *Engineering and Mining Journal* 76 (December 31, 1903), 1000; and May 1, 1900, report from Ignacio Bonillas to the Governor of Sonora, tomo 1584, expediente 2, Archivo General del Estado de Sonora (hereafter referred to as AGES), Hermosillo, Sonora.

3. For treatment north of the border, see *Tombstone Epitaph*, April 8, 1900; and *Nogales Oasis*, April 14, 1900.

4. May 1, 1900, Ignacio Bonillas report; and October 4, 1899, contract between the State of Sonora and the Cananea Consolidated Copper Company, and S. M. Aguirre to Secretary of the Governor, April 21, 1901, AGES, tomo 1584, expediente 2.

5. Frank M. King, *Pioneer Western Empire Builders* (Pasadena: Trail's End, 1946), 164–65; *Tombstone Epitaph*, April 8, 1900; *Nogales Oasis*, April 14, 1900; and *Bisbee Daily Review*, January 21, 1904.

6. *Tombstone Epitaph*, April 8, 1900; and Steven M. Aguirre to Secretary of the Governor, April 12, 1901, AGES, tomo 1584, expediente 2. For Kosterlitzky's friendship with Greene, see Emilio Kosterlitzky to William C. Greene, January 17, 1901, Documentación Procedente de la Compañía Minera de Cananea, Centro INAH Sonora, Instituto Nacional de Antropología e Historia (hereafter referred to as CMC), microfilm 71/147, folder 16.

7. G. Cosio, Secretary of State and Office of Interior, to the Governor of Sonora, June 13, 1902, AGES, tomo 1704, expediente 7.

8. Government of Sonora to the Secretary of Interior, Mexico City, April 7, 1903, AGES, tomo 1704, expediente 7; and Presidente Municipal of Cananea to Col. Benjamin Hill, February 26, 1912, AGES, tomo 2777, expediente 1.

9. Government of Sonora to the Secretary of Interior, Mexico City, April 7, 1903; and Residents of Cananea to Porfirio Díaz, President of Mexico, and Rafael Izábal, Governor of Sonora, May 27, 1902, AGES, tomo 1704, expediente 7.

10. Angel L. Coronado to Porfirio Díaz, March 23, 1902, Bonifacio Romero Rubio to Por-

firio Díaz, March 25, 1902, and undated memo from Robert Mitchell, AGES, tomo 1704, expediente 7; and Cosio to Governor of Sonora, June 13, 1902.

11. William C. Greene to George Mitchell, November 29, 1901, CMC, microfilm 69/147, folder 14; Allen C. Bernard to Antonio A. Martínez, June 21, 1902, CMC, microfilm 69/147, folder 1; Cosio to Governor of Sonora, June 13, 1902; Governor of Sonora to G. Cosio, June 23, 1902, AGES, tomo 1704, expediente 7; and Pablo Rubio to Secretary of State of Sonora, September 29, 1902, AGES, tomo 1705, expediente 3.

12. Residents of Cananea to Díaz and Izábal, May 27, 1902; and Cosio to Governor of Sonora, June 13, 1902.

13. Petition from residents of Cananea to Filiberto Barroso, Municipal President, Cananea, April 6, 1906, AGES, tomo 2138, expediente 1; Tomás Rico and other butchers of Cananea to the Governor of Sonora, January 13, 1906, AGES, tomo 2129, expediente 1; and Zacarías de la Torre to Filiberto Barroso, April 3, 1906, AGES, tomo 2138, expediente 1.

14. June 21, 1906, contract between the State of Sonora and the Cananea Cattle Company, AGES, tomo 2107, expediente 1.

15. *Tombstone Epitaph*, August 2, 1896; and Shelley Ann Bowen Hatfield, *Chasing Shadows: Indians Along the United States–Mexico Border, 1876–1911* (Albuquerque: University of New Mexico Press, 1998), 121–22, for the Apache Kid. For Billy Stiles, see *Bisbee Daily Review*, May 13, 1904; and Bill O'Neal, *The Arizona Rangers* (Austin: Eakin Press, 1987), 2.

16. Frazier Hunt, *Cap Mossman: Last of the Great Cowmen* (New York: Hastings House, 1951), 143–45.

17. For the Rangers in the copper borderlands, see O'Neal, *Arizona Rangers*, 7, 34, 118. For the *rurales*, see Paul J. Vanderwood, *Disorder and Progress: Bandits, Police, and Mexican Development* (Lincoln: University of Nebraska Press, 1981), and for the Gendarmería Fiscal, a branch of the Department of Treasury, see Carlos J. Sierra and Rogelio Martínez Vera, *El resguardo aduanal y la gendarmería fiscal, 1850–1925* (Mexico City: Secretaría de Hacienda y Crédito Público, 1971).

18. For Kosterlitzky's career in the copper borderlands, see Samuel Truett, "Transnational Warrior: Emilio Kosterlitzky and the Transformation of the U.S.–Mexico Borderlands, 1873–1928," in *Continental Crossroads: Remapping U.S.–Mexico Borderlands History*, ed. Samuel Truett and Elliott Young (Durham: Duke University Press, 2004), 241–70.

19. Judith Deutsch Kornblatt, *The Cossack Hero in Russian Literature: A Study in Cultural Mythology* (Madison: University of Wisconsin Press, 1992), 4; and Jules Verne, *Michael Strogoff, The Courier of the Czar* (New York: Scribner, Armstrong, 1877). For Kosterlitzky's linguistic skills, see "Kosterlitzky Retires as U.S. Agent," unidentified clipping in Emilio Kosterlitzky Papers, University of Arizona, Tucson.

20. September 27, 1902, certificate and September 2, 1893, certificate, Kosterlitzky Papers; Daniel Nugent, *Spent Cartridges of Revolution: An Anthropological History of Namiquipa, Chihuahua* (Chicago: University of Chicago Press, 1993); and Ana María Alonso, *Thread of Blood: Colonialism, Revolution, and Gender on Mexico's Northern Frontier* (Tucson: University of Arizona Press, 1995). For Sonora's "Apache fighting"

families, see James E. Officer, *Hispanic Arizona, 1536–1856* (Tucson: University of Arizona Press, 1987); and Stuart F. Voss, *On the Periphery of Nineteenth-Century Mexico: Sonora and Sinaloa, 1810–1877* (Tucson: University of Arizona Press, 1982).

21. Joe Wise to Ernest Kosterlitzky, n.d., Kosterlitzky Papers; Britton Davis, *The Truth About Geronimo*, ed. M. M. Quaife (New Haven: Yale University Press, 1929), 231; *Cananea Herald*, December 14, 1902; Hatfield, *Chasing Shadows*, 98; and *Tombstone Epitaph*, February 15, 1890.

22. Allan A. Erwin, *The Southwest of John H. Slaughter, 1841–1922* (Glendale, Calif.: Arthur H. Clark, 1965), 167–267; *Tombstone Epitaph*, October 15, 1929; *Tucson Citizen*, August 5, 1911; "Allen C. Bernard," in James H. McClintock, *Arizona: Prehistoric —Aboriginal—Pioneer—Modern*, vol. 3, *Biographical* (Chicago: S. J. Clarke, 1916), 871; and Mildred Young Wallace, *We Three: Papa's Ladies* (San Antonio: Naylor, 1957), 60. For militias in Sonora, see Officer, *Hispanic Arizona*.

23. *Bisbee Daily Review*, March 4, 1903; *Douglas Daily International*, November 22, 1904; and *Bisbee Daily Review*, July 6, 1907.

24. O'Neal, *Arizona Rangers*, 64; Joe Wise to Ernest Kosterlitzky, n.d., Kosterlitzky Papers; and Joe H. Pearce, "Line Rider," typewritten reminiscence in J. H. Pearce Papers, Arizona Historical Society, 111, 114.

25. For Apaches, see Howard Carroll Groton, "Riding the Flying Tortilla: Recollections of a Gringo Storekeeper in Mexico," *Journal of Arizona History* 31 (Summer 1990), 213–14; and Grenville Goodwin and Neil Goodwin, *The Apache Diaries: A Father–Son Journey* (Lincoln: University of Nebraska Press, 2000). For Yaquis, see Evelyn Hu-DeHart, *Yaqui Resistance and Survival: The Struggle for Land and Autonomy, 1821–1910* (Madison: University of Wisconsin Press, 1984); Edward H. Spicer, *The Yaquis: A Cultural History* (Tucson: University of Arizona Press, 1980); and Francisco P. Troncoso, *Las guerras con las tribus Yaqui y Mayo* (Mexico City: Instituto Nacional Indigenista, 1977).

26. *Bisbee Daily Review*, June 7, 1902, January 21, 1904, May 26, 1903, March 1, 1905. Kosterlitzky was involved with the Greene Consolidated Gold Company; see Emilio Kosterlitzky to William C. Greene, January 17, 1901, CMC, microfilm 71/147, folder 16. He also owned (with Americans) the Queatica Mining Company near Cananea. *Cananea Herald*, July 12, 1906. Kosterlitzky and Fenochio were also awarded lands by Díaz for campaigns against alleged bandits and Indians, lands they sold to Mormon colonists in 1892. Thomas H. Naylor, "The Mormons Colonize Sonora: Early Trials at Colonia Oaxaca," *Arizona and the West* 20 (Winter 1978), 329.

27. U.S. Consul Albert R. Morawitz to U.S. Assistant Secretary of State Robert Bacon, November 3, 1905, U.S. Department of State, *Despatches from United States Consuls in Nogales, 1889–1906* (hereafter DUSC-N), microfilm roll 4, vol. 4, National Archives, National Archives and Records Service (Washington, 1959).

28. Guillermo B. Puga to the Mining Agent of Magdalena, Sonora, December 30, 1905, DUSC-N microfilm roll 4, vol. 4; *Douglas Daily International*, January 15, 1906, January 11, 1906, January 23, 1906. Woodward had a motivation to squelch all stories about Yaqui depredations where he lived because he employed Yaqui workers.

29. Report from Rafael Izábal, Governor of Sonora, to the Department of Government,

Mexico City, in *El Diario Oficial*, February 27, 1906, in Ambassador David E. Thompson to Secretary of State Elihu Root, June 6, 1906, U.S. Department of State, *Despatches from United States Ministers to Mexico, 1823–1906*, (hereafter DUSM), microfilm roll 178, vol. 183, National Archives, National Archives and Records Service (Washington, 1955).

30. Testimony of Allen C. Bernard, J. H. Lesser, and J. C. Townsend in February 27, 1906, report from Rafael Izábal; and *Douglas Daily International*, February 21, 1906.

31. Testimony of P. Penelli, F. H. Seymour, and R. I. Horitt, in February 27, 1906, report from Rafael Izábal; and *Douglas Daily International*, January 3, 1906, December 26, 1905, January 10, 1906.

32. February 27, 1906, report from Rafael Izábal.

33. The strike at Cananea in 1906 has generated significant scholarly attention on both sides of the border. The best published source on the strike is Manuel González Ramírez, *La huelga de Cananea*, vol. 3, *Fuentes para la historia de la Revolución Mexicana* (Mexico City: Fondo de Cultura Económica, 1956) (hereafter referred to as *HC*).

34. Municipal President Filiberto Barroso to the Second Judge of the First Instance, June 1, 1906, *HC*, 32–33; and William C. Greene, "Brief Resume of the Recent Disorders in Cananea," June 11, 1906, and Statement by Arthur S. Dwight, June 8, 1906, CMC, microfilm 72/147, folder 19.

35. Rafael Izábal and Alberto Cubillas to Secretary of Government, June 19, 1906, *El Correo de Sonora*, July 9, 10, 11, 1906, *HC*, 95–96; Esteban Baca Calderón, *Juicio sobre la guerra del Yaqui y génesis de la huelga de Cananea* (Hermosillo: Contrapunto 14, 1997), 74–75; and *Douglas Daily International*, June 4, 1906. Some Americans did assign blame to the Metcalfs; see I. Kemperman to David Cole, July 24, 1906, CMC, microfilm 69/147, folder 7; and Thomas Rynning, *Gun Notches: The Life Story of a Cowboy-Soldier* (New York: Frederick A. Stokes, 1931), 306.

36. Dwight Statement; Barroso to Second Judge; Izábal and Cubillas to Secretary of Government; Testimony of Plácido Ríos, *HC*, 31–33, 96, 138–40; "Brief Resume"; and Vice Consul Albert W. Brickwood, Jr. to Assistant Secretary of State Robert Bacon, June 22, 1906, DUSC-N.

37. U.S. Consular Agent W. J. Galbraith to U.S. Department of State, June 1, 1906, DUSC-N; William C. Greene to Rafael Izábal, June 1, 1906, and F. López Linares to Rafael Izábal, June 1, 1906, *HC*, 28, 27; Calderón, *Juicio*, 76; *Douglas Daily International*, June 2, 1906; Luis E. Torres to Vice President Ramón Corral, June 5, 1906, *HC*, 75–76; Rynning, *Gun Notches*, 291–92; and *Douglas Daily International*, June 2, 1906.

38. Izábal and Cubillas to Secretary of Government; Brickwood to Bacon, June 22, 1906; Izábal's testimony in Torres to Izábal, June 5, 1906; Rynning, *Gun Notches*, 291–92; Adrián M. Cubillas to Ramón Corral, June 5, 1906, *HC*, 29–30; and C. I. McReynolds to Greene, June 6, 1906, CMC, microfilm 69/147, folder 7.

39. Izábal's testimony in Torres to Izábal; and Rynning, *Gun Notches*, 292–99. Rynning was himself a former rough rider. O'Neal, *Arizona Rangers*, 32–33.

40. Rynning, *Gun Notches*, 298–99; Brickwood to Bacon, June 22, 1906; Izábal's testimony in Torres to Izábal; and *Douglas Daily International*, June 3, 1906, June 7,

1906. I refer to Izábal's testimony as his "most candid report" because soon afterward he changed his story, claiming that Americans just happened to take the same train. Ramón Corral to Rafael Izábal, June 8, 1906, *HC*, 85–86.

41. "Brief Resume"; *Douglas Daily International*, June 3, 1906; Filiberto Barroso to the Second Judge of the First Instance, Cananea, June 2, 1906, Luis E. Torres to Municipal President of Guaymas, June 4, 1906, and Rafael Izábal to Ramón Corral, June 3, 1906, *HC*, 42–43, 68, 72; and James C. Scott, *Domination and the Arts of Resistance: Hidden Transcripts* (New Haven: Yale University Press, 1990), 105.

42. *Douglas Daily International*, June 2, 1906. "Kosterlitzky wasn't noways feeling friendly towards the world at large," Rynning later recalled. "Anyways he rode up to me and says: 'Get the hell out of Mexico, Tom, or I'll shoot you out!'" Rynning, *Gun Notches*, 307. See also Scott, *Hidden Transcripts*, 105. "A ruling stratum whose claim to authority rests on the provision of institutionalized justice under law with honest judges," notes Scott, "will have to go to exceptional lengths to hide its thugs, its hired assassins, its secret police, and its use of intimidation."

43. *Douglas Daily International*, June 2, 1906; photograph #4362, Pictures—Out of State—Mexico—Riots (Cananea), Arizona Historical Society; Mrs. I. L. Burgess to Ernest Kosterlitzky, September 19, 1947, Kosterlitzky Papers; and *Douglas Daily International*, August 13, 1906.

44. *Douglas Daily International*, July 13, 1906, August 13, 1906; Emilio Kosterlitzky to George Young, July 31, 1907, and Emilio Kosterlitzky to George Young, April 10, 1907, CMC, microfilm 71/147, folder 16.

45. *Mining World* 21 (December 24, 1904), front page; and *Engineering and Mining Journal* 83 (January 5, 1907), 6. Years later, Cananea officials were still trying to shake the specter of Greene's mismanagement, his reckless appetite, and his mishandling of events in 1906. George Young to Horace J. Stevens, March 21, 1912, CMC, microfilm 71/147, folder 11.

46. David M. Pletcher, *Rails, Mines, and Progress: Seven American Promoters in Mexico, 1867–1911* (Ithaca: Cornell University Press, 1958), 252–53; *Mining World* 26 (January 19, 1907), 59–60; and William C. Greene to Stockholders of the Greene Consolidated Copper Company, August 11, 1906, William H. Brown Collection, Yale University.

47. *Engineering and Mining Journal* 82 (December 22, 1906), 1183, 1192, and 83 (January 5, 1907), 6, 43.

48. "Louis D. Ricketts: An Interview," in T. A. Rickard, *Interviews with Mining Engineers* (San Francisco: Mining and Scientific Press, 1922), 431–43; and George Young to L. D. Ricketts, February 2, 1907.

49. *Engineering and Mining Journal* 84 (November 2, 1907), 842, and (November 9, 1907), 895.

50. *Mining World* 29 (September 12, 1908), 393, and (August 8, 1908), 224.

51. *Mining World* 29 (September 12, 1908), 393; *Engineering and Mining Journal* 86 (November 14, 1908), 954–56; and *Mining World* 30 (May 8, 1909), 869–70.

52. *Mining World* 21 (December 10, 1904), 581–82; *Bisbee Daily Review*, September 8, 1905; Greene Consolidated Copper Company, *1906 Annual Report*; and "Remarks of

President W. C. Greene at the Meeting of the Stockholders of the Greene Consolidated Copper Co. held at 24 Broad Street, New York, February 10th, 1906," CMC, microfilm 70/147, folder 19.

53. Morris B. Parker, *Mines, Mules and Me in Mexico, 1895–1932*, ed. James M. Day (Tucson: University of Arizona Press, 1979), 97; and *Bisbee Daily Review*, September 20, 1905.

54. *Douglas Daily International*, May 14, 1906; and Winthrop E. Scarritt, "On the Road to Ocampo," 2–5, undated typed manuscript, Robert F. Torrance Papers, box 2, folder 20, Arizona Historical Society.

55. Scarritt, "Road to Ocampo," 6–7.

56. W. H. Webb to Ignacio Macmanus, May 18, 1907, and Ignacio Macmanus to Mercantile Banking Company, May 27, 1907, CMC, microfilm 71/147, folder 15; *Douglas Daily International*, December 6, 1907; *Annual Report of the Greene Consolidated Copper Company, for the Year Ending July Thirty-First, 1907*, 5; L. D. Ricketts to John A. Campbell, November 14, 1907, CMC, microfilm 70/147, folder 12; and *Engineering and Mining Journal* 86 (August 1, 1908), 252, (August 15, 1908), 350, and (September 5, 1908), 494.

57. *Engineering and Mining Journal* 86 (July 25, 1908), 159–60.

58. Ibid., 160.

59. Parker, *Mules*, 97–98, 100.

60. *Engineering and Mining Journal* 86 (October 17, 1908), 786, and (November 7, 1908), 929; *Douglas Daily International*, May 17, 1909; and Parker, *Mules*, 99.

7. INSURGENT LANDSCAPES

1. *Bisbee Daily Review*, September 23, 1905; and *Douglas Daily International*, March 2, 1905, July 26, 1906, August 6, 1906. For *Magonistas* in the copper borderlands, also see discussions in Ward S. Albro, *Always a Rebel: Ricardo Flores Magón and the Mexican Revolution* (Fort Worth: Texas Christian University Press, 1992); and W. Dirk Raat, *Revoltosos: Mexico's Rebels in the United States, 1903–1923* (College Station: Texas A&M University Press, 1981).

2. *Douglas Daily International*, August 9, 1906, August 13, 1906, September 5, 1906, September 13, 1906, September 18, 1906, September 19, 1906.

3. *Douglas Daily International*, September 13, 1906, September 17, 1906, September 18, 1906, September 19, 1906.

4. *Douglas Daily International*, June 17, 1910; Emilio Kosterlitzky to Porfirio Díaz, August 1, 1910, Emilio Kosterlitzky Papers, University of Arizona Library, Special Collections; *Douglas Daily International*, June 18, 1910, June 20, 1910, June 21, 1910.

5. U.S. Consul Luther T. Ellsworth to U.S. Secretary of State Philander C. Knox, October 27, 1910, *Records of the Department of State Relating to Internal Affairs of Mexico* (hereafter RDS-RIAM), 1910–29, National Archives Microfilm Publications, microcopy no. 274 (Washington: National Archives and Records Service, 1959), roll 10, 812.00/411; Emilio Kosterlitzky to Porfirio Díaz, August 1, 1910, Kosterlitzky Papers; Luther T. Ellsworth to Philander C. Knox, November 11, 1910, and F. W. Berkshire

to Luther T. Ellsworth, November 9, 1910, RDS-RIAM, roll 10, 812.00/422; Emilio Kosterlitzky to William H. Brophy, November 23, 1910, Frank Cullen Brophy Papers, box 31, folder 952, Arizona Historical Society; *Douglas Daily International,* November 24, 1910; U.S. Marshal C. M. Foraker to U.S. Attorney General George W. Wickersham, December 31, 1910, RDS-RIAM, roll 10, 812.00/624; and *Douglas Daily International,* January 3, 1911.

6. Morris B. Parker, *Mules, Mines and Me in Mexico, 1895–1932* (Tucson: University of Arizona Press, 1979), 104–05; and Alan Knight, *The Mexican Revolution* (Lincoln: University of Nebraska Press, 1986), 1:175–78.

7. Knight, *Mexican Revolution,* 1:181–82; U.S. Consul Alexander V. Dye to Philander C. Knox, March 4, 1911, RDS-RIAM, roll 11, 812.00/907; Luther T. Ellsworth to Philander C. Knox, March 4 and 7, 1911, RDS-RIAM, roll 11, 812.00/907 and 812.00/924; and *Douglas Daily International,* March 10, 1911, March 14, 1911, March 17, 1911.

8. Inez Horton, *Copper's Children: The Rise and Fall of a Mexican Copper Mining Camp* (New York: Exposition Press, 1968), 67; Alexander V. Dye to Philander C. Knox, April 14, 1911, RDS-RIAM, roll 12, 812.00/1333; J. E. Morrison to George W. Wickersham, April 14, 1911, RDS-RIAM, roll 12, 812.00/1418; and *Douglas Daily International,* April 14, 1911, April 16, 1911.

9. *Douglas Daily International,* April 18, 1911, April 19, 1911.

10. *Douglas Daily International,* April 18, 1911, May 5, 1911.

11. Alexander V. Dye to Philander C. Knox, April 18, 1911, RDS-RIAM, roll 12, 812.00/1376; and *Douglas Daily International,* April 19, 1911, April 24, 1911, April 25, 1911.

12. Knight, *Mexican Revolution,* 1:201–04.

13. William C. Greene to U.S. Secretary of State Philander C. Knox, May 13, 1911, RDS-RIAM, roll 13, 812.00/1749; U.S. Consul Alexander V. Dye to U.S. Secretary of State Philander C. Knox, May 12, 1911, RDS-RIAM, roll 13, 812.00/1737; U.S. Consular Agent George A. Wiswall to U.S. Secretary of State Philander C. Knox, May 13 and 14, 1911, RDS-RIAM, roll 13, 812.00/1754 and 812.00/1757; U.S. Consul Alexander V. Dye to U.S. Secretary of State Philander C. Knox, May 17, 1911, RDS-RIAM, roll 13, 812.00/1893; John C. Greenway to Thomas F. Cole, May 16, 1911, John C. Greenway Papers, Arizona Historical Society, box 182, folder 2408; and *Douglas Daily International,* May 10, 1911, May 13, 1911, May 15, 1911, May 16, 1911.

14. U.S. Consul Alexander V. Dye to U.S. Secretary of State Philander C. Knox, May 21, 1911, RDS-RIAM, roll 13, 812.00/1954; and *Douglas Daily International,* April 2, 1911, June 8, 1911, May 19, 1911.

15. *Engineering and Mining Journal* 92 (July 29, 1911), 209, and (October 7, 1911), 689.

16. For political conditions in Sonora and the Orozquista revolt, see Susan M. Deeds, "José María Maytorena and the Mexican Revolution in Sonora (Part I)," *Arizona and the West* 18 (Spring 1976), 30–39; but also see Michael C. Meyer, *Mexican Rebel: Pascual Orozco and the Mexican Revolution, 1910–1915* (Lincoln: University of Nebraska Press, 1967).

17. Deeds, "José María Maytorena," 38–39; *Douglas Daily International,* August 5, 1912; U.S. Bureau of Investigation Special Agent's Report, El Paso, August 8, 1912, RDS-

RIAM, roll 20, 812.00/4669; U.S. Consul Alexander V. Dye to U.S. Secretary of State Philander C. Knox, August 8, 1912, roll 19, 812.00/4591; *Douglas Daily International*, August 6, 1912; U.S. Consul Alexander V. Dye to U.S. Secretary of State Philander C. Knox, August 20, 1912, RDS-RIAM, roll 20, 812.00/4671; and U.S. Consul Thomas D. Bowman to U.S. Secretary of State Philander C. Knox, August 19, 1912, RDS-RIAM, roll 20, 812.00/4665.

18. *Douglas Daily International*, August 26, 1912, August 27, 1912, August 29, 1912; U.S. Consul Thomas D. Bowman to U.S. Secretary of State Philander C. Knox, September 7, 1912, RDS-RIAM, roll 20, 812.00/4888; U.S. Consul Alexander V. Dye to U.S. Secretary of State Philander C. Knox, September 2, 1912, RDS-RIAM, roll 20, 812.00/4765; and *Douglas Daily International*, September 3, 1912, September 4, 1912, September 8, 1912.

19. Second Assistant Secretary of State Alvey A. Adee to U.S. Consul Alexander V. Dye, September 5, 1912, RDS-RIAM, roll 20, 812.00/4771; U.S. Bureau of Investigation Special Agent's Report, Douglas, September 4, 1912, RDS-RIAM, roll 20, 812.00/5110; U.S. Consul Alexander V. Dye to U.S. Secretary of State Philander C. Knox, September 4, 1912, RDS-RIAM, roll 20, 812.00/4807; *Douglas Daily International*, September 5, 1912, September 6, 1912; and U.S. Bureau of Investigation Special Agent's Report, Douglas, September 6, 1912, RDS-RIAM, roll 20, 812.00/5110.

20. U.S. Bureau of Investigation Special Agent's Report, Douglas, September 4, 1912, RDS-RIAM, roll 20, 812.00/5110.

21. *Douglas Daily International*, September 13, 1912.

22. *Douglas Daily International*, August 20, 1912; and *Engineering and Mining Journal* 94 (September 7, 1912), 431–32.

23. Knight, *Mexican Revolution*, 329; but also see Álvaro Obregón, *Ocho mil kilómetros en campaña* (Mexico City: Fondo de Cultura Económica, 1959), 22–66; Héctor Aguilar Camín, *La frontera nómada: Sonora y la Revolución Mexicana*, 2d ed. (Mexico City: Cal y Arena, 1997); and Linda B. Hall, *Álvaro Obregón: Power and Revolution in Mexico, 1911–1920* (College Station: Texas A&M University Press, 1981).

24. Emilio Kosterlitzky to Antonio F. Torres, February 12, 1912, and undated 1912 circular from Emilio Kosterlitzky, Kosterlitzky Papers; U.S. Consul Alexander V. Dye to U.S. Secretary of State Philander C. Knox, July 17, 1912, RDS-RIAM, roll 19, 812.00/4458; Emilio Kosterlitzky to Juán N. Rondero, April 21, 1912, Kosterlitzky Papers; Emilio Kosterlitzky to U.S. Consul Alexander V. Dye, July 11, 1912, RDS-RIAM, roll 19, 821.00/4458; and *El Paso Herald*, August 28, 1912. For Apache fighting identities in Chihuahua, see Daniel Nugent, *Spent Cartridges of Revolution: An Anthropological History of Namiquipa, Chihuahua* (Chicago: University of Chicago Press, 1993); and Ana María Alonso, *Thread of Blood: Colonialism, Revolution, and Gender on Mexico's Northern Frontier* (Tucson: University of Arizona Press, 1995). For Yaquis as soldiers in the Mexican revolution, see Edward H. Spicer, *The Yaquis: A Cultural History* (Tucson: University of Arizona Press, 1980), 227–35; and Evelyn Hu-DeHart, *Yaqui Resistance and Survival: The Struggle for Land and Autonomy, 1821–1910* (Madison: University of Wisconsin Press, 1984), 206–10.

25. Knight, *Mexican Revolution*, 2:1–17; Frederick Simpich to U.S. Secretary of State,

February 21, 1913, RDS-RIAM, roll 23, 812.00/6303; Thomas D. Bowman to U.S. Secretary of State, February 24, 1913, RDS-RIAM, roll 23, 812.00/6342.

26. See discussions of motivations in Knight, *Mexican Revolution,* 2:16–17; and Susan M. Deeds, "José María Maytorena and the Mexican Revolution in Sonora (Part II)," *Arizona and the West* 18 (Summer 1976), 125–32.

27. Knight, *Mexican Revolution,* 2:11–17, 24–30; and Deeds, "Maytorena and the Mexican Revolution," 127–36.

28. Knight, *Mexican Revolution,* 2:218–19, 276–78; and Deeds, "Maytorena and the Mexican Revolution," 138–42.

29. Brigadier General Tasker H. Bliss, "Report for the week ending October 10, 1914," RDS-RIAM, roll 41, 812.00/13545.

30. Brigadier General Tasker H. Bliss, "Report for the week ending October 17, 1914," RDS-RIAM, roll 41, 812.00/13586; Brigadier General Tasker H. Bliss, "Report for the week ending October 10, 1914," RDS-RIAM, roll 41, 812.00/13545; and C. K. Schafer, Inspector in Charge, Naco, to Supervising Inspector, Immigration Service, El Paso, October 13, 1914, RDS-RIAM, roll 43, 812.00/14065.

31. Governor George W.P. Hunt to U.S. Secretary of State William Jennings Bryan, October 3, 1914, RDS-RIAM, roll 41, 812.00/13386; and U.S. Vice Consul Frederick Simpich to U.S. Secretary of State William Jennings Bryan, October 13, 1914, RDS-RIAM, roll 41, 812.00/13485.

32. Wheeler's testimony was taken during the late 1910s as part of a larger hearing by Albert Bacon Fall to study claims by U.S. citizens against the Mexican government. See "Testimony of Capt. Harry Wheeler," in U.S. Senate, *Investigation of Mexican Affairs. Hearing Before a Subcommittee of the Committee on Foreign Relations . . . to Investigate the Matter of Outrages on Citizens of the United States in Mexico, Part 12* (Washington: GPO, 1919), 1878.

33. "Testimony of Capt. Harry Wheeler," 1878.

34. Secretary of State William Jennings Bryan to William C. Carothers, August 13, 1914, RDS-RIAM, roll 40, 812.00/12836; Brigadier General Tasker H. Bliss, "Report for the week ending August 15, 1914," RDS-RIAM, roll 40, 812.00/12972; U.S. Vice Consul Frederick Simpich to U.S. Secretary of State William Jennings Bryan, September 4, 1914, RDS-RIAM, roll 40, 812.00/13147.

35. U.S. Consular Agent Charles Montague to U.S. Consul Frederick Simpich, February 28, 1915, RDS-RIAM, roll 44, 812.00/14863.

36. Ibid.

37. U.S. Consul Frederick Simpich to U.S. Secretary of State William Jennings Bryan, April 6, 1915, RDS-RIAM, roll 44, 812.00/14863. For a brief history of the Yaqui Indians and their role in the Mexican Revolution to this date, see Anonymous author (likely Frederick Simpich) from Nogales in Major General Frederick Funston, "Report for the week ending May 15, 1915," RDS-RIAM, roll 45, 812.00/15074.

38. F. W. Berkshire, Supervising Inspector, El Paso, to Commissioner-General of Immigration, Washington, D.C., June 11, 1915, *Records of the Immigration and Naturalization Service, Series A: Subject Correspondence Files, Part 2: Mexican Immigra-*

tion, 1906–1930 (Bethesda, Md.: University Publications of America, 1993) (hereafter *RINS-MI*), microfilm 5, frame 0301.

39. Frank W. Heath, Inspector in Charge, Douglas, Arizona, to Supervising Inspector, Immigration Service, El Paso, June 17, 1915, *RINS-MI*, microfilm 5, frame 0255.

40. For the Plan de San Diego uprising, see Benjamin Heber Johnson, *Revolution in Texas: How a Forgotten Uprising and Its Bloody Suppression Turned Mexicans into Americans* (New Haven: Yale University Press, 2003).

41. U.S. Consul Frederick Simpich to U.S. Secretary of State Robert Lansing, September 15, 1915, RDS-RIAM, roll 48, 812.00/16188; U.S. Consul Frederick Simpich to U.S. Secretary of State Robert Lansing, September 4, 1915, RDS-RIAM, roll 48, 812.00/16068; and Major General Frederick Funston, "Report for the week ending September 11, 1915," RDS-RIAM, roll 48, 812.00/16256.

42. J. W. Heard, Department Adjutant, "Report for the week ending January 9, 1915," RDS-RIAM, roll 43, 812.00/14241.

43. Knight, *Mexican Revolution*, 2:333–34; Major General Frederick Funston, "Report for the week ending October 9, 1915," RDS-RIAM, roll 49, 812.00/16526.

44. U.S. Consul Frederick Simpich to U.S. Secretary of State Robert Lansing, October 14, 1915, RDS-RIAM, roll 49, 812.00/16481; Major General Frederick Funston, "Report for the week ending October 16, 1915," RDS-RIAM, roll 49, 812.00/16600; U.S. Consular Agent Charles L. Montague to U.S. Secretary of State Robert Lansing, October 23, 1915, RDS-RIAM, roll 49, 812.00/16582; Major General Frederick Funston, "Report for the week ending October 23, 1915," RDS-RIAM, roll 49, 812.00/16667; Oscar K. Goll, Secretary, Douglas Chamber of Commerce and Mines, to U.S. Secretary of State Robert Lansing, October 25, 1915, RDS-RIAM, roll 49, 812.00/16590; and U.S. Consular Agent George C. Carothers to U.S. Secretary of State Robert Lansing, October 29, 1915, RDS-RIAM, roll 49, 812.00/16627.

45. Knight, *Mexican Revolution*, 2:333–34.

46. These kinds of fears are abundantly illustrated by the correspondence files in the Records of the Department of State Relating to the Internal Affairs of Mexico, 1910–29 for 1916 and 1917.

47. For the Bisbee Deportation, see James W. Byrkit, *Forging the Copper Collar: Arizona's Labor Management War of 1901–1921* (Tucson: University of Arizona Press, 1982); George Soule, "The Law of Necessity in Bisbee," *Nation* 113 (1921), 21–23; Colleen O'Neill, "Domesticity Deployed: Gender, Race, and the Construction of Class Struggle in the Bisbee Deportation," *Labor History* 34 (Spring 1993), 256–73; David M. Kennedy, *Over Here: The First World War and American Society* (New York: Oxford University Press, rev. ed., 2004); and Katherine Benton-Cohen, "Docile Children and Dangerous Revolutionaries: The Racial Hierarchy of Manliness and the Bisbee Deportation of 1917," *Frontiers: A Journal of Women's Studies* 24 (Fall 2003), 30–50.

48. Testimony of Harry C. Wheeler, Sheriff of Cochise County, *Papers of the President's Mediation Commission, 1917–1919* (hereafter *PMC*), ed. Melvyn Dubofsky, rev. ed. (Frederick, Md.: University Publications of America, 1986), reel 2, 141. Perhaps the

best discussion of Mexicans in the Bisbee Deportation is Benton-Cohen, "Docile Children and Dangerous Revolutionaries."

49. "Testimony of Capt. Harry Wheeler," *Investigation of Mexican Affairs*, 1883, 1885; but also see "Testimony of Harry C. Wheeler," *PMC*, reel 2, 141.

50. "Testimony of Harry C. Wheeler," *PMC*, reel 2, 143. Most historians have anchored the Loyalty League directly in the context of World War I without bothering to trace its beginnings.

EPILOGUE. REMAPPING THE BORDERLANDS

1. Maud Kenyon-Kingdon, *From Out the Dark Shadows* (San Diego: Frye and Smith, 1925), 233. For bilingual lawyers, see Delbert Haff to George Young, Documentación Procedente de la Compañía Minera de Cananea (hereafter referred to as CMC), microfilm 69/147, folder 12, Centro INAH Sonora, Instituto Nacional de Antropología e Historia, Hermosillo, Sonora. For Sonorenses in Mexico City in the 1920s, see Héctor Aguilar Camín, "The Relevant Tradition: Sonoran Leaders in the Revolution," in *Caudillo and Peasant in the Mexican Revolution*, ed. David A. Brading (Cambridge: Cambridge University Press, 1980).

2. P. L. Bell and H. Bentley Mackenzie, *Mexican West Coast and Lower California: A Commercial and Industrial Survey* (Washington: GPO, 1923), 1; *Engineering and Mining Journal-Press* 116 (September 8, 1923), 408, and 116 (October 27, 1923), 719–22.

3. H. H. Horton, "Memorandum for the Directors," September 6, 1926, Moctezuma Copper Company Papers (hereafter referred to as MCC Papers), Labor Disputes and Strikes, Phelps Dodge Corporation Archives, Phoenix Arizona.

4. Ibid.

5. P. G. Beckett to Walter Douglas, December 12, 1923, MCC Papers, Labor Disputes and Strikes; Walter Douglas to A. T. Thompson, April 13, 1918, MCC Papers, Dwelling Houses and Quarters, 1918; and Frank Ayer to P. G. Beckett, April 30, 1927, MCC Papers, Industrial Relations.

6. H. T. Hamilton to P. G. Beckett, February 22, 1923, H. T. Hamilton to P. G. Beckett, December 4, 1923, H. T. Hamilton to P. G. Beckett, December 14, 1923, and Frank Ayer to P. G. Beckett, February 17, 1925, MCC Papers, Labor Disputes and Strikes.

7. For progressive ideals infusing Phelps Dodge company town planning at this time, see Margaret Crawford, *Building the Workman's Paradise: The Design of American Company Towns* (London: Verso, 1995).

8. Simón Russek to H. T. Hamilton, December 26, 1923, and Frank Ayer to P. G. Beckett, January 8, 1924, MCC Papers, Labor Disputes and Strikes.

9. H. T. Hamilton to P. G. Beckett, December 4, 1923, and December 24, 1923, MCC Papers, Labor Disputes and Strikes; and Ralph McA. Ingersoll, *In and Under Mexico* (New York: Century, 1924), 38–44, 67–69, 75–78.

10. Morris B. Parker, *Mules, Mines and Me in Mexico, 1895–1932* (Tucson: University of Arizona Press, 1979), 140–41; and Inez Horton, *Copper's Children: The Rise and Fall of a Mexican Copper Mining Camp* (New York: Exposition Press, 1968), 186–

92. Phelps Dodge reopened Pilares in the late 1930s, briefly returning to full-scale production after World War II but closing down for the last time in 1950. Carlos A. Schwantes, *Vision and Enterprise: Exploring the History of Phelps Dodge Corporation* (Tucson: University of Arizona Press, 2000), 229.

11. Josiah McC. Heyman, *Life and Labor on the Border: Working People of Northeastern Sonora, Mexico, 1886–1986* (Tucson: University of Arizona Press, 1991), 111; Leslie Hewes, "Huepac: An Agricultural Village of Sonora, Mexico," *Economic Geography* 11 (July 1935), 292; William A. Evans, *Two Generations in the Southwest* (Phoenix: Sims, 1971), 17; and Isaac F. Marcosson, *Anaconda* (New York: Dodd, Mead, 1957), 255–56.

12. For the rise of the border patrol, see Joseph Nevins, *Operation Gatekeeper: The Rise of the "Illegal Alien" and the Making of the U.S.–Mexico Boundary* (New York: Routledge, 2002). For repatriation, see Abraham Hoffman, *Unwanted Mexican Americans in the Great Depression: Repatriation Pressures, 1929–1939* (Tucson: University of Arizona Press, 1974); and Francisco E. Balderrama, *Decade of Betrayal: Mexican Repatriation in the 1930s* (Albuquerque: University of New Mexico Press, 1995). For the deportation of Chinese in Sonora, see Leo Michael Dambourges Jacques, "The Anti-Chinese Campaigns in Sonora, Mexico, 1900–1931" (PhD diss., University of Arizona, 1974); and José Angel Espinoza, *El ejemplo de Sonora* (Mexico City, 1932).

13. See discussions in John Francis Bannon, *Herbert Eugene Bolton: The Historian and the Man, 1870–1953* (Tucson: University of Arizona Press, 1978); Samuel Truett, "Epics of Greater America: Herbert Eugene Bolton's Quest for a Transnational American History," in *Interpreting Spanish Colonialism: Empires, Nations, and Legends*, ed. Christopher Schmidt-Nowara and John Nieto-Phillips (Albuquerque: University of New Mexico Press, 2005), 213–47; and Suzanne Forrest, *The Preservation of the Village: New Mexico's Hispanics and the New Deal* (Albuquerque: University of New Mexico Press, 1989).

14. Mary Kay Vaughan, *Cultural Politics in Revolution: Teachers, Peasants, and Schools in Mexico, 1930–1940* (Tucson: University of Arizona Press, 1997), 38–45, 190; but also see Thomas Benjamin, *La Revolución: Mexico's Great Revolution as Memory, Myth, and History* (Austin: University of Texas Press, 2000).

BIBLIOGRAPHY

ARCHIVAL SOURCES

Archivo General del Estado de Sonora. Hermosillo, Sonora.

Archivo General de Notarías del Estado de Sonora. Archivo General del Estado de Sonora. Hermosillo, Sonora.

Bisbee Mining and Historical Museum. Bisbee, Arizona.

Blake, William P. Collection. Yale University. New Haven, Connecticut.

Brophy, Frank Cullen. Papers. Arizona Historical Society. Tucson, Arizona.

Brown, William H. Collection. Yale University. New Haven, Connecticut.

Documentación Procedente de la Compañía Minera de Cananea. Centro INAH Sonora, Instituto Nacional de Antropología e Historia. Hermosillo, Sonora.

Douglas, James. Papers. Arizona Historical Society. Tucson, Arizona.

Gray, John Pleasant. "When All Roads Led to Tombstone." 1940 manuscript, Arizona Historical Society. Tucson, Arizona.

Greene Cananea Copper Company Collection. Arizona Historical Society. Tucson, Arizona.

Greenway, John C. Papers. Arizona Historical Society. Tucson, Arizona.

Hayden Arizona Pioneer Biographies Collection. Arizona Collection, Department of Archives and Manuscripts, Arizona State University Library. Phoenix, Arizona.

Hill, Robert T. Papers. DeGolyer Library. Southern Methodist University. Dallas, Texas.

Kosterlitzky, Emilio. Papers. University of Arizona. Tucson, Arizona.

Milton, Jeff. File. Tombstone Courthouse State Historic Park, Law Office Annex. Tombtone, Arizona.

Moctezuma Copper Company Papers. Phelps Dodge Corporation Archives. Phoenix, Arizona.

Park, Joe. Collection. Arizona Historical Society. Tucson, Arizona.

Parker, Morris B. Papers. Huntington Library. San Marino, California.

Pearce, J. H. Papers. Arizona Historical Society. Tucson, Arizona.

Phelps Dodge Corporation Archives. Phoenix, Arizona.

Robinson, Don Juan A. Statement. Bancroft Library, Mexican Manuscript 375.
Steinfeld, Albert. "Copper Queen History as told by A. Steinfeld." Recollections in the form of clip books. Arizona Historical Society. Tucson, Arizona.
Torrance, Robert F. Papers. Arizona Historical Society. Tucson, Arizona.

PERIODICALS

Arizona Citizen (Tucson)
Arizona Daily Star (Tucson)
Arizona Quarterly Illustrated (Tucson)
Arizona Weekly Star (Tucson)
Cananea Herald (Cananea)
Cochise Review (Bisbee)
Congressional Globe (Washington, D.C.)
La Constitución (Hermosillo)
Daily Alta California (San Francisco)
Douglas Daily International (Douglas)
El Fronterizo (Tucson)
El Paso Herald (El Paso)
Engineering and Mining Journal (New York)
Mining and Metallurgy (New York)
Mining World (Chicago)
New York Daily Tribune (New York)
Nogales Oasis (Nogales)
San Francisco Call (San Francisco)
Tombstone Epitaph (Tombstone)
Tombstone Daily Nugget (Tombstone)
Weekly Alta California (San Francisco)
Weekly Arizonian (Tubac)

CORPORATE ANNUAL REPORTS

Annual Report of the Greene Consolidated Copper Company. New York. 1902–07.
Atchison, Topeka, and Santa Fe Railroad. *Annual Reports*. 1883–89.
Greene Gold-Silver Company. New York. 1905.

GOVERNMENT DOCUMENTS

Letters Received Relating to Disturbances Along the Mexican Border, December 13, 1878–January 25, 1884. Interior Department Territorial Papers, Arizona, 1868–1913. Microcopy no. 429, roll 3. Washington, 1963.
Papers of the President's Mediation Commission, 1917–1919. Edited by Melvyn Dubofsky. Revised edition. Frederick, Md.: University Publications of America, 1986.

Papers Relating to the Foreign Relations of the United States, December 4, 1882. Washington: GPO, 1883.

Records of the Department of State Relating to Internal Affairs of Mexico, 1910–29. National Archives Microfilm Publications, Microcopy no. 274. Washington: National Archives and Records Service, 1959.

Records of the Immigration and Naturalization Service, Series A: Subject Correspondence Files, Part 2: Mexican Immigration, 1906–1930. Bethesda, Md.: University Publications of America, 1993.

Report of the Postmaster General for 1861. Washington: GPO, 1862.

U.S. Congress. *Papers Relating to the Foreign Relations of the United States.* Washington: GPO, 1879–80.

U.S. Department of Interior. *Annual Report of the Secretary of Interior. Report of the Governor of Arizona Territory.* Washington: GPO, 1864–1910.

U.S. Department of State. *Commercial Relations of the United States with Foreign Countries.* Washington, D.C.: GPO, 1864–1900.

U.S. Department of State. *Commercial Relations of the United States. Reports from the Consuls of the United States on the Commerce, Manufactures, etc., of their Consular Districts.* Washington: GPO, 1864–1900.

U.S. Department of State. *Despatches from United States Consuls in Nogales, 1889–1906.* Microfilm series T-323. Washington: National Archives, 1959.

U.S. Department of State. *Despatches from United States Ministers to Mexico, 1823–1906.* National Archives and Records Service. General Services Administration. Washington, 1955.

U.S. House of Representatives. Thirty-Sixth Congress, First Session. Executive Document. *Message from the President of the United States in the Two Houses of Congress at the Commencement of the First Session of the Thirty-Sixth Congress.* Volume 2. Washington: George W. Bowman, 1860.

U.S. House of Representatives. Fortieth Congress, First Session. *Executive Document No. 33.* Washington: GPO, 1867.

U.S. Senate. *Investigation of Mexican Affairs. Hearing Before a Subcommittee of the Committee on Foreign Relations . . . to Investigate the Matter of Outrages on Citizens of the United States in Mexico.* 23 volumes. Washington: GPO, 1919.

U.S. War Department. *Report of the Secretary of War for 1859.* Washington: George W. Bowman, 1860.

U.S. War Department. *Report of the Secretary of War.* Washington: GPO, 1885.

PUBLISHED SOURCES, DISSERTATIONS, AND THESES

Acuña, Rodolfo. *Sonoran Strongman: Ignacio Pesqueira and his Times.* Tucson: University of Arizona Press, 1974.

Adorno, Rolena, and Patrick Charles Pautz. *Álvar Núñez Cabeza de Vaca: His Account, His Life, and the Expedition of Pánfilo de Narváez.* 3 volumes. Lincoln: University of Nebraska Press, 1999.

Aguilar, José de, Gobernador de Sonora. *Memoria en que el gobierno del estado libre de Sonora, da cuenta de los ramos de su administración al congreso del mismo estado, con arreglo a lo dispuesto en el artículo 27 de La Constitución.* Ures: Imprenta del Gobierno del Estado, a cargo de Jesús P. Siquieros, 1850.

Aguilar Camín, Héctor. "The Relevant Tradition: Sonoran Leaders in the Revolution." In *Caudillo and Peasant in the Mexican Revolution.* Edited by David A. Brading. Cambridge: Cambridge University Press, 1980.

———. *La frontera nómada: Sonora y la Revolución Mexicana.* Second edition. Mexico City: Cal y Arena, 1997.

Aguirre, Mamie Bernard. "Spanish Trader's Wife." *Westport Historical Quarterly* 4 (December 1968), 5–22.

Aguirre, Manuel J., ed. *Cananea: Las garras del imperialismo en las entrañas de México.* Mexico City: Libro Mex, 1958.

Albro, Ward S. *Always a Rebel: Ricardo Flores Magón and the Mexican Revolution.* Fort Worth: Texas Christian University Press, 1992.

Allyn, Joseph Pratt. *The Arizona of Joseph Pratt Allyn: Letters from a Pioneer Judge: Observations and Travels, 1863–1866.* Edited by John Nicholson. Tucson: University of Arizona Press, 1974.

Almada, Francisco R. *Diccionario de historia, geografía, y biografía sonorenses.* Third edition. Hermosillo: Instituto Sonorense de Cultura, 1990.

Alonso, Ana María. *Thread of Blood: Colonialism, Revolution, and Gender on Mexico's Northern Frontier.* Tucson: University of Arizona Press, 1995.

Atondo Rodríguez, Ana María, and Martha Ortega Soto. "Entrada de colonos españoles en Sonora durante el siglo XVII." In *Tres siglos de historia sonorense (1530–1830),* coordinated by Sergio Ortega Noriega and Ignacio del Río. Mexico City: Universidad Nacional Autónoma de México, 1993.

Austin, W. Lawrence. "Silver Milling in Arizona." *Transactions of the American Institute of Mining Engineers* 11 (1883), 91–106.

Axford, Joseph "Mack." *Around Western Campfires.* Tucson: University of Arizona Press, 1969.

Baca Calderón, Esteban. *Juicio sobre la guerra del Yaqui y génesis de la huelga de Cananea.* Hermosillo: Contrapunto 14, 1997.

Bahre, Conrad J. *A Legacy of Change: Historic Human Impact on Vegetation in the Arizona Borderlands.* Tucson: University of Arizona Press, 1991.

———. "Wild Hay Harvesting in Southern Arizona: A Casualty of the March of Progress." *Journal of Arizona History* 28 (Spring 1987), 69–78.

Bahre, Conrad J., and Charles F. Hutchison. "The Impact of Historic Fuelwood Cutting on the Semidesert Woodlands of Southeastern Arizona." *Journal of Forest History* 29 (October 1985), 175–86.

Bailey, Lynn R. *Tombstone, Arizona, "Too Tough to Die": The Rise, Fall, and Resurrection of a Silver Camp, 1878 to 1990.* Tucson: Westernlore Press, 2004.

———. *The Valiants: The Tombstone Rangers and Apache War Frivolities.* Tucson: Westernlore Press, 1999.

———. *"We'll All Wear Silk Hats": The Erie and Chiricahua Cattle Companies and the*

Rise of Corporate Ranching in the Sulphur Spring Valley of Arizona, 1883–1909. Tucson: Westernlore Press, 1994.

Bailey, Lynn R., and Don Chaput. *Cochise County Stalwarts: A Who's Who of the Territorial Years.* Volume 1, A-K. Tucson: Westernlore Press, 2000.

———. *Cochise County Stalwarts: A Who's Who of the Territorial Years.* Volume 2, L-Z. Tucson: Westernlore Press, 2000.

Balderrama, Francisco E. *Decade of Betrayal: Mexican Repatriation in the 1930s.* Albuquerque: University of New Mexico Press, 1995.

Ball, Eve. *Indeh: An Apache Odyssey.* Norman: University of Oklahoma Press, 1988.

Bakewell, Peter J. *Silver Mining and Society in Colonial Mexico: Zacatecas, 1546–1700.* Cambridge: Cambridge University Press, 1971.

Bannon, John Francis. *Herbert Eugene Bolton: The Historian and the Man, 1870–1953.* Tucson: University of Arizona Press, 1978.

Bannon, John Francis. *The Mission Frontier in Sonora, 1620–1687.* New York: United States Catholic Historical Society, 1955.

Bartlett, John Russell. *Personal Narrative of Explorations and Incidents in Texas, New Mexico, California, Sonora, and Chihuahua.* 2 volumes. New York: D. Appleton, 1854.

Bartlett, S. C. "Arizona Development." *The Golden Era* 38 (June 1889), 245–47.

Baud, Michiel, and Willem Van Schendel. "Toward a Comparative History of Borderlands." *Journal of World History* 8 (Fall 1997), 211–42.

Bell, P. L., and H. Bentley Mackenzie. *Mexican West Coast and Lower California: A Commercial and Industrial Survey.* Washington: GPO, 1923.

Benjamin, Thomas. *La Revolución: Mexico's Great Revolution as Memory, Myth, and History.* Austin: University of Texas Press, 2000.

Benton, Katherine A. "What about Women in the 'White Man's Camp'?: Gender, Nation, and the Redefinition of Race in Cochise County, Arizona, 1853–1941." PhD diss., University of Wisconsin-Madison, 2002.

Benton-Cohen, Katherine A. "Docile Children and Dangerous Revolutionaries: The Racial Hierarchy of Manliness and the Bisbee Deportation of 1917." *Frontiers: A Journal of Women's Studies* 24 (Fall 2003), 30–50.

Bernstein, Marvin D. *The Mexican Mining Industry, 1890–1950: A Study of the Interaction of Politics, Economics, and Technology.* Albany: State University of New York Press, 1964.

Billington, Ray Allen. *The Genesis of the Frontier Thesis: A Study in Historical Creativity.* San Marino, Calif: Huntington Library, 1971.

Bolton, Herbert Eugene. *Coronado on the Turquoise Trail: Knight of Pueblos and Plains.* Albuquerque: University of New Mexico Press, 1949.

Botting, Douglas. *Humboldt and the Cosmos.* New York: Harper and Row, 1973.

Bourke, John Gregory. *On the Border with Crook.* New York: Charles Scribner's Sons, 1891.

———. *An Apache Campaign in the Sierra Madre.* New York: Charles Scribner's Sons, 1886.

Boyd, Consuelo. "Twenty Years to Nogales: The Building of the Guaymas–Nogales Railroad." *Journal of Arizona History* 22 (Autumn 1981), 305–24.

Breakenridge, William M. *Helldorado: Bringing the Law to the Mesquite.* Boston: Houghton Mifflin, 1928.

Brewster, Jane Wayland. "The San Rafael Cattle Company: A Pennsylvania Enterprise in Arizona." *Arizona and the West* 8 (Summer 1966), 133–56.

Brinckerhoff, Sidney B., and Odie B. Faulk, trans. and eds. *Lancers for the King: A Study of the Frontier Military System of Northern New Spain, With a Translation of the Royal Regulations of 1772.* Phoenix: Arizona Historical Foundation, 1965.

Brown, Clara Spalding. *Tombstone from a Woman's Point of View: The Correspondence of Clara Spalding Brown, July 7, 1880, to November 14, 1882.* Edited by Lynn R. Bailey. Tucson: Westernlore Press, 1998.

Browne, J. Ross. *Adventures in the Apache Country: A Tour Through Arizona and Sonora.* New York: Harper and Brothers, 1869.

Buck, Edward N. *Douglas: Its Resources and Development.* Douglas: Nacozari Railroad, 1904.

Burns, Barney T., and Thomas H. Naylor. "Colonia Morelos: A Short History of a Mormon Colony in Sonora, Mexico." *The Smoke Signal* 27 (Spring 1973), 142–80.

Byrkit, James W. *Forging the Copper Collar: Arizona's Labor Management War of 1901– 1921.* Tucson: University of Arizona Press, 1982.

Carr, C. C. C. "The Days of the Empire—Arizona, 1866–1869." *Journal of the United States Cavalry Association* 2 (March 1889), 3–22.

Chadwick, R. "New Extraction Processes for Metals." In *A History of Technology.* Edited by Charles Singer et al. Volume 5, *The Late Nineteenth Century c1850 to c1900.* Oxford: Clarendon Press, 1958.

Cincinnati and Sonora Mining Association. *Geological Report and Map of the San Juan del Rio Ranche, in Sonora, Mexico.* Cincinnati: Wrightson, 1866.

Cleland, Robert Glass. *A History of Phelps Dodge, 1834–1950.* New York: Alfred A. Knopf, 1952.

Clements, Eric L. *After the Boom in Tombstone and Jerome, Arizona: Decline in Western Resource Towns.* Reno: University of Nevada Press, 2003.

Clum, John P. *Apache Days and Tombstone Nights: John Clum's Autobiography, 1877–1887.* Edited by Neil B. Carmony. Silver City, N.M.: High Lonesome Books, 1997.

Colquhoun, James. *The History of the Clifton-Morenci District.* London: John Murray, 1924.

Coolidge, Dane. *Fighting Men of the West.* New York: C. P. Dutton, 1932.

Cooke, Philip St. George. *The Conquest of New Mexico and California.* Oakland: Bio-books, 1952.

Corral, Jesus C. *Caro Amigo: The Autobiography of Jesus C. Corral.* Tucson: Westernlore Press, 1984.

Corral, Ramón. *Memoria de la administración pública del estado de Sonora.* 2 volumes. Guaymas: Gaxiola, 1891.

———. *Obras históricas.* Hermosillo, 1959.

Cott, Kennett. "Mexican Diplomacy and the Chinese Issue, 1876–1910." *Hispanic American Historical Review* 67 (February 1987), 63–85.

Craib, Raymond. *Cartographic Mexico: A History of State Fixations and Fugitive Landscapes.* Durham: Duke University Press, 2004.

Cram, Captain T. J. *Memoir Showing How to Bring the Lead, Copper, Silver and Gold of*

Arizona into the Marts of the World, and Project of a Rail Road Through Sonora, to Connect With the Pacific Rail Road in Arizona. Troy, N.Y.: R. V. Wilson, 1858.

Crawford, Margaret. *Building the Workman's Paradise: The Design of American Company Towns.* London and New York: Verso, 1995.

Cronon, William. *Nature's Metropolis: Chicago and the Great West.* New York: W. W. Norton, 1991.

Daggett, Stuart. *Chapters on the History of the Southern Pacific.* New York: Ronald Press, 1922.

Dambourges Jacques, Leo Michael. "The Anti-Chinese Campaigns in Sonora, Mexico, 1900–1931." PhD diss., University of Arizona, 1974.

Davis, Britton. *The Truth About Geronimo.* Edited by M. M. Quaife. New Haven: Yale University Press, 1929.

Deeds, Susan M. *Defiance and Deference in Mexico's Colonial North: Indians under Spanish Rule in Nueva Vizcaya.* Austin: University of Texas Press, 2003.

———. "José María Maytorena and the Mexican Revolution in Sonora (Part I)." *Arizona and the West* 18 (Spring 1976), 21–40.

———. "José María Maytorena and the Mexican Revolution in Sonora (Part II)." *Arizona and the West* 18 (Summer 1976), 125–48.

Delgado, Grace Peña. "At Exclusion's Southern Gate: Changing Categories of Race and Class among Chinese *Fronterizos*, 1882–1904." In *Continental Crossroads: Remapping U.S.–Mexico Borderlands History*, edited by Samuel Truett and Elliott Young. Durham: Duke University Press, 2004.

DePalma, Anthony. *Here: A Biography of the New American Continent.* New York: PublicAffairs, 2001.

Deutsch, Sarah. *No Separate Refuge: Culture, Class, and Gender on an Anglo-Hispanic Frontier in the American Southwest, 1880–1940.* New York: Oxford University Press, 1987.

Dickson, Christina E. M., and Robert Henry Dickson. *Dickson Saga: Story of our Married Life.* Sun City, Ariz.: Robert H. Dickson, 1970.

Dobyns, Henry F. *Tubac Through Four Centuries: An Historical Resume and Analysis.* Phoenix: Arizona State Parks Board, 1959, typescript manuscript in the Arizona State Museum Library, Tucson, Arizona.

Dodge, Fred. *Under Cover for Wells Fargo: The Unvarnished Recollections of Fred Dodge.* Edited by Carolyn Lake. Boston: Houghton Mifflin, 1969.

Douglas, James. "Conservation of Natural Resources." *Transactions of the American Institute of Mining Engineers* 40 (1910), 419–31.

———. "The Copper Queen Mine, Arizona." *Transactions of the American Institute of Mining Engineers* 29 (1899), 511–46.

———. *The Cupola Smelting of Copper in Arizona.* Department of the Interior, U.S. Geological Survey. Washington: GPO, 1885.

———. "Notes on the Operation of a Light Mineral Railroad." *Transactions of the American Institute of Mining Engineers* 28 (1899), 600–04.

Douglas, James, et al. "The Copper Queen Mines and Works, Arizona, U.S.A." *Transactions of the Institution of Mining and Metallurgy* 22 (1913), 532–90.

Dunn, Mary Maples. "Introduction." In *Political Essay on the Kingdom of New Spain,* by

Alexander von Humboldt. Abridged edition. 1972; Reprint, Norman: University of Oklahoma Press, 1988.

Eldredge, James. *A Short Description of the Frontier State of Sonora, One of the States of the Republic of Mexico: With Some Notices on its Climate, Soil, and Productions, and of its Future Commercial Importance, From its Immediate Proximity to the United States of America, and its Proposed Railway from Guaymas in the Gulf of California to Tucson in the Territory of Arizona.* London, 1872.

Elías Chomina, Armando. *Compendio de datos históricos de la familia Elías.* Hermosillo, 1986.

Emmons, S. F. "Cananea Mining District of Sonora, Mexico." *Economic Geology* 5 (1910), 312–56.

———. "The Mining Work of the United States Geological Survey." *Transactions of the American Institute of Mining Engineers* 10 (1882), 412–24.

Emory, William H. *Lieutenant Emory Reports: A Reprint of Lieutenant W. H. Emory's Notes of a Military Reconnaissance.* Edited by Ross Calvin. Albuquerque: University of New Mexico Press, 1951.

———. *Report on the United States and Mexican Boundary Survey: Made Under the Direction of the Secretary of the Interior.* 2 volumes. Washington: A. O. P. Nicholson, 1857–59.

Erwin, Allan A. *The Southwest of John H. Slaughter, 1841–1922.* Glendale, Calif.: Arthur H. Clark, 1965.

Escandón, Patricia. "Economía y sociedad en Sonora, 1767–1821." In *Tres siglos de historia sonorense (1530–1830)*, coordinated by Sergio Ortega Noriega and Ignacio del Río. Mexico City: Universidad Nacional Autónoma de México, 1993.

Espinoza, José Angel. *El ejemplo de Sonora.* Mexico City, 1932.

Etter, Patricia A. *To California on the Southern Route, 1849: A History and Annotated Bibliography.* Spokane: Arthur H. Clark, 1998.

Evans, William A. *Two Generations in the Southwest.* Phoenix: Sims, 1971.

Exposición hecha al supremo gobierno de la unión por los representantes de los estados de Chihuahua, Sonora, Durango, y Territorio del Nuevo-Mejico, con motivo de los desastres que sufren por la guerra de los bárbaros. Mexico City: Galvan, 1832.

Ezell, Paul H. "History of the Pima." In *Handbook of North American Indians*, edited by William C. Sturtevant. Volume 10, *Southwest*, edited by Alfonso Ortiz. Washington: Smithsonian Institution Press, 1983.

Farish, Thomas Edwin. *History of Arizona.* 8 volumes. San Francisco: Filmer Brothers, 1915–18.

Faulk, Odie B. *Destiny Road: The Gila Trail and the Opening of the Southwest.* New York: Oxford University Press, 1973.

———. *Tombstone: Myth and Reality.* New York: Oxford University Press, 1972.

Fenn, Alward Forster. *A House by the Side of the Road; Memoirs: The Story of Alvah and Carmen Forster Fenn.* Phoenix: Image Printers, 1974.

Fischer, Robert. "Humboldt in New Spain." *Américas* 26 (February 1974), 25–31.

Flint, Richard, and Shirley Cushing Flint, eds. *The Coronado Expedition to Tierra Nueva: The 1540–1542 Route Across the Southwest.* Niwot: University Press of Colorado, 1997.

Fong, Lawrence Michael. "Sojourners and Settlers: The Chinese Experience in Arizona." *Journal of Arizona History* 21 (Autumn 1980), 227–55.

Fontana, Bernard L. "Calabazas of the Río Rico." *The Smoke Signal* 24 (Fall 1971), 65–88.

———. "History of the Papago." In *Handbook of North American Indians,* edited by William C. Sturtevant. Volume 10, *Southwest,* edited by Alfonso Ortiz. Washington: Smithsonian Institution Press, 1983.

———. "Pima and Papago: Introduction." In *Handbook of North American Indians,* edited by William C. Sturtevant. Volume 10, *Southwest,* edited by Alfonso Ortiz. Washington: Smithsonian Institution Press, 1983.

Forbes, Robert H. *Crabb's Filibustering Expedition into Sonora, 1857.* Tucson: Arizona Silhouettes, 1952.

Forrest, Suzanne. *The Preservation of the Village: New Mexico's Hispanics and the New Deal.* Albuquerque: University of New Mexico Press, 1989.

Fulton, Richard W. "Millville-Charleston, Cochise County, 1878–1889." *Journal of Arizona History* 7 (1966), 9–22.

Garate, Donald T. *Juan Bautista de Anza: Basque Explorer in the New World.* Reno: University of Nevada Press, 2003.

García y Alva, Federico. *"México y sus progresos": Álbum-Directorio del Estado de Sonora.* Hermosillo: Antonio B. Monteverde, 1905–07.

Gerhard, Peter. *The North Frontier of New Spain.* Revised edition. Norman: University of Oklahoma Press, 1993.

Gilmore, N. Ray. "Henry George Ward, British Publicist for Mexican Mines." *Pacific Historical Review* 32 (February 1963), 35–47.

Gird, Richard. "True Story of the Discovery of Tombstone." *Out West* (July 1907), 39–50.

González Ramírez, Manuel. *La huelga de Cananea.* Volume 3, *Fuentes para la historia de la Revolución Mexicana.* Mexico City: Fondo de Cultura Económica, 1956.

Goodwin, Grenville, and Neil Goodwin. *The Apache Dairies: A Father–Son Journey.* Lincoln: University of Nebraska Press, 2000.

Gordon, Robert B., et al. *Toward a New Iron Age?: Quantitative Modeling of Resource Exhaustion.* Cambridge: Harvard University Press, 1987.

Gran Banquete dado en Nueva York al Ministro de la República Mejicana. New York, 1864.

Granger, Byrd Howell. "Southwest Chronicle: The Journal of Charles D. Poston, 1850–1899." Parts 1–3. *Arizona Quarterly* 13 (1957), 152–63, 251–61, 353–62.

Gray, Andrew B. *Southern Pacific Railroad: Survey of a Route for the Southern Pacific R.R. on the 32nd Parallel, by A. B. Gray, for the Texas Western R.R. Company.* Cincinnati: Railroad Record Print, 1856.

Griffen, William B. *Apaches at War and Peace: The Janos Presidio, 1750–1858.* Albuquerque: University of New Mexico Press, 1988.

Griffiths, David. "Range Improvement in Arizona." U.S. Department of Agriculture, Bureau of Plant Industry, Bulletin no. 4. Washington: GPO, 1901.

Groton, Howard Carroll. "Riding the Flying Tortilla: Recollections of a Gringo Storekeeper in Mexico." *Journal of Arizona History* 32 (Summer 1990), 183–216.

Gutiérrez, Edgar O. "Comerciantes marítimos del noroeste de México, 1810–1835." *Siglo XIX* 13 (September–December 1995), 49–62.

Hackett, Charles Wilson, ed. *Historical Documents Relating to New Mexico, Nueva Vizcaya, and Approaches Thereto, to 1773.* 3 volumes. Washington: Carnegie Institution of Washington, 1923–37.

Hadley, Diana. "Border Boom Town—Douglas, Arizona, 1900–1920." *Cochise Quarterly* 17 (Fall 1987), 3–47.

Hadley, Diana, and Thomas E. Sheridan. *Land Use History of the San Rafael Valley, Arizona (1540–1960).* Fort Collins, Colo.: U.S. Department of Agriculture, U.S. Forest Service, Rocky Mountain Forest and Range Experiment Station, 1995.

Hafen, LeRoy R., ed. *The Mountain Men and the Fur Trade of the Far West.* 9 volumes. Glendale, Calif.: Arthur H. Clark, 1965–72.

Hale, Charles A. *Mexican Liberalism in the Age of Mora, 1821–1853.* New Haven: Yale University Press, 1968.

———. *The Transformation of Liberalism in Late Nineteenth-Century Mexico.* Princeton: Princeton University Press, 1989.

Hall, John Denton. *Travels and Adventures in Sonora; Containing a Description of its Mining and Agricultural Resources and Narrative of a Residence of Fifteen Years.* Chicago: J. M. W. Jones, 1881.

Hall, Linda B. *Álvaro Obregón: Power and Revolution in Mexico, 1911–1920.* College Station: Texas A&M University Press, 1981.

Hammond, George P., and Agapito Rey, eds. *Narratives of the Coronado Expedition, 1540–1542.* Albuquerque: University of New Mexico Press, 1940.

———. *Obregón's History of Sixteenth Century Explorations in Western America.* Los Angeles: Wetzel, 1928.

Hardy, Lieutenant R. W. H. *Travels in the Interior of Mexico, in 1825, 1826, 1827, and 1828.* London: Henry Colburn and Richard Bentley, 1829.

Hardy, R. Carmon. "Cultural 'Encystment' as a Cause of the Mormon Exodus from Mexico in 1912." *Pacific Historical Review* 34 (1965), 439–53.

Hatch, Nelle Spilsbury, and B. Carmon Hardy, compilers. *Stalwarts South of the Border.* El Paso: Ernestine Hatch, 1985.

Hatfield, Shelley Ann Bowen. *Chasing Shadows: Indians along the United States–Mexico Border, 1876–1911.* Albuquerque: University of New Mexico Press, 1998.

Haymore, Millard. "A Letter to a Niece." *Cochise Quarterly* 22 (Winter 1993), 4–5.

Heath, Hilarie J. "British Merchant Houses in Mexico, 1821–1860: Conforming Business Practices and Ethics." *Hispanic American Historical Review* 73 (May 1993), 261–90.

Hewes, Leslie. "Huepac: An Agricultural Village of Sonora, Mexico." *Economic Geography* 11 (July 1935), 284–92.

Heyman, Josiah McC. *Life and Labor on the Border: Working People of Northeastern Sonora, Mexico, 1886–1986.* Tucson: University of Arizona Press, 1991.

Hicks, Lewis Wilder, comp. *The Biographical Record of the Class of 1870, Yale College, 1870–1911.* Boston: Thomas Todd, 1912.

Hill, Robert T. "The Wonders of the American Desert." *World's Work* 3 (March 1902), 1818–32.

Hine, Robert V. *Bartlett's West: Drawing the Mexican Boundary.* New Haven: Yale University Press, 1968.

Hinton, Richard J. *The Hand-book to Arizona: Its Resources, History, Towns, Mines, Ruins, and Scenery*. San Francisco: Payot, Upham; New York: American News Co., 1878.

Hinton, Thomas B. *A Survey of Indian Assimilation in Eastern Sonora*. Volume 4, *Anthropological Papers of the University of Arizona*. Tucson: University of Arizona Press, 1959.

Hoffman, Abraham. *Unwanted Mexican Americans in the Great Depression: Repatriation Pressures, 1929–1939*. Tucson: University of Arizona Press, 1974.

Holden, Robert H. *Mexico and the Survey of Public Lands: The Management of Modernization, 1976–1911*. DeKalb: Northern Illinois Press, 1994.

Horton, Inez. *Copper's Children: The Rise and Fall of a Mexican Copper Mining Camp*. New York: Exposition Press, 1968.

Howe, Walter. *The Mining Guild of New Spain and its Tribunal General, 1770–1821*. Cambridge: Harvard University Press, 1949.

Hrdlicka, Ales. "Notes on the Indians of Sonora, Mexico." *American Anthropologist* 6 (January–March 1904), 51–89.

Hu-DeHart, Evelyn. "Immigrants to a Developing Society: The Chinese in Northern Mexico, 1875–1932." *Journal of Arizona History* 21 (Autumn 1980), 275–312.

———. *Missionaries, Miners, and Indians: Spanish Contact with the Yaqui Nation of Northwestern New Spain, 1533–1820*. Tucson: University of Arizona Press, 1981.

———. *Yaqui Resistance and Survival: The Struggle for Land and Autonomy, 1821–1910*. Madison: University of Wisconsin Press, 1984.

Humboldt, Alexander von. *Political Essay on the Kingdom of New Spain*. Translated by John Black. 5 volumes. London: Longman, Hurst, Rees, Orme, and Brown, 1811.

Hunt, Frazier. *Cap Mossman: Last of the Great Cowmen*. New York: Hastings House, 1951.

Ingersoll, Ralph McA. *In and Under Mexico*. New York: Century, 1924.

Izábal, Rafael. *Memoria de la administración pública del Estado de Sonora, 1903–1907*. Hermosillo: Antonio Monteverde, 1907.

Johnson, Benjamin Heber. *Revolution in Texas: How a Forgotten Uprising and Its Bloody Suppression Turned Mexicans into Americans*. New Haven: Yale University Press, 2003.

Jones, Oakah L., Jr. *Nueva Vizcaya: Heartland of the Spanish Frontier*. Albuquerque: University of New Mexico Press, 1988.

———. *Los Paisanos: Spanish Settlers on the Northern Frontier of New Spain*. Norman: University of Oklahoma Press, 1979.

Katz, Friedrich. "Labor Conditions on Haciendas in Porfirian Mexico: Some Trends and Tendencies." *Hispanic American Historical Review* 54 (February 1974), 1–47.

Keane, Melissa, A. E. Rogge, and Bradford Luckingham. *The Chinese in Arizona, 1870–1950: A Component of the Arizona Historic Preservation Plan*. Phoenix: Arizona State Historic Preservation Office, 1992.

Kendrick, Charles W. "The Mormons in Mexico." *American Monthly Review of Reviews* 19 (June 1899), 702–05.

Kennedy, David M. *Over Here: The First World War and American Society*. Revised edition. New York: Oxford University Press, 2004.

Kenyon-Kingdon, Maud. *From Out the Dark Shadows*. San Diego: Frye and Smith, 1925.

King, Frank M. *Pioneer Western Empire Builders*. Pasadena, Calif.: Trail's End, 1946.

King, Thomas Butler. *First Annual Report to the Board of Directors of the Southern Pacific Railroad Company.* New York: American Railroad Journal Office, 1856.

Knight, Alan. *The Mexican Revolution.* 2 volumes. Lincoln: University of Nebraska Press, 1986.

Kornblatt, Judith Deutsch. *The Cossack Hero in Russian Literature: A Study in Cultural Mythology.* Madison: University of Wisconsin Press, 1992.

Lawson, Thomas William. *Report on the Property of the Santa Rita Mining Company.* Boston: T. W. Lawson, 1909.

Lee, Erika. *At America's Gates: Chinese Immigration During the Exclusion Era, 1882–1943.* Chapel Hill: University of North Carolina Press, 2003.

Liggett, Wm. (Bill), Sr. *My Seventy-five Years Along the Mexican Border.* New York: Exposition Press, 1964.

Lister, Florence C., and Robert H. Lister. *The Chinese of Early Tucson: Historic Archaeology from the Tucson Urban Renewal Project.* Tucson: University of Arizona Press, 1989.

Logan, Walter S. *Irrigation for Profit.* New York: Albert B. King, n.d.

Logan, Walter S. *Mining for a Profit.* New York: W. S. Logan, 1891.

———. *Yaqui: The Land of Sunshine and Health; What I Saw in Mexico.* New York: Albert B. King, 1894.

Logan, Walter S., and John Nichol Irwin. *Arizona and Some of Her Friends: The Toasts and Responses at a Complimentary Dinner Given by Walter S. Logan, at the Marine and Field Club, Bath Beach, N.Y., Tuesday, July 28th, 1891, to Hon. John N. Irwin, Governor of Arizona, and Herbert H. Logan, of Phoenix, Arizona.* New York: Albert King, 1891.

Logan, Walter S., and Matías Romero. *A Mexican Night: The Toasts and Responses at a Complimentary Dinner Given by Walter S. Logan, at the Democratic Club, New York City, December 16th, 1891, to Señor Don Matías Romero, Mexican Minister to the United States.* New York: Albert B. King, 1892.

Longwell, Alden Richard. "The Cananea Ejidos: From Private Ranch to Collective in Sonora." PhD diss., University of Nebraska, 1974.

López Mañón, Edgardo, and Ignacio del Río. "La reforma institucional borbónica." In *Tres siglos de historia sonorense (1530–1830),* coordinated by Sergio Ortega Noriega and Ignacio del Río. Mexico City: Universidad Nacional Autónoma de México, 1993.

Lowitt, Richard. *A Merchant Prince of the Nineteenth Century, William E. Dodge.* New York: Columbia University Press, 1954.

Mange, Juan Matheo. *Luz de tierra incógnita en la América septentrional y diario de las exploraciones en Sonora.* Publicaciones del Archivo General de la Nación, tomo 10. Mexico City: Talleres Gráficos de la Nación, 1926.

Marcosson, Isaac F. *Anaconda.* New York: Dodd, Mead & Company, 1957.

Mattison, Ray H. "Early Spanish and Mexican Settlements in Arizona." *New Mexico Historical Review* 21 (October 1946), 273–327.

McGaw, William Cochran. *Savage Scene: The Life and Times of James Kirker, Frontier King.* New York: Hastings House, 1972.

McClintock, James H. *Arizona: Prehistoric—Aboriginal—Pioneer—Modern.* 3 Volumes. Chicago: S. J. Clarke, 1916.

Mecham, J. Lloyd. *Francisco de Ibarra and Nueva Vizcaya*. Durham: Duke University Press, 1927.

Meinig, D. W. *The Shaping of America: A Geographical Perspective on Five Hundred Years of History*. Volume 3, *Transcontinental America, 1850–1915*. New Haven: Yale University Press, 1998.

Meskus, Winifred G. "Some Cochise County Pioneers: As Seen by One of Them." *Cochise Quarterly* 15 (Spring 1985), 18–19

Meyer, Michael C. *Mexican Rebel: Pascual Orozco and the Mexican Revolution, 1910–1915*. Lincoln: University of Nebraska Press, 1967.

Miller, Darlis A. *Soldiers and Sutlers: Military Supply in the Southwest, 1861–1885*. Albuquerque: University of New Mexico Press, 1989.

Miller, Robert Ryal. "Matias Romero: Mexican Minister to the United States during the Juárez-Maximilian Era." *Hispanic American Historical Review* 45 (May 1965), 228–45.

Mitchell, Olive Kimball B. *Life Is a Fulfilling: The Story of a Mormon Pioneer Woman— Sarah Diantha Gardner Curtis and Her Part in the Colonization of the San Pedro Valley in Southern Arizona, the Homeland of the Powerful, Antagonistic Apache*. Provo: Brigham Young University Press, 1967.

Moisés, Rosalio. *A Yaqui Life: The Personal Chronicle of a Yaqui Indian*. Edited by Jane Holden Kelley and William Curry Holden. Lincoln: University of Nebraska Press, 1977.

Moody, W. G. *A Comparison of the Northern and Southern Mines in Mexico: With a Description of Two of the Mining Districts in North-Eastern Sonora*. San Francisco: Towne and Bacon, 1863.

Moorhead, Max L. *New Mexico's Royal Road: Trade and Travel on the Chihuahua Trail*. Norman: University of Oklahoma Press, 1958.

———. *The Presidio: Bastion of the Spanish Borderlands*. Norman: University of Oklahoma Press, 1975.

Mora Torres, Gregorio. "Los comerciantes de Guaymas y el desarrollo económico de Sonora, 1825–1910." In *Memoria: VII Simposio de historia de Sonora*. Hermosillo: Instituto de Investigaciones Históricas, 1984.

Mowry, Sylvester. *Arizona and Sonora: The Geography, History, and Resources of the Silver Region of North America*. 3d edition. New York: Harper and Brothers, 1864.

Myrick, David F. *Railroads of Arizona*. Volume 1, *The Southern Roads*. Berkeley: Howell-North Books, 1975.

Navin, Thomas R. *Copper Mining and Management*. Tucson: University of Arizona Press, 1978.

Naylor, Thomas H. "The Mormons Colonize Sonora: Early Trials at Colonia Oaxaca." *Arizona and the West* 20 (Winter 1978), 325–42.

Naylor, Thomas H., and Charles W. Polzer, eds. *The Presidio and Militia on the Northern Frontier of New Spain: A Documentary History*, Volume 1, 1570–1700. Tucson: University of Arizona Press, 1986.

Nentvig, Juan. *Rudo Ensayo: A Description of Sonora and Arizona in 1764*. Translated by Alberto Francisco Pradeau and Robert R. Rasmussen. Tucson: University of Arizona Press, 1980.

Nevins, Joseph. *Operation Gatekeeper: The Rise of the "Illegal Alien" and the Making of the U.S.–Mexico Boundary.* New York: Routledge, 2002.

New York Bar Association. *Proceedings of the Thirtieth Annual Meeting.* Albany: Argus, 1907.

North, Diane M. T., ed. *Samuel Peter Heintzelman and the Sonora Exploring and Mining Company.* Tucson: University of Arizona Press, 1980.

Nugent, Daniel. *Spent Cartridges of Revolution: An Anthropological History of Namiquipa, Chihuahua.* Chicago: University of Chicago Press, 1993.

Obregón, Álvaro. *Ocho mil kilómetros en campaña.* Mexico City: Fondo de Cultura Económica, 1959.

Och, Joseph. *Missionary in Sonora: The Travel Reports of Joseph Och, S.J., 1755–1767.* Edited and translated by Theodore E. Treutlein. San Francisco: California Historical Society, 1965.

Officer, James E. *Hispanic Arizona, 1536–1856.* Tucson: University of Arizona Press, 1987.

———. "Yanqui Forty-Niners in Hispanic Arizona: Interethnic Relations on the Sonoran Frontier." *Journal of Arizona History* 28 (Summer 1987), 101–34.

O'Neal, Bill. *The Arizona Rangers.* Austin: Eakin Press, 1987.

O'Neill, Colleen. "Domesticity Deployed: Gender, Race, and the Construction of Class Struggle in the Bisbee Deportation." *Labor History* 34 (Spring 1993), 256–73.

Ortega Soto, Martha. "La colonización española en la primera mitad del siglo XVIII." In *Tres siglos de historia sonorense (1530–1830),* coordinated by Sergio Ortega Noriega and Ignacio del Río. Mexico City: Universidad Nacional Autónoma de México, 1993.

Owen, Roger C. *Marobavi: A Study of an Assimilated Group in Northern Sonora.* Volume 3, *Anthropological Papers of the University of Arizona.* Tucson: University of Arizona Press, 1959.

Pailes, Richard A. "An Archaeological Perspective on the Sonoran Entrada." In *The Coronado Expedition to Tierra Nueva: The 1540–1542 Route Across the Southwest,* edited by Richard Flint and Shirley Cushing Flint. Niwot: University Press of Colorado, 1997.

Park, Joseph F. "The Apaches in Mexican–Indian Relations, 1848–1861: A Footnote to the Gadsden Treaty." *Arizona and the West* 3 (Summer 1961), 129–46.

———. "The History of Mexican Labor in Arizona during the Territorial Period." MA thesis, University of Arizona, 1961.

Parker, Morris B. *Mules, Mines, and Me in Mexico, 1895–1932.* Tucson: University of Arizona Press, 1979.

Parkhill, Forbes. "Antoine Leroux." In *The Mountain Men and the Fur Trade of the Far West,* edited by LeRoy R. Hafen. Volume 4. Glendale, Calif.: Arthur H. Clark, 1965–72.

Parsons, George Whitwell. *The Devil Has Foreclosed: The Private Journal of George Whitwell Parsons: The Concluding Arizona Years, 1882–87.* Edited by Lynn R. Bailey. Tucson: Westernlore Press, 1997.

———. *A Tenderfoot in Tombstone: The Private Journal of George Whitwell Parsons: The Turbulent Years, 1880–82.* Edited by Lynn R. Bailey. Tucson: Westernlore Press, 1996.

Paul, Rodman Wilson. *Mining Frontiers of the Far West, 1848–1880.* Revised edition. Albuquerque: University of New Mexico Press, 2001.

Peset, José Luis. "The Reception of Modern Scientific Mining in an Enlightened Mexico."

In *Geoscience and Man*. Volume 33, *In Quest of Mineral Wealth: Aboriginal and Colonial Mining and Metallurgy in Spanish America*, edited by Alan K. Craig and Robert C. West. Baton Rouge: Geoscience Publications, 1994.

Pesqueira P., Héctor Alfredo. *Parentescos Extendidos de Sonora S.A.* Morelia: H. A. Pesqueira P., 1998.

Pfefferkorn, Ignaz. *Sonora: A Description of the Province*. Edited by Theodore E. Treutlein. Albuquerque: University of Arizona Press, 1949.

Pletcher, David M. "The Development of Railroads in Sonora." *Inter-American Economic Affairs* 1 (March 1948), 3–44.

———. *The Diplomacy of Trade and Investment: American Economic Expansion in the Hemisphere, 1865–1900*. Columbia: University of Missouri Press, 1998.

———. "Mexico Opens the Door to American Capital, 1877–1880." *The Americas* 16 (July 1959), 1–14.

———. *Rails, Mines, and Progress: Seven American Promoters in Mexico, 1867–1911*. Ithaca: Cornell University Press, 1958.

Polzer, Charles W., and Thomas E. Sheridan, eds. *The Presidio and the Militia on the Northern Frontier of New Spain: A Documentary History*. Volume 2, Part 1, *The Californias and Sinaloa–Sonora, 1700–1765*. Tucson: University of Arizona Press, 1997.

Portrait and Biographical Record of Arizona. Chicago: Chapman, 1901.

Poston, Charles D. *Building a State in Apache Land: The Story of Arizona's Founding Told by Arizona's Founder*. Edited by John Myers Myers. Tempe: Aztec Press, 1963.

Pratt, Mary Louise. *Imperial Eyes: Travel Writing and Transculturation*. London: Routledge, 1992.

Proceedings of a Meeting of Citizens of New York to Express Sympathy and Respect for the Mexican Republican Exiles. New York: John A. Gray and Green, 1865.

Pumpelly, Raphael. *Across America and Asia: Notes of a Five Years' Journey Around the World and of Residence in Arizona, Japan, and China*. New York: Leypoldt and Holt, 1870.

Raat, W. Dirk. *Revoltosos: Mexico's Rebels in the United States, 1903–1923*. College Station: Texas A&M University Press, 1981.

Radding, Cynthia. "Las reformas borbónicas en la Provincia de Sonora: El régimen de propiedad en la sociedad colonial." *Noroeste de México* 10 (1991), 51–57.

———. *Wandering Peoples: Colonialism, Ethnic Spaces, and Ecological Frontiers in Northwestern Mexico, 1700–1850*. Durham: Duke University Press, 1997.

Randall, Robert W. *Real del Monte: A British Mining Venture in Mexico*. Austin: University of Texas Press, 1972.

Ransome, F. L. "Copper Deposits of Bisbee, Ariz." In *Contributions to Economic Geology, 1902*. U.S. Geological Survey, Bulletin no. 213. Washington: GPO, 1903.

Reales ordenanzas para la dirección régimen y gobierno del importante cuerpo de la minería de Nueva-España, y de su Real Tribunal General. Madrid: Ibarra, 1783.

Reff, Daniel T. *Disease, Depopulation, and Culture Change in Northwestern New Spain, 1518–1764*. Salt Lake City: University of Utah Press, 1991.

Reid, John Coleman. *Reid's Tramp, or a Journal of the Incidents of Ten Months Travel Through Texas, New Mexico, Arizona, Sonora, and California*. Selma: John Hardy, 1858.

Reséndez, Andrés. *Changing National Identities at the Frontier: Texas and New Mexico, 1800–1850.* Cambridge: Cambridge University Press, 2005.

Rickard, T. A. *Interviews with Mining Engineers.* San Francisco: Mining and Scientific Press, 1922.

Riesgo, Juan M. and Antonio J. Valdez. *Memoria estadística del estado de Occidente.* Guadalajara: C. E. Alatorre, 1828.

Río, Ignacio del. "El noroeste novohispano y la nueva política imperial española." In *Tres siglos de historia sonorense (1530–1830),* coordinated by Sergio Ortega Noriega and Ignacio del Río. Mexico City: Universidad Nacional Autónoma de México, 1993.

Rippy, J. Fred. "Latin America and the British Investment 'Boom' of the 1820s." *Journal of Modern History* 19 (March-December 1947), 122–29.

Roberts, Virginia Culin. *With Their Own Blood: A Saga of Southwestern Pioneers.* Fort Worth: Texas Christian University Press, 1992.

Rockfellow, John A. *Log of an Arizona Trial Blazer.* 1933. Reprint, Tucson: Arizona Silhouettes, 1955.

Rodgers, William M. "Historical Land Occupance of the Upper San Pedro River Valley Since 1870." MA thesis, University of Arizona, 1965.

Romero, Matías. *Artículos sobre México publicados en los Estados Unidos de América por Matías Romero en 1891–1892.* México: Oficina Impresora de Estampillas, 1892.

———. *Diario personal (1855–1865).* Edited by Emma Cosío Villegas. Mexico City: Colegio de México, 1960.

———. *Mexican Lobby: Matías Romero in Washington, 1861–1867.* Edited by Thomas D. Schoonover. Lexington: University Press of Kentucky, 1986.

———. *Mexico and the United States: A Study of Subjects Affecting Their Political, Commercial, and Social Relations, Made with a View to Their Promotion.* New York: G. P. Putnam, 1898.

Romney, Thomas Cottam. *Life Story of Miles P. Romney.* Independence: Zions, 1948.

———. *The Mormon Colonies in Mexico.* Salt Lake City: Deseret Book Company, 1938.

Ruiz, Ramón Eduardo. *The People of Sonora and Yankee Capitalists.* Tucson: University of Arizona Press, 1988.

Rynning, Thomas. *Gun Notches: The Life Story of a Cowboy-Soldier.* New York: Frederick A. Stokes, 1931.

Sacks, Benjamin. "New Evidence on the Bascom Affair." *Arizona and the West* 4 (Autumn 1962), 261–78.

Safford, A. P. K., et al. *Resources of Arizona Territory, with a Description of the Indian Tribes; Ancient Ruins; Cochise, Apache Chief; Antonio, Pima Chief; Stage and Wagon Roads; Trade and Commerce, etc.* San Francisco: Francis and Valentine, 1871.

Santa Rita Silver Mining Company. *Second Annual Report of the Santa Rita Silver Mining Company, Made to the Stockholders, March 18, 1860.* Cincinnati: Railroad Record Print, 1860.

Schaafsma, Curtis F., and Carroll L. Riley, eds. *The Casas Grandes World.* Salt Lake City: University of Utah Press, 1999.

Schoonover, Thomas D. "Dollars over Dominion: United States Economic Interests in Mexico, 1861–1867." *Pacific Historical Review* 45 (February 1976), 23–45.

Schrader, Frank C. *Mineral Deposits of the Santa Rita and Patagonia Mountains, Arizona.* U.S. Geological Survey Bulletin 582. Washington: GPO, 1915.

Schwantes, Carlos A. *Vision and Enterprise: Exploring the History of Phelps Dodge Corporation.* Tucson: University of Arizona Press, 2000.

Scott, James C. *Domination and the Arts of Resistance: Hidden Transcripts.* New Haven: Yale University Press, 1990.

———. *Seeing Like a State: How Certain Schemes to Improve the Human Condition Have Failed.* New Haven: Yale University Press, 1998.

Segesser, Philipp. "The Relation of Philipp Segesser." Edited by Theodore Treutlein. *Mid-America* 27 (July 1945), 139–87 and (October 1945), 257–60.

Sheridan, Thomas E. *Los Tucsonenses: The Mexican Community in Tucson, 1854–1941.* Tucson: University of Arizona Press, 1986.

Shillingberg, William B. *Tombstone, A.T.: A History of Early Mining, Milling, and Mayhem.* Spokane: Arthur H. Clark, 1999.

Sierra, Carlos J., and Rogelio Martínez Vera. *El resguardo aduanal y la gendarmería fiscal, 1850–1925.* Mexico City: Secretaría de Hacienda y Crédito Público, 1971.

Singer, Charles, et al., eds. *A History of Technology.* Volume 5, *The Late Nineteenth Century c1850 to c1900.* Oxford: Clarendon Press, 1958.

Skinner, Brian J. "Copper Resources." In *Toward a New Iron Age?: Quantitative Modeling of Resource Exhaustion,* edited by Robert B. Gordon et al. Cambridge: Harvard University Press, 1987.

Smith, Jesse Nathaniel. *The Journal of Jesse Nathaniel Smith: Six Decades in the Early West, Diaries and Papers of a Mormon Pioneer, 1834–1906.* Edited by Oliver R. Smith. Provo: Jesse N. Smith Family Association, 1970.

Smith, Ralph Adam. *Borderlander: The Life of James Kirker, 1793–1852.* Norman: University of Oklahoma Press, 1999.

Sonnichsen, C. L. *Colonel Greene and the Copper Skyrocket.* Tucson: University of Arizona Press, 1974.

Sonora Exploring and Mining Company. *First Annual Report of the Sonora Exploring and Mining Company, Made to the Stockholders, March 16, 1857.* Cincinnati: Railroad Record Print, 1857.

———. *Possessions and Prospects of the Sonora Silver Mining Co. Report of the Sonora Exploring and Mining Co., Made to the Stockholders, September 1857.* Cincinnati: Railroad Record Print, 1857.

———. *Report of Frederick Brunckow, Geologist, Mineralogist, and Mining Engineer, to a Committee of the Stockholders of the Sonora Exploring and Mining Co. upon the History, Resources, and Prospects of the Company in Arizona.* Cincinnati: Railroad Record Print, 1859.

———. *Second Annual Report of the Sonora Exploring and Mining Co., Made to the Stockholders, March 29, 1858.* Cincinnati: Railroad Record Print, 1858.

———. *Sonora and the Value of Its Silver Mines. Report of the Sonora Exploring and Mining Co., Made to the Stockholders. December 1856.* Cincinnati: Railroad Record Print, 1856.

———. *Third Annual Report of the Sonora Exploring and Mining Co., Made to the Stock-holders, March, 1859.* New York: W. Minns, 1859.

Soule, George. "The Law of Necessity in Bisbee." *Nation* 113 (1921), 21–23.

Southworth, J. R. *Las Minas de México: Historia—Geología—Antigua Minería—y Descripción General de los Estados Mineros de la República Mexicana.* Liverpool: Blake and Mackenzie, 1905.

Spicer, Edward H. *Cycles of Conquest: The Impact of Spain, Mexico, and the United States on the Indians of the Southwest, 1533–1960.* Tucson: University of Arizona Press, 1962.

———. *Pascua: A Yaqui Village in Arizona.* Tucson: University of Arizona Press, 1967.

———. *The Yaquis: A Cultural History.* Tucson: University of Arizona Press, 1980.

Spring, John. *John Spring's Arizona.* Edited by A. M. Gustafson. Tucson: University of Arizona Press, 1966.

Spude, Robert Lester. "Mineral Frontier in Transition: Copper Mining in Arizona, 1880–1885." MA thesis, Arizona State University, 1976.

Stern, Peter, and Robert Jackson. "*Vagabundaje* and Settlement Patterns in Colonial Northern Sonora." *The Americas* 44 (April 1988), 461–81.

Stevens, Horace J. *The Copper Handbook: A Manual of the Copper Industry of the World.* Volume 4. Houghton, Mich.: Horace J. Stevens, 1904.

Stokes, Richard. "Bisbee, No Good for Chinaman." *Cochise Quarterly* 3 (December 1973), 6–9.

Stone, Charles P. *Notes on the State of Sonora.* Washington: Henry Polkinhorn, 1861.

Strickland, Rex W. "The Birth and Death of a Legend: The Johnson 'Massacre' of 1837." *Arizona and the West* 18 (Autumn 1976), 257–86.

———. "Robert McKnight." In *The Mountain Men and the Fur Trade of the Far West,* edited by LeRoy R. Hafen. Volume 9. Glendale, Calif.: Arthur H. Clark, 1965–72.

Swann, Michael M. "Migration, Mobility, and the Mining Towns of Colonial Northern Mexico." In *Migration in Colonial Spanish America,* edited by David J. Robinson. Cambridge: Cambridge University Press, 1990.

Sweeney, Edwin R. *Cochise: Chiricahua Apache Chief.* Norman: University of Oklahoma Press, 1991.

———. *Mangas Coloradas: Chief of the Chiricahua Apaches.* Norman: University of Oklahoma Press, 1998.

Thomas, Estelle Webb. *Uncertain Sanctuary: A Story of Mormon Pioneering in Mexico.* Salt Lake City: Westwater Press, 1980.

Thompson, Gerald E., ed. "Railroads and Mines in Arizona: The Cram Memoir of 1858." *Arizona and the West* 10 (Winter 1968), 363–76.

Thrapp, Dan L. *The Conquest of Apacheria.* Norman: University of Oklahoma Press, 1967.

Tinker Salas, Miguel. *In the Shadow of the Eagles: Sonora and the Transformation of the Border during the Porfiriato.* Berkeley: University of California Press, 1997.

Titcomb, Edward. "A Yankee Odyssey: Edward Titcomb's Adventures in Mexico and the Southwest." *Journal of Arizona History* 30 (Spring 1989), 73–100.

Treutlein, Theodore E. "The Economic Regime of the Jesuit Missions in Eighteenth Century Sonora." *Pacific Historical Review* 8 (1939), 289–300.

Troncoso, Francisco P. *Las guerras con las tribus Yaqui y Mayo.* Mexico City: Instituto Nacional Indigenista, 1977.

Truett, Samuel, "Epics of Greater America: Herbert Eugene Bolton's Quest for a Transnational American History." In *Interpreting Spanish Colonialism: Empires, Nations, and Legends,* edited by Christopher Schmidt-Nowara and John Nieto-Phillips. Albuquerque: University of New Mexico Press, 2005.

———. "Transnational Warrior: Emilio Kosterlitzky and the Transformation of the U.S.–Mexico Borderlands, 1873–1928." In *Continental Crossroads: Remapping U.S.–Mexico Borderlands History,* edited by Samuel Truett and Elliott Young. Durham: Duke University Press, 2004.

Truett, Samuel, and Elliott Young. "Making Transnational History: Nations, Regions, and Borderlands." In *Continental Crossroads: Remapping U.S.–Mexico Borderlands History,* edited by Samuel Truett and Elliott Young. Durham: Duke University Press, 2004.

Truett, Samuel, and Elliott Young, eds. *Continental Crossroads: Remapping U.S.–Mexico Borderlands History.* Durham: Duke University Press, 2004.

Tullis, F. LaMond. *Mormons in Mexico: The Dynamics of Faith and Culture.* Logan: Utah State University Press, 1987.

Turner, Frederick J. "The Significance of the Frontier in American History." In *Annual Report of the American Historical Association for the Year 1893.* Washington: GPO, 1894.

Turner, Thompson M. *Latest from Arizona! The Hesperian Letters, 1859–1861.* Edited by Constance Wynn Altshuler. Tucson: Arizona Pioneers' Historical Society, 1969.

Underhill, Lonnie E., ed. "The Tombstone Discovery: The Recollections of Ed Shieffelin and Richard Gird." *Arizona and the West* 21 (Spring 1979), 37–76.

Utley, Robert M. "The Bascom Affair: A Reconstruction." *Arizona and the West* 3 (Spring 1961), 59–68.

Vanderwood, Paul J. *Disorder and Progress: Bandits, Police, and Mexican Development.* Lincoln: University of Nebraska Press, 1981.

Vaughan, Mary Kay. *Cultural Politics in Revolution: Teachers, Peasants, and Schools in Mexico, 1930–1940.* Tucson: University of Arizona Press, 1997.

Vaughan, Tom. "Bisbee's Transition Years: 1899–1918." *Cochise Quarterly* 14 (Winter 1984), 3–42.

Velasco, José Francisco. *Noticias estadísticas del estado de Sonora.* Mexico City: Imprenta de Ignacio Cumplido, 1850.

Verne, Jules. *Michael Strogoff, The Courier of the Czar.* New York: Scribner, Armstrong, 1877.

Voss, Stuart F. *On the Periphery of Nineteenth-Century Mexico: Sonora and Sinaloa, 1810–1877.* Tucson: University of Arizona Press, 1982.

Wagoner, J. Jay. *History of the Cattle Industry in Southern Arizona, 1540–1940.* University of Arizona Social Science Bulletin no. 20. Tucson: University of Arizona Press, 1952.

Walker, Henry Pickering. "Freighting from Guaymas to Tucson, 1850–1880." *Western Historical Quarterly* 1 (July 1970), 291–304.

Wallace, Mildred Young. "I Remember Chung." *Journal of Arizona History* 20 (Spring 1979), 35–46.

———. *We Three: Papa's Ladies*. San Antonio: Naylor, 1957.

Wang, Wensheng. "The First Chinese in Tucson: New Evidence on a Puzzling Question." *Journal of Arizona History* 43 (Winter 2002), 369–80.

Ward, Henry G. *Mexico in 1827*. 2 volumes. London: Henry Colburn, 1828.

Warren, T. Robinson. *Dust and Foam, or Three Oceans and Two Continents*. New York: Charles Scribner, 1859.

Way, Phocion R. "Overland Via 'Jackass Mail' in 1858: The Diary of Phocion R. Way." Edited and annotated by William A. Duffen. *Arizona and the West* 2 (Summer 1960), 147–64; (Autumn 1960), 279–92; and (Winter 1960), 353–70.

Weber, David J. *The Mexican Frontier, 1821–1846: The American Southwest Under Mexico*. Albuquerque: University of New Mexico Press, 1982.

———. *The Spanish Frontier in North America*. New Haven: Yale University Press, 1992.

Wentworth, Frank L. *Bisbee and the Big B*. Iowa City: Mercer, 1938.

West, Robert C. *The Mining Community in Northern New Spain: The Parral Mining District*. Ibero-Americana 30. Berkeley: University of California Press, 1949.

———. *Sonora: Its Geographical Personality*. Austin: University of Texas Press, 1993.

White, Philip L. *The Beekmans of New York in Politics and Commerce, 1647–1877*. New York: New-York Historical Society, 1956.

White, Richard. "Frederick Jackson Turner and Buffalo Bill." In *The Frontier in American Culture: An Exhibition at the Newberry Library, August 26, 1994–January 7, 1995*, edited by James R. Grossman. Chicago: Newberry Library; Berkeley: University of California Press, 1994.

———. *The Organic Machine: The Remaking of the Columbia River*. New York: Hill and Wang, 1995.

Wilson, Neill C., and Frank J. Taylor. *Southern Pacific: The Roaring Story of a Fighting Railroad*. New York: McGraw-Hill, 1952.

Wilson, Robert Anderson. *Mexico: Its Peasants and Its Priests; or Adventures and Historical Researches in Mexico and Its Silver Mines During Parts of the Years 1851-52-53-54*. New York: Harper, 1856.

Worcester, Donald E. "The Beginnings of the Apache Menace of the Southwest." *New Mexico Historical Review* 16 (January 1941), 1–14.

Zakin, Susan. "The Hunters and the Hunted: The Arizona–Mexico Border Turns into the 21st Century Frontier." *High Country News*, October 9, 2000.

Zúñiga, Ignacio. *Rapida ojeada al estado de Sonora, dirigida y dedicada al supremo gobierno de la nación*. Mexico City: Juan Ojedo, 1835.

INDEX

Acapulco (Guerrero), 34–35
Aconchi (Sonora), 163
agriculture, 16, 21–24, 31, 35, 37, 39; 1850s–
    80s, 41–42, 44, 47, 57, 72; copper
    borderlands, 72, 84, 89, 95, 107–08,
    117–19, 120–23, 127–29; in Mexican
    Revolution and 1920s, 159, 161–62,
    169–70, 178, 180–81
Agua Prieta (Sonora), 111, 158, 160–61,
    170–73; battles of, 159–60, 172–73
Aguascalientes, 109
Aguilar, José de, 29
Aguirre: Epifanio, 95; Stephen, 95, 135
Ahumada, Secundino, 101–02
Ajo Mountains, 89, 160, 162, 175, 208n30
Ake: Felix Grundy, 41, 46; William, 46, 65
Alldredge, Isaac, 128
Altar (Sonora), 27, 43
Álvarez Tuñon y Quirós, Gregorio, 27
Amalgamated Copper Company, 149
American Museum of Natural History, 99
Apache fighting: identity and, 28, 85–86,
    139–40, 149, 165
Apache Kid, 138
Apaches (Indians), in colonial era, 18,
    20, 22, 25–28, 40, 78–79, 192n9; and
    early Mexico, 14–15, 28–30, 35–37, 41,
    79, 200n18; and Tubac, 39–41, 47–49;
    after 1860, 59–63, 65–67, 73, 139–40,

142, 200n18; and Mexican Revolution,
    159–60, 162, 164–65, 174–76
Apaches de paz, 28, 190n44
Arivaca (Arizona), 40, 45–46, 49
Arizona. *See specific places*
Arizona and South Eastern Railroad, 72,
    74, 82–83
Arizona Rangers, 138–42, 146, 148, 164
Arizpe (Sonora), 20, 63
Aros River, 99
Arvallo: José María, 79, 101; heirs, 101,
    210n56
Atchison, Topeka, and Santa Fe Railroad,
    59–60, 70, 74–75
Atlanta mine, 69, 72
Axford, Joseph "Mack," 84–85

Babiácora (Sonora), 21
Bacanuchi (Sonora), 18, 78
Bacerac (Sonora), 127
Bacoachi (Sonora), 25, 63
Baja California, 109
Bajo (Sonora), 111, 211n15
Banco de Cananea, 95, 154
banditry, 5, 64–66, 118–19, 138, 141; in
    Mexican Revolution, 159–61, 164–65
Barrio Libre (Arizona), 119
Barroso, Filiberto, 147
Bartlett, John Russell, 13–15, 29–30, 32

Bascom, George N., 48
Baud, Michiel, 7
Bavispe (Sonora), 26, 65, 127
Bavispe River valley, 18, 104, 126–28, 159, 161
Beckett, P. G., 179
Benson (Arizona), 70, 75, 83, 120, 123
Berkshire, Frank W., 170
Bernard, Allen C., 94, 136, 140
Bisbee (Arizona), 66–73, 133, 138, 174–76, 183; transportation ties to, 71–72, 74–75, 81–83; and rural ties, 72–74, 84; environmental limits in, 72–76, 82–83; Mexicans, 111–12, 116, 158, 162, 183; Chinese, 120, 123–24; and Mexican Revolution, 158–59, 167
Bisbee Butcher Shop, 72
Bisbee Deportation, 174–76
Bisbee "volunteers," 146–49, 158, 164
Blanco, José de la Luz, 159
Bolton, Herbert Eugene, 182
Bonillas, Ignacio, 133–34
boosters: visions of, 1–4, 80, 83, 91 fig. 11, 92–93, 108
border: mapping of, 13; surveillance of, 120–25, 138–42, 157–59, 163–68, 182; reciprocal crossing of, 65, 138, 142
Bourbon reforms, 27–28, 30–31, 33
Bourke, John Gregory, 57
Bourne, Simon, 34–36, 38, 105
Brewery Gulch, 73, 111, 183
Brickwood, Albert W., Jr., 146
British entrepreneurs, 33–36, 42, 59, 143
Brooks, John, 141
Brown, Clara Spalding, 66
Browne, J. Ross, 44–45, 49–50, 92
Brunckow, Frederick, 61
Buenavista (Sonora), 109, 113, 116, 150
Bureau of Investigation, 158, 163–64
Byrd, Greenbury, 46

Cabeza de Vaca, Álvar Núñez, 16–17
Caborca (Sonora), 45, 56
Cabral, Juan, 161, 166

Cahuabi mine, 43
Calabasas (Arizona), 41
California, 15, 36–39, 56–58, 67, 107; gold rush, 29, 37, 41, 43; exports, 42, 56, 58, 62, 74, 114, 127
California Land and Cattle Company, 64
Calles, Plutarco Elías, 166, 168, 173, 178; and *Callistas*, 167, 169
Camou, Juan Pedro, 84
Campa, Emilio, 163–64
Camp Wallen (Arizona), 57
Cananea (Sonora): 4, 14, 63–64, 78–80, 150, 180–81, 183; and Pesqueiras, 63–64, 78–80, 86–87; Greene in, 84–88, 133–36; Mexican lands and, 86–87, 94–96, 99–102, 135–36; CCCC in, 87–93, 96–98, 133, 135–37; views of, 88–93, 106–08, 133–38; transportation ties to, 88–89, 95, 97–98, 128–29; and rural ties, 89, 93–102, 108–09, 117–19, 121–23, 127–29; and Mexicans, 94–95, 106–10, 112–13, 116–17; corporate control of, 95–97, 135–37; Chinese, Mormons, and Americans and, 106, 112, 121–25, 127–29; Mexican Revolution and, 157–61, 163, 165, 168–69, 173–75
Cananea Cattle Company, 93–95, 98, 101, 123, 137, 143; and Mexican Revolution, 159, 163
Cananea Central Copper Company, 149–50
Cananea Consolidated Copper Company (CCCC), 87–94, 178–83; transforms Cananea, 87–93, 96–98, 133; Mexican state and, 90–92, 97–99, 134–38; and Cananea Cattle Company, 94–95, 101–02; and Mexican elites and lands, 94–96, 99–102, 135; railroad, 97–98; and Mexican labor, 109–10; and Chinese, 123; and police, 135–36, 109, 149; and monopolies, 95–97, 135–38; and strike of 1906, 145–49; and Greene Cananea takeover, 149–54; Mexican Revolution and, 161, 168–69, 173–74, 180

Cananea Copper Company, 87
Cananea Mountains, 79, 89, 94, 97
Cananea–Naco railroad, 93, 97–98, 128, 138
Cananea Realty Company, 94
Cananea strike of 1906, 144–52, 157–58, 164–65, 176
Cananea Vieja (Sonora), 94, 150
Canoa ranch, 40, 47
Caraway, Henry T., 86–87
Carlos III, King, 27
Carlos IV, King, 33
Carranza, Venustiano, 166, 173; and *Carrancistas*, 173
Carretas Pass, 26, 28, 104
Carson, Kit, 47
Casas Grandes (Chihuahua), 20, 104, 125, 129; River valley, 126
Catalina (Sonora), 101
caudillos, 28–29, 67, 80, 166
Charleston (Arizona), 62–64, 72, 120, 123
Charley (Chinese farmer), 123
Chávez, Joaquín, 159
Chihuahua, 4, 104–05; colonial, 17, 20, 25–26, 39, 79; early Mexican, 28–29, 33–34, 36–37, 95; Mexican elites and workers from, 95, 109, 116; Greene in, 98–100, 152–56; Mormons and, 125–26, 128–29; and Mexican Revolution, 159–63, 165, 169, 171
Chihuahua Hill (Arizona), 111, 113, 162
China, 34–35, 120–21, 124
Chinese: in Arizona, 62, 72, 120, 123–25; in Sonora, 106, 112–13, 115, 120–25, 160, 169, 214n40; and smuggling networks, 123–25, 182, 214n43
Chinese Exclusion Act, 120–21, 123
Chiricahua Apache Reservation, 60–61
Chiricahua Mountains, 60, 62, 72, 74, 160
Chivatera (Sonora), 107, 113, 116
Church, William, 69
Cienega de Heredia, Exedencias de, 101–02

Cieneguilla (Sonora), 37
Citizens' Protective League, 174
Ciudad Juárez (Chihuahua), 161
Clanton family, 64
Clifford, E. G. "Lige," 81–82
Clifton-Morenci (Arizona), 68–69, 81, 111, 157–58, 160
Cobre Grande mine, 136
Cochise, 48, 60
Cocóspera (Sonora), 14, 21, 43
Cole, Thomas F., 149–50
Columbus (New Mexico), raid on, 173
commerce: colonial, 18, 23–25, 34, 43; and Pacific and Santa Fe trades, 29, 34–36, 59, 95; from 1840s to 1870s, 37, 42–45, 49, 57–58; in Tombstone and Bisbee, 63–65, 74; in Sonora after 1900, 89–90, 97, 117–18, 121–23, 127–28, 137, 169; in arms and ammunition, 36, 57, 119, 141–42, 158, 160
Comstock Lode (Nevada), 62
Concheño (Chihuahua), 153–55
confidence, relations of, 40–41, 58, 61, 70, 134, 138–39, 142–44, 158; and investors, 45, 65, 87–88, 102, 149–51, 161, 173
Connell, Charles T., 123–24
Constitutionalists, 166, 171
Contention City (Arizona), 62
Cooke, Philip St. George, 37
copper: and uses, 4, 56, 67–68; and markets, 67–72, 80–82, 149–52, 178; and refining, 68–69, 80, 183; and geological factors, 69–70. *See also* mining and metallurgy
copper borderlands, 6, 8
Copper Queen Consolidated Copper Company, 69–70, 72–74, 174, 176. *See also* Phelps, Dodge, and Company
Copper Queen Mercantile Company, 74, 119, 157–58, 163
Copper Queen Mining Company, 67, 69
Corella: Rafael Angel, 48; Ignacio, 63
Coronado, Angel F., 136
Coronado, Francisco Vázquez de, 17, 20

Corral: Jesús, 106–07, 113, 129, 177;
   Emilio, 107; family, 107–08, 113, 177
Corral, Ramón, 80–81, 90, 134–35, 142,
   166, 206n9
Cosmos Club, 87
Crabb, Henry, 45–46, 56, 65, 176
Cram, Thomas J., 58
Cranz, William S., 86
Crocker, Charles, 58
Crook, George, 60, 65, 140
Cubillas, Adrián, 158
Cucurpe (Sonora), 18, 42–43, 46–47
Cuerpo de Minería, 30, 33, 92
Cumpas (Sonora), 35, 79, 105, 127–28, 162,
   170
Cuquiárachi (Sonora), 21
custom: relations of, 28, 57, 84–88, 101,
   105, 167, 176; rhetoric of, 85–87, 138
customs, 23, 85; inspectors and houses, 58,
   63–64, 81, 85; guards, 64, 85–86, 126,
   134, 137, 139–40, 158; brokers, 95. See
   also *gendarmería fiscal*
Cutler, Cornelius T., 64, 80

D'Aumaile, Robert, 79–80
Dedrick (Chihuahua). *See* Madera
Deming (New Mexico), 58
Díaz, Porfirio, 3–4, 59, 80–81, 119, 126,
   138–39, 142; and Mexican Revolution,
   157–59, 161–62
Díaz, Ramón, 101–02
disease and epidemics, 21–22, 26, 28, 59,
   67; in mining camps, 111, 113
Dodge, William E., Jr., 55–56, 68–69, 76;
   William E., 56
Douglas (Arizona), 83, 104–05, 119, 123,
   138, 145, 183; railroad to, 83, 97; *barrios*,
   111; Mexican Revolution and, 157–64,
   170–71, 176
Douglas: James, 69–73, 75–77, 80–84,
   181; James S. "Rawhide Jimmy," 163–65;
   Walter, 163, 174, 179
Dragoon Mountains, 60–61
Duluth (Minnesota), 150

Dun, R. G., and Company, 143
Durango, 29, 33, 37, 109
Dwight, Arthur S., 109
Dye, Alexander, 161

Edison, Thomas, 68, 108
Edmunds Act, 125
Ehrenberg, Herman, 38–39
Eldredge, James, 59
Elguea, Francisco, 79, 205n2
Elhúyar, Fausto de, 33
Elías: Angel, 139; family, 28, 85, 95, 139;
   José Juan, 48; Rafael, 102; ranch, 85,
   102. *See also* Calles, Plutarco Elías
El Paso (Texas), 123–24, 152, 162; and rail-
   roads, 58–59, 83, 97, 99, 104, 109, 111, 173
El Paso and Southwestern Railroad, 73
   fig. 7, 83, 88, 109, 111, 174, 206n15; and
   Cananea, 88, 97; contractors for, 97,
   109, 111
El Tigre (Sonora), 127, 159
Empire Ranch, 128
environmental limits to development, 23,
   25–27; floods and, 22, 73, 111, 117, 169;
   drought and, 22, 74; wild animals and,
   22, 26; rains and, 25, 42, 44, 71, 82, 97,
   155, 162; fires and, 26, 111; in mining
   and metallurgy, 34, 45, 79, 99; food and
   supply shortages and, 42, 44, 72–76, 161,
   169
Erie Cattle Company, 72
Evans, Tindall, 121
Ewell, R. S., 47
expansionism: territorial, 1, 15, 37, 45, 56,
   77; economic, 1–4, 55–58, 77

Fairbank (Arizona), 62, 70–72, 74, 81, 120,
   123–24
Fall, Albert Bacon, 175
Fayant, Frank H., 99
Fenn, Alvah, 128
Fenochio, Juan, 86, 126, 140, 176, 218n26
filibusters: Crabb, 45–46, 56, 176; Phelps
   Dodge, 163–64

Flores Magón brothers, 157
Fort Buchanan (Arizona), 41–43, 47–49, 56
Fort Huachuca (Arizona), 61, 84
Fort Yuma (California), 39
Foster, Lt. John, 141
Freiberg (Saxony), 33, 45
freighting, 24–26, 43, 68, 128–29, 155, 159;
    at Tombstone, Bisbee, 62–63, 70–72,
    75 fig. 8; at Cananea, Nacozari, 81–83,
    88–89, 95, 97, 105, 117
French intervention, 55–57, 64
Fresnal mine, 43
Fronteras (Sonora), 27, 30, 60, 63, 65,
    81–82, 105
Fronteras River valley, 18, 82
frontier: views of, 1–4, 6, 27–28, 37, 133–
    34, 137, 178; and investor confidence,
    45, 87–88; rhetoric and identities, 6,
    85–86, 139–40, 146, 149, 176; imagery
    and Mexican Revolution, 160, 164–65,
    167, 176
fundo legal, 135–36

Gabilondo, Eduardo, 86 fig. 9
Gadsden Purchase, 38–39
Galbraith, W. J., 145
gambusinos, 31, 49, 79, 102. *See also*
    prospectors
Gándara, José, 46
García, Telésforo, 99
García y Alva, Federico, 92–93, 95
Gates, Egbert, 94
Gendarmería Fiscal, 134, 139–40, 165;
    gendarmes of, 139, 141–42, 145, 148–49,
    158. *See also* Emilio Kosterlitzky; Juan
    Fenochio
Germany, 38–39, 173–74; and mining
    professionals, 30, 33, 38, 45, 61
Geronimo, 65–66, 71, 125, 133, 140, 165,
    175 fig. 27
Gila River valley, 18, 37, 43, 45
Gin, Wo, 124
Gird, Richard, 61, 64
Globe (Arizona), 105

Goliad (Texas), 14
Graveyard claim, 61
Gray, Andrew B., 58
Gray, John, 73–74
Greene, Ella (Roberts), 84, 156
Greene, William Cornell, 4, 83–88, 93–
    94, 98, 152, 156, 209n43; and Mexican
    and U.S. elites, 86–88, 94–95, 99, 149–
    50, 153, 183; CCCC and, 87–89, 90,
    93, 101, 149–54; and frontier persona,
    88, 94, 133, 140, 149; and Chihuahua,
    98–100, 152–56; imperial vision of, 99,
    150, 152–54; and 1901 invasion of Cana-
    nea, 133–35; and strike of 1906, 145–49;
    decline of, 149–56
Greene Cananea Copper Company, 150
Greene Cattle Company, 94
Greene Consolidated Copper Company,
    87, 88, 149. *See also* Cananea Consoli-
    dated Copper Company
Greene Gold-Silver Company, 98–99,
    152–56
Groton, Howard Carroll, 117–18
Guadalajara (Jalisco), 23–24
Guadalupe (Arizona), 120
Guaymas (Sonora), 14, 34, 36, 56–60, 74,
    121, 143, 169
Guggenheim family, 81
Guzmán, Núño Beltrán de, 16–17

Hall, John, 31, 41, 43, 46–47, 64
Hallihan, J. P., 97
Hardy, Robert, 34–36, 38, 105
Hathaway, Eugene, 65
Haymore family, 128
Heath, Frank W., 170
Heintzelman, Samuel Peter, 39, 44–45
Heintzelman mine, 42, 44, 46, 49
Hereford (Arizona), 84, 120, 123
Hermanas (New Mexico), 174
Hermosillo (Sonora), 34–35, 44, 57, 91,
    121, 143, 180
Herreras, León, 40
Hilburn, Bob, 163

Hill, Benjamin, 166
Hill, Robert T., 87–88, 90, 99, 133, 208n27
Hohstadt, John, 64
Hopkins, Mark, 58
Hop Sing, 123–24, 129
Horitt, R. I., 143
Horton: Inez, 159; Herman, 179
Hovey, Edmund O., 99
Huachinera (Sonora), 127
Huachuca Mountains, 62, 72, 74, 133
Huásabas (Sonora), 25, 140
Huatabampo (Sonora), 164
Huépac (Sonora), 117, 181
Huerta, Victoriano, 165–66
Huish, William Claude, 128
Humboldt, Alexander von, 33–36, 38, 99
Hunt, George W. P., 167
Huntington, Collis P., 58

Ibarra, Francisco de, 17, 20
Imuris (Sonora), 41, 145
Industrial Workers of the World, 174
Ingersoll, Ralph, 113–14, 116, 212n20
Izábal, Rafael, 80, 142–48, 166, 220n40

Jalisco, 169
Janos (Indians), 18, 25
Jarvis, Frances Godfrey, 128
Jesuit expulsion, 28
Jesuit order, 14, 18, 20–24, 36, 45, 118
Jocomes (Indians), 18, 25
Juan Lung Tain y Compañía, 121–22
Juárez, Benito, 55

Kansas City, Mexico, and Orient Railroad, 129
Kearny, Stephen, 37, 47
Kenyon-Kingdon, Maud, 105–07, 112, 116, 123, 178
Kibbey, Joseph H., 146
King, Sam, 134
Kingdon, George, 105–06, 211n5
Kino, Eusebio Francisco, 18
Kirk, James, 140, 145

Kirker, James, 36
Knight, Alan, 164
Kosterlitzky, Emilio, 126, 134, 139–43, 158, 164–65, 218n26; Cananea strike of 1906 and, 145, 147–49, 152, 220n42

labor, 21–26, 41–47, 62, 67, 196n32; in copper borderlands, 89, 92, 106–14, 116–23, 127–29, 142, 150; movements and strikes, 144–49, 152, 157–58, 174–75; Mexican Revolution and, 161–62, 168–69
La Dura (Sonora), 107
La Junta (Colorado), 68
Lamb, Mark R., 154–55
land: privatization of, 28, 31; common and private claims on, 31, 101, 135–36; expropriation of, 92, 95, 135, 183; and Mexican surveyors, 95, 99, 121
land grants, 28, 30, 40: Arivaca, 40; Canoa, 40; San Rafael del Valle, 84, 94
Laredo (Texas), 59
Las Cruces (New Mexico), 68
Las Delicias (Sonora), 63–65
Las Nutrias ranch, 123
Lee Quong, 124
León de la Barra, Francisco, 161
Leroux, Antoine, 37
Lesinsky family, 68
Lewis Springs (Arizona), 123
Lillywhite family, 127 fig. 20
Logan, Walter S., 1–4, 55, 84, 87–88
Longfellow mine, 68
Long Island (New York), 1, 69
López, Red, 159–60
López Linares, F., 145
Loreto (Baja California), 35
Los Angeles (California), 74, 114, 124
Lucky Tiger mine, 109

Macmanus: family, 95, 99; Ignacio, 95, 209n45; Tomás, 95
Madera (Chihuahua), 153
Madero, Francisco I., 158–59, 161–62, 165–66

Magdalena (Sonora), 7, 41–43, 45, 86–87, 121–22, 134, 145, 150
Magdalena River valley, 18
Mangas Coloradas, 41, 48
Manila trade, 120
Martínez: Antonio A., 95, 136; Morales de, Mariana, 95
Maximilian, Ferdinand, 55
Mayo (Indians), 18
Maytorena, José M., 161, 166–68, 170–71; and *Maytorenistas*, 167, 169
Maza, Antonio, 158
Mazatlán (Sinaloa), 34–35
McClellan: William Carroll, 125; David Alvin, 128
McKinley Tariff, 85
McKnight, Robert, 36
McLaury family, 64
Mecham: Lucien Mormon, 128; Laura Ann Hardy, 128
Mendoza, Antonio de, 17
Mercer, George, 46
merchants, 24–25, 27–29, 34–37, 42–44, 46–47, 57, 95; as mining investors, 24–25, 34, 43, 79; in copper borderlands, 67–68, 74, 86, 117, 119, 136–37, 158; Chinese, 120–22, 169, 214n40
Metcalf: George, 144–45; William, 144–45
Mexican: state, 29–30, 56, 59, 80–81, 90–93, 102, 138–44, 178–83; workers, 41–47, 67, 89, 106–18, 150, 161–62, 168–69, 196n32; entrepreneurs, 34–38, 43, 63–65, 78–80, 94–95, 101–02, 136–37, 181
Mexican Central Railroad, 59, 109
Mexican National Railroad, 59
Mexican Revolution, 157–76, 180–83
Mexican Rurales, 138–39, 145–47, 158
Mexico City, 23–24, 29, 33, 55, 95, 139, 183; Mexican Revolution and, 165–66, 171
Michigan: copper region of, 68, 149
militias, 19, 27, 65, 140, 167
Millville (Arizona), 62

mining and metallurgy: colonial, 17–18, 24–26, 30, 193n17; expertise, 17, 30, 44–45, 81; and resource hinterlands, 24, 62, 72–76, 89, 96–97, 99, 152–54; and limits of control, 24–26, 44–45, 41–42, 70, 79, 99, 181; ordinances, 30–31, 191n52; technologies and methods, 42, 44–45, 62, 70, 75, 82, 89, 152
Mitchell, George, 87
mobility, 15, 20–22, 25, 29, 31–32, 123–25, 128–29; wage worker, 45–47, 67, 106–09, 116–20, 150, 177, 180–81; entrepreneurial, 64, 82, 84–85, 101–02, 104–06, 152, 156; Mexican Revolution and, 160–62, 168–70
Moctezuma (Sonora), 35–36, 64, 105, 139, 142–44, 150, 158, 170
Moctezuma River valley, 18
Montague, Charles, 169
Moody, W. G., 79
Morawitz, Albert, 142
Mormon colonies: Oaxaca, 104, 126–27; Morelos, 105, 126–27, 159; Díaz, 126; Juárez, 126; Pacheco, 126; Dublán, 126; García, 126; Chuhuichupa, 126
Mormons, 62, 72, 81, 104–05, 125–29, 215n47: in Mexican Revolution, 159, 161–62
Mossman, Burt, 138
Mowry, Sylvester, 31, 42–43, 45, 56
Mowry mine, 42, 44–45, 47, 57, 98
Mule Mountains, 60, 67–68, 72–73, 75–76, 111
Mule Pass, 67, 70. *See also* Bisbee
Munguía Villela family, 78
Murphy, Nathan, 138

Naco (Arizona/Sonora), 81–83, 88, 93, 123–24, 128, 146; Cananea railroad and, 97–98, 109, 128, 138, Mexican Revolution and, 158, 166–68
Nacozari (Sonora), 21, 104–05, 108, 144, 150, 179–81; early years of, 18, 26, 34–36, 38, 56, 64, 79–80; and Tombstone,

Nacozari (Sonora) (continued)
64, 67; Phelps Dodge and, 76–77, 80–
83; and hinterlands, 117–18, 127–29;
Mexican Revolution and, 144, 150,
158–59, 163, 173
Nacozari Creek, 129
Nacozari Railroad, 82–83, 109, 117, 128,
144, 170
Nana, 65
Nentvig, Juan, 24–26
New Braunfels (Texas), 39
New Mexico, 14, 17, 28–29, 33–34, 36–
37; after 1854, 58, 68, 83, 104, 125–26,
173–74
New Spain, 16–18, 23, 120
New York City, 1–4, 55–56, 87, 134, 149
Nogales (Arizona/Sonora), 26, 86, 95, 145,
158, 163, 171, 178
Nueva Vizcaya, 17–18

Obregón, Álvaro, 164, 166, 171, 178
Obregón, Baltasar de, 17, 20–21
Ocampo (Chihuahua), 100 fig. 14, 153,
155, 159
Ochoa, Esteban, 63, 81, 105
Ochoaville (Arizona), 63
Ojitos Ranch, 128
Ojo de Agua (Sonora), 96, 101, 121, 123
Ojo de Agua grant, 101
Oklahoma, 152
O'Neal, Bill, 141
Opatas (Indians), 8, 16, 18, 20–25, 27,
37, 40, 118n22; post–1854, 42–43, 65,
117–18, 127, 129, 140, 163, 212n27
Orozco, Pascual, 159, 162, 165; and *Oroz-
quistas*, 162, 164, 166, 173, 176
Ortíz: family, 28, 40; Celedonio, 134–35;
Ignacio, 40; Tomás, 40

Packard, Burdette A., 84–85, 94, 140,
207n19
Padrés, Francisco, 43
Palominas Ranch, 94

Panic of 1857, 48
Panic of 1907, 149–50, 152, 181
Parker, Morris B., 82, 104–05, 119, 126, 153,
155, 159
Parral (Chihuahua), 18, 23–24
Parsons, George Whitwell, 63–67, 80
Pascua Village (Arizona), 119
Paso del Norte (Chihuahua), 14
Patagonia mine, 41–42, 46–47. *See also*
Mowry mine
patron-client relations, 27–28, 84–85, 121,
149, 181
Pearce, Joe H., 141
Pearce, W. D., 162
Pennington: Elias Green, 41; family, 41
Pennsylvania, immigrants from, 62, 84
Perea: Pedro de, 18; family, 78
Pérez: family, 28; José, 79
Pesqueira: Ignacio P., 166; Alfredo, 87;
Doña Elena, 86–87; family, 28, 86–87;
Ignacio, 56, 59, 63–64, 78–80, 94
Pfefferkorn, Ignaz, 22–24, 26–27, 34, 79
Phelps, Dodge, and Company (Phelps
Dodge), 56; in Arizona, 69–76, 138,
146, 183; in Sonora, 76, 81–83, 114–17,
150, 178–81; railroads, 71–75, 82–83, 97,
104–05, 109, 128, 206n15; and Mexican
Revolution, 163–64, 174
Phelps Dodge Mercantile, 117
Piedras Verdes River valley, 126
Pilares (Sonora), 82, 105–06, 109, 113–16,
119, 179–81
Pilares de Teras (Sonora), 127
Pilares mine, 81, 150
Pimas (Indians), 16, 18, 20–22, 24–27,
39–40; post–1854, 43, 78, 118
Pimería Alta, 7, 18, 43
Pino Suárez, José María, 165
Pitic (Sonora). *See* Hermosillo
place-names, 20–21, 61, 78, 96, 111, 210n47
Plan de San Diego, 170, 173, 175; uprising,
170–71
Pleasanton (New Mexico), 125

Polk, James K., 39

Poston, Charles Debrille, 38–41, 43, 45, 49–50, 61, 194n26

pragmatism, 15, 23, 29–32, 86, 93–94, 111, 118–19, 160

presidio, 19, 27–28, 190n44; Fronteras, 27, 30; officers, 27–28; Santa Cruz, 30, 37; Tubac, 39–40

prospectors, 17–18, 25, 39, 61, 64, 68, 105, 183. See also *gambusinos*

Puga, Guillermo B., 142

Púlpito Pass, 104, 126, 162

Pumpelly, Raphael, 44, 49, 51

Ragtown (Arizona), 111, 160

railroad, 75–76, 83, 88, 171; speculation and dreams, 58–59, 80–81, 91 fig. 11; concessions, 59, 80, 82–83, 90

Ramsey, John P., 105

ranching: colonial, 14, 18, 24, 26–28, 39–40, 78–79; from 1850s to 1880s, 39–41, 45–47, 50, 57; Tombstone and copper borderlands, 61–65, 72–74, 85–86, 95, 101–02, 123–25, 128, 138; and Greene, 85–86, 89, 93–96, 98, 101–02, 123, 135, 156, 183; Phelps Dodge, 115; Mexican Revolution and, 163, 169, 171–73, 179

Ray, James Wilford, 128

Rayón district (Chihuahua), 159

Regeneración, La, 157

regional community, 43, 116–17, 120, 124

Reventon ranch, 45–46

Ricketts, Louis D., 76, 81, 105, 150, 154

Riesgo, Juan M., 36

Río, Andrés Manuel del, 33

Rio Grande, Sierra Madre, and Pacific Railroad, 99, 105, 126, 153

roads and road building, 25–26, 35–37, 41, 44, 49, 58, 153–55, 171; Sonora, 63, 81–83, 104–05, 117–18, 126–28, 183; Bisbee, 70–71

Roberts: Ed J., 84; family, 84, 94

Robinson, John A., 36

Rockfellow, John A., 57

Rodríguez, Enrique, 109

Rojas, Antonio, 163–64

Romero, Matías: 3–4, 55–56, 76–77, 120

Romero Rubio, Bonifacio, 136

Romney: Thomas, 126; Miles P., 128

Romo de Vivar family, 78

Ronquillo (Sonora), 94, 96 fig. 12, 113, 137, 146, 150

Roods, William B., 41

Royal School of Mining (Mexico City), 30, 33

Rubio, Pablo, 109, 136

ruins, 14–15, 20, 33; and rhetoric of conquest, 15, 37; mining, 30–31, 35, 40, 49–51, 79–80

Russek, Simón, 180

Ryan, John D., 149–50

Rynning, Thomas, 146, 148, 220n42

Safford, A. P. K., 61

St. David (Arizona), 62, 72, 125

St. Helena Gold Mine, 65

Salcido, Abrán, 157–58

San Antonio (Texas), 14, 39

San Bernardino ranch, 14, 37, 65, 86, 123

San Blas (Nayarit), 34

San Carlos Reservation, 60–62, 65–66

Sánchez Ochoa, Gaspar, 59

San Diego (California), 37, 58–59

San Francisco (California), 38, 42, 44, 56–58, 67, 79–80, 124

San Francisco, festival of, 45, 196n38

San Ignacio (Sonora), 41

San José Mountains, 158

San Juan Bautista (Sonora), 18, 34–36, 38

San Luis Potosí, 109

San Luis Valley, 39, 43, 63

San Miguel de Horcasitas (Sonora), 29

San Miguel River valley, 18, 116

San Pedro customshouse, 63, 64, 81, 85

San Pedro de Palominas ranch, 102

San Pedro mine, 104

San Pedro ranch, 28

San Pedro River valley, 57, 61–64, 70, 81, 89, 183; pre–1854, 14, 18, 26, 30, 37, 40; ranching in, 63, 72–74, 84, 98; Chinese and Mormon farmers in, 62, 72, 120, 123–24, 125

San Rafael del Valle land grant, 84, 94

San Rafael Valley, 98

San Simon valley, 160

Santa Cruz (Sonora), 30, 37, 39–40, 42–43, 45–46; post–1861, 57, 63, 95, 163

Santa Cruz County (Arizona), 171

Santa Cruz River valley, 18, 26, 39–41, 46, 62, 95, 120

Santa Fe (New Mexico), 49

Santa Fe trade, 34, 36, 95

Santa María Soamca (Sonora), 39

Santa Rita copper mines (Chihuahua), 79

Santa Rita mines (Arizona), 42, 44, 46

Santa Rita Mining Company, 42–43

Santa Rita Mountains, 42

Saracachi (Sonora), 25

Sáric (Sonora), 49

Scarritt, Winthrop, 153–54

Schieffelin, Edward, 61, 67

Scott, James C., 146, 220n42

Secretan Syndicate, 70

Segesser, Philipp, 22, 25–26

Seward, John, 99

Sierra, Antonio F., 158

Sierra Madre Land and Lumber Company, 99, 152–54

Sierra Madre Mountains, 16–18, 58, 125–26, 129; as Apache and bandit refuge, 26, 65, 138–39, 142, mining in, 98–100, 104, 152, Mexican Revolution and, 159, 162, 171

Silver City (New Mexico), 68

Simpich, Frederick, 169–70

Sinaloa, 16–18, 38, 169, 178

Siu Fo Chon, 121

Skeleton Canyon, 65

Slaughter, John, 86, 140, 176

smuggling, 36, 58, 64–65, 120, 124

Sobaipuris (Indians), 18

Sobas (Indians), 18

Solis, Angel, 113–14

Sonoita Massacre, 45–47, 56, 176

Sonoita ranch, 40

Sonoita valley, 40–41, 46

Sonora. *See specific places*

Sonora Exploring and Mining Company, 39, 41–42, 194n19

Sonora Railway, 59–60, 109, 166

Sonora River valley, 18, 20, 63, 96, 101, 116–17; in Mexican Revolution, 169

Southern Pacific Railroad, 58, 60–61, 70, 73–74, 83, 120; in Mexico, 100 fig. 14, 129, 138, 150, 178

Spanish-American War, 77

Spring, John, 57

Stanford, Leland, 58

Steinfeld, Albert, 67–68

Stephens, David Alma, 129

Stiles, Billy, 138

Storman, J. B., 86–87

Sulphur Spring Valley, 62–64, 72–73, 83

Sumas (Indians), 18, 25

Swansea (Wales), 80

Temosachic (Chihuahua), 153–54

Terrazas (Chihuahua), 99

Terrenate (Sonora), 27

Texas, 13–14, 16, 38–39, 73, 152–53, 170–71; immigrants from, 37, 62, 64; livestock from, 73

Texas and Pacific Railroad Company, 58

Texas Oil Company, 152

Texas Rangers, 138, 170

Texas Western Railroad Company, 39, 58, 194n19

Thomas, Estelle Webb, 127

Thompson, Pete, 163

Thompson, Thomas, 41

Tigre Mountains, 127

timber and woodcutting industries, 24, 40–42, 47; in copper borderlands, 62, 72–74, 76, 89, 95, 169, 208n30; ties to

outside markets, 56, 62, 74, 89, 153; in Chihuahua, 99, 129, 152–54; charcoal making and, 24, 44, 72
Tintown (Arizona), 111, 113, 116, 158, 162
Tohono O'odham (Indians), 8, 18, 21–22, 42, 195n31
Tombstone (Arizona), 61–67, 70–74, 80, 175–76, 183; and "cow-boys," 64–66, 133, 183; and Greene, 83–84, 94; and Chinese, 120, 123, 125
Tombstone Canyon, 73
Tombstone claim, 61
Tombstone Rangers, 66
Tombstone Stock Growers' Association, 74
Torres, Luis E., 80, 142, 158, 166
Townsend, J. C., 143
traction engines, 71, 82, 88, 154
Transvaal Mining Company, 162
Treadwell, George A., 87
Treaty of Ciudad Juárez, 161
Tritle, Frederick A., 65
Tubac (Arizona): 27, 39–49, 117; U.S. entrepreneurs at, 40–51, 58, 61–62, 78
Tucson (Arizona), 7, 27, 40, 119–20, 123, 171; border economy and, 37, 41, 57–61, 67–68
Tumacácori (Arizona), 21, 40, 46
Turkey Track Cattle Company, 94
Turkey Track Ranch, 128
Turner, Frederick Jackson, 1–3, 76

U.S. Department of Commerce, 178
U.S. Geological Survey, 87, 207n26
U.S. Secret Service, 158

Valdez, Antonio J., 36
Valenzuela, Pastor, 114
Van Schendel, Willem, 7
Velasco, Carlos I., 59
Veracruz (Veracruz), 23, 158
Vickers, John J., 84, 207n19

Vickers, R. S., 143
Victorio, 48, 65
vigilantism, 5, 46, 66, 146–48, 163–65, 170, 174–76, 183; and "home guards," 164–65, 167, 176
Villa, Pancho, 159, 162, 166, 171, 173; and *Villistas*, 171, 174–75

Wah Kee, 124
Walker, Robert J., 39
Wallace, Mildred Young, 112–13, 121, 123
Ward, Henry, 35, 38
Wheeler, Harry, 164–68, 174–76
White, Scott, 94
Whitewater Draw, 83, 104, 111
Willard, Alexander, 57
Wiswall, George A., 159
Wong: Ah Yot, 124; Took Lung, 124
Woodward, George F., 64, 105, 143, 218n48
Wordsworth, William, 41
Workmen's Loyalty League, 174, 176

Yaqui River valley, 18, 22, 116, 118–19
Yaquis (Indians), 18, 25, 107, 118–20, 129; as workers, 42–43, 46, 119, 142, 218n28; war against, 59, 119, 142–43; Mexican Revolution and, 165–67, 169–70
Yee: Jung Hung, 125; Sack, 125; Woo, 125; Yin, 124
Young: George, 101–02, 112–13, 121; family, 113; Mildred, *see* Wallace, Mildred Young
Yruretagoyena, Tadeo, 86–87, 207n24
Yuma (Arizona), 58

Zacatecas (Zacatecas), 17
Zacatecas Canyon (Arizona), 111, 116, 183
Zeckendorf, Louis, 67–68
Zimmerman Telegram, 173
Zúñiga, Ignacio, 36–37